LEARNING ON DEMAND

ADL and the Future of e-Learning

LEARNING ON DEMAND

ADL and the Future of e-Learning

Edited by

Robert A. Wisher
Naval Postgraduate School

Badrul H. Khan
Consultant, ADL Initiative

Advanced Distributed Learning Initiative
2010   Washington, DC

Production Editor:	Julianne Lammersen Baum
Editorial Assistant:	Shenan Hahn
Cover Design:	Kiril Tchangov and Erin Avvento

Library of Congress Cataloging-in-Publication Data

Learning on demand: ADL and the future of e-learning / Robert A. Wisher and Badrul H. Khan.
    p. cm.
Includes bibliographic references and indexes
International Standard Book Number: 978-0-578-05734-7
1. Distance Education-International.
2. Internet in Education and Training-International
Printed in the United States of America

This book is dedicated to the memory of Philip V.W. Dodds
Chief Architect, ADL Initiative
Colleague and Friend

Learning on Demand: ADL and the Future of e-Learning

Table of Contents

SECTION III: ADL and New Technologies

SECTION IV: Implementation Strategies

SECTION V: ADL—The Way Ahead

Preface

The Advanced Distributed Learning (ADL) Initiative was launched in 1997 as a visible commitment to incorporate into practice the benefits of technology-based instruction, generally referred to as e-learning. The goal of the ADL Initiative is to ensure access to high quality education, training, and job support, tailored to individual needs, and delivered on demand anytime and anywhere. Moreover, the goal is to do this in a way that harmonizes standards for the delivery of e-learning. The Sharable Content Object Reference Model, or SCORM, is an early ADL example of a harmonized standard. Since its launch, ADL has attracted significant attention from many segments in the learning, education, and technology space, well beyond its origins in military training and education.

This book offers an historical account of the activities of ADL since its inception. This story has not been told, at least in a single volume. The book covers the origins of ADL, the policies that govern its application, how it is being implemented in the United States and other nations, and considerations for incorporating new technologies into its future technical infrastructure. Rather than develop a technical infrastructure to suit the requirements of military training, ADL has adopted a strategy of openness, collaboration, and partnerships. ADL has substantial implications for the structures, processes, and activities of civilian education and for nearly all learning organizations. The story presented here can have parallels in other governments, agencies, institutions, and organizations. Hopefully, others will be able to apply the methods and guidelines described here to their own projects and organizations.

ADL is establishing a common technical framework for computer and Web-based learning that fosters the creation of reusable learning content as instructional objects. These objects will be discoverable and reusable, with the capability to be shaped into precise learning experiences suited to an individual learner, and delivered on demand. ADL is preparing for a world where communications networks and personal delivery devices are pervasive and inexpensive, where learning can be delivered on demand.

We want to thank the authors, all of whom have actively engaged in the ADL Initiative, some from the very beginning, for their contributions and willingness to share their perspectives with the global e-learning community. As editors, one of our tasks was to cross reference chapters, another task was to offer a broader perspective on the business of ADL (RAW) and its position in a global e-learning framework (BHK). We thank the authors for their patience and feedback during this formulation and throughout the effort.

Thanks are due to senior leadership within the Department of Defense for making ADL a reality and supporting its development, namely Dr. David S.C. Chu, Dr. Paul Mayberry, Dr. Sam Kleinman, Mr. Mike Parmentier, and Mr. Dan Gardner. There are many others inside and outside of DoD who played vital roles in its formation and early successes. The editors are grateful to the excellent editorial support from Julie

Baum, whose commitment from start to finish made this book possible. We also thank Shenan Hahn for her sharp editorial eye.

The views and opinions expressed are those of the authors and do no necessarily represent the views, opinions, or policies of the U.S. Department of Defense or the Advanced Distributed Learning Initiative.

Robert A. Wisher

Badrul H. Khan

ADL CHRONOLOGY

Kristin M. Hasselbrack, Michael A. Parmentier and Robert Downes

November 1997
The Advanced Distributed Learning Initiative was established to standardize and modernize the delivery of training and education across the Department of Defense and other federal agencies. A kick-off meeting held in Arlington, Virginia, sponsored by the White House Office of Science and Technology Policy, attracts more than 300.

January 1999
Executive Order 13111, "Using Technology to Improve Training Opportunities for Federal Government Employees," is signed by President William Clinton. This assigns the Department of Defense as the federal lead for developing consensus standards for training software.

January 1999
The Office of the Secretary of Defense, the Department of Labor, and the National Guard Bureau established the ADL Co-Laboratory (now called the ADL Co-Lab Hub) in Alexandria, Virginia, as a forum for cooperative research, development and assessment of new learning technology prototypes, guidelines and specifications.

April 1999
Department of Defense Strategic Plan for ADL submitted to Congress.

November 1999
The Joint ADL Co-Laboratory is established in Orlando, Forida. It serves as the ADL Initiative's organization for adopting and implementing ADL across DoD Component organizations.

January 2000
Academic ADL Co-Laboratory is established at the University of Wisconsin in Madison, Wisconsin as an academic link to test, evaluate, and demonstrate ADL-compliant tools and next-generation technologies to enhance teaching and learning.

January 2000
Sharable Content Object Reference Model (SCORM) Version 1.0 released.

May 2000
ADL Implementation Plan submitted to Congress.

June 2000

Plugfest 1 was held at the ADL Co-Laboratory in Alexandria, Virginia. Plugfest 1 focused on understanding the initial SCORM release and the technical ramifications.

August 2000

Plugfest 2 was held at the Academic ADL Co-Laboratory on the campus of University of Wisconsin in Madison, Wisconsin. Plugfest 2 showcased the official release of the SCORM Version 1.0 Test Suite software and focused on interoperability demonstrations among advanced early adopters of the SCORM.

November 2000

Plugfest 3 was held in conjunction with the Interservice/Industry Training, Simulation and Education Conference (I/ITSEC), in Orlando, Florida. The goal of Plugfest 3 was to demonstrate interoperability and reuse of content in the spirit of the SCORM.

January 2001

SCORM Version 1.1 released.

May 2001

Plugfest 4 was held at the ADL Co-Laboratory in Alexandria, Virginia. This Plugfest was designed to synchronize development of commercial authoring tools, learning management systems and Web-based courses with the evolution of the SCORM open-architecture specifications.

October 2001

SCORM Version 1.2 released.

November 2001

Plugfest 5 was held in conjunction with the I/ITSEC Conference in Orlando, Florida. Plugfest 5 brought e-learning organizations and experts together to refine the SCORM and other e-learning practices.

April 2002

United Kingdom ADL Partnership Lab established in Telford, England.

July 2002

Plugfest 6 was held on the campus of the Defense Acquisition University at Fort Belvoir, Virginia. The focus of Plugfest 6 was to introduce the latest sequencing and application profile specifications.

December 2002

Plugfest 7 was held in conjunction with the I/ITSEC Conference in Orlando, Florida. Plugfest 7 shared lessons learned, experiences in SCORM Version 1.2 and early SCORM Version 1.3 demonstrations.

October 2003

Plugfest 8 was held on the campus of Carnegie Mellon University in Pittsburgh, Pennsylvania. Plugfest 8 differed from other Plugfests with an increased focus on e-learning content which implements SCORM Version 1.2 and/or Beta Version 1.3 specifications.

November 2003

Workforce ADL Co-Laboratory established at the FedEx Institute of Technology, University of Memphis to support the ADL vision by advancing the development of emerging e-learning technologies to commercial implementations.

January 2004

SCORM 2004 released.

January 2004

Canada ADL Partnership Lab established in Ottawa, Ontario, Canada.

February 2004

International Plugfest I was held at the ETH Zurich (Swiss Federal Institute of Technology) in Zurich, Switzerland. Participating international organizations briefed the community on the current status of their adoption and implementation of e-learning standards the SCORM.

July 2004

SCORM 2004 2nd Edition released.

February 2005

Plugfest 9 was held, in conjunction with the Workshop on SCORM Sequencing & Navigation at the National Institute of Standards and Technology in Gaithersburg, Maryland. Plugfest 9 focused on content, tools, and LMSs that were implementing SCORM 2004.

January 2006

International Plugfest II was held, in conjunction with the 2006 International Conference on SCORM 2004 on the Tamsui Campus of Tamkang University in Taipei, Taiwan. International Plugfest II focused on content, tools, and LMSs that are implementing SCORM 2004.

May 2006

Australia ADL Partnership Lab established in Melbourne, Australia.

June 2006

Depatement of Defense releases policy on the Development, Management, and Delivery of Distributed Learning. Policy requires DoD Components to share training resources, including SCORM-compliant objects, to the maximum extent possible.

October 2006

SCORM 2004 3rd Edition Released.

December 2006

Release of ADL-Registry 1.0

January 2007

Latin American & Caribbean Region ADL Partnership Lab established in Mexico City, Mexico

January 2007

Korea ADL Partnership Lab established in Seoul, Korea

April 2007

Joint Knowledge Online officially launched as the DoD portal for joint individual training with SCORM-conformant learning content

May 2008

Norway ADL Partnership Lab established in Oslo, Norway

October 2008

President Bush signed the National Defense Authorization Act of 2009. One provision of the new law permits, for the first time, distribution to certain foreign personnel of U.S. education and training materials and information technology designed to enhance interoperability between our armed forces and the military forces of friendly foreign nations.

January 2009

Romania ADL Partnership Lab established in Bucharest, Romania.

April 2009

Release of ADL-Registry Version 1.7

April 2009

SCORM 2004 4th Edition released. This edition adds more than 75 new test cases to improve interoperability across LMSs through more stringent testing of LMSs. In addition, 4th Ed. allows more flexible persistence of data during sequencing.

Section I

ADL—FROM THE START

Chapter 1

Introduction to ADL
Robert A. Wisher

The potential of computers to aid instruction has long fascinated those in the field of learning, education, and training. Researchers and analysts have published hundreds of technical reports and journal articles illustrating clear advantages in terms of reducing instructional time and increasing effectiveness. Human resource managers, manpower analysts, and educational policymakers are enticed by the possibilities. When designed properly, using sound instructional principles, computer-based instruction can generally reduce training time by about one third, or increase learning outcomes by about one third, a finding detailed as the Rule of Thirds (Fletcher, this volume).

In the 1970s and the early 1980s, when computers were relatively expensive and communication networks limited, the U.S. Department of Defense was at the forefront of this research and analysis. The enormous training and education requirements of the military, with billions of dollars spent each year at training centers, staff colleges, reserve centers, and training ranges, offered fertile ground for the Rule of Thirds to pay dividends. Despite the empirical evidence, however, the implementation of computer-based instruction in the military was low, a notable exception being high-end weapons training devices. In an analysis reported in 1997 (Office of the Under Secretary of Defense, Personnel and Readiness, 1997), only four percent of the thousands of military courses for individual training were using computers for instructional delivery.

This lack of payoff was noted in a comprehensive strategic review of the strategies and priorities of the Department of Defense required by the U.S. Congress on a quadrennial basis (QDR, 1997). An examination conducted to account for the low computer usage rate in military training identified the *lack of interoperability* as the key obstacle. This chapter describes the influence of the ADL Initiative towards overcoming this obstacle.

This chapter overarches all other chapters within this volume. It serves as an organizing framework reflecting a shift from singular approaches to a strategy of wide-scale implementation of training technologies within the Department of Defense. A notional business paradigm, presented later, arrays the various chapters into a whole picture. As described by Khan (this volume), this business paradigm is consistent with other global views of educational technology.

The Interoperability Key

Interoperability refers to the ability of different sytems to exchange and use the same information, assuming that content is readily accessible. In the context of computer-based instruction, instructional delivery systems use specialized software called learning management systems as their runtime environment. A runtime environment supports programs while they execute in order to enable platform-independent programming. In computer-based learning systems, runtime activities include the loading of content and linking of student records and progress, and, of course, the execution of the programs. Hundreds of learning management systems entered the marketplace over the past three decades. Early on, there were no specifications or standards to ensure interoperability.

In the initial phases of implementing computer-based instruction, companies developed learning management systems largely independently of each other, selling their products and services to the military Services and other Defense components. Subsequently, learning content developed on one specific system, designed, say, for a specific Navy schoolhouse, could not be shared with other schoolhouses unless they used the same system. Vendors designed systems that were proprietary, hoping to gain market share through promotion and pricing, and through added features.

Learning content was chained to a particular delivery system, unable to function, or interoperate, in other runtime environments. There was little incentive to change this business model, and many reasons to keep it. The strength of the ADL Initiative to invoke the use of standards and specifications for interoperability made the exchange of courses and learning content between learning management systems possible. From a student's perspective, the learning experiences across systems for a given course were essentially identical. This benefit has started to be realized on a large scale in the Department of Defense, has extended to other federal agencies, and is now openly available to all others in the learning, education, and training communities.

The Influence of the Internet
In the 1990s, the Internet, spawned from research sponsored by the military, became widely accessible. A separate but related advancement, the World Wide Web, enabled the spread of information over the Internet through the use of a common format, hypertext markup language, or html. Together they provided a common infrastructure for delivering learning content and a convention for its appearance.

Learning content could now be delivered through any number of Web browsers (Kearsley, 1996). Although this was not its intention, the Web formatting imposed constraints on instructional design which proved to be restrictive. For example, displays of instructional material could appear differently on different systems (Hannum, 2001). There were no common provisions for tracking students' progress. The systematic identification and exchange of learning content was not practical. To enable true interoperability, three elements were still needed: first, a common set of specifications for packaging the learning content and allowing that content to work across multiple learning management systems; second, a repository architecture that allows discovery and access to quality learning content; and third, a stimulus to motivate their implementation.

These factors demonstrated the need to inaugurate a program such as the ADL Initiative to develop options to increase the penetration of computer-based instruction in the U.S. military. Many outside of DoD were similarly interested in a Web-based delivery capability for learning, education, and training (Khan, 1997). Researchers, however, cautioned against overly optimistic views of what technology can do for instruction. Clark (1983), for example, identified the fundamental importance of sound pedagogy and design of instruction as the critical factor for instructional effectiveness, warning against overconfidence in the glittering technology which simply delivers instruction (Sitzmann & Ely, this volume; Gamor, this volume). Proponents of learning technologies have paid too little attention to important instructional design issues, focusing on media rather than learning objectives (Kozlowski & Bell, 2007). The ADL Initiative was well aware of this predisposition.

The Role of the Department of Defense

In 1997, the inability of learning systems and content to withstand infrastructure changes, due simply to the lack of standards, presented the major challenge to wide-scale implementation of education and training technology within the DoD. One military Service could not take advantage of what another Service developed. An inability to easily access quality content which could be repurposed for similar learning or performance objectives, and a lack of incentives for reusing content, further hindered progress. The same or similar courses were being developed multiple times. As a result of its 1997 review, the DoD recognized the need to address the learning needs of warfighters, operators, and Defense civilians in more effective and efficient ways.

In 1997, there was no single rallying point in the industry to lead a broad-scale attempt to change the existing condition. The aviation industry formed an industry-wide computer-based training committee in 1988, but it was geared toward the requirements of its members (Robson & Richards, this volume). There was a compelling need to develop standards and specifications to enable participants in the broader educational and training technology industry to create technical tools and solutions that would overcome the interoperability obstacle. The DoD responded to this need by initiating a program to accelerate large-scale development of dynamic and cost-effective learning tools and environments and to stimulate a vigorous global market for these products.

Formation of ADL

At a meeting sponsored by the White House Office of Science and Technology Policy in November 1997, the Advanced Distributed Learning (ADL) Initiative was formally launched to find a way to close the gap between the potential benefits of using computers in instruction on a broad scale and the current benefits realized with the existing state of usage. More than 350 policymakers, technology experts, educators, and training professionals attended the event and defined the ADL vision of developing the capability to deliver high quality instruction, delivered anytime, anywhere

7

set forth a new paradigm based on a structured, adaptive, collaborative effort between the public and private sectors to develop the standards and tools for the future learning environment. By establishing a common technical framework for computer-based and Web-based learning, ADL would foster an environment and the tools for the creation of reusable learning content.

For ADL to succeed, the Initiative needed partners who could collaborate to develop consensus on technical matters of interoperability, instructional designers and evaluators to check for solid pedagogical practice and to verify learning efficiencies and effectiveness, vendors to supply interoperable products, and buyers to demand such products be procured and implemented. ADL needed all stakeholders to work in concert towards a common goal. Developers and users had reciprocal interests. Missing was an overarching effort to channel these interests into a functioning, mutually supportive paradigm.

Executive Order

In 1999, President William J. Clinton issued an executive order (Executive Order No. 13111, 1999) directing the DoD to lead Federal participation in business and university organizations charged with developing consensus standards for training software and associated services. The order further directed the DoD to provide guidance to Defense agencies and advise the civilian agencies, as appropriate, on how best to use these standards for large-scale development and implementation of efficient and effective distributed learning technologies (Bardack, Koch, & Smith, this volume).

The U.S. Congress required the Department of Defense to develop a strategic plan for guiding and expanding distance learning initiatives. The directive stated that the Secretary may take into account the ongoing collaborative effort between the DoD, other Federal agencies, and private industry already known as the Advanced Distributed Learning Initiative, but must focus on the education and training goals and objectives of the DoD. The Strategic Plan for ADL was submitted to Congress in April 1999.

The ADL Vision

The ADL vision is to provide access to the highest quality education and training, tailored to individual needs, delivered cost effectively, anytime and anywhere. This vision has remained in place throughout the Initiative, and is worth keeping in mind collectively while charting the future course for ADL.

ADL's vision can be achieved affordably, and made feasible, primarily through the use of technology—specifically computer technology. Since computer technology is constantly evolving, ADL is preparing for a world where communications networks personal delivery devices are pervasive and inexpensive, as well as transparent in terms of ease of use and portability. ADL is determining how to best technology infrastructure for learning on demand in operational to experience.

Training for future military operations, which embody all characteristics of the information age, depends on access to the right information, making learning on demand a vital part of any training strategy (Alberts & Hayes, 2003). Training for such net-centric operations will rely on technology, as exemplified by ongoing efforts at the Joint Forces Command (Camacho, West, & Vozzo, this volume).

Similarly, the rapidly changing requirements and practices of the commercial sector are a substantial driver in advancing distributed learning into the workforce (Paradise, 2008). Academic and industrial laboratories continue to offer new insights into the science of learning (Fiore & Salas, 2007) and innovations abound from all corners of the globe (Khan, this volume). The force of these contributors must be channeled and coupled to the greatest extent possible if ADL is to serve as a model for providing high quality training and education to learners from all sectors.

A Notional Business Paradigm

The lofty vision of ADL required a new approach to doing business, one based not on a belief of "build it and they will come," but on a belief that sustainable advances in e-learning could be best achieved through cooperative efforts. Specifying an end state and requesting bidders to build a solution for others to apply was deemed impractical. The end state, such as a universal learning management system, depended on a point of view, a set of fixed requirements, and a means to maintain and upgrade the end state. Rather, the best approach appeared to be to sharpen the focus of the spectrum of users towards a common vision.

From the start, ADL engaged many partners and stakeholders in the learning-education-training field from government, industry, and academia, openly and in a collaborative spirit. Parties outside of the DoD had ongoing interests in contributing to certain elements of the common goal of accessibility and interoperability, most notably specification and standards bodies (Robson & Richards, this volume). To create value, ADL needed a business approach that incorporated two fundamental aspects, one technical and the other dealing with relationships across the sectors of stakeholders.

The ADL Initiative is wholly funded by the U.S. government and operates as a cost center rather than a profit-or-loss activity. Describing its setup in terms of a business approach shows ADL's pivotal and active role in fostering change. It also underscores the need for ADL to maintain neutrality in judging or recommending products from industry. Conformance to open standards and specifications endorsed by ADL is what matters.

Technical Aspect
The technical aspect of the notional model identifies interoperability across learning management systems as a first component. Here, interoperability is a general reference to the functional requirements of accessibility, interoperability, durability, and reusability which are described later. A second component of the technical aspect

concerns the art of sound instructional design, research on pedagogical models, as well as advances in the learning sciences that affect learning outcomes.

Sector Relationship Aspect

On the other hand, the sector relationships aspect represents a reach-out to parties external to ADL, also divided into two components. The first is represented by those who partner directly with ADL as advocates and supporters of common standards and specifications. The second component is represented by those forming the marketplace of buyers, and those developing and selling products and services that conform to the standards and specifications advocated by ADL.

Graphical Representation of the ADL Business Paradigm

The model of the ADL business paradigm may be depicted as a parallelogram, a four-sided figure in which the opposite sides are parallel and congruent. A notional representation of this model appears in Figure 1-1.

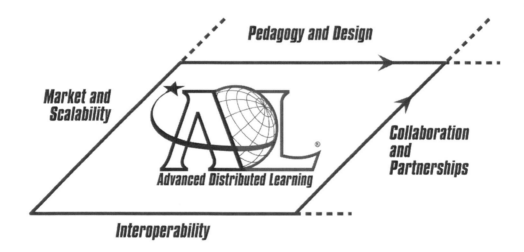

Figure 1-1. Graphic model of notional ADL business paradigm. The parallelogram depicts a structural design component above an interoperability component, and a market and scalability component opposite a collaboration and partnership component.

The solid lines, arbitrary in length, represent the current state of the paradigm. The future state is implied through dashed lines of arbitrary length. Note that the horizontal axes, reflecting the technical aspect, have dashed lines to the right only, implying durability. The thinking is that what has already been developed will sustain until it is improved. In contrast, the vertical axes, representing external relationships, have dashed lines that are bi-directional, implying that relationships can either grow or shrink over time. The thinking is that ADL can gain or lose support from its

10

stakeholders. The intention here is to have the figure serve as a notional model that frames ADL with providers, users, and technical developers.

Horizontal Axes

The two horizontal axes relate to the technical elements of ADL. The base of the figure is termed the Interoperability Line. Above and in parallel is the Pedagogy and Design Line. Advances in the base make possible new pedagogical approaches to instructional design. For example, a future compatibility of SCORM with online games opens new instructional design possibilities that can be accessed, shared, and reused (Xu, this volume). As one capability grows, so does the other; thus they are congruent. A key to making this happen is that users want such capabilities, and the marketplace offers them.

Vertical Axes

The vertical axes represent sector relationships. They are the Collaboration and Partnerships Line, arbitrarily positioned on the right, in parallel with the Market and Scalability Line. Together they reflect ADL's mutual interests with external organizations and customer needs. As the collaboration towards pursuing a common vision increases, and the partnerships with governments, industry, and academia expand, a marketplace for industry to offer products and services emerges. More buyers scale to more sellers. A growing marketplace can attract new partners and increase the level of collaboration; thus there is a congruence. Roughly speaking, ADL occupies the area inside this notional parallelogram. Elements of this business paradigm are referenced in all ensuing chapters.

The sector relationship aspect reflects the partnerships and collaborative activities needed to design, critique, and build the technical requirements. These relationships span the public, non-profit, industrial, and academic sectors. The relationships also concern those who design learning content compatible with the ADL runtime environment and are ready to make this content available to others for reuse or repurposing (Shanley et al., this volume). The relationship aspect concerns further those who risk capital, the vendor community, and enterprise developers in the learning-education-training marketplace. It concerns those who dispense resources to satisfy learning needs, such as agencies and corporations. Vendors profit from the sales of compatible systems, tools, and content. The buyers and users achieve their organizational goals in delivering quality instruction in affordable ways. Together, these become a loosely coupled collective business practice with a common interest in realizing the potential of computers for instruction and ultimately achieving the ADL vision.

Functional Requirements

An important factor in achieving the ADL vision is the re-shaping of what traditionally and conveniently has been called a "course" into a set of constituent "learning objects" (Fletcher, this volume). A learning object is an entity (learning material) that can be used, re-used, or referenced in technology supported learning environments. From the student's perspective, they can be modules, lessons, units, chapters, sections, and assignments. Learning objects include multimedia content, instructional content, learning objectives, instructional software and software tools, instructional interventions, and persons, organizations, or events referenced in technology-supported learning. An early industry champion of the learning object construct, Cisco Systems, viewed a learning object as a single learning or performance objective that can be tested through assessments (Barritt & Alderman, 2004).

Learning objects are called sharable content objects (SCOs) in the terminology of ADL (Gallagher, this volume). These SCOs are individually tagged with defining terms, according to a standard, and housed in repositories for later discovery and use (Lannom, this volume). A fixed sequence of these objects may constitute a traditional course, but the power of ADL technology allows them to be sequenced in ways unique to an individual's prior knowledge, learning patterns, and goals, and, ultimately, on demand.

Sharable Content Objects—Functions

Sharable content objects need to meet specific criteria that represent the essential functional requirements that are at the heart of ADL. The most prominent requirements are:

Accessibility. It must be possible to find needed and sharable content objects. They must be accessible.

Interoperability. Once found, the objects should be usable. This means that they must be interoperable and portable across most, if not all, platforms, operating systems, browsers, and course development tools.

Durability. Once implemented, the objects should continue to operate reliably. If the underlying platform, operating system, or browser is modified (for instance when a new version is released and installed), the objects should continue to operate as before. They should be durable.

Reusability. Finally, objects should be reusable. Multiple platforms, operating systems, browsers, and courseware tools should be able to reuse, and even modify as needed, the original content objects.

Certainly, there are many views and perspectives on how these functional requirements can or should be accomplished. Ideas abound on the impact technology has on learning, education, and training. No one organization has the answers. From its inception, ADL followed an approach of community development. The stakes were high not only within the DoD, but to the many other interested parties across sectors willing to invest time and resources to achieve a common goal.

ADL Method of Work

The global marketplace for technology-based tools for learning is massive. Before the ADL Initiative took the lead, there were no common standards for creating tools that work in harmony and on a large scale. Collaboration was essential. Certain communities, such as the aviation industry, had already recognized the value of standards within their vertical market, but the vast enterprises representing education and training were locked into approaches and products that were proprietary. There was a clear need to spur industry to build a consensus to develop learning management systems, content, and tools that could be freely exchanged, to the advantage of all. ADL was in a unique position to serve this role due to the buying power of the DoD. The long-term value proposition was high quality education and training at a low cost.

The decisive first function of the Initiative was to contribute to the development, evaluation, and promotion of standards. This was done through working relationships with and participation in technical working groups and specifications and standards bodies (Robson & Richards, this volume). The Sharable Content Object Reference Model (SCORM) was the first product of the extensive public-private collaborative effort advocated by ADL, beginning in 1999. SCORM, at a high level, is a reference model—a collection of interrelated technical specifications and guidelines. It applies proven, but limited, developments in training technology through use of a specific content model to enable consistent formatting, packaging, and delivery of training across the e-learning community. In the opinion of numerous experts external to DoD, SCORM has become the global *de facto* standard for developing and delivering e-learning with tremendous possibilities for extensions to more recent advances.

Working the Technical Aspect

The business paradigm has at its base a consensus of technical specifications, standards, and architectures which define interoperability. Industry, through partnerships and collaborations with ADL, expressed a willingness to build conforming systems and develop conforming content. One of ADL's assumed roles is to compose a reference model that unifies various specifications into a harmonized whole, rigorously defined and testable. Learning content, media assets, entire courses, and even training interventions can be easily exchanged among users. This harmonized technical infrastructure allows different learning management systems to deliver, track, report on, and manage learning content and learner progress in a common way. Additionally, it sets the stage for making content discoverable, accessible, and reusable. Extensions to the base must permit backward compatibility, so that content is durable. The Interoperability Line in the ADL business paradigm represents this technical base.

Parallel to the base, the important contributions from instructional designers in creating learning experiences needs representation in the business paradigm. However, there can be a disparity between what a designer may have in mind and what the specifications allow. The early phases of the interoperability work limit what is possible in the design using SCORM (Roberts & Gallagher, this volume), so designs using peer feedback, for example, are not included. Eventually this will be overcome through additions and new technical approaches. Such capabilities can be handled in various ways with learning management systems, but interoperability and content sharing are lost.

Requirements for advanced instructional designs will, in time, influence the extension of the technical base. For example, intelligent tutoring systems can lead to higher learning outcomes, but how should the technical base be extended to make this possible (Hu, Graesser, & Fowler, this volume)? Change can be accommodated but interoperability of systems and durability of content must be maintained. This aspect is referred to as the Instruction and Pedagogy Line in the ADL business paradigm.

There is, thus, a congruence between the Interoperability Line and the Instruction and Pedagogy Line: The instructional design can push the technical base to require certain functionality. In contrast, technical advances arising from progress in information sciences can pull new instructional design approaches. For example, the capabilities available in a virtual world environment have much appeal but how to best harmonize this environment for interoperability and apply it to learning is not yet clear (Gamor, this volume; Fowler, this volume). What is evident is that as the interoperability base extends, so too do the possibilities for innovative approaches to instructional design.

ADL practice is to work with others to identify and refine a common ground for a specification or standard. ADL plays a vital role in harmonizing the raw specifications. Alternate approaches to the specification approach are possible in the future, such as through architectures, services, and data models external to the learning management system (Panar, Rehak, & Thropp, this volume).

Working the Sector Relationship Aspect
The ADL business paradigm also involves relationships between those who develop the technical features, those who design instruction, and those who build the systems, tools, and content to make this all work. The ADL strategy depends on collaboration and partnerships. In 1999, the ADL Initiative established the first of several collaboration laboratories (ADL Co-Labs) in Alexandria, Virginia, to foster partnerships, resource sharing, and large-scale collaboration among the public and private sectors. The Department of Labor and the National Guard Bureau provided staff to support the mission to seek common tools, standards, content, and guidelines for the ADL Initiative (Bardack, Koch, & Smith, this volume).

Examples of ADL's formal activities that contributed to this business system include the sponsorship of technical working groups on SCORM, participation in specification and standards bodies, hosting a succession of Plugfests that brought together hundreds of participants from the broad e-learning community to discuss their concerns and demonstrate their solutions, and the provisioning of an active Web site and help desk. ADL also provided the test suite for all versions of SCORM and established independent test centers to conduct the testing. Less formal activities included participation in the many e-learning conferences, such as providing keynote speakers, information booths, pre-conference workshops, and so forth. The ADL Co-Labs hosted hundreds of groups, including visiting researchers and government policy makers, some for periods of more than a year. Webinars are a more recent addition to ADL's informal outreach. Throughout, ADL has remained vendor-neutral.

Plugfests

Beginning in 2000, ADL began sponsoring a series of events, Plugfests, inviting the participation of all those active in the field of Web-based learning. The Plugfest events were cooperative efforts designed to offer "no-fault" interoperability testing for vendors, content providers, and tool makers. Participants plugged into a local area network and tested their wares with other providers, seeking to verify or reject interoperability claims, function by function, feature by feature. The ten Plugfests hosted in the United States were interspersed to coincide with enhancements to SCORM (Hasselbrack, Parmentier, & Downes, this volume). Two international Plugfests, one in Europe and one in Asia, served to broaden the commitment to the reference model.

The ADL Network

For the business aspect, partnerships and collaboration are required to gain traction in creating a marketplace and supply chain for systems, tools, and content. ADL's creation of a network of Collaborative Laboratories, or Co-Labs, is a leading example of collaboration.

ADL Collaborative Laboratory (Co-Lab) Network. Since the first ADL collaborative laboratory was founded in 1999, the initiative has sponsored three additional co-labs that focus on specific communities of interest. The ADL Co-Lab Hub in Alexandria, Virginia, focuses on all ADL activities whereas the Joint ADL Co-Lab in Orlando, Florida, focuses on U.S. military applications of ADL. The Academic ADL Co-Lab in Madison, Wisconsin, and the ADL Memphis Intelligent Tutoring Systems Center (formerly called the Workforce ADL Co-Lab) in Memphis, Tennessee focus on higher education and workforce development. What the Co-Labs have in common is support for a common reference model and assisting their respective sectors in implementation activities.

ADL Partnership Labs. Another innovation within the business aspect is the creation of an international network of ADL Partnership Laboratories. These were not envisioned during the initial strategic plan submitted to the U.S. Congress in 1999. Based on the practices surrounding ADL and the progress and name recognition coming from SCORM, other nations were interested in establishing a more formal relationship with ADL, such as Norway and Romania (Roceanu & Isaksen, this volume), Korea (Park, Ho, & Yun, this volume), and the Latin America region (Cartas, this volume). Starting with the United Kingdom in 2002, several nations have volunteered to champion the ADL cause, namely Canada, Korea, Australia, Norway, Romania, Germany, and a consortium of 14 Latin American and Caribbean nations. Some translate the ADL documentation into their native languages, others develop internal compliance test centers, and others share content.

Additional Affiliations.   Not formally affiliated as an ADL Partnership Lab is the ADL Working Group under the Consortium of Defense Academies and Security Studies Institutes, headquartered in Geneva, Switzerland (Synytsya & Staub, this volume). The Working Group has developed dozens of online courses through cooperative development teams across nations such as the Ukraine, Switzerland, Bulgaria, and Estonia. In October 2008, President George W. Bush signed the National Defense Authorization Act of 2009. One provision of the new law supports selective distribution of U.S. education and training materials and information technology to foreign personnel in order to enhance interoperability between our armed forces and the military forces of friendly foreign nations.

The global interest in ADL incubates a marketplace for the buying, selling, or exchanging of products and services. Industry must be willing to make up-front investments to ensure that their systems comply with the common technical infrastructure. Tool makers are needed to refine the common framework, incorporating functions and extending features needed by some but not necessarily all. Designers and content producers are needed to contribute best practices and quality learning content in order to achieve the economies of scale that make all this affordable. All are needed at the planning table to chart the next big steps for ADL.

The ADL Marketplace

Along with many organizations and much industry participation, ADL has accomplished much. The ADL vision is long term, and the progress must be steady. The ADL chronology (Hasselbrack, Parmentier, & Downes, this volume) illustrates a steady path of progress, from the launch of ADL to the issuance of its most recent edition of a reference model that incorporates numerous standards and specifications into a harmonized, working package.

ADL is the steward of the Sharable Content Object Reference Model (SCORM) which makes possible the interoperability of learning content, its initial goal (Gallagher, this volume). ADL has created a large following, evidenced not only by participation in the many Plugfests and the growth of its Co-Laboratory and international partnership networks, but especially by the number of vendors who develop products that are SCORM-conformant. The table below illustrates the interest in developing such products, starting with the earliest version of SCORM to its current version, 2004 4th edition. Each product has been independently certified through a third party test center (Panar, Brannon, & Poltrack, this volume).

Table 1-1

Certified SCORM products

Version of SCORM	Products Formally Certified
SCORM 1.2	158
SCORM 2004 2nd Ed.	65
SCORM 2004 3rd Ed.	63

Note: SCORM Version 1.2 was the first official specification with the option to certify. SCORM 2004 4th Ed. certification is expected in early 2010.

Finding Learning Content

One functional requirement of ADL is that learning content be accessible. SCORM does not address finding and reusing learning objects after they have been created. ADL researchers investigated the difficulties of creating learning objects, storing them, and managing them for discovery and access. This investigation drew from the fields of library science, computer and network systems design, and publishing (Dodds & Lewis, 2008).

Through a partnership with the Corporation for National Research Initiatives, the investigation resulted in the Content Object Discovery and Registration/Resolution Architecture (CORDRA). The first instance of this architecture is the ADL Registry, where learning objects are centrally registered and stored in repositories distributed throughout the DoD (Lannom, this volume). The architecture is open and available to others to replicate. A long term goal is to federate the various registries, creating a truly global resource for learning objects and other content packages that can play on SCORM-compatible delivery devices.

ADL Applications

ADL is being broadly implemented within the DoD (Murray & Marvin, this volume). During a recent one-year reporting period, more than ten million online courses had been completed by Service members and DoD civilians. These courses would otherwise require classroom space, time for transportation, instructors, and so forth to meet the same learning objectives. ADL is having a significant impact on training within the U.S. military.

One application area concerns the integration of content authored in SCORM environments with content in the form of technical publication data residing in S1000D™ common source database. An international body of researchers and engineers, led by the ADL Job Performance Technology Center, are defining requirements for a specification for such an integration of content sources (Gafford & Heller, this volume). Given that technical publications serve as the authoritative source of much technical

17

training content, the specification will enable a government to acquire, manage, and produce integrated training and technical information in vendor-neutral formats (International S1000D-SCORM Bridge Project Team, 2009). If widely adopted, a change in a technical publication can lead to an immediate, corresponding change in online technical training.

Defense Acquisition University

Another example of an application is the work at the Defense Acquisition University (DAU), which is a corporate university that trains the acquisition, technology, and logistics workforce of 125,000 people within the Department of Defense. Faced with the need to provide training as quickly and as cost effectively as possible, DAU has made strategic decisions that have allowed it to experience both growth and budget efficiencies simultaneously (Anderson, Hardy, & Leeson, 2008).

The enterprise provides workforce support in critical areas: certification training, performance support, communities of practice, and continuous learning. Each of these areas is supported by the learning network architecture that enables delivery of content in multiple modes, enriching interaction between learners, instructors, and content. By focusing on content as a strategic asset and implementing SCORM, DAU plans to benefit from the system's scalability by identifying opportunities for reuse and sharing of assets across multiple organizations.

The metrics are truly impressive. From 2001 to 2006, student enrollment increased from 46,000 to 113,000 per year while the average training cost per student dropped from $3,000 to $958. At the end of 2008, more than 240 continuous learning modules were available online and more than 330,000 completions were recorded. To accomplish this, DAU implemented its Performance Learning Model—a model through which traditional classroom training, distance learning, knowledge sharing, and other workforce resources are connected and aligned with mission and goals. DAU learning products are available around the clock—more than just a convenience, a necessity with a global, deployed workforce located across several continents and at sea.

Summary

The ADL Initiative has grown from a concept in 1997 to a global undertaking. The expansion of the use of technology in military training has increased tremendously, either for stand-alone delivery or in blend with other forms of instruction (Wisher, 2005). An unexpected consequence is the extent of global adoption of the ADL approach by other governments, for military as well as civilian training and education. The activities described in this chapter, and in the entire volume, are by no means comprehensive but rather demonstrative of the many ingredients of ADL.

The business paradigm used to describe ADL depended on solid technical ideas coupled with solid support from collaborators, partners, sellers and buyers, and steady funding from the U.S. Department of Defense. Since its inception, ADL has hopefully made permanent strides towards providing high quality education and training, delivered on demand, and has done so in a manner that is open and fair. As ADL explores new technologies and new approaches toward achieving the vision, the future of e-learning is definitely bright.

References

Alberts, D. S., & Hayes, R. E. (2003). *Power to the edge: Command, control in the information age.* DoD Command and Control Research Program. Vienna, VA: ERB.

Anderson, F. J., Hardy, C. R., & Leeson, J. (2008). *Leading a learning revolution: The story behind Defense Acquisition University's reinvention of training.* San Francisco: Pfeiffer.

Barritt, C., & Alderman, F. L. (2004). *Creating a reusable learning objects strategy.* San Francisco: Pfeiffer.

Clark, R.E. (1983). Reconsidering research on learning from media. *Review of Educational Research*, 53, 445-460.

Dodds, P., & Lewis, S. (2008). *The ADL Registry and CORDRA: Vol. 1. General overview* (IDA Document NS D-3597). Alexandria, VA: Institute for Defense Analyses.

Executive Order No. 13111. (1999). *Using technology to improve training opportunities for Federal government employees.* Retrieved October 27, 2009 from http://www.opm.gov/pressrel/1999/eo.htm

Fiore, S. M., & Salas, E. (2007). *Toward a science of distributed learning.* Washington, DC: American Psychological Association.

Fletcher, J. D., Tobias, S., & Wisher, R. A. (2007). Learning anytime, anywhere: advanced distributed learning and the changing face of education. *Educational Researcher*, *36*(2), 96-102.

Hannum, W. (2001). Web-based training: advantages and limitations. In B. H. Kahn (Ed.), *Web-based training* (pp. 13-20). Engelwood Cliffs, NJ: Educational Technology Publications.

International S1000D-SCORM Bridge Project Team. (2009). *A technical development strategy for bridging S1000D and SCORM.* Alexandria, VA: Advanced Distributed Learning Initiative.

Kearsley, G. (1996, winter). The World Wide Web: Global access to education. *Educational Technology Reviews, 5*, 26-30.

Khan, B. H. (Ed.). (1997). *Web-based instruction.* Engelwood Cliffs, NJ: Educational Technology Publications.

Kozlowski, S.W. & Bell, B.S. (2007). A theory-based approach for designing distributed learning system. In S.M. Fiore & E. Salas (Eds.), *Toward a science of distributed learning.* Washington, DC: American Psychological Association.

Office of the Under Secretary of Defense, Personnel and Readiness. (1997). *Distance learning in the Department of Defense* (Report to the House Committee on Appropriations). Washington, DC: Author.

Paradise, A. (2008). *State of the industry report 2008.* Alexandria, VA: American Society for Training & Development.

U.S. General Accounting Office. (2003). *United States General Accounting Office report to the congressional committees: Military transformation: Progress and challenges for DOD's advanced distributed learning programs, February 2003* (Report No. GAO-03-393). Washington, DC: Author.

Wisher, R. A. (2005). Blended learning in military training. In C. J. Bonk & C. R. Graham (Eds.), *Handbook of blended learning environments* (pp. 519-532). San Francisco: Pfeiffer.

The Author

Dr. Robert Wisher is a Research Professor at the Naval Postgraduate School in the Modeling, Virtual Environments and Simulation (MOVES) Institute. From 2002 to 2009 he was Director of the Advanced Distributed Learning Initiative within the Office of the Secretary of Defense.

Chapter 2

Why ADL? Research Foundations
J. D. Fletcher

About 1.1 million U.S. forces are dispersed across the continental United States with an additional 1.4 million forces spread across 50 foreign countries. Individuals in these forces need to be capable of independent thought and action. They also need to continue their training and career growth when they are far removed from military schoolhouses, expert mentors, or even others in their own career specialties.

Additional complications arise from the rapid growth in the amount and complexity of information that individuals at all levels must integrate and prioritize. The trend has produced an increasing demand for what Wulfeck and Wetzel-Smith (2008) and Wetzel-Smith and Wulfeck (2010) have described as "Incredibly Complex Tasks." Today about 15 percent of military tasks are abstract, multidimensional, non-linear, dynamic, and interdependent. The dynamic nature of these tasks and the evolving operational environment means that individuals must continually receive up-to-date training and performance assistance.

Finally, the difficulty of all military tasks is exacerbated by the dispersal of units and the individuals serving within them. Human decisions and actions must increasingly be coordinated within and across teams whose members may be globally dispersed, serving other nations and other cultures, at widely varied levels of command. Ability to communicate, coordinate, and perform tasks under these conditions may not guarantee success, but the consequences of its absence are severe.

These operational conditions have created an imperative to ensure that "learning"—education, training, and task, job, and decision aiding—is rapidly available on demand, anytime and anywhere, to individuals and teams, uniformed and civilian, at all levels of responsibility.

The Technical Opportunity: A Third Revolution in Learning

In response to this requirement, advanced distributed learning (ADL), enabled through computer technology, is riding and contributing to a third revolutionary wave in learning. The first of these revolutions occurred about 5,000 years ago with the invention of writing—the use of graphic tokens to represent syllables of sound. Prior to writing, learning activity appears to have been conducted as a tutorial conversation between a learner and a sage, or at least someone with the knowledge and skill the learner sought to acquire. With writing, it became possible for a learner to access knowledge and skill without this face-to-face interaction. Writing allowed the content of ideas and instruction to transcend time and place.

The second revolution in learning occurred with the invention of books printed from moveable type—first in China around 1000 AD and then in Europe in the mid-1400s (Kilgour, 1998). With them, the dissemination of knowledge and skills through writing became scalable. Once content was produced, it could be made widely available and increasingly inexpensive as printing technology developed.

But with writing and printing the dissemination of content was still passive. It lacked the tutorial interactivity that had been the foundation of learning for the previous 100,000 years or so of human existence.

Enter computer technology with its ability to adapt rapidly, in real time, to the changing demands, needs, and circumstances of learners and learning. Computer technology allows not just content but also instructional strategies, techniques, and interactions to become inexpensively ubiquitous and available on demand, anytime, anywhere. It may be fomenting a third revolution in learning. ADL is both a response and a contributor to this third revolutionary possibility.

"Learning" in ADL, then, is used as a catch-all designator for education, training, and performance/decision aiding. "Distributed" in ADL is not just another word for distance. It signifies learning that can be provided in classrooms with a teacher present, in the field linking together widely dispersed instructors and students, and standing alone with no instructor other than the computer itself present. Finally, "Advanced" in ADL implies affordable, interactive, adaptive, on-demand instruction delivered using computer technology so that it is available anytime, anywhere. ADL relies on computer technology to accomplish its goals.

The purpose of the ADL Initiative has, from its inception, been to ensure access to the highest quality education, training, and performance/decision aiding tailored to individual needs, and delivered cost effectively, anytime and anywhere. The purpose of this chapter is to present a rationale for pursuing the ADL vision. This rationale is based on a foundation of empirical evidence reported by leading researchers in the field.

Evidence: Research and Development Foundations

What evidence is there that computer technology might be effecting this third revolution? What have we learned from research on computer uses in instruction? Some key findings may be summarized as follows:

- Although individualized learning tailored to the needs of individual students has long been viewed as an imperative, it has also been viewed as unaffordable (Scriven, 1974). With few exceptions we cannot afford one instructor for every student—an Aristotle for every Alexander. Computer technology can make this imperative affordable. A core argument for ADL, then, is not for technology, but for making individualization affordable.

- The instructional technologies targeted by ADL have been found to be more effective than typical classroom instruction across many instructional objectives and subject matters.

- ADL is generally less costly, offering greater return on investment than current instructional approaches, especially at scale where many widely dispersed students must be served.

- ADL allows education, training, and performance/decision aiding and problem solving to be delivered from the same knowledge bases on platforms ranging from hand-held devices to large desktop computers to capabilities embedded in operational equipment.

These arguments have been made for the computer-assisted approaches used by ADL for the last 40-50 years (e.g., Alpert & Bitzer, 1970; Atkinson, 1968; Coulson, 1962; Galanter, 1959; Suppes, 1966). They have been repeatedly validated by empirical research and practical experience. Statistical findings from this work have been summarized by a "Rule of Thirds" (Fletcher, 1997, 2004). It states that application of the technologies on which ADL is based reduces the cost of instruction by about one-third. Additionally it can *either* reduce instructional time to reach instructional goals by about one-third, *or* increase the skills and knowledge acquired by about one-third while holding instructional time constant.

The following sections discuss more specifically the research and development behind these arguments and the Rule of Thirds.

Individualization: Tutorial Instruction
The argument for ADL technology begins with an issue that arises independently from applications of technology. It concerns the effectiveness of classroom instruction, involving one instructor for 20-30 (or more) students, compared to individual tutoring, involving one instructor for each student. Empirical results from comparisons of this sort are shown in Figure 2-1 adapted from Bloom (1984).

Bloom combined findings from three empirical studies comparing tutoring with one-on-many classroom instruction. That such comparisons would show the tutored students to have learned more is not surprising. What is surprising is the size of the difference. Overall, as Figure 2-1 suggests, the difference was found to be two standard deviations. It suggests that, with instructional time held constant, one-on-one tutoring can raise the performance of mid-level 50th percentile students roughly to that of 98th percentile students. These and similar empirical findings suggest that differences between one-on-one tutoring and typical classroom instruction are not only likely, but very large.

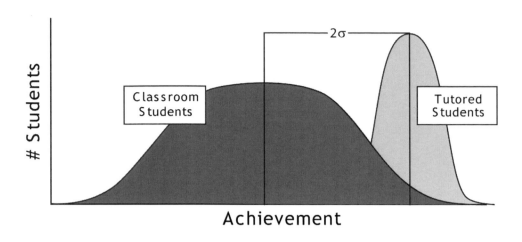

Figure 2-1. Delivery Mode Comparison. This figure demonstrates achievement gains from individual tutoring compared to classroom instruction.

Most importantly for training applications, the shapes of these distributions support Corno and Snow's (1986) suggestion that the individualization provided by tutorial instruction helps guarantee that all learners reach some basic level of competency.

What accounts for the success of one-on-one tutoring? Research summarized below suggests that it is primarily due to: (1) the capability of tutors and their students to engage in many more interactions per unit of time than is possible in a classroom, and (2) the capability of tutors to tailor pace, sequencing, and content to the needs, capabilities, goals, interests, and values of individual students.

Individualization: Interactivity

With regard to the first tutorial capability, intensity of instructional interaction, Graesser and Person (1994) reported the following:

- Average number of questions by a teacher of a class in a classroom hour: 3

- Average number of questions asked by a tutor and answered by a student during a tutorial hour: 120-145

- Average number of questions asked by any one student during a classroom hour: 0.11

- Average number of questions asked by a student and answered by a tutor during a tutorial hour: 20-30

These data show great differences in interactivity and intensity between tutorial and classroom instruction. This level of interactivity, by itself, may account for a substantial portion of the success of tutorial over classroom instruction.

Is this level of interactivity found in instruction using ADL technology? Early studies of computer-assisted reading and arithmetic instruction found that students in grades K-6 were answering 8-10 individually selected and assessed questions each minute (Fletcher & Atkinson, 1972; Fletcher & Suppes, 1972). This level of interactivity extrapolates to 480-600 such questions an hour, if students were to sustain this level of interaction for 60 minutes.

Individualization: Pace

With regard to the second tutorial capability, it is worth noting that tutors adjust the content, sequence, and difficulty of instruction to the needs of their students. All these adjustments relate to pace—the rate or speed with which students are allowed to proceed through instructional material.

Many classroom instructors have been struck by the differences in the pace with which their students learn. Their observations are confirmed by research. For instance, consider some findings on the time it takes for different students to reach the same instructional objectives:

- Ratio of time needed by fastest and slowest students to reach mathematics objectives: 4 to 1 (Suppes, Fletcher, & Zanotti, 1975, 1976)

- Overall ratio of time needed by fastest 10 percent and slowest 10 percent of K-8 students to reach objectives in a variety of subjects: 5 to 1 (Gettinger, 1984)

- Ratio of time needed by fastest and slowest undergraduates in a major research university to learn a programming language: 7 to 1 (Private communication, Corbett, 1998)

That there are differences among students in the speed with which they learn is not surprising, but, as with tutoring, the magnitudes of the differences are surprising. Although the speed with which different students reach instructional objectives is not independent of ability, research has found it most directly keyed to prior knowledge (Dochy, Segers, & Buehl, 1999; Tobias, 1989). Students in military education and training bring with them a wide variety of backgrounds and life experiences—often much wider than that found among K-12 students. Adjusting the pace of instruction to their individual needs may be especially important for them.

The challenge this diversity presents to classroom instructors is daunting. Typically they focus on some of their students and leave the others to fend for themselves. This is especially true in training settings where the primary task is to enable as many learners as possible to cross a specific threshold of knowledge and skill. Technology alleviates this difficulty by allowing each learner to proceed as rapidly or as slowly as needed. Learners can skip what they already know and concentrate on what they have yet to learn.

Individualization: Sequencing and Content

The degree to which individualization matters is to some degree addressed by studies comparing individualized branching with fixed-content, linear sequencing.

Two early studies were performed by Fowler (1980) and Verano (1987), both of whom used computer-controlled videodisc instruction in their experiments. Fowler compared branched presentations with linear instruction in which precisely the same materials were held to a fixed-content, linear sequence. She reported an effect size of 0.72 (roughly, an improvement from the 50th to 76th percentile) in ability to operate and locate faults on a movie projector. Verano also compared an interactive, adaptive, branching approach with a strictly linear approach for presenting instructional material in beginning Spanish. He reported an effect size of 2.16 (roughly, an improvement from the 50th to 98th percentile) in end-of-course knowledge. These two studies, among others, suggest that individualization of sequence and content matters, perhaps a great deal.

Technology Assisted Learning: Time Savings

One of the most stable findings in comparisons of technology-based instruction with conventional instruction using lecture, text, and experience with equipment concerns instruction time savings. These findings are presented in Table 2-1.

Table 2-1

Percent Time Savings for Technology-Based Instruction

Study (Reference)	Number of Studies Reviewed	Average Time Saved (Percent)
Orlansky and String (1977) (Military Training)	13	54
Fletcher (1991) (Higher Education)	8	31
Kulik (1994) (Higher Education)	17	34
Kulik (1994) (Adult Education)	15	24

As the table shows, Orlansky and String (1977) reported that reductions in time to reach instructional objectives averaged about 54 percent in their review of technology-based military training. Fletcher (1997) reported an average time reduction of 31 percent in six assessments of interactive multimedia instruction applied in higher education. Kulik reported time reductions of 34 percent in 17 assessments of technology used in higher education and 24 percent in 15 assessments of adult education (Kulik, 1994). Each of these reviews covered different sets of evaluation studies comparing technology-based instruction to conventional classroom instruction involving lecture, texts, and perhaps laboratory examples. Overall, it seems reasonable to expect technology-based instruction to reduce the time it takes students to reach a variety of objectives by about 30 percent.

An example of the cost benefits of this reduction in time to learn may be seen in residential, specialized skill training. The DoD spends about $6.5 billion a year on this training, which is the "schoolhouse" training individuals receive after Basic, or initial accession, training. It qualifies individuals for the many technical jobs (e.g., wheeled vehicle mechanics, radar operators, avionics technicians, medical technicians) needed to perform military operations. It does not include the costs of aircraft pilot training, officer education, or training provided in military units.

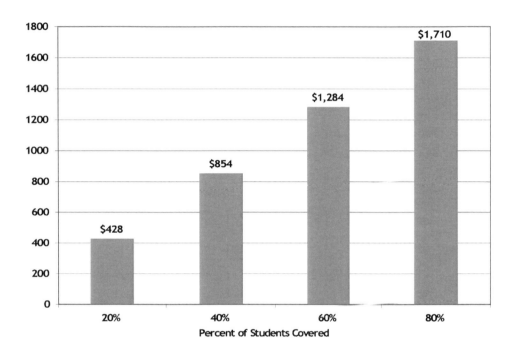

Figure 2-2. Cost Savings in millions $ (2008). This figure depicts savings in specialized skill training assuming a 30 percent reduction in training time.

Extrapolated from an earlier analysis by Angier and Fletcher (1991), Figure 2-2 shows the annual reductions in costs that would result if instruction time were reduced by 30 percent for 20, 40, 60, and 80 percent of military personnel who complete residential, specialized skill training each year. For instance, if the DoD reduced by 30 percent the time to train 20 percent of the personnel undergoing specialized skill training, it would save about $428 million per year. If it were to do so for 60 percent of these personnel, it would save about $1,284 million per year, or about 20 percent of the funds allocated for specialized skill training. Specialized skill training is particularly amenable to the use of ADL technologies. Use of ADL capabilities by 60 percent of specialized skill trainees is not an unreasonable expectation.

Saving 30 percent of training time may be a conservative target. Commercial enterprises that develop technology-based instruction for the DoD regularly base their bids on the expectation that they can reduce instructional time by 50 percent. Noja (1991) has reported time savings through the use of technology-based instruction as high as 80 percent in training operators and maintenance technicians for the Italian Air Force.

Two other sources of cost savings with ADL technologies are not considered in the Figure 2-2 data. First, the cost models behind Figure 2-2 assume reductions in time to train in residential settings, but they take no account of using ADL technologies to distribute some of that training to operational units, thereby reducing change of station or temporary duty costs. Second, ADL technologies can be used to simulate expensive equipment, operational environments, and interpersonal situations—thereby not just reducing costs, but increasing safety, enhancing visualization, and allowing time to be sped up or slowed down as needed for the training.

Perhaps more importantly for military applications, ADL technologies can prepare individuals more quickly for operational duty. In this way they act as a force multiplier, increasing readiness and operational effectiveness without increasing personnel costs.

Instructional Effectiveness

Research data suggest that savings in using ADL technologies do not come at the expense of instructional effectiveness. Empirical findings report the opposite. Figure 2-3 shows effect sizes from several reviews of studies that compared conventional instruction with technology-based instruction.

In the figure, "Computer-based instruction" summarizes results from 233 studies that involved straightforward application of computer presentations using text, graphics, and some animation—as well as some degree of individualized interaction. The effect size of 0.39 standard deviations suggests, roughly, an improvement of 50th percentile students to the performance levels of 65th percentile students.

"Interactive multimedia instruction" involves more elaborate interactions adding audio, animation, and video, and generally taking advantage of the Multimedia Effect (Fletcher & Tobias, 2005; Mayer, 2005). These added capabilities evidently increase achievement. They show an average effect size of 0.50, which suggests an improvement of 50th percentile students to the 69th percentile of performance.

"Intelligent tutoring systems" involve a capability that has been developing since the late 1960s (e.g., Carbonell, 1972; Sleeman & Brown, 1976). In this approach an attempt is made to directly mimic the one-on-one dialogue that occurs in tutorial interactions. A key goal of these systems is to generate computer presentations and responses in real-time and on-demand as needed or requested by learners. Instructional designers do not need to anticipate and pre-store them. This approach is computationally more sophisticated and more expensive to produce than standard computer-based instruction. However, its costs may be justified by the increase in average effect size to 0.84 standard deviations, which suggests, roughly, an improvement from 50th to 80th percentile performance. As discussed a little later in this chapter, return on investment is much more sensitive to scaling and delivery costs of instruction than to the initial costs to design and develop it.

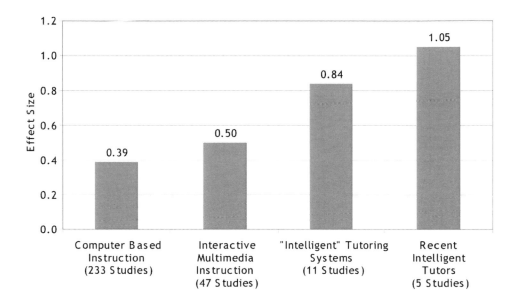

Figure 2-3. Technology-based instruction effects. This graphic illustrates effect sizes from selected studies comparing technology-based instruction with more conventional approaches.

A selected group of intelligent tutoring systems were considered just to see how far they are progressing. The average effect size of 1.05 standard deviations for these applications is promising. It represents, roughly, an improvement of the performance of 50th percentile students to 85th percentile performance.

The more extensive tailoring of instruction to the needs of individual students that can be obtained through the use of generative, intelligent tutoring systems can only be expected to increase. Such systems may raise the bar for the ultimate effectiveness of ADL instruction. It may well surpass Bloom's 2-Sigma challenge.

Student Attitudes

The attitudes of students toward instruction can affect its effectiveness and efficiency. Many evaluations of technology-based instruction simply ask students if they prefer it to more conventional classroom approaches. Greiner (1991) reviewed these evaluations and found overall that 70-80 percent of students who were polled

29

preferred technology-based approaches over others. When students reported that they did not, the reasons were usually traced to implementation or technical problems with the technology, not the instructional approach itself.

McKinnon, Nolan, and Sinclair (2000) completed a thorough three-year study of student attitudes toward the use of technology-based learning and productivity tools such as spreadsheets, databases, graphics, desktop publishing, and statistical processing. The attitudes of the students toward technology use slackened as the novelty of using the technology wore off. However, their attitudes remained positive and significantly more positive than those of students who did not have access to the technology throughout the three years of the study.

Return on Investment

Knowing that we can use ADL technologies to reliably reduce learning time, particularly time to learn journeyman skills such as remembering, understanding, and applying facts, simple concepts, and straight-forward procedures, what might an investment in it return?

One way to answer this question is by applying the findings presented earlier in Figure 2-2, which only considered savings. Using the analysis underlying that figure we can wrap in both the savings and the costs to achieve them using a return on investment (ROI) model. This model simply reduces to the ratio of the net return (savings in this case) to the costs as shown in the following:

$$\frac{(\text{Savings} - \text{Costs})}{\text{Costs}}$$

We can begin by assuming (conservatively) a 30 percent reduction in training time achieved through the use of ADL technologies by (conservatively again) 40 percent of residential specialized training students. From Figure 2-2 and the analysis on which it is based (Angier & Fletcher, 1991), these assumptions suggest annual savings of $854 million. Given this result the next step is to determine the costs to design, develop, and deliver ADL instruction to 40 percent of residential specialized skill training students.

How much would it cost to render with ADL technology the training needed by 40 percent of specialized skill students? The 2002 Military Manpower Training Report is the last such report issued by the Office of the Under Secretary of Defense for Personnel and Readiness. Changes in specialized skill training since 2002 are assumed to have been small. This analysis uses training and manpower data from the 2002 report, but 2008 cost data for personnel and ADL course development and delivery. According to the 2002 Military Manpower Training Report, the average Specialized

Training course length across all four Services was about 57 training days. If that were reduced by 30 percent it would amount to 40 days. Military personnel in training billets may be required to perform additional duties, but, assuming 8 hours a day in course training, that amounts to about 320 hours of training. About 357,700 officers and enlisted personnel completed Specialized Training in FY02. Forty percent of that number amounts to 143,080 learners. In effect then, 320 hours of ADL training would have to be produced and then delivered to 143,080 learners.

Estimates to produce an hour of computer-assisted training range widely depending on the content, instructional strategy used, and pay and allowances for subject matter experts, "authors," and computer programmers/analysts. One source of estimates comes from the Joint Knowledge Development and Distribution Capability (JKDDC), which is producing Web-based individual training programs for joint assignments and operations. As of May 2008, JKDDC had produced more than 200 courses with more than 65,000 course completions (Camacho, 2008). In the first quarter of FY 2008 the costs for JKDDC to develop an hour of instruction were about $14,000 and about $4 to deliver it. For an update, see Camacho, West, and Vozzo (this volume).

We might then assume that it would cost about $4.48 million to produce 274 hours of ADL specialized skill training and an additional $183.14 million to deliver it to 143,080 students. The investment for the first year of this training would be about $87.64 million.

Plugging these data and assumptions into an ROI calculation yields a value of ($821.94 − $187.62)/$187.62 = $3.38. Under these assumptions, an investment in ADL technology will return about $3.38 for every dollar invested.

Under current practice each of 143,080 learners is spending the full 456 hours in the 57 days of courses instead of saving 30 percent of that time – a savings that amounts to 19.57 million hours. Average hourly pay for learners at this level is $42. The return on investing in ADL technology under these assumptions is then about $821.94 million.

After the first year, the costs to develop the instruction would be reduced to whatever is required to maintain and update the course, but the ROI is not particularly sensitive to development costs. It seems far more sensitive to delivery costs. They are included in this analysis for the delivery of the ADL instruction but not for the classroom instruction it replaces. If the savings in training delivery costs were fully considered in this calculation, the ROI would increase substantially. Also, as suggested earlier, 30 percent time savings is likely to be an underestimate of the student time in training that can be saved. Further, even though this analysis assumes Web-based capability for delivering the instruction, it does not take into account reductions in travel and temporary duty costs, which, if included, would further increase ROI. Finally, the administrative efficiencies, improved tracking and assurance of student progress, and other benefits provided by ADL technology that were not considered in the above analysis have their place and would continue to argue for its use.

Less time in school means more time on the job. Savings in time needed to reach training objectives not only reduce training costs, but also increase the supply of people for operational forces without increasing the number of people in uniform—they amount to a force multiplier. Ways to account for accompanying increases in readiness and effectiveness due to force multiplication remain to be determined, but they, rather than savings in training costs, may be the most significant impact of reducing time to reach performance levels required by operational forces.

In short, a significant return seems likely to result from an investment to convert some proportion of training to ADL technology. This value arises primarily from the reduction of student time spent in the training infrastructure. Even with ADL, seasoned military personnel must provide additional training, mentoring, and monitoring for people early in their careers. Certainly efforts must be made to preserve the camaraderie and *espirit de corps* gained by students undergoing the rigors of training together. The argument for ADL is not to suggest massive replacement of people with technology. It is, instead, that ADL both reduces costs to train and increases force effectiveness by releasing people sooner from the training infrastructure and ensuring their competencies. A cost-effective, optimal balance between the use of ADL and more people-intensive approaches to training and education remains to be determined.

Technology Assisted Learning: Performance Aiding

Most of the discussion to this point has focused on education and training applications using ADL technology. Something remains to be said about its use in providing on demand performance aiding. The term Interactive Electonic Technical Manual is a generic label for such a device (Gafford & Heller, this volume). Fletcher and Johnston (2002) presented data on effectiveness and costs of several portable, electronic maintenance performance systems, one of which was the Integrated Maintenance Information System (IMIS).

IMIS is a wearable computer-based performance aid for avionics maintenance. Thomas (1995) compared the performance of 12 Avionics Specialists and 12 Airplane General (APG) Technicians in troubleshooting three F-16 avionics subsystems. Within each of the two groups of subjects, six of the fault isolation problems were performed using paper-based Task Orders (Air Force technical manuals) and six were performed using IMIS.

Training for APG Technicians includes all aspects of aircraft maintenance, only a small portion of which concerns avionics. In contrast, Avionics Specialists must meet higher selection standards and receive 16 weeks of specialized training focused on avionics maintenance. Costs to train APG Technicians are about half those for Avionics Specialists. Results of the study are shown in Table 2-2.

As shown in the table, findings of the study were:

Table 2-2

Maintenance performance of 12 Air Force Avionics Specialists and 12 General (APG) Technicians using Task Orders (TOs) and IMIS.

Technicians/ Performers	Correct Solutions (Percent)		Time to Solution (Minutes)		Average Number of Parts Used		Time to Order Parts (Minutes)	
	TOs	IMIS	TOs	IMIS	TOs	IMIS	TOs	IMIS
Avionics Specialists	81.9	100.0	149.3	123.6	8.7	6.4	19.4	1.2
APG Technicians	69.4	98.6	175.8	124.0	8.3	5.3	25.3	1.5

- Avionics Specialists using Task Orders compared with those using IMIS. The Avionics Specialists using IMIS found more correct solutions in less time, used fewer parts to do so, and took less time to order them. All these results were statistically significant. The results concerning time to order parts are to be expected because IMIS automated much of this process.

- APG Technicians using Task Orders compared with those using IMIS. The APG Technicians using IMIS found more correct solutions in less time, used fewer parts to do so, and took less time to order them. All these results were statistically significant.

- APG Technicians using IMIS compared with Avionics Specialists using Task Orders. The APG Technicians using IMIS found more correct solutions in less time, used fewer parts to do so, and took less time to order them than did Avionics Specialists using paper-based Task Orders. All these results were statistically significant.

- APG Technicians using IMIS compared with Avionics Specialists using IMIS. In these comparisons, the APG Technicians performed just about as well as the Avionics specialists, and even slightly better in the number of parts used. None of these comparisons were statistically significant.

The economic promise suggested by these results could well vanish if the costs to provide the performance aid (IMIS) exceed the costs they otherwise save. Teitelbaum and Orlansky (1996) estimated IMIS reductions in depot-level maintenance, organizational-level maintenance, and maintenance and transportation of inventories of spare parts. They found annual savings from the use of IMIS at about $38 million for the full Air Force fleet of F-16s. Teitelbaum and Orlansky assumed an eight-year useful life for IMIS and estimated about $18 million per year to maintain and update it and amortize its development costs. The result is a benefit of about $20 million per year in net savings or an ROI of about 1.11, which excludes the significant impact of IMIS on sortie rate, readiness, and operational effectiveness.

The ADL Vision

The long-term vision of ADL is an extrapolation from such developments as portable, increasingly accessible computing (including hand-held, worn, or even implanted computers), the global information infrastructure (currently manifest in the World Wide Web with its multitude of search engines), modular object-oriented architectures, Web 2.0 technologies, and natural language processing. The march toward devices that might be described as personal learning associates seems inevitable.

As currently envisioned, these devices will act as personal accessories. They will respond to each individual's needs on demand for education, training, and performance aiding by assembling relevant objects from the global infrastructure and engaging the user in guided conversations (such as those described by Hu, Graesser, and Fowler in this volume) to enhance the user's knowledge and skills and/or problem solving capabilities. Learning in these cases is not a matter of just working through pre-specified lessons, but a return to the 100,000 year old tutorial practice of an individual and a sage working together to enhance knowledge and skill. In this case, the human sage is supplanted by a computational device with access to something approaching the whole of human knowledge carried throughout the global information infrastructure.

As described by Dodds and Fletcher (2004) and by Wisher in this volume, objects drawn from the global infrastructure must be portable, durable, reusable, and accessible. A number of researchers writing in this volume discuss the history and development of the Sharable Object Reference Model (SCORM), which can ensure that objects have the first three of these qualities (Gallagher, this volume).

Additionally, the objects must be accessible. As discussed by Wisher and in more detail by Lannom and others in this volume, the development of the Content Object Repository Discovery Registration/Resolution Architecture (CORDRA) and its use by the ADL Registry provide global visibility for objects while allowing their developers to retain control over access to them. They are then available for reuse or repurposing (Shanley et al., this volume).

These developments have provided ways for objects to be identified and collected for local use from the global information infrastructure. The continued operation of Moore's Law predicting continual advances in computing power per unit cost, and the market-driven effort to imbue computer-technology with natural language understanding should ensure development of affordable, mobile, conversation-capable computing. The major issue that remains for ADL is development of the envisioned individualized tutorial capabilities. Progress and promise can be seen in this area (e.g., Graesser, Olney, & Cade, in press; Hu, Graesser, & Fowler, this volume). It remains key for realizing the full ADL vision.

Conclusion

In short, the above research suggests that use of ADL technology:

- Can increase instructional effectiveness.

- Can reduce time needed to learn.

- Can ensure that all students learn.

- Is preferred by students.

- Is effective and efficient for distributing instruction anytime, anywhere.

Most of the research and data to support these conclusions has been available for some time. The usual lag between research findings and their application in practice is observable here as elsewhere. As argued first by Fletcher (1992, 1997) and later by Corbett (2001), ADL technology may make Scrivin's educational imperative and Bloom's tutorial instruction affordable.

The "Rule of Thirds" that emerges from empirical evaluations of technology-based instruction was mentioned earlier in this article. The Rule of Thirds is strictly a statistical statement. It summarizes a large body of empirical findings, but it does not directly address cause and effect.

Clark's often quoted statement (1983) that "The best current evidence is that media are mere vehicles that deliver instruction but do not influence student achievement any more than the truck that delivers our groceries causes changes in our nutrition" (p. 445) does address cause and effect. This point of view seems both fair and unequivocal. The presence of any technology is no guarantee that effective instructional content, effective ways to present it, or even that the unique strengths of the technology itself will be present or used. On the other hand, the absence of technology, including ADL technology, is a reasonable guarantee that its unique functionalities will be unavailable.

Another statement to take into account is that "If you don't have a gadget called a 'teaching machine,' don't get one. Don't buy one; don't borrow one; don't steal one. If you have such a gadget, get rid of it. Don't give it away, for someone else might use it. …. If you begin with a device of any kind, you will try to develop the teaching program to fit that device" (Gilbert, 1960, p. 478).

Gilbert seems both right and wrong. He is certainly correct in suggesting that instructional designers and developers who adopt a "teaching machine" will try to fit the teaching program to it. The new functionalities such a device makes available motivates its adoption and adaptations to it in the first place.

It is less certain that such adaptations are to be avoided. They might well be enthusiastically sought, just as printed textbooks were long ago. If properly applied, technology should improve, if not revolutionize, the effectiveness and efficiency of teaching programs. It is up to researchers, developers, and instructors, not the technology itself, to see that it does.

Finally there is the Columbus effect. In keeping with technologies that made carriages go without horses and telegraphs transmit without wires, the Columbus effect will doubtless apply to our efforts to provide tutorial instruction without humans. We envision the development of personal learning associates and are building toward them, but just as Columbus headed for the East Indies and ended up with something entirely unexpected, so we may end up with something as unforeseen and different from horseless carriages and wireless telegraph as automobiles and radio—to say nothing of the Santa Monica Freeway and Wolfman Jack. Nonetheless, making education, training, and problem solving aids as affordable and universally accessible as possible seems as good a start as any.

References

Alpert, D. I., & Bitzer, D. L. (1970). Advances in computer-based education. *Science, 167*, 1582-1590.

Angier, B., & Fletcher, J. D. (1991). *Interactive courseware (ICW) and the cost of individual training* (IDA Paper No. P-2567). Alexandria, VA: Institute for Defense Analyses.

Atkinson, R. C. (1968). Computerized instruction and the learning process. *American Psychologist, 23*, 225-239.

Bloom, B. S. (1984). The 2 sigma problem: The search for methods of group instruction as effective as one-to-one tutoring. *Educational Researcher, 13*, 4-16.

Camacho, J. (2008). *Joint Knowledge Online brief to the NoD Education Command ADL Conference.* Retrieved from www.mil.no/multimedia/archive/00123/ Joe_Camacho_plenary_123167a.pdf

Carbonell, J. R. (1970). AI in CAI: An artificial intelligence approach to computer-assisted instruction. *IEEE Transactions on Man-Machine Systems, 11*, 190-202.

Clark, R. E. (1983). Reconsidering research on learning from media. *Review of Educational Research, 53*, 445-459.

Corbett, A. (2001). Cognitive computer tutors: Solving the two-sigma problem. In M. Bauer, P. J. Gmytrasiewicz, & Y. Vassileva (Eds.), *User modeling* (pp. 137-147). Berlin: Springer-Verlag.

Corno, L., & Snow, R. E. (1986). Adapting teaching to individual differences among learners. In M. C. Wittrock (Ed.), *Handbook of research on teaching* (3rd ed., pp. 605–629). New York: Macmillan.

Coulson, J. E. (Ed.) (1962). *Programmed learning and computer-based instruction.* New York: John Wiley.

Dochy, F., Segers, M., & Buchl, M. (1999). The relation between assessment practices and outcomes of studies: The case of research on prior knowledge. *Review of Educational Research, 69*(2), 145-186.

Dodds, P. V. W., & Fletcher, J. D. (2004). Opportunities for new "smart" learning environments enabled by next generation web capabilities. *Journal of Education Multimedia and Hypermedia, 13*(4), 391-404.

Fletcher, J. D. (1991). Effectiveness and cost of interactive videodisc instruction. *Machine Mediated Learning, 3*, 361-385.

Fletcher, J. D. (1992). Individualized systems of instruction. In M. C. Alkin (Ed.), *Encyclopedia of educational research* (6th ed., pp. 613-620). New York: Macmillan.

Fletcher, J. D. (1997). What have we learned about computer based instruction in military training? In R. J. Seidel & P. R. Chatelier (Eds.), *Virtual reality, training's future?* (pp. 169-177). New York: Plenum Publishing.

Fletcher, J. D. (2004). Technology, the Columbus Effect, and the third revolution in learning. In M. Rabinowitz, F. C. Blumberg, & H. Everson (Eds.), *The design of instruction and evaluation: Affordances of using media and technology* (pp. 139-157). Mahwah, NJ: Lawrence Erlbaum Associates.

Fletcher, J. D., & Atkinson, R. C. (1972). An evaluation of the Stanford CAI program in initial reading (Grades K through 3). *Journal of Educational Psychology, 63*, 597-602.

Fletcher, J. D., & Johnston, R. (2002). Effectiveness and cost benefits of computer-based aids for maintenance operations. *Computers in Human Behavior, 18*, 717-728.

Fletcher, J. D., & Suppes, P. (1972). Computer-assisted instruction in reading: Grades 4-6. *Educational Technology, 12*, 45-49.

Fletcher, J. D., & Tobias, S. (2005). The multimedia principle. In R. E. Mayer (Ed.), *The Cambridge handbook of multimedia learning* (pp. 117-133). New York: Cambridge University Press.

Fowler, B. T. (1980). *The effectiveness of computer-controlled videodisc-based training.* Unpublished doctoral dissertation, University of Iowa, Iowa City.

Galanter, E. (Ed.) (1959). *Automatic teaching: The state of the art.* New York: John Wiley.

Gettinger, M. (1984). Individual differences in time needed for learning: A review of the literature. *Educational Psychologist, 19*, 15-29.

Gilbert, T. F. (1960). On the relevance of laboratory investigation of learning to self-instructional programming. In A. A. Lumsdaine & R. Glaser (Eds.), *Teaching machines and programmed learning: A source book* (pp. 475-485). Washington, DC: National Education Association of the United States.

Graesser, A. C., & Person, N. K. (1994). Question asking during tutoring. *American Educational Research Journal, 31*, 104-137.

Graesser, A. C., Olney, A., & Cade, W. (in press). Instruction based on tutoring. In R. E. Mayer & P. A. Alexander (Eds.), *Handbook of research and learning on instruction*. New York: Routledge Press.

Greiner, J. M. (1991). Interactive multimedia instruction: What do the numbers show? In *Proceedings of the Ninth Annual Conference on Interactive Instruction Delivery* (pp. 100-104). Warrenton, VA: Society for Applied Learning Technology.

Kilgour, F. G. (1998). *The evolution of the book*. New York: Oxford University Press.

Kulik, J. A. (1994). Meta-analytic studies of findings on computer-based instruction. In E. L. Baker & H. F. O'Neil, Jr. (Eds.), *Technology assessment in education and training*. Hillsdale, NJ: Lawrence Erlbaum Associates.

Mayer, R. E. (Ed.) (2005). *The Cambridge handbook of multimedia learning*. New York: Cambridge University Press.

McKinnon, D. H., Nolan, C. J. P., & Sinclair, K. E. (2000). A longitudinal study of student attitudes toward computers: Resolving an attitude decay paradox. *Journal of Research on Computing in Education, 32*, 325-335.

Defense Manpower Data Center, U.S. Department of Defense. (2002). *Military manpower training report*. Washington, DC: Author.

Noja, G. P. (1987). New frontiers for computer-aided training. In R. J. Seidel & P. D. Weddle (Eds.), *Computer-based instruction in military environments* (pp. 215-229). New York: Plenum Press.

Orlansky, J., & String, J. (1977). *Cost effectiveness of computer-based instruction in military training* (IDA Paper No. P-1375). Arlington, VA: Institute for Defense Analyses.

Scriven, M. (1975). Problems and prospects for individualization. In H. Talmage (Ed.), *Systems of individualized education* (pp. 199-210). Berkeley, CA: McCutchan.

Sleeman, D., & Brown, J. S. (Eds.) (1982). *Intelligent tutoring systems*. New York, NY: Academic Press.

Suppes, P. (1966). The uses of computers in education. *Scientific American, 215*, 206-220.

Suppes, P., Fletcher, J. D., & Zanotti, M. (1975). Performance models of American Indian students on computer-assisted instruction in elementary mathematics. *Instructional Science, 4,* 303-313.

Suppes, P., Fletcher, J. D., & Zanotti, M. (1976). Models of individual trajectories in computer-assisted instruction for deaf students. *Journal of Educational Psychology, 68,* 117-127.

Thomas, D. L. (1995). *Integrated Maintenance Information System: User field demonstration and test executive summary* (Tech. Rep. No. AL/HR-TR-1995-0033). Wright-Patterson Air Force Base, OH: Human Resources Directorate, Logistics Research Division. (DTIC/NTIS ADA 293 250)

Teitelbaum, D., & Orlansky, J. (1996). *Costs and benefits of the Integrated Maintenance Information System (IMIS)* (IDA Paper No. P-3173). Alexandria, VA: Institute for Defense Analyses. (DTIC/NTIS ADA 312 884)

Tobias, S. (1989). Another look at research on the adaptation of instruction to student characteristics. *Educational Psychologist, 24,* 213-227.

Verano, M. (1987). *Achievement and retention of Spanish presented via videodisc in linear, segmented, and interactive modes.* Unpublished doctoral dissertation, University of Texas, Austin. (DTIC No. ADA 185 893).

Wetzel-Smith, S. K., & Wulfeck, W. H. (2010). Training incredibly complex tasks. In J. V. Cohn & P. E. O'Connor (Eds.), *Performance enhancement in high risk environments.* Westport, CT: Praeger.

Wulfeck, W. H., & Wetzel-Smith, S. K. (2008). Use of visualization techniques to improve high-stakes problem solving. In E. Baker, J. Dickieson, W. Wulfeck, & H. F. O'Neil, (Eds.), *Assessment of problem solving using simulations* (pp. 223–238). Florence, KY: Taylor and Francis–Lawrence Erlbaum Associates.

The Author

J. D. Fletcher is a Research Staff Member with the Institute for Defense Analyses. He developed the technical background and goals for establishing ADL and assembled the team that produced SCORM, CORDRA, and the ADL Registry.

Chapter 3

Standards—The Agony and Ecstasy of ADL
Robby Robson and Tyde Richards

Standards, by which we mean technical standards that enable systems to work together, are at the foundation of modern existence. Standardized parts are a pre-condition for mass production, economies of scale, commoditization, and the development of supply chains. Modern technology relies on standards for weights, measures, units of time, fasteners, electricity, paper, televisions and telephony, currency, and thousands of other things. Standards are unquestionably important and ubiquitous, but what have they to do with *learning*?

At first glance, learning and standards seem to be at opposite ends of the spectrum. Standards are about uniformity and universality, whereas few things are more personalized or context-dependent than learning. The thought of standardized learning systems, rolling off assembly lines like so many tanks, is an anathema to learning professionals. Instructional designers and developers of training content are artisans who feel most comfortable producing highly customized learning experiences. They roll their eyes at the "cookie cutter content" to which standardization must, in their opinion, inevitably lead.

But first impressions can be very wrong. An important lesson of the learning industry is that personalization and standardization go hand in glove. When properly conceived and implemented, standards can provide the foundation for innovation and creativity while reducing costs and enabling supply chains. This chapter is the story of the efforts that helped achieve these goals for the ADL Initiative and, in particular, the efforts that played into the development of SCORM.

Taking Off with the Aviation Industry CBT Committee

In the 1980s, hardware was not "plug-and-play," and PCs were not commodities. Training developed for one configuration of graphics cards, audio drivers, video displays, and memory would not run on another. This was a problem for the aviation industry, where computer-based training (CBT) was starting to take hold. To address this problem, a group of training professionals formed the Aviation Industry CBT Committee (AICC) in 1988. Their goal was to standardize platforms used for CBT, and they soon turned to the problem of standardizing the way in which CBT could be delivered on a Local Area Network (LAN).

At that time, and indeed throughout the early 1990s, there was little notion of training content being different than the system which delivered it. The AICC recognized this as a fundamental roadblock and developed a set of standards for *Computer Managed Instruction (CMI)* that laid the foundation for interoperability among learning management systems (LMS) and learning content for years to come. The AICC CMI standards introduced many revolutionary ideas. They:

- Introduced the idea that training *content* was different from a training *system*.

- Defined roles that training and training content played in a CBT environment. In the AICC approach it was the job of the LMS to house and deliver training content to student computers and to record data such as test results, whereas the training content was responsible for the student experience and for reporting results.

- Defined how training content running on a learner's computer communicates with the LMS that put it there as well as what data could be communicated.

- Defined a paradigm for determining what content an LMS should deliver to the learner based on an instructional model. In this model, content is broken into chunks with objectives and prerequisites. In the AICC approach, the LMS is given a list of blocks and instructed to show the learner the first block for which all prerequisites have been met. This reflects an instructional model that measured performance by interactions with multimedia content and progress is guided both by a predetermined curriculum and the objectives that a learner has mastered.

- Defined how descriptive information such as the title of a course could be recorded and given to an LMS. This information is called *metadata* and has played a central role in the history of learning technology standards.

When ADL turned its attention to the problem of developing portable training content that could be used by any system, it was natural to adopt the CMI standards as the basis for SCORM.

The New Kids on the Block

The AICC was the first kid on the block to develop viable interoperability standards for e-learning. But as the Web started to explode in the late 1990s, at least a dozen others joined the fray. The two organizations that would play the largest role in the development of SCORM were the IEEE Learning Technology Standards Committee (IEEE LTSC) and the IMS project (IMS) which later was renamed the IMS Global Learning Consortium (IMS GLC).

The IEEE LTSC operates under the auspices of the Institute of Electrical and Electronic Engineers (IEEE) Standards Association. The IEEE is a strong brand in the information technology standards world, responsible for standards such as Ethernet and WiFi, but the real significance of this parentage is that the IEEE LTSC is an accredited Standards Development Organization. This means that its standards are developed using an open consensus process that safeguards against domination by any one company or stakeholder group, and that the standards distinguish between *normative* language (parts of a standard that set out requirements) and *informative* language (the parts that explain the requirements).

The IMS started as the Instructional Management System Project under an organization called Educom. Educom soon merged with Educause which is "a nonprofit association whose mission is to advance higher education by promoting the intelligent use of information technology" (Educause, 2010), and which also controls who may use the .edu extension on their domain name. Structurally, the IMS GLC is an industry consortium. Industry consortia differ from accredited standards bodies in decision making, participation rights, and legal requirements, but the processes used to develop standards are very similar.

Strange Bedfellows

Early on ADL made the decision to build SCORM from existing standards if possible, and SCORM 2004 is derived almost entirely from work done in the AICC, IEEE LTSC, and IMS. These four organizations are strange bedfellows. The AICC is an informal consortium focused on solving problems in a single vertical industry. IMS members are primarily academic institutions, educational technology vendors, and educational publishers. The IEEE LTSC has only individual memberships and draws from academia, research organizations, e-learning vendors, training organizations, and the public sector.

In the late 1990s ADL was able to pull all of these organizations and constituencies together around standards development activities. It did this by contributing time, resources, meeting space and, in the case of the IMS, significant financial investments. It also galvanized the e-learning vendor community through its Plugfests, which served as a reality check to ensure that the standards being developed could be implemented on a practical level. However, over time this coalition ran into trouble.

One issue was the significant overlap among the people participating in all four organizations. This drained resources and encouraged individuals who did not get their way in one venue to take the fight to another. Another, more common problem arose over ownership and intellectual property. This is not just an ego issue: Changes in a standard can have far-reaching deleterious effects. Imagine what would happen if all online courses in the world stopped accurately reporting test scores and certification statuses! In the world of standards, where different organizations have different processes and intellectual property rights policies, joint work is difficult and turf wars are common.

The Ecstasy of SCORM 1.2

Returning to the story of standards and SCORM, we start with the observation that content designed for delivery by an LMS has several components, including:

- The underlying multimedia (text, graphics, audio, and video) that is displayed to the learner

- Instructions for how and when and in what order the content is displayed

- Descriptive information (metadata) that give context to the content

- Methods for communicating information with an LMS

The AICC CMI work laid the foundation for standardizing all of these components, but by the time the ADL, IEEE LTSC, and IMS were getting going, drawbacks were apparent. The first was the method used by the AICC to communicate information in a Web-based environment. This method seemed difficult for content developers to implement. With encouragement from ADL, the AICC developed a new method that overcame this obstacle and that would eventually be standardized through the IEEE LTSC. In a bizarre twist, the older AICC method was a first instance of a "Web service," and is in many ways more modern than the subsequent one incorporated into SCORM.

The new method (called the SCORM run-time API, or application programming interface) was designed specifically for Web content delivered through a Web browser. It also made implicit architectural and technological assumptions that were not universally valid and that are less and less valid today. But it had two major advantages: It was easy for content developers to use and it worked.

A second challenge with adopting the AICC work concerned the means by which content was transferred from an authoring environment to an LMS. In the AICC method, the control files were separate from the content itself. This was due in part to the AICC's emphasis on pedagogical structures rather than the portability of content. The IMS, meanwhile, had developed a packaging specification that enabled all of this information to be bundled together. It had several technical advantages, including the ability to represent Web content with dependent resources, and it fit better with the conceptual notion of a course or module being a self-contained package. It also was backed by major technology vendors, including Microsoft, Apple, and Sun Microsystems, who were IMS members.

When SCORM 1.2 was released, it was based on the AICC CMI work (as modified by the IEEE LTSC) and on IMS content packaging. It also included IEEE LTSC Learning Object Metadata, or LOM. Metadata enables you to discover properties of an object without examining the object directly, such as in the case of library catalog cards or tags added to images, videos, wikis, and blogs. The first project undertaken by both the IMS and IEEE LTSC was developing a metadata standard. Much of the early work was done collaboratively and was based on contributions from a European organization called ARIADNE. Later the efforts would diverge and then be reconciled. Here again ADL played a key role in ensuring convergence among potentially divergent standards.

From an industry perspective, SCORM 1.2 was a resounding success. It was not perfect and even today SCORM 1.2 content is not guaranteed to work flawlessly in an LMS without some adjustment. But it passed the litmus test of being "good enough" to be widely adopted. Because of the work of ADL, AICC, IMS, and IEEE LTSC, there is now an industry where thousands of e-learning content developers supply hundreds of thousands of organizations that deliver e-learning to hundreds of millions of learners using whatever LMS they choose.

The Agony of SCORM 2004

In addition to packaging, metadata, and a communication protocol, SCORM 1.2 specifies what data can be communicated between content and an LMS. This is done by defining a large set of instructionally relevant data elements, carried over from the original AICC work. Some are universal in nature, such as the name of a student, the score on a test, and the time a learner has spent interacting with a particular piece of content. Others were included in the AICC CMI specification to support the instructional model of progressing through a course based on objective-based prerequisites.

From the vantage point of ADL, the instructional model seemed too limiting and the data dictionary too complex. Representatives from the AICC, IMS, ADL, and IEEE LTSC agreed at contentious session to remove the unused and overly complex data elements when moving to a standardized version. This simplified the standard, but it also rendered it unsuitable for some aviation industry use cases. As mentioned earlier, joint work among standards organizations is very difficult, and the predictable result of the contention was the opening of a rift among all of them.

The final challenge of adopting the AICC work was the instructional model. SCORM 1.2, while solving the problem of content portability, did not include a standardized method for encoding instructional design. To many this was a giant step backwards. They observed that the intelligent tutoring systems of the 1980s could deliver more adaptive (and presumably more effective) learning experiences than the Web-based LMS twenty years later.

At the time SCORM 1.2 was released, the IMS was in the throes of developing a more flexible framework for encoding the instructional design of a course. One approach was based on a specification developed at the Open University in the Netherlands called "learning design." The learning design specification concerned itself at the macro level with activities, actors, and the context in which learning took place. The other approach, called "simple sequencing," focused on the problem of determining what an LMS should next show based on the results of previous interactions. It had its roots in yet another learning technology industry consortium known as Customized Learning Experiences Online (CLEO). CLEO was organized under a different branch of the IEEE known as the IEEE Industry Standards and Technology Organization and included Microsoft, CICSO Systems, IBM, and Thomson NETg. The simple sequencing specification was developed with heavy participation from active members of the ADL, AICC, and IEEE LTSC communities, and was intended to serve as an instructional design component in SCORM.

Simple Sequencing

Simple sequencing took a long time to develop within the IMS GLC. The specification was difficult to understand and harder to implement. ADL invested significant resources in clarifying it in the SCORM 2004 documentation, which has gone through four editions, largely to address problems with this portion.

The idea behind simple sequencing, its AICC predecessor, and IMS Learning Design is deep and significant. They provide a standardized way of representing and changing the navigational and instructional structure of a learning experience without touching the actual content. But SCORM 2004 has not had the same adoption as SCORM 1.2. The reason is this: Standards work well when they solve pressing business problems and are conceptually accessible to practitioners. They fail otherwise.

The Impact of Standards

This chapter has discussed standards used in SCORM, but the learning technology standards program has always been far more ambitious. Most of the major relevant organizations have at one time or another started on comprehensive sets of standards meant to define and enable a broad range of functionality required by distributed learning systems. These include representations of tests, descriptions of accessibility traits, numerous standards for exchanging data and plugging and playing different components, standards for communicating student results, quality standards, standardized vocabularies, standards for adaptable interactive multimedia components, standards for other types of content, and many more. ADL itself launched a second major standards-related activity, the Content Object Repository Discovery and Registration/Resolution Architecture (CORDRA) in 2004 (Lannom, this volume) and was instrumental in forming the international federation for Learning, Education and Training Systems Interoperability (LETSI) to look at future directions in standards.

The impact of standards in learning technology has been enormous. SCORM is one example, but even the many standards with minimal adoption have influenced the construction and functionality of learning management systems, assessment engines, learning content management systems, repositories, and other learning technologies. In the year 2000, an ISO standards committee (ISO/IEC JTC1 SC36) was formed to standardize information technology for learning, education, and training. As with all ISO committees, representation is by National Body, i.e., by country, and its standards are recognized and often incorporated into laws by governments around the world. It has a broad agenda that brings a level of legitimacy to the learning technology industry.

The Nice Thing About Standards

It is often said that "the nice thing about standards is that there are so many to choose from." Having different standards for things like electrical plugs and mobile telephony is at best an inconvenience and at worst a significant expense. But in a field such as learning technology multiple standards may not be such a bad thing.

Standards reflect the environment in which they were conceived, and technology changes rapidly. ADL was born into an information technology world dominated by monolithic enterprise systems that handled human resource, financial, customer relations, and other functions. The Web was a slow and clunky content delivery system, and if you wanted to find something you would probably have used Alta Vista, Lycos, or Yahoo! and certainly not Google. As this is being written, software is transitioning from a product to a service, enterprise architectures have become distributed and service-oriented, and the Web has become a ubiquitous, mobile, social, media-rich, and user-generated tool for commerce, entertainment, information, and learning.

SCORM was a good start towards solving problems of interoperability, durability, and reusability. It helped establish the feasibility and desirability of standard specifications for sharable objects. However, with the continued rapid advancement of technology in this area, the original architectural assumptions on which SCORM was based, along with SCORM itself, are now in need of review and updating (Panar, Rehak, & Thropp, this volume). SCORM will continue to be useful for some time, but it is necessary to begin this review and make plans for its evolution. As an aggregator of standards, ADL should have a wide choice of standards—and futures—to choose from.

Web Resources

Aviation Industry CBT Committee. http://www.aicc.org/pages/down-docs-index.htm

Educause. http://www.educause.edu

ARIADNE. http://www.ariadne-eu.org

The Authors

Robby Robson, PhD, is the president of Eduworks Corporation based in Corvallis, Oregon. He chaired the IEEE Learning Technology Standards Committee from 2000 to 2008, has served on the IEEE Standards Association Standards Board, and has contributed to numerous IMS and IEEE specifications and standards.

Tyde Richards is a senior technologist at Eduworks Corporation and former global program manager of learning technology standards for IBM. He has served on the

IMS Technical Board, chaired the IEEE Learning Technology Standards Committee CMI Working Group, served on the executive committee of the Aviation Industry CBT Committee, and served on the U.S. National Body and as ADL liaison to ISO-IEC standardization committee on information technology for learning, education, and training.

Chapter 4

The Development of SCORM
Patrick Shane Gallagher

Section I
Introduction and Executive Summary

The SCORM, or Sharable Content Object Reference Model, is an underlying technology and product of the ADL Initiative. SCORM makes possible the sharing of distributed learning content across learning management systems that conform to the SCORM. Its development and implementation was clearly a vital first step in achieving the long-term vision of providing high quality training and education on demand.

The purpose of this chapter is to describe, in general terms, SCORM, how it was developed, and how it works. This chapter has two sections. The first is introductory and non-technical, intended for those who need only a familiarity with the basics of SCORM. This section ties together the provisions of a learning management system with that of a learning object, also known as a sharable content object (SCO) in ADL terminology. The second section provides more details on the mechanics of SCORM – its main components, how they evolved, and how they all work in harmony. The challenges to SCORM from both a pedagogical and technical perspective are presented elsewhere (Roberts & Gallagher, this volume). In the context of the ADL business paradigm, the present chapter squarely addresses the Interoperability portion of the technical elements.

The Emergence of Learning Management Systems

As information and communication technology (ICT), specifically the Internet and Web technology, gained traction in education and training activities, it was increasingly viewed as a tool to support learning in a variety of learning experiences, ranging from formal self-directed autonomous courses to virtual classrooms (Gallagher, 2007). Because of the evolution and integration of ICT within education and training, lower costs, and ease of implementation, large server-based databases such as learning management systems (LMSs) have emerged from the remnants of early mainframe-based computer-managed instruction. There are hundreds of LMSs in the global marketplace today.

A learning management system is an organization-wide, networked software package that enables the management and delivery of learning content and resources to students. Most LMSs are Internet/intranet-based to facilitate anytime, anywhere access to learning content and also administer functions such as enrollment and student tracking through a Web browser. The Learning Systems Architecture Lab at Carnegie Mellon University stated that, "A Learning Management System (LMS) is a software package used to administer one or more courses to one or more learners. An (sic) LMS is typically a web-based system that allows learners to authenticate themselves, register for courses, complete courses and take assessments" (LSAL, 2004, p. 5). LMSs are based on a variety of development platforms, such as Java Enterprise Edition or Microsoft .NET, and usually employ a robust database. Most systems are commercially developed with license fees and code restrictions. However, free and open-source models also exist (EduTools, 2007; Wikipedia-contributors, 2006).

Learning Objects

Also evolving was the concept of learning objects as a unit of learning content managed by a LMS. Learning objects (LOs), as currently conceived, have their roots in computer science and are elements of computer-based instruction derived from the object-oriented paradigm in computer science (Downes, 2001; Wiley, 2001). Online courses and learning objects are just another application from the perspective of software engineering which considers designing applications from scratch to be inefficient (Downes, 2001), thereby embracing object-oriented design. The object-oriented paradigm is seen as facilitating a "design for reuse" strategy (Sutcliffe, 2002) and, therefore, has reusability as one of its primary attributes. This intention has been transferred to the concept of an LO and is one of the primary tenets of ADL.

With high perceived return-on-investment, LMSs (and LOs) are implemented to help increase organizational efficiency. Even though they possess a rich heritage in learning theory, this has largely been lost or understated by commercial ventures. There are, however, several benefits that are attributed to LMSs such as:

- Reducing costs through decreased training redundancy and reduced operational errors and down-time

- Maximizing efficiency through the integration of content delivery such as safety issues, operating procedures, maintenance packages, environmental standards, and job reference, reducing complexity and costs of auditing

- Leveraging existing resources by including established policies and procedures, and utilizing existing training material and links to "off-the-shelf" commercial computer-based courseware (Szabo & Flesher, 2002)

Despite the perceived benefits of using a LMS, many of the first Web-based LMS products used proprietary middleware and data models to track learner performance. The concept of proprietary systems actually worked against the value proposition of a LMS implementation, creating inefficiencies and higher costs. Examples of these problems included:

- Learning content (LOs) that could not be moved from one LMS environment to another

- LMS products that could not integrate learning content created for other systems

- Inability to create searchable content or content repositories

In other words, the LMSs were not interoperable, with interoperability being defined as the ability of a system or components to work with other systems or components without special effort on the part of the end user (Miller, 2000). Interoperability can be thought of as enabling information that originates in one context to be used in another in ways that are as highly automated as possible. Lego blocks provide an analogy. Lego blocks are interlocking plastic bricks that can be assembled and connected in many ways. They can be used to build a variety of structures because of their standardized interface. Therefore, they are considered to be interoperable, at least in the Lego environment. Similarly, LOs can be connected in many ways for different learning objectives, and be interoperable within SCORM. Interoperability of LOs is an attribute of the standardization of their communication structures and protocols required to function across multiple LMS and their variations (Gallagher, 2007).

In this context, interoperability refers mainly to the interactions between learning objects and learning management systems but may extend to interaction between LOs as well. More specifically, interoperability can be defined as the ability of objects from multiple and unknown or unplanned sources to work or operate technically when put together with other objects or systems (Duval & Hodgins, 2003).

To solve the interoperability issue as well as other issues, the ADL team envisioned a new approach for ICT-based learning where LOs could be reusable, searchable, durable, and accessible. They further imagined an approach that would enable customized learning experiences that match a learner's needs. Such learning experiences would be assembled "on the fly" and would adapt intelligently to the learner. LOs comprising such experiences could include assessments, simulations, performance support, as well as directed learning experiences (adlCommunity, 2007c).

The Components of SCORM

As Internet and Web technologies became inherent in education and training, learning management systems (LMS) became the enterprise system of choice to deliver and manage Web-based learning content. However, the learning content only worked with specific LMSs and therefore could not be shared (interoperate) or reused. The Sharable Content Object Reference Model, SCORM, was developed to solve several problems including those of interoperability and reusability. Prior to SCORM, LMSs were proprietary and tightly coupled with the learning content designed to run on them. With the introduction and adoption of SCORM, learning content could now be developed for and delivered on multiple systems without redevelopment. This attribute enabled the ability for content to be used over time, or be durable, as well be reused or reusable. It also enabled learning content to be more accessible to broader audiences, fostering the ADL attribute of accessibility.

SCORM is a reference model that is essentially a collection of standards and specifications that have been profiled to work together and are described in the SCORM Bookshelf – i.e., SCORM Overview, Content Aggregation Model (CAM), Runtime Environment (RTE), and Sequencing and Navigation (S&N). The SCORM Bookshelf is available at the ADL Web site and is fully downloadable. The bookshelf describes in detail the complete technical architecture of SCORM and how each component works together.

To ensure conformance to SCORM and to help with those interested in SCORM development, the Sample Runtime Environment (SRTE) and the SCORM Test Suite have been developed and released with each version of SCORM. These are executable files and are also found on the ADL Web site, available for download by anyone.

Even though SCORM has been successful at solving major restrictions in e-learning, there still exist issues with SCORM in the form of perceived limitations and gaps in capabilities (Roberts & Gallagher, this volume). These issues begin in the technical architecture resulting in pedagogical constraints. However, it is generally accepted that SCORM works well for single-learning self-directed learning experiences that do not require extensive higher-order learning outcomes.

As the ubiquity of online learning continues to grow, so does its significance within the education and training communities. With online learning taking on more and more roles in corporations, higher education, and the military, the importance of standardizing online learning content development with models such as SCORM has emerged. SCORM is now recognized as a *de facto* standard and is used globally by governments, industry, and academia to support learning content developers in the reuse, repurposing, and establishment of interoperability across LMSs, thereby creating efficiencies and cost savings.

The Development of SCORM

Section II
The Mechanics of SCORM

During 1998, and after attending many technical meetings, ADL noticed that there were a number of parallel efforts to standardize various aspects of Internet-based learning systems. Unfortunately, these efforts were not initially coordinated and there was a great deal of confusion about where each of the working groups was headed (adlCommunity, 2007c). Over time, however, it was apparent some communities were beginning to standardize learning object characteristics, usages, and reusability through what is called a learning object content model (LOCM) (Gallagher, 2007), resulting in the development of specifications for components of the LOCM.

These efforts were limited within particular domains and organizations and were not being coordinated between communities. ADL determined that for the specifications and standards being developed to work together, there should be an integrated application profile or reference model. It was thought that the development of a reference model could also focus the activities of the various communities facilitating coordination. It was within this context that the Sharable Content Object Reference Model or SCORM was developed.

SCORM and Existing Standards and Specifications

To better understand SCORM it is important to understand what specifications and standards for learning are, who develops them, and why they are necessary (Robson & Richards, this volume). For learning experiences to be managed, tracked, and reusable, they must be standardized in the way they are described and implemented (Strijker, 2004; Sutcliffe, 2002). For reuse to occur across multiple organizations and enterprise systems, this standardization is based upon defined specifications and standards published by existing bodies such as the Alliance of Remote Instructional Authoring and Distribution Networks for Europe (ARIADNE), the Instructional Management Systems (IMS) Global Learning Consortium, the IEEE Learning Technology Standards Committee (LTSC), or the Dublin CORE (Duval, 2004; Wiley, 2001).

Specifications are developed by organizations such as the IMS or the Aviation Industry Computer-Based Training (CBT) Committee (AICC) which may or may not feed into existing or upcoming standards. Existing standards organizations may work with specifications bodies and/or implementers (industry) to develop and recommend specifications to higher standards organizations for new standards. Specific implementations may consist of one or more standards or specifications, a unique model, or some combination of standards, specifications, and models. As an example of this fuzzy delimitation, IMS LO metadata is a specification which has become the basis for the IEEE Learning Object Metadata (LOM) standard but is also used in its entirety as a basis for specific implementations of the complete specification. SCORM is a model consisting of standards and specifications from IEEE, IMS, and (historically) AICC with a defined implementation strategy or application profile. Any implementation or reference model concerned with the overarching issues of reuse and interoperability then may be based entirely or in part upon these standards and/or specifications.

SCORM is closely related to the other specific implementations or LOCMs prevalent in online learning. It is implemented globally not only in the DoD and other U.S. Government agencies (Bardack, Koch, & Smith, this volume), but across Europe, Asia, Africa, and Latin America by governmental departments and institutions concerned with e-learning. Besides being implemented by most e-learning content providers and major corporations and institutions worldwide, SCORM is also extremely well-documented and is referenced in thousands of articles in scholarly and peer-reviewed journals, books and conference proceedings (Google, 2006) and is considered a *de facto* standard in the literature (Gallagher, 2007).

The Advantage of Standards

There are many advantages to having specifications and standards in learning technology. Typically these advantages center on the idea of interoperability or the ability for learning content to be used across different organizations or enterprises employing one or multiple learning management systems (LMSs). This concept can significantly reduce costs of development and redevelopment of learning content.

A related but still mostly unrealized advantage to interoperability is that of reuse. Reuse can be, and is, defined in multiple ways but in the context of online learning it encompasses the idea of learning content being accessed in original or altered states by many different learners and/or authors/designers for multiple purposes many times. In other words, it is about reusing developed content over and over in the same or different context. The latter can also be referred to as repurposing (Doerksen, 2002). Reuse of online learning content, however, is mostly unrealized to date due to the lack of policy and infrastructure that currently exists across organizations as well as cultural barriers (Shanley et al., this volume). Other ADL initiatives such as CORDRA (Content Object Repository Discovery and Registration/Resolution Architecture), when fully implemented, are anticipated to have a positive impact on reusability. As with interoperability, the concept of reuse is part of the efficiency and economies-of-scale arguments for realizing e-learning as a means to lower training costs (Gallagher, 2007).

SCORM 2004

Comprised of specific standards and specifications, the Sharable Content Object Reference Model or SCORM is a Web-based learning content aggregation model and run-time environment for learning objects (ADL & UK, 2007). SCORM now has approximately 193 adopters globally and its development was supported by a technical working group of over 70 members. It has gained world-wide acceptance and is poised to transcend from the sole support of ADL to a global stewardship organization (adlCommunity, 2007a).

Introduction

Essentially a reference model in its sixth release state, SCORM is a model that references a set of interrelated technical specifications, guidelines, and standards designed to meet the DoD's high-level requirements for e-learning content (ADL, 2004b). SCORM is recognized as a learning object content model or LOCM (Katz et al., 2004; Verbert et al., 2005; Verbert & Duval, 2004; Verbert et al., 2004) and was one of the models used in Verbert et al's comparative analysis of LOCMs (Verbert & Duval, 2004; Zouaq et al., 2007) with a shareable content object (SCO) described as a learning object. As the basic building block for online learning using SCORM 2004, a SCO is recognized as a learning object (Advanced Distributed Learning Partnership Lab UK, 2007; Kilby, 2004) and may exhibit an innate instructional design. In the context of SCORM, ADL envisaged Internet users and heterogeneous LMSs using the

Web as a universal platform for accessing and launching sharable content objects and for establishing close communication, interaction, and coordination among content object developers, course authors, content users, and course administrators (Su & Lee, 2003).

Technical Architecture

SCORM was designed to facilitate heterogeneous Web-based LMSs to interoperate, access common repositories of executable content, and launch content that is authored using tools from different vendors (ADL, 2001a). From its inception until version 1.2, SCORM has been based upon a technical architecture composed of a Content Aggregation Model (CAM) for aggregating learning resources to form learning modules and courses and a Run-Time Environment (RTE) for launching learning resources and enabling the communication between learning resources and LMSs.

With the evolution to SCORM 2004, the architecture expanded to include sequencing and navigation functionality. The use of simple sequencing directs a LMS to automate the selection, sequencing, and progression of a learner through a defined collection of SCOs. The sequencing information for each course is contained within XML (extensible markup language) data as part of the course manifest, and reusable sequencing data are defined with usage suggestions as part of the ADL Best Practices Guide for Content Developers (ADL, 2008). In its implementation, it is beginning to be understood that sequencing data snippets can be defined and reused as specific patterns. These patterns could be representative of interactions and branching decisions that, together with specific types of SCOs, may instantiate or facilitate specific pedagogical models. However, defining SCO types and other specifics is considered part of a SCORM implementation strategy but not specified within SCORM itself.

The overall collection of functionality is referred to by ADL as the SCORM Bookshelf and is contained within a set of four books corresponding to each component plus an overarching document called the SCORM Overview. The SCORM Bookshelf is maintained and released with each version of SCORM as it evolves.

SCORM Evolution

Initial contributions to SCORM came from the various components of the AICC CMI specification, with the addition of metadata (from IMS and ARIADNE) to describe learning materials. In the initial release, SCORM focused on the interchange and interoperability of courses versus more granular units. Also, due to the lack of an available specification to draw upon, SCORM included its own course/content model eventually evolving into the present LOCM. An illustration of the contributors to SCORM and at what points in the SCORM evolution their contributions occurred is found in Figure 4-1 below.

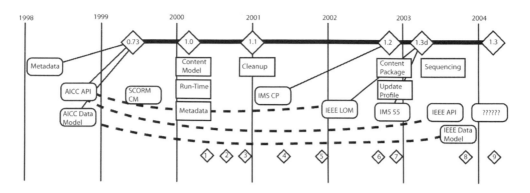

Figure 4-1. The evolution of SCORM. SCORM evolved through the inclusion of developing standards (Rehak, 2003).

In 2000, the initial SCORM 1.0 release was followed by the first maintenance release (SCORM 1.1) that removed features of the CMI model not considered widely used. The intention was to replace them with improved alternative approaches as SCORM evolved. The removal of features in the movement to SCORM 1.1 was somewhat controversial with confusion over the implications of removing features and an incomplete understanding of how and where the features targeted for removal were being used. To ADL this indicated that the impact of SCORM evolution on the community would need to be carefully considered before going forward (Rehak, 2003).

SCORM 1.2, released in late 2002, presented the first prominent technical change to SCORM with the inclusion of the IMS Content Packaging specification. It also provided the basis for most current implementations and content. SCORM 1.2 is the most widely adopted version of SCORM to date, spanning corporate, educational, and international implementation (Rehak, 2003).

SCORM 1.3 (renamed to SCORM 2004) was officially released in 2004 and continued to add new components and features by adding the IMS Simple Sequencing specification to the SCORM Bookshelf. SCORM 2004 has been released in four editions with its 3rd edition considered to be the most widely implemented. SCORM 2004 4th Edition was released in 2009 with only minor changes to the 3rd edition and most changes occurring to add more rigor to conformance certification testing. SCORM 2004 3rd Edition will be used to describe the SCORM technical architecture as this chapter progresses.

The approach for the inclusion of components into SCORM is to adopt existing standards and specifications as the basis for the reference model. SCORM adds both the critical profiling of the specification for the community and the description of how the individual data models and behaviors from the underlying standards and specification components fit into an overall framework for a complete learning delivery environment.

SCORM evolution is also moving from more than just the inclusion of new standards and features into SCORM. Support documents, test suites, prototype implementations, etc., are all key components to be provided with each new release of the model and must be planned and coordinated with the technical evolution of the reference model itself (Rehak, 2003).

SCORM 2004

Using common standards and specifications as well as custom models, SCORM 2004 3rd Edition has incorporated and harmonized the specifications and standards identified in Table 4-1.

Table 4-1

The Specifications and Standards of SCORM

Specification or Standard	Provider	Reference
Standard for Learning Object Metadata	IEEE	IEEE LTSC, 2005
SCORM Content Aggregation Model	ADL	ADL, 2006d
ECMAScript API for Content to Runtime Services	IEEE	IEEE, 2004
Data Model for Content to LMS Communication	IEEE	IEEE, 2005
IMS Content Packaging Specification	IMS GLC	IMS GLC, 2005
IMS Simple Sequencing Specification	IMS GLC	IMS GLC, 2003a
SCORM Navigation Model	ADL	ADL, 2006c

Manifest File

Using these specifications and standards, SCORM specifies how reusable Web-based content objects called sharable content objects (SCOs) can be aggregated into a portable package that includes a manifest to form a larger self-contained content object (Ostyn, 2007). The manifest includes metadata to describe each level of the aggregation as well as prescriptive data defining the sequencing or order of content accessibility. The types of objects that can be described and utilized as a content package are outlined in the SCORM CAM as Assets, SCOs, and Content Organization (activities). Within the SCORM nomenclature, Assets and SCOs are both considered Resources. Activities are considered learning activities. An Activity Tree represents the data structure that an LMS implements to reflect the hierarchical, internal representation of the defined learning activities. Content Organization represents an Activity Tree describing the organization and sequencing of Items (Activities and Resources) (ADL, 2006c).

Content Aggregation Model

The term "Content Aggregation" can be used as both an action and as a way of describing a conceptual entity. "Content Aggregation" can be used to describe the action or process of composing a set of functionally related content objects or, in terms of the SCORM Content Model, the entity created as part of this action or process. The term is also used informally to describe the content package. The aggregation can then be used to deliver the content and prescribed content structure, transferred between systems or even stored in a repository (ADL, 2006d). The Content Aggregation Model (CAM) is the set of object descriptions and specifications.

According to the SCORM 2004 CAM book, Assets, the basic building blocks, are an electronic representation of media, such as text, images, sound, assessment objects, or any other piece of data that can be rendered by a Web client and presented to a learner. Assets can be collected together to build other assets and may be launched independently if necessary. Using the IEEE LOM or other defined schema, Assets can be described with metadata for search and discovery (ADL, 2006d).

A SCO is a collection of one or more Assets representing a single, launchable learning resource (i.e., learning object) that can communicate with an LMS using the run-time environment, and can be described by metadata for search and discovery. SCOs communicate with an LMS using the IEEE ECMAScript API for Content to Runtime Services Communication standard and are the lowest level of object tracked by an LMS using the SCORM Run-Time Environment Data Model. The communication and tracking functionality together are the basis for the SCORM RTE. An illustration depicting the conceptual makeup of a SCO and its component Assets is presented in Figure 4-2 below.

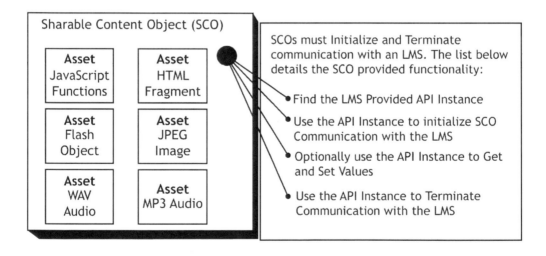

Figure 4-2. Conceptual Makeup of a SCO (ADL, 2006d). This figure depicts the basic functionality and makeup of a SCO.

There are specific expectations and requirements of a SCO by the RTE. This implies that a SCO must be able to locate an API Instance provided by the LMS and must invoke at a minimum the API methods *Initialize* and *Terminate*. There are, however, no requirements to use any other of the API methods, and they are usually only implemented as required by the learning content. The reasoning behind forcing a SCO to utilize the RTE actually lies with the LMS. By having content that behaves in a standardized fashion, and with the tracking and management capabilities of the RTE, the following gains can be realized:

- Any LMS that supports the SCORM RTE can launch SCOs and track them, regardless of where they originated.

- Any LMS that supports the SCORM RTE can track any SCO and know when it has been started and when it has ended.

- Any LMS that supports the SCORM RTE can launch any SCO in the same way.

ADL loosely describes an Activity as a meaningful unit of instruction and as what the learner does while progressing through instruction. As described in SCORM, an Activity may provide a learning resource (SCO or Asset) to the learner or it may be composed of several sub-Activities. Activities may be nested in multiple levels and consist of other Activities or sub-Activities, which may themselves consist of other Activities. There is no set limit to the number of levels of nesting for Activities.

Although activities are often associated with educational levels such as a unit, module, or course, these levels are not a requirement for SCORM. If an Activity does not consist of other Activities, it will have an associated learning resource (SCO or Asset) that is used to perform the Activity. A resource is launched when an Activity that references that resource is started (Ostyn, 2007). Multiple Activities can reference the same resource. As with the other levels of aggregation, each Activity in a Content Organization (i.e., complete collection of Activities and learning resources in a package) can reference metadata to allow for search and discovery (ADL, 2006d).

Sequencing of learning content by the LMS only applies at the Activity level (ADL, 2006d). Through the use of the Simple Sequencing specification, SCO and Asset sequence rules can be defined in the Content Organization and applied at run-time. Sequencing also allows for a limited variable defined as an objective status that can be tracked within a defined sequence (ADL, 2006c). Typically, when a SCO is launched, the tracking data provided can influence the result of sequencing rules. For example, a passing score for a SCO may result in skipping some other Activity (Ostyn, 2007).

Run-Time Environment (RTE)

One of the most essential functions of SCORM is that of communicating with an LMS. What performs the communication is defined by the CAM. The RTE and, to a lesser degree, the Sequencing and Navigation model, define how and when communication occurs. However, by defining how and when communication occurs, limits are naturally imposed. The inability to launch and maintain persistent SCOs, no direct SCO to SCO communication, and the CMI data model are some of the limits imposed with potential constraining effect. The RTE contains three components: the

Launch model, the API, and the RTE (CMI) Data Model. The Launch Model and the API are closely related and are discussed together in the following section.

Application Programming Interface (API). "In its simplest terms, the API is merely a set of defined functions that the SCO can rely on being available" (ADL, 2006b, p. RTE 3-4). The RTE is based upon a client/server relationship and is shared between both the server (LMS) and the client (Web browser). It relies on an instance of the API object provided by the LMS and instantiated in the document object model of the Web browser. The SCO is required to locate the API object upon launch, establishing communication with the LMS. For the connection to occur, the LMS must make the API object available in the DOM (Document Object Model) context of the Web browser before it launches the SCO. The SCO must then look for an instance of this API object by searching frames and windows in a very specific order defined by the IEEE standard. Once the SCO has found the object, it calls methods (functions) of the object to start a communication session with that object. The sharing relationship and the API's place are illustrated by the SCORM RTE Conceptual Model in Figure 4-3.

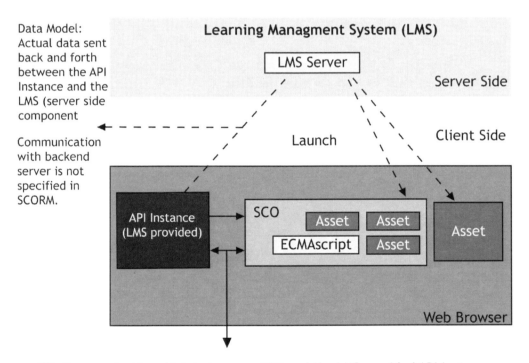

API: Communications Link between a SCO and the LMS provided API Instance

Data Model: Data is requested to be retrieved from and stored in the LMS from the SCO.

Figure 4-3. SCORM RTE Conceptual Model (ADL, 2006b). This figure depicts the communications relationships in the SCORM Run-Time Environment.

A SCO initializes a communication session by calling the corresponding method or function of the API instance. After the session has been successfully initialized, a SCO can get and set data (send and set a variable) to and from the LMS through corresponding methods or functions of the API instance. To end the session, a SCO must terminate the communication session by calling the corresponding function. There is only one communication session allowed for every launch of a SCO by the runtime environment. An error will be caused if a SCO tries to initialize a new communication session after terminating the session. In effect this means that only one SCO can be launched at a time.

Within an API instance, there are eight functions divided into three broad categories that can be called. These include functions for launching and terminating a SCO called Session Methods, functions for exchanging data model values between a SCO and a LMS called Data-Transfer Methods, and functions for auxiliary communications such as error handling call Support Methods (ADL, 2006b). These functions are illustrated below in Table 4-2.

Table 4-2

Illustration of API, API Instance and API Implementation (ADL, 2006b)

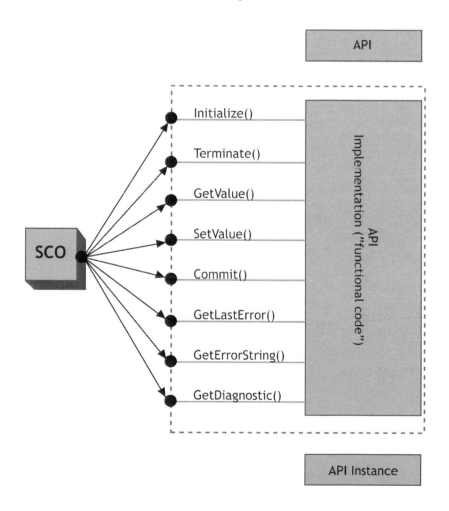

RTE Data Model. The CMI communication data model defines the data that can be sent back and forth between a SCO and the LMS using the API. Each data element is specified whether the data contained within it can be retrieved by a SCO from the LMS or sent from a SCO to the LMS or both. Data retrieved from a SCO include requests about how it is being launched, other initialization data, and learner data. Data used as signals, markers, or requests to the RTE, such as the time elapsed in the SCO or SCO suspend data requests, are sent from the SCO to the LMS. However, most of the data elements defined in the CMI data model may be retrieved or sent.

Score data may be sent to the LMS, which is sent back later in the same communication session, or data describing an existing objective status for a particular learner may be updated and sent to the runtime environment to facilitate LMS tracking or sequencing of content (ADL, 2006b; Ostyn, 2007).

Data Elements

There are 24 main data elements defined within the CMI data model. SCOs are not required to implement every data element, but they must all be implemented by the RTE (Phelps, 2004). These elements represent several data categories that support specific SCO/LMS functionality. The categories (Ostyn, 2007) have been characterized as:

- SCO status, including completion and success status

- Score data

- Score thresholds

- Objective data and object status data

- Data about various types of interactions and their status and learner responses

- Comments

- Limited learner information

- Common learner preferences

- Suspend data and location (used for bookmarking)

- Entry and exit status

Sequencing

Sequencing defines a method for representing the intended behavior of designed learning activities, allowing any LMS to sequence discrete learning resources in a consistent manner (ADL, 2006c). The Sequencing Definition Model allows a learning activity to be defined as an Activity Tree (a hierarchical organization of learning content) having sequencing control modes associated with its items, called Activities (ADL, 2006c; Su & Lee, 2003).

Using Activities, sequencing functionality is designed to allow instructional designers to define the manner in which a learner accesses SCOs and allows a designer to specify what is presented to a learner, when it is presented, and the attributes or functions the SCOs entail. Sequencing is also designed to track the learner's choices and performance (LSAL, 2004).

Movement between SCOs

As SCORM does not permit one SCO to "call" or access another SCO directly, through sequencing the LMS controls the movement of the learner from SCO to SCO. This control, described as "branching," is based upon behaviors defined by the designer. The resulting sequencing rules are a part of the manifest in the "organization" element and read by the LMS at run-time. This functionality allows the same set of SCOs to be sequenced in many different ways, depending upon the designer and the learner (LSAL, 2004).

Implicit objectives exist within the design of every activity and, if they are explicated, success in achieving those objectives can be recorded. Sequencing allows the implicit objective for an activity to become explicit and to map it to other objectives associated with other Activities in the Activity Tree (LSAL, 2004). To accomplish this, sequencing uses a global variable called an objective. For sequencing purposes, the objective global variable allows the LMS to share status values between SCOs. Depending on a designer's needs, the objective may or may not track actual learner objectives, skills, or abilities.

The objective refers to the method by which a SCO can pass two types of MasteryStatus parameters to the LMS: PassFail and NormalizedScore. The criteria the SCO will use to report these parameters are determined by the designer. The PassFail data type reports only true or false values and the NormalizedScore reports a value for an OBJ (objective) to any decimal value between -1 and +1. Either parameter can have values set based on a response to a single question, a complete assessment, or simply whether the SCO has actually been viewed. It is possible to set or read multiple objectives by any SCO, and it is possible to set or read a single objective by multiple SCOs (LSAL, 2004).

Activity Trees

LMSs read sequencing data represented by an Activity Tree - an instance of hierarchical learning activities and specified sequencing behaviors. An Activity Tree is a static structure that represents the data structure that an LMS implements to reflect defined learning activities. The Activity Tree is defined within a SCORM manifest as a Content Organization or, more simply, the organization. The organization contains one or more activities that can be nested to any depth as sub-activities (ADL, 2006c).

As the content structure and the method or sequence that a learner is expected to access is represented by the Activity Tree, the tree can either be a parent activity in a cluster of sub-activities or a leaf activity with no children. Leaf activities reference a resource launched when the activity has begun. A leaf activity may reference only a single resource, Asset, or SCO (Ostyn, 2007).

For sequencing to occur, there must be a defined structure of learning activities, the Activity Tree; a defined sequencing strategy, the Sequencing Definition Model; and the application of defined behavior to external and system triggered events, and SCORM Sequencing Behaviors (ADL, 2006c). A unit of learning defined by an Activity Tree is static in as much as it has a fixed structure, predefined control modes, and sequencing and roll-up rules, which are to be followed by an LMS occurring for each and every enactment of the tree (i.e., all instances of its processing) (Su & Lee, 2003). To successfully design the Activity Tree, sequencing strategy, and the sequencing behaviors requires the creation of a content structure diagram (ADL, 2008).

Content structure diagrams as a means of facilitating sequence design can be constructed as templates and reused. These templates can be based upon useful and common instructional processes such as a remediation process or different types of branching conditions (LSAL, 2004). Templates can also be made to embody combinations of proven learning patterns (Ostyn, 2007) or even instructional strategies or pedagogical models (Gallagher, 2006).

According to the Learning Systems Architecture Laboratory (LSAL, 2004), "Any template or combination of templates can be 'overlaid' on or combined with another template, creating a more complex instructional strategy for a course or a lesson. Combining the templates …will give you viable sequencing models that you can adapt to meet your particular training and educational requirements" (p. 8).

SCORM Conformance

An important concept for using SCORM is the idea of conformance. To ensure interoperability at some level all systems relying on SCORM must conform to its underlying specifications and standards as applied within the model. This has traditionally taken on the form of conforming or conformance because SCORM does not specify every conceivable implementation pathway, allowing for greater latitude for communities to implement SCORM in ways best fitting to each community. This approach, however, also tends to allow for SCORM-dependent systems to implement SCORM somewhat uniquely, degrading the level of interoperability that may be attained in practice.

SCORM conformance has typically been tested by a test suite developed in parallel with each SCORM version by ADL and freely available on ADL's Web site. This test suite contains test packages (SCORM content) loaded into a target LMS and designed to test a specific use case for SCORM conformance. If an LMS runs the packages without throwing errors, it is said to be conformant. The testing for SCORM conformance is covered in detail in Panar, Brannon, and Poltrack (this volume).

Perceived Limitations

Even though SCORM in its ubiquity may be developing into a *de facto* standard (Olivier & Liber, 2003), it is seen as being limited in many areas. Although it is self-described as focusing on individual self-directed learning (Dodds & Fletcher, 2004; Kraan & Wilson, 2002), this is seen as a limitation for collaborative learning models which have taken hold and are dictating new work in developing collaboration SCOs and services within the SCORM environment (Ip & Canale, 2003; Oliver & McLoughlin, 2003). The use of learning models other than those that are content-centric or based on intelligent tutoring within the SCORM environment is seen as limited and, consequentially, new models are emerging (Conlan, Wade, Bruen, & Gargan, 2002; Harper et al., 2005; Oliver & McLoughlin, 2003; Olivier & Liber, 2003)

References

ADL, & UK, P. L. (2007). SCORM overview. Retrieved September 15, 2007 from http://www.learninglab.org.uk/adl/scorm.asp?ses=

adlCommunity. (2007a). LETSI working area. Retrieved September 17, 2007 from http://adlcommunity.net/course/view.php?id=18

adlCommunity. (2007b). Main section for adlCommunity. Retrieved July 17, 2007 from http://adlcommunity.net/user/view.php?id=5&course=14

adlCommunity. (2007c). SCORM: ADL background from Philip Dodds. Retrieved December 14, 2009 from http://adlcommunity.net/mod/resource/view. php?id=462

ADLNet. (2006). DoD publications. Retrieved May 5, 2006 from https://adlregistry. dtic.mil/2/index4.htm

Advanced Distributed Learning. (2004). *Sharable Content Object Reference Model (SCORM) Run-Time Environment (RTE) Version 1.3.1*. Retrieved from http:// www.adlnet.org.

Advanced Distributed Learning. (2004a). *Sharable Content Object Reference Model (SCORM) 2004: Overview* (2nd ed.). Alexandria, VA: ADL, United States Government.

Advanced Distributed Learning. (2004b). *Sharable Content Object Reference Model (SCORM): Run-Time Environment (RTE) Version 1.3.1* (2nd ed.). Alexandria, VA: ADL, United States Government.

Advanced Distributed Learning. (2006a). *Sharable Content Object Reference Model (SCORM) 2004 3rd Edition: Overview* (3rd ed.). Alexandria, VA: ADL, United States Government.

Advanced Distributed Learning. (2006b). *Sharable Content Object Reference Model (SCORM) 2004 3rd Edition: Run-Time Environment Version 1.0* (3rd ed.). Alexandria, VA: ADL, United State Government.

Advanced Distributed Learning. (2006c). *Sharable Content Object Reference Model (SCORM) 2004 3rd Edition: Sequencing and Navigation Version 1.0* (3rd ed.). Alexandria, VA: ADL, United State Government.

Advanced Distributed Learning [ADL]. (2006d). *Sharable Content Object Reference Model (SCORM) 2004 3rd Edition:Content Aggregation Model (CAM) Version 1.0* (3rd ed.). Alexandria: ADL, United States Government.

Advanced Distributed Learning. (2006e). *Sharable Content Reference Model (SCORM) 2004 3rd Edition: Impact Summary* (3, Trans.). Alexandria, VA: ADL, United States Government.

Advanced Distributed Learning Partnership Lab UK. (2007). SCORM overview. Retrieved September 15, 2007 from http://www.learninglab.org.uk/adl/scorm.asp.

Conlan, O., Wade, V., Bruen, C., & Gargan, M. (2002). Multi-model, metadata driven approach to adaptive hypermedia services for personalized elearning. Services for Personalized eLearning. In *Proceedings of the Second International Conference on Adaptive Hypermedia and Adaptive Web-Based Systems* (AH2002), (p.100-111).

Dodds, P., & Fletcher, J. D. (2004). Opportunities for new "smart" learning environments enabled by next-generation Web capabilities. *Journal of Educational Multimedia and Hypermedia, 13*, 391-404.

Doerksen, T. L. (2002). Content repurposing: Supporting models, methodology, and content development techniques. *MAI, 41*(5), 125.

Downes, S. (2001). Learning objects: Resources for distance education worldwide. *International Review of Research in Open and Distance Learning.* Retrieved 1, 2, from http://www.icaap.org/iuicode?149.2.1.2

Duval, E. (2004). Learning technology standardization: making sense of it all. *Computer Science and Information Systems, 1*(1), 33-43.

Duval, E., & Hodgins, W. (2003, May). *A LOM research agenda.* Paper presented at the WWW2003 Conference, Budapest, Hungary.

Gallagher, P. S. (2002). *Distributed learning: Best practices in industry, academia, and governmental agencies.* Paper written for SAIC in support of the US AF ADL Strategic Plan.

Gallagher, P. S. (2005, June). *Design for knowledge management.* Paper presented at the Innovations in E-Learning Symposium 2005, Fairfax, VA.

Gallagher, P. S. (2007). *Assessing SCORM 2004 for its Affordances in Facilitating a Simulation as a Pedagogical Model.* Doctoral Dissertation, George Mason University, Fairfax, VA.

Google. (2006). Google Scholar SCORM search. Retrieved May 3, 2006 from http://scholar.google.com/scholar?q=SCORM&ie=UTF-8&oe=UTF-8&hl=en&btnG=Search

Harper, B., Bennett, S., Lukasiak, J., & Lickyer, L. (2005). *Learning designs to support educationally effective e-learning using learning objects.* Wollongong, Australia: Research Centre for Interactive Learning Environments, Telecommunications and Information Technology Research Institute, University of Wollongong.

Institute of Electrical and Electronics Engineers. (2004). IEEE Std. 1484.11.2 - 2003 - IEEE Standard for Learning Technology - ECMAScript application programming interface for content to runtime services communication. Retrieved September 3 2007 from http://ieeexplore.ieee.org/servlet/opac?punumber=8972

Institute of Electrical and Electronics Engineers. (2005). IEEE Std 1484.11.1 - 2004 IEEE Standard for Learning Technology - Data Model for Content to Learning Management System Communication [Electronic Version]. Retrieved September 3, 2007 from http://ieeexplore.ieee.org/servlet/opac?punumber=9661

IMS Global Learning Consortium, I. (2003). IMS simple sequencing specification. Retrieved August 14, 2007 from http://www.imsglobal.org/simplesequencing/index.html

IMS Global Learning Consortium, I. (2005). IMS content packaging overview. Retrieved 15 August, 2007, from http://www.imsglobal.org/content/packaging/cpv1p2pd/imscp_oviewv1p2pd.html

IMS Global Learning Consortium, I. (2006). IMS Shareable State Persistence Information Model. Retrieved June 20, 2007 from http://www.imsglobal.org/ssp/

Ip, A., & Canale, R. (2003, May). *Supporting collaborative learning activities with SCORM.* Paper presented at EDUCAUSE, Adelaide, Australia.

Jonassen, D., & Churchill, D. (2004). Is there a learning orientation in learning objects? *International Journal on E-Learning, 3*(2), 32-41.

Katz, H., Worsham, S., Coleman, S., Murawski, M., & Robbins, C. (2004). Reusable learning object model design and implementation: Lessons learned. *Proceedings of the World Conference on E-Learning in Corporate, Government, Healthcare, and Higher Education 2004* (pp. 2483-2490). Chesapeake, VA: AACE.

Kilby, T. (2004). Overview of e-learning standards. Retrieved June 3, 2007 from http://www.webbasedtraining.com/primer_standards.aspx

Kraan, W., & Wilson, S. (2002). Dan Rehak: "SCORM is not for everyone." Retrieved 4/1/06, 2006, from http://www.cetis.ac.uk/content/20021002000737

Learning Systems Architecture Lab. (2004). *SCORM Best practices guide for content developers* (2004 ed.). Pittsburgh: Carnegie Mellon University.

Miller, P. (2000). Interoperability. What is it and why should I want it? *Ariadne*. Retrieved January 1, 2006 from http://www.ariadne.ac.uk/issue24/interoperability/intro.html

Oliver, R., & McLoughlin, C. (2003). Pedagogical designs for scalable and sustainable online learning. In A. Littlejohn (Ed.), *Reusing online resources: A sustainable approach to e-learning* (pp. 94-105). London: Kogan Page.

Olivier, B., & Liber, O. (2003). Learning content interoperability standards. In A. Littlejohn (Ed.), *Reusing online resources: A sustainable approach to e-learning* (pp. 146-155). London: Kogan Page.

Ostyn, C. (2007). *In the eye of the SCORM: An introduction to SCORM 2004 for content developers*. Retrieved August 13, 2007 from http://www.ostyn.com/standards/docs/Eye_Of_The_SCORM_draft.pdf

Phelps, S. (2004). *JKDDC interim distribution capability data model assessment: Vol.1*. Unpublished manuscript. McLean, VA: SAIC.

Rehak, D. (2003). *Technical evolution of SCORM*. Pittsburgh, PA: Learning Systems Architecture Lab, Carnegie Mellon University.

Strijker, A. A. (2004). *Reuse of learning objects in context: Human and technical aspects*. Unpublished doctoral dissertation, University of Twente, Enschede, The Netherlands.

Su, S., & Lee, G. (2003, November). *A Web-service-based, dynamic and collaborative learning management system*. Paper presented at the World Conference on E-Learning in Corporate, Government, Healthcare, and Higher Education 2003, Phoenix, AZ.

Sutcliffe, A. (2002). *The domain theory: Patterns for knowledge and software reuse*. Mahwah, NJ: L. Erlbaum Associates.

Szabo, M., & Flesher, K. (2002, October). *CMI theory and practice: Historical roots of learning management systems*. Paper presented at the World Conference on E-Learning in Corporate, Government, Healthcare, and Higher Education 2002, Montreal, Quebec, Canada.

Verbert, K., Dragan, G., Jovanovi, J., & Duval, E. (2005, May). *Ontology-based learning content repurposing*. Paper presented at the special interest tracks and posters of the 14th International Conference on World Wide Web, Chiba, Japan.

Verbert, K., & Duval, E. (2004, June/July). *Towards a global architecture for learning objects: A comparative analysis of learning object content models*. Paper presented at the World Conference on Educational Multimedia, Hypermedia and Telecommunications 2004, Lugano, Switzerland.

Verbert, K., Klerkx, J., Meire, M., Najjar, J., & Duval, E. (2004). *Towards a global component architecture for learning objects: An ontology based approach.* In R. Meersman (Ed.), *OTM workshops 2004*, LNCS 3292 (pp.713–722). Berlin: Springer-Verlag.

Wikipedia-contributors (2005, January 1, 2006). Application programming interface. Retrieved from http://en.wikipedia.org/w/index.php?title=Application_programming_interface&oldid=32973825

Wiley, D. A. (2001). Learning objects need instructional design theory. In A. Rossett (Ed.), *The ASTD e-learning handbook* (pp. 115-126). New York: McGraw-Hill.

Wiley, D. A. (2001). Learning objects need instructional design theory. In A. Rossett (Ed.), *The ASTD e-learning handbook* (pp. 115-126). New York: McGraw-Hill.

Web Resources

The ADL Initiative. www.adlnet.gov

The Author

Patrick Shane Gallagher, PhD, is currently the program director for the Advanced Distributed Learning (ADL) Technical PMO and is employed by Serco Learning and Human Capital Business Unit as a SCORM researcher.

Chapter 5

Instructional Design and SCORM
Nina Pasini Deibler and Peter Berking

Instructional design in most e-learning development settings simply refers to the process used to define learning requirements and outcomes, plan, develop, and deploy the learning content, and monitor and ensure the success of that plan. The same process applies to learning content developed using the Sharable Content Object Reference Model (SCORM) developed by ADL. The purpose of this chapter is to suggest how SCORM can be effectively integrated into instructional design. It also addresses certain misperceptions, ones that instructional designers often may not fully appreciate. This chapter focuses on the pedagogical and design aspect of the ADL business paradigm (Wisher, this volume).

Training Design and Development

Training professionals frequently refer to a five-phased generic process for training design and development called ADDIE—an acronym for Analysis, Design, Development, Implementation, and Evaluation (Grafinger, 1988). Using the ADDIE process model as a reference, an instructional designer, also called an instructional systems designer (ISD), follows an ordered sequence of steps, with the outcome of each step feeding into the next.

ADDIE Process Sequence
The ADDIE model defines an intellectually rigorous process that provides a systematic, solid framework for developing training and instruction.

Analysis. The designer determines the organization, stakeholder, and learner requirements for the training.

Design. The designer creates the plan for the e-learning using storyboards and other documents.

Development. The developer creates and tests the e-learning files, with oversight from the designer to ensure that it follows the design.

Implementation. The developer or administrator deploys the e-learning to the target learners in the final delivery environment.

Evaluation. The designer collects data on the viability of the product and on the success of the learning, evaluates the data, and makes changes as necessary on a regular, ongoing basis.

Instructional designers apply best practices in each of these phases of the ADDIE process. For example, theories of learning that have been pedagogically tested and validated guide the Design phase of ADDIE (Fletcher, this volume); for each type of learner, learning objective, learning context, etc., there are associated best-practice approaches. SCORM integrates some new best practices to support the successful implementation of ADDIE, enabling ISDs to find, import, share, reuse, and export learning content.

Gallagher (this volume) describes SCORM and the general framework within which it operates. This chapter elaborates on SCORM to show how it fits within the instructional design framework and how to combine it with instructional design best practices when implementing SCORM. For more information about how to implement SCORM, consult the *ADL Guidelines for Creating Reusable Content Using SCORM 2004*, available for download at the ADL Initiative's Web site.

The Precedence of Instructional Design
Instructional designers and SCORM have had a somewhat tenuous relationship. Some instructional designers complained that adding SCORM to their process adds extra work with little visible benefit to the learner. There are several reasons some instructional designers may not have seen the fulfillment of the benefits of SCORM in their projects.

Limitations of authoring tools. Technical complexities of developing robust SCORM content with limited authoring tools made implementing SCORM labor intensive and confusing.

Limited reuse of SCOs. ISDs may have developed Sharable Content Objects (SCOs) for their courses that were never reused. In some cases, the SCOs were reused, but the original designer may not have been aware of reuse that occurred after the completion of the original project (Shanley et al., this volume). In addition, some designers did not fully grasp the reusability paradigm and did not look for reusable content to use in their courses.

Change in LMS. The designers may not have been aware that their e-learning was moved from one learning management system (LMS) to another after project completion, thereby taking advantage of SCORM-enabled interoperability.

Misperceptions arising from these factors sometimes resulted in a lackluster integration of SCORM into instructional design, since some ISDs used SCORM only to meet the minimum technical requirements. Subsequently, others did not find the SCOs to be reusable because of weak initial implementations.

Another factor contributing to this tenuous relationship is the fact that instructional design was an established discipline long before the advent of SCORM, with a precedence and long-standing practices in place (Dick & Carey, 1985; Smith & Ragan, 1993). As with any new technology, SCORM was often retrofitted into the established best practice framework of instructional design without a comprehensive understanding of SCORM's technical requirements and the synergistic efficiencies of integrating it into instructional design.

Value of SCORM to Instructional Design

SCORM is neutral on many aspects of instructional design that are key concerns for instructional designers. For example, SCORM says nothing about learning theory, instructional best practices, and assessments. SCORM can be implemented in the design of a course in many different ways. The value of SCORM to instructional designers is not in how it can increase the instructional effectiveness of the product, since there are many areas over which it has no control, but in how it increases the efficiency of using the technology. This requires an expanded view of instructional design, one that is not limited to purely instructional concerns but also includes a key stakeholder concern—cost efficiency.

Optimizing Cost Efficiencies

SCORM can be layered with many different instructional designs. It will not inherently impede or augment e-learning designs or functionality. It can be added after the instructional design is complete by making only a few changes to design documentation. Learners should see no difference between a SCORM or non-SCORM treatment of the same course.

However, optimizing for ADL's functional requirements of accessibility, interoperability, durability, and reusability (Wisher, this volume; Gallagher, this volume) for maximizing cost efficiency starts with a proper integration of SCORM into instructional design, one that begins in the first few minutes of conceptualization of the e-learning product by the ISD and ends with delivery of a learning experience that is both engaging and effective from a learning perspective while being at the same time highly cost effective and efficient.

Designing Reusable Content

The aspect of SCORM that is most relevant to instructional design is reusability (Barritt & Alderman, 2004). It is both a key benefit of SCORM to the training community, and a key advantage of SCORM to the instructional design process, since designers can save significant amounts of time by reusing existing content instead of building it from scratch (Shanley et al., this volume).

When people hear the term *reuse*, they usually equate it with the direct, unchanged use of what is typically highly contextualized content designed for a specific group of individual learners. Given the cost of designing and developing new content, any savings that can be generated through reuse has merit. Designing reusable content implies creating smaller, more granular pieces. Smaller pieces of content can be assembled in many different ways, and can also enable more individualized instruction than is possible with larger pieces of content.

Categories of Reuse

There are four basic categories of reuse. Figure 5-1 illustrates the categories using a consistent example of changing a flat tire. These concepts describe how instructional designers combine, present, and alter reusable content independently of the instructional decisions made about the appropriate learning context and audience.

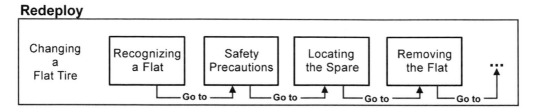

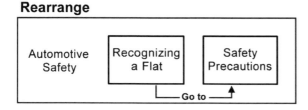

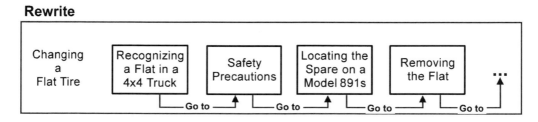

Figure 5-1. Categories of Reuse. This figure depicts the four categories of reuse in instructional design.

The four categories of reuse in instructional design are:

Redeploy. This is the ability to run content, without modification, in multiple LMSs.

Rearrange. This involves reordering existing content for new uses or new contexts.

Repurpose. This category of reuse involves using a piece of content in new contexts or in different ways.

Rewrite. This category of reuse requires modifying relevant materials and changing the examples, graphics, or writing style, or removing irrelevant information.

The ability to use these concepts is proportional to how granular the SCOs are; producing a reusable "Changing a Flat Tire" course relies on small, very specific SCOs designed to be swapped out with the SCOs used in "Recognizing a Flat in a 4x4 Truck" and "Locating the Spare on a Model 891s." These would be designed for different car types and models, for example, "Recognizing a Flat in a Minivan" to replace "Recognizing a Flat in a 4x4 Truck" and "Locating the Spare on a Model 791s" to replace "Locating the Spare on a Model 891s." Granularity of SCOs is a fundamental concept in integrating SCORM into instructional design. This also raises the issue of context.

Context

Context is an essential component of learning—people learn best when instruction is presented in the context in which it will be used. Good instructional design builds knowledge incrementally, using previous knowledge as the foundation for moving from the known to the unknown. This is typically accomplished with a reference to a previous instruction, such as, "In the last lesson you learned…" Statements such as these hamper reuse because they may not apply within a different content context and must be removed for it to be reused.

To maximize the potential for reusability, the content must be context-neutral, or not specific to any one audience, item, or subject area. Since this philosophically contradicts what designers know about creating good content, there are concerns about the validity of context-neutral learning content.

Not all content can or should be context-neutral, just as not all content can or should be reusable. However, careful attention to principles for integrating SCORM will help designers create instructionally-sound, context-neutral, reusable content while allowing them to weave context into their content by placing the context around the reusable pieces rather than inside them.

Target Audience and Designing for Reusability

The first step in designing reusable content is determining which, if any, portions of the content could be useful for someone other than the target audience. If the members of an automobile association are the target audience for content about flat tires, the content could be designed for all drivers, since the members of an automobile association also represent the general public; there are no unique characteristics about them or their driving habits. The same content may be reused in different industries by different learners to achieve the same or even different outcomes. Likewise, if the target audience is truck drivers who must be certified to transport hazardous materials, the designer could reuse existing content on hazardous materials and hazardous materials classification developed for, or used by, emergency responders.

Since reusable content is intended to be inherently small, a piece of content that addresses a broad subject like "Operating Your Car" might be too comprehensive to be reusable for most audiences. However, a smaller piece of content, such as "Before Starting Your Engine," may be reusable because the procedures one follows are fairly consistent and usually unrelated to the type of vehicle one is operating.

After identifying the pieces of content that can be reused, designers can add context to their content by weaving in pieces that are context specific. For example, in developing a composite course using existing modules from the military services, Brooks and Jesukiewicz (2006) recognized the need to create small "segue SCOs" when shifting topics, alerting the learner to a change in context. When content is limited to a single, granular, well-written learning objective, it is easier to make it context-neutral. Where context-specific instruction is required, instructional designers can create context-specific objectives such as "In accordance with the owner's manual, state the location of the spare tire in a Model 891s, without assistance."

The ADDIE Process and SCORM

Designers do not need to master all of the technical nuances of a SCORM implementation. Their primary responsibility should remain designing effective instructional materials that work within the SCORM technical guidelines. This section and the ones that follow correspond to each part of the ADDIE process. They provide a basic understanding of how specific SCORM features and requirements impact, and are integrated into, the design process for SCORM-conformant e-learning, addressing the question: "How is developing SCORM-conformant e-learning different from developing non-SCORM-conformant e-learning?" Note that since SCORM has no direct impact that affects the Evaluation phase, that section is not included.

Integrating SCORM into the Analysis Phase

In the analysis phase of the ADDIE process, the primary SCORM task is to search for existing content that the designer may be able to reuse. Content repositories and registries are two key sources. A content repository contains the e-learning files themselves (course screens, media assets, etc.) whereas a registry only contains metadata for e-learning objects and provides pointers to the content in their native content repositories. Two prominent DoD sources of reusable content are the ADL Registry (Lannom, this volume) and the Defense Automated Visual Information System/Defense Instructional Technology Information System content repository, also known as DAVIS/DITIS. These sources are available to designers seeking to identify existing content or media for reuse (see Web Resources).

Integrating SCORM into the Design Phase

Effective integration of SCORM requires that the instructional designer incorporate SCORM design guidelines into the design phase of the process. These include:

Granularity and context-neutrality. In practical terms, this means designing smaller, context-neutral SCOs and using SCORM 2004 sequencing capabilities to add context-specific SCOs.

Data collection and tracking requirements. ISDs should outline basic data collection and tracking requirements defined in the SCORM data model (see *Using the SCORM Data Model* section of this chapter).

Content structure diagram and rules table. Instructional designers should employ a content structure diagram (flow chart) and rules table for SCORM 2004 sequencing (see *Using SCORM 2004 Sequencing* section of this chapter) that organizes the SCOs and aggregations, and depicts their relationships to one another.

Creating the content structure diagram early in the process speeds development by allowing the programmer to begin developing and testing the sequencing rules using generic sample content in a skeleton (containing basic mock content to simulate functionality) while the team continues to refine and develop the actual content. A clearly defined set of sequencing rules should accompany the diagram.

In addition to the standard activities associated with the instructional design process, designers should also consider these questions:

- How will I maximize the potential for content to be redeployed, rearranged, repurposed, and rewritten?

- Will SCOs cover a single learning objective or multiple learning objectives, or will the mapping of SCOs to learning objectives vary as needed for the project?

- Will SCOs include an embedded assessment, or will the assessment be a separate SCO?

- How will SCOs be divided, structured, and sequenced?

- When, where, and how will I collect evaluation data (e.g., per SCO, aggregation, entire course organization?)

- How many navigation options will be provided in the SCO versus the standard navigation options provided by a typical LMS?

- How will the use of templates and cascading style sheets impact rearranging, repurposing, and rewriting the content?

Integrating SCORM into the Development Phase

This phase is more focused on the technical implementation of SCORM than on the instructional design and is generally performed by a content developer rather than an instructional designer. However, designers should be aware of relevant best practices related to the instructional design during this phase.

While the developers are building the content, the programmer should be using the content structure diagram to code the sequencing rules in a functioning prototype or skeleton, using generic content. This will allow multiple iterations to test the sequencing rules before the actual content development is completed. This method will help to ensure that the sequencing rules will work properly when the content is ready to be deployed. The designer will then review the results of the development phase to ensure it adheres to the design specifications.

ADL provides a SCORM Conformance Test Suite that allows designers and developers to self-test LMSs, SCOs, and content packages to determine if they are SCORM conformant. By self-testing SCOs and content packages, ISDs and programmers can ensure that the product will work as intended. The test suite systematically checks the product and produces a report that indicates whether or not the product conforms to SCORM requirements (Panar, Brannon, & Poltrack, this volume).

Integrating SCORM into the Implementation Phase

The implementation phase begins by deploying the content in a testing area on the target LMS to ensure that learner data is being recorded as the ISD intended, per the SCORM data model. After successful testing, the content package can be uploaded to the production area of the LMS and beta testers from the target audience can run the content and note discrepancies.

If the target LMS is unavailable, ADL provides an option for testing content on its Sample Run-Time Environment (SRTE) in "learner mode." The SRTE is an example of a basic LMS that has implemented the SCORM data model and the minimum functionality specified in SCORM to achieve conformance. It is not intended to be a functioning LMS. Designers can use the SRTE to display and sequence their content in the same way that learners would experience it. If content successfully passes using the SCORM Test Suite, then it should run properly in the SRTE. ISDs and programmers should verify that the content sequences correctly and that the data model elements are receiving and setting the correct values.

If there are multiple LMSs targeted for implementation, the designer must test in as many of them as possible. The ADL Co-Lab Hub maintains an assortment of SCORM-certified LMSs in its Learning Technology Lab for those who need to test their content on multiple systems. The implementation phase ends when the content is deployed to actual learners via the LMS.

Designers who are developing content for a DoD organization must also register the content in the ADL Registry and store their content packages and SCOs in a searchable content repository (Lannom, this volume).

Using the SCORM Data Model

The SCORM data model elements, described in detail in the *SCORM RTE* book, facilitate the collection of learner information as learners progress through a SCO. SCORM 2004 LMSs are required to support all of the data model elements, but instructional designers are not required to use any of them. Designers do need to know what kinds of data can be communicated via the SCORM data model elements so they can tell their programmers which of the elements they want to use and how.

Here are some examples of information an ISD might want to retrieve from the LMS to customize their learners' experiences:

- The learner's name for use inside the content (e.g., Well done, Jane Doe.)

- The last location in the content the learner viewed (e.g., Do you want to start where you left off?)

- The learner's language, presentation, or other preferences

Examples of learner-related information an ISD might want to store in the LMS include score, total time spent in a SCO, time spent in a single session of a SCO, completion status, responses to assessment items, interactions within a SCO, and pass/fail status.

Creating Assessments

SCORM does not directly address the design and development of assessments nor does it provide guidance about when and how assessments should be made into SCOs. As a result, many organizations deliver assessments using proprietary assessment solutions provided by their LMS. This is not the ideal solution because assessments and assessment metrics defined within a given LMS solution are not interoperable or reusable in other LMSs.

Creating SCOs for Assessments
SCORM assessments can be structured in two ways: as a single SCO containing multiple test items or as multiple SCOs, each of which contains a single test item. Each assessment SCO must report a score and completion status, regardless of its structure. The pros and cons of each are described in the *ADL Guidelines for Creating Reusable Content with SCORM 2004*. In most cases, ADL recommends creating a single SCO assessment.

The SCORM data model element called *cmi.interactions* provides an interoperable way for a SCO to send assessment data about a learner's performance to the LMS. It provides a detailed model enabling designers and programmers to collect metrics about learner response or performance within a SCO, particularly data related to performance on assessments such as correct response, learner's response, duration taken to respond, and weight of the particular item relative to the overall assessment score.

Using *cmi.interactions,* instructional designers can collect metrics for formative and summative evaluation reporting, and can link *cmi.interactions* and other data model elements to sequencing rules to create remediation or adaptive learning strategies that further customize learning experiences. This may significantly improve learner performance and optimize individualized learning by allowing designers to better match performance on individual learning objectives with remediation and feedback strategies. For example, a learner might select response A on a multiple choice question for which the correct response is actually C. Selecting A, an incorrect response, could indicate that the learner does not understand a specific concept.

Using *cmi.interactions* in combination with other data model elements, the course design could individualize the learning by sending the learner to a specific SCO that addresses the weakness identified during the initial assessment. The course could be designed to then reassess the learner, and, based on the results, either assign further remediation or return him or her to the original learning path.

Using SCORM 2004 Sequencing and Navigation

In traditional multimedia and computer-based training, branching enabled (or sometimes forced) learners to move from one piece of content to another relatively seamlessly. If learners failed to understand a certain concept, the course could send them to new or existing content for remediation. Learners may or may not have known they were moving from one lesson or module to another. This was possible because robust authoring and delivery systems gave designers and developers nearly limitless programming options for structuring and branching their content. The functionality was hard-coded, whether based on a linear or an adaptive model. If you removed one piece of content from the whole, the branching rules would break.

In the early versions of SCORM, learners received a set of SCOs, typically via a table of contents, and learners could select the SCOs they wanted to see in any order. Some instructional designers found this aspect of SCORM frustrating; they were being asked to design granular SCOs, but with granular SCOs they were unable to ensure that learners received the SCOs in the order they prescribed. This was particularly problematic for procedural content that required learners to experience the content in the order they would perform the procedure.

To overcome this limitation, some designers created very large SCOs that had internal branching. This enabled them to conform to SCORM without sacrificing control over the learners' experiences. However, these SCOs were often too big to be reusable, which went against the spirit of SCORM. Other designers used the proprietary sequencing functionality provided by the LMS, which meant that the sequencing was lost when the content package was moved to another LMS.

Hard-Coded Rules

Since ADL promotes interoperability and reusability, hard-coding functionality within or between SCOs contradicts the architectural functionality. Content was often not interoperable when hard-coded sequencing rules were present or when sequencing rules were defined using an LMS's proprietary functionality because the sequencing functionality of one LMS could not be processed by another. Likewise, content was not reusable when individual SCOs relied directly on the presence of other SCOs. Hard-coding also limits the ability to create new or custom content structures from the same instructional materials.

Sequencing in SCORM

The sequencing capabilities of SCORM 2004 enable designers to prescribe the manner in which learners receive individual pieces of content from the LMS while supporting interoperability. As a result, designers can create more granular content, allowing the LMS to control the movement of learners from SCO to SCO in accordance with the behaviors the designer specifies. This increases the possibility that the SCOs will be reusable because there is no need to modify hard-coded rules in the SCOs. Sequencing can also be used with highly granular reusable content to add context to context-neutral SCOs.

Before structuring the content for sequencing, designers need to determine their assessment and remediation requirements and how they want learners to experience the content. After defining these requirements, designers can begin to structure the content and define the sequencing behaviors. The relevant questions in defining sequencing requirements are:

- Will learners be able to choose the content they see, or will you prescribe the order in which they see it?

- Do you want to adapt the learner's experience according to their choices or decisions?

- How will you determine when the learner has completed the content?

The sequencing features of SCORM 2004 are technically complex. Designing a course that takes full advantage of SCORM 2004 sequencing capabilities requires a designer to work closely with a programmer to determine implementation options. This usually requires creating a flow diagram and rules table. Figure 5-2 shows a sample flow diagram.

The *ADL Guidelines for Creating Reusable Content Using SCORM 2004* has a collection of sequencing templates representing typical course scenarios. Figure 5-2 offers one example. These templates can be used for ideas, inspiration, and documentation.

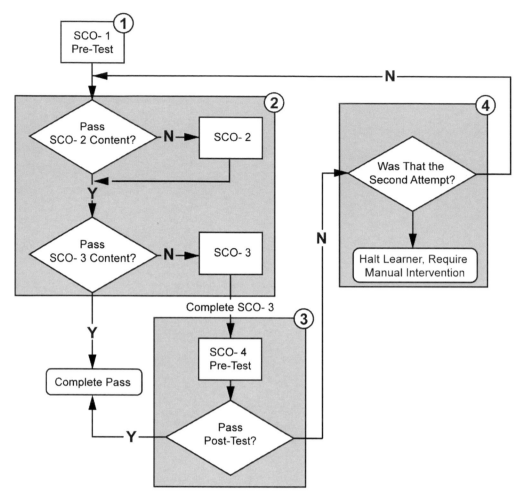

Figure 5-2. Example template for reusable content. Templates can be used as is, or adapted to specific course scenarios.

Integration of SCORM into Instructional Design – A Case Study

In 2003, the Chrysler Academy used the transition from SCORM 1.2 to SCORM 2004 to work with their instructional designers and developers to re-think how courses should be designed. The design team began looking at courses as an assembly of learning objects and designed them accordingly. Over time, instructional designers were educated on the underlying principles of SCORM. In the meantime, Chrysler worked with its LMS provider to create administrative tools and a SCORM 2004 run-time environment with sequencing and navigation rules and global shared objectives (a SCORM function that allows learner performance to be tracked persistently across SCOs, sessions, and courses).

Chrysler expected cost reductions from reuse and repurposing of SCOs. While this has happened, even greater cost reductions came from the reuse of media assets and sequencing templates along with the implementation of the course shell. SCORM has also facilitated course maintenance and multi-lingual support.

Chrysler improved the learner experience by focusing development on learning objectives rather than framing devices, and by shifting from large packages to very small SCOs. Leveraging global shared objectives reduced learner seat time and training redundancy. If a learner views content about Chrysler's satellite radio in a Jeep Liberty course, that SCO is tagged as complete when the learner accesses a Dodge Ram course with the same satellite radio SCO.

Best Practices

The Chrysler Academy's approach and experiences provides several examples of best practices in instructional design:

Standards documentation. The Academy wrote design and development standards specific to Chrysler.

Expert support. SCORM-educated ISDs provided guidance on content development to the design team.

Model course shell. Chrysler developed a generic course shell (for standard navigational controls, menus, SCO display size and placement) whose look and feel could be customized.

Design library. The Chrysler team created a library of design patterns, including templates for sequencing models.

LMS education. Chrysler ensured that all team members had an in-depth understanding of the delivery system provided by the LMS.

More details on this and other cases are available at the ADL Initiative's Web site (See Web Resources).

Conclusion

In SCORM, ADL has provided a reference model that serves as a technical guide to creating and delivering training and education in a way that addresses cost effectiveness and technological efficiency. SCORM is neutral in its application to, and impact on, learning effectiveness and strategy, hence on instructional design.

Cost-effectiveness is a primary concern for stakeholders, thus for instructional designers. For this reason alone, SCORM implementation is worth the time and effort designers expend to integrate it into their instructional designs. However, this chapter shows that there is more to SCORM than cost-effectiveness. When integrated properly into the instructional design process, it can also support and enhance instructional effectiveness and provide many benefits to learners.

References

Barritt, C. & Alderman, F. L. (2004). *Creating a reusable learning objects strategy*. San Francisco: Pfeiffer.

Brooks, J., & Jesukiewicz, P. (2006). SCORM reuse: current reality, challenges, and best practice. *Proceedings of the Interservice/Industry Training, Simulation & Education Conference (I/ITSEC) 2006*.

Dick, W., & Carey, L. (1985). *The systematic design of instruction* (2nd ed.). Glenview, IL: Scott, Foresman & Co.

Grafinger, D. J. (1988). Basics of instructional systems development. *InfoLine 8803*, 1-16.

Jonassen, D. H. (1999). Designing constructivist learning environments. In C. M. Reigeluth (Ed.), *Instructional Design Theories and Models*. Vol. 2 (pp. 215–240). Mahwah, NJ: Erlbaum.

Smith, P. L., & Ragan, T. J. (1993). *Instructional design*. New York: Macmillan.

Web Resources

ADL Initiative. *www.ADLNet.gov*

ADL Registry. *http://adlregistry.ADLNet.gov/*

The Authors

Peter Berking leads the Instructional Capabilities team at the ADL Co-Lab Hub in Alexandria, Virginia.

Nina Deibler is Outreach lead at the ADL Co-Lab Hub in Alexandria, Virginia.

Chapter 6

Metrics and Evaluation:
Increasing Training Effectiveness and Efficiency
Traci Sitzmann and Katherine Ely

Evaluation is fundamental to ensuring the success of e-learning courses. Training evaluation is a planned and systematic effort to determine whether a training program met the stated objectives. After all, how do organizations know if their training is beneficial unless they stop to examine changes produced by their efforts? Evaluation efforts are invaluable for providing diagnostic feedback to designers, trainers, and trainees. Organizations can use the information gleaned from an evaluation to make decisions about whether to revise a course and may even use evaluation outcomes, such as trainee satisfaction, to promote the training program (Kraiger, 2002).

Without training evaluation, organizations may repeatedly invest in programs that do not produce meaningful changes in employee attitudes, job performance, and work efficiency. In a well planned evaluation effort, the information obtained in the evaluation feeds back into the next cycle of training, creating a continual process of improving training effectiveness and increasing training efficiency.

The Advanced Distributed Learning (ADL) Initiative assists members of the Department of Defense (DoD) community and other federal agencies in using advanced technologies to improve training effectiveness and increase training efficiency. Training effectiveness refers to whether the course accomplished its intended purpose such as changing trainees' attitudes, increasing their knowledge base, or improving their job performance. Training efficiency refers to completing training with a minimal expenditure of time and cost. Efficiency can refer to both the cost that the organization invests in developing the course as well as to trainees' investment in participating in training. ADL's Research and Evaluation Team conducts empirical research to examine ways to increase the effectiveness and efficiency of training delivered with advanced learning technologies.

This chapter provides a broad overview of evaluation research conducted at ADL and describes how technology and evaluation metrics can be used to reform and continuously improve learning in the modern work environment. It highlights specific projects that ADL has undertaken and describes how the research results can be used to make informed decisions regarding choosing between e-learning and classroom instruction, designing effective training courses, gaining time efficiencies from e-learning, implementing learning interventions, and interpreting training evaluation data. This chapter also discusses the tradeoff between training effectiveness and efficiency. Each of these research streams is summarized in the following sections along with specific examples of how the research can be used to evaluate and improve the effectiveness of training courses.

Effectiveness of ADL Technologies

ADL's vision is to provide access to the highest quality training and education that can be tailored to individual needs and delivered cost effectively, anywhere and anytime. ADL's Research and Evaluation Team collects evaluation metrics in order to examine the effectiveness of educational technology. The team also conducts empirical research to examine ways to increase the effectiveness and efficiency of training delivered with advanced learning technologies, as well as to examine how organizations can use technology to its fullest potential and maximize the value added by their investments. The United States DoD, in 2008, had 10 million e-learning course completions by members of the active duty, reserve, and civilian workforce. Research on the effectiveness and efficiency of training is of critical importance.

An initial training evaluation project was a large-scale statistical summary on the effectiveness of e-learning. The team conducted a meta-analysis (i.e., a statistical technique for summarizing the research in a literature domain) to compare the effectiveness of e-learning and classroom instruction for teaching factual and skill-based knowledge with data from 26,460 trainees and 208 training courses (Sitzmann, Kraiger, Stewart, & Wisher, 2006). All of the courses were adult work-related training, and included both organizational and university courses. Many of the courses included an asynchronous component, such as email to an instructor. Also they were generally of fixed length and not purely computer-based training, so a comparison to the Rule of Thirds (Fletcher, this volume) is not possible.

The results revealed that, overall, e-learning was 6 percent more effective than classroom instruction for teaching factual knowledge. This suggests that if the average test score in classroom instruction is 75 percent, then the average test score in the comparison e-learning course would be 81 percent. However, the two delivery media were equally effective for teaching skill-based knowledge and trainees were equally satisfied with e-learning and classroom instruction.

The Role of Delivery Media

Educational theory can be used to shed light on the meaning of the current results. Richard Clark (1983) proposed that delivery media are "mere vehicles that deliver instruction but do not influence student achievement any more than the truck that delivers our groceries causes change in our nutrition" (p. 445). In making this assertion, Clark (1983, 1994) noted the need to distinguish between the effects of instructional methods and delivery media on learning outcomes. Instructional methods are techniques used to convey course content such as lecture, group discussion, reading, and assignments. Delivery media are technological devices such as computers, video-teleconferencing, and the Internet used for the purpose of instruction.

Clark argued that while delivery media influence the cost and accessibility of material, the medium used is inconsequential in affecting learning—trainees' learning outcomes are driven by the instructional methods. Clark's theory suggests our finding that e-learning is 6 percent more effective than classroom instruction for teaching factual knowledge is driven by the instructional methods incorporated in e-learning, rather than a true difference in the effectiveness of the delivery media. Thus, if identical instructional methods are used in both e-learning and classroom versions of a course, the two delivery media should be equally effective for teaching factual knowledge.

To test Clark's (1983, 1994) theory, ADL's Research and Evaluation Team isolated studies that compared the effectiveness of e-learning and classroom instruction for teaching factual knowledge and used similar instructional methods in the two versions of the course. Studies utilized similar instructional methods when all of the instructional methods included in the e-learning version of the course had a comparable instructional method in the classroom version of the course (e.g., when lecture is provided in classroom instruction, a comparable instructional method in e-learning is an online video of the lecture). Studies used different instructional methods in the two versions of the course when an instructional method was present in e-learning or classroom instruction, and there was not a comparable instructional method in the other delivery medium. The results support Clark's theory, and indicate e-learning and classroom instruction were equally effective for teaching factual knowledge when similar instructional methods were used.

This finding suggests instructional methods rather than delivery media are the causal factor in determining trainees' achievement levels. Therefore, course designers should choose instructional methods that will maximize learning outcomes. When courses used the instructional advantages of the Internet, e-learning was up to 19 percent more effective than classroom instruction for teaching factual knowledge. The following sections discuss the course design features that were associated with higher learning outcomes from e-learning courses.

Guidelines for Designing Effective e-Learning Courses

The results of the meta-analysis revealed that the most effective e-learning courses were not merely Internet versions of classroom instruction. Rather, the most effective e-learning courses leveraged the instructional advantages afforded by the delivery medium. We examined trends across the courses included in the meta-analysis to determine which course design characteristics are associated with trainees learning more, or less, from e-learning. These analyses enabled the ADL team to develop six empirically-derived guidelines for designing more effective e-learning courses.

Active Engagement
The first guideline is that trainees should be actively engaged in learning the course material. Trainees are active when they are completing assignments, participating in online simulations, and collaborating with other trainees. The Small Group Scenario Trainer (SGST) is one example of a system that promotes active learning. SGST is a configurable online mission rehearsal system in which trainees

assume roles within a military unit and coordinate their efforts to successfully complete the exercise. Instructors are actively involved in the learning exercise as they monitor trainees' performance, provide feedback, and facilitate communication. Trainees are also active as they communicate with other members of their team, access information relevant to the scenario, rehearse for upcoming missions, and complete after action reviews. The United States Northern Command is currently using SGST for Initial Qualification Training.

Instructional Methods

Course designers should incorporate a variety of instructional methods (e.g., lecture, assignments, games, discussion, and tutorials) in e-learning courses. One of the main advantages of using the Internet to deliver training is the ability to customize the instruction to the needs of individual trainees. Through the incorporation of a variety of instructional methods, e-learning provides trainees with the opportunity to continue to review content in different ways when they are having difficulty understanding the material. For example, if learners miss key points in an online lecture, they could post questions on a discussion board, read articles on the topic, email the instructor, or complete tutorials related to the lecture in order to fully grasp the training content.

Computer Skills Training

Organizations should offer a computer and Internet skills course to trainees before they participate in e-learning. Organizations need to be aware that some trainees may not have the computer and Internet skills required to navigate e-learning courses. Providing trainees with access to computer and Internet skills courses may enable all trainees to be successful in e-learning.

Synchronous Learning Opportunities

Incorporate synchronous human interaction in e-learning. Synchronous communication occurs in real time and includes communication media such as voice chat and instant messaging. Asynchronous communication involves a delay in communicating with the instructor or other trainees, such as with email or discussion boards. When engaged in asynchronous discussions, the lack of immediate feedback may result in trainees withdrawing from the discussion. However, synchronous communication provides immediate feedback to trainees and can reduce the frustration associated with lengthy time delays between asking a question and receiving a response. Thus, incorporating synchronous communication periodically throughout e-learning courses can be beneficial to trainees and increase learning.

Learner Control

Provide trainees with control over the content, sequence, and pace of instruction. One of the benefits of using technology-delivered instruction is the ability to customize training programs (Brown & Ford, 2002). Learner-controlled environments allow trainees to spend as much time as they want, or need, learning the material. This allows trainees to tailor the experience to meet their specific needs and interests as well as accommodates differences in trainees' knowledge levels. Additionally, providing trainees with control should reduce frustration and boredom, since trainees can skip sections of the material with which they are already familiar.

Practice and Feedback

Trainees should practice using their knowledge and skills, and receive feedback on their performance during training. Practice is essential for skill acquisition and trainees must receive feedback in order to know whether they are effectively using their newly acquired knowledge and skills. Moreover, frequent practice should increase the likelihood that trainees will automate skills by the end of training, leading to better performance by the end of the course and higher levels of training transfer. Transfer of training is defined as the successful application of knowledge, skills, and attitudes gained in a training context to the job.

This investigation of the effectiveness of e-learning is just one example of how ADL is using empirical data to improve the effectiveness of e-learning courses. By following these guidelines, organizations can make informed decisions on designing and delivering e-learning, which should maximize learning outcomes. Elsewhere in this volume, information is presented on intelligent tutors (Hu, Graesser, & Fowler, this volume), virtual worlds (Gamor, this volume), games (Xu, this volume), and social media (Fowler, this volume) as advanced training technologies for teaching work-related knowledge and skills.

Training Efficiency

In addition to learning outcomes, another key evaluation metric is training efficiency. Within the ADL framework, training efficiency refers to time and cost savings organizations can realize by using the Sharable Content Object Reference Model (SCORM) to design reusable and adaptable e-learning content. SCORM provides e-learning specialists with the specifications necessary to produce online learning content that is accessible, interoperable, durable, and reusable. By using SCORM, online courses can be built as a series of small interoperable building blocks, called Sharable Content Objects (SCOs), that can come from a variety of content sources. Course designers can select and combine SCOs to support a broad range of learning experiences and reuse content in multiple ways. This section describes two case studies that highlight the efficiencies that the ADL model of e-learning promotes.

Efficiencies in Developing Course Content

By designing courses as a series of SCOs, organizations can reuse instructional content and integrate it into different courses without modification, leveraging the savings e-learning affords. For example, if a one-hour course takes 100 hours to produce, at $100 an hour, even if an organization only reuses 5 percent of that content, it would save $500 on course development. However, in order to realize this benefit, organizations must develop their course content with reusability in mind. That is, course designers must create a SCO as a standalone object—containing all the material relevant to that learning objective without referencing previous or subsequent lessons that may not be included in future courses (Deibler & Berking, this volume).

Organizations have realized time and cost savings from using the ADL model of reusability. Specifically, some companies working under contract to the DoD have gained development efficiencies by designing SCOs at a highly granular level to facilitate reuse. That is, SCOs were designed as a standalone lesson—containing all the material relevant to that learning objective without referencing previous or subsequent lessons that may not be included in future courses. In 2007, one company repurposed 24 SCOs multiple times across four courses, thereby lowering both the development time and the production cost of the courseware. The company was then able to pass the savings resulting from reuse on to their customers.

The Joint Knowledge Development and Distribution Center (JKDDC) has also realized significant time and cost savings through content reuse (Camacho, West, & Vozzo, this volume).

Implementation Efficiencies
Research has shown that when instructional designers leverage the features technology affords, such as providing learners with control over their instructional experience, they maximize the benefits of online instruction. Classroom instruction assumes that all trainees begin a course with the same knowledge level and requires trainees to learn the same content within the same timeframe. However, SCORM standards enable dynamic customization and remediation during the training program. Using SCORM, instructional designers can create courses such that correct responses to assessments allow trainees to progress to new material while incorrect responses cue remediation to the lessons covering the learning objectives that they have not mastered. This tailored approach to training has the potential to reduce training time and increase training efficiency. The following section describes the results of an analysis conducted by the Research and Evaluation Team examining the potential time efficiencies that can result from e-learning (Ely, Sitzmann, & Falkiewicz, 2009).

Navy Study
As part of a move towards online instruction, the Navy's Center for Surface Combat Systems converted several of their Apprentice Technical Training (ATT) courses from traditional classroom instruction to self-paced e-learning. This ADL case study focuses on 111 electronics technicians participating in ATT. Training consisted of 33 self-paced modules covering a variety of topics such as electricity and circuits. Before trainees could advance to the next module, they had to pass a knowledge test and a performance exam. When delivered via classroom instruction, the training lasted 86 days. However, in the e-learning version of the course, trainees finished in an average of 45 days—a 48 percent reduction in time to train (see Figure 6-1).

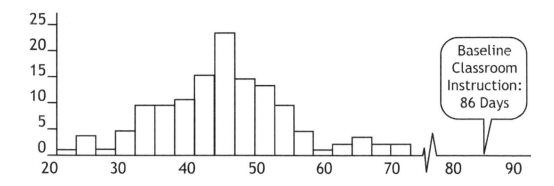

Figure 6-1. Variability in time to train in online instruction. This figure shows the range in time to train online, with reference to the average time to train in a classroom environment.

Although trainees varied in the amount of time it took them to complete the course (lengths ranged from 21 to 72 days), the amount of time spent in training did not predict trainees' knowledge levels. Trainees who completed the course in a relatively short amount of time had knowledge levels similar to trainees who spent a relatively longer amount of time in training. In addition, even the slowest-paced trainee completed the e-learning course in less time than those in classroom instruction. These findings demonstrate that when e-learning enables learners to train at their own pace, they can save time while still achieving the same level of content mastery as classroom instruction.

Reusable Training Interventions

Another way the ADL model can potentially cut training costs and increase efficiencies is by repurposing training interventions. In the context of training, interventions are techniques designed to help trainees maximize their potential during training. For example, trainees can participate in a study skills course to ensure they are aware of techniques that optimize retention of training material. Based on both primary research and a review of the literature, the Research and Evaluation Team found a plethora of evidence suggesting that training interventions can have a large effect on learning outcomes.

Interventions can also assist trainees in self-regulating while participating in e-learning. Self-regulation permits trainees to exert control over their affect, cognition, and behavior during training. Although trainees can control these processes, they do not consistently engage in self-regulation during training. Trainees occasionally get distracted by off-task thoughts and rely on learning strategies (i.e., rehearsal rather than deep processing) that are not optimal for learning the material.

Self-Regulation

One training intervention addresses these tendencies by asking questions during training to encourage trainees to reflect on their cognitive activities. The questions ask trainees about gaps in their understanding of the course material, about their ability to concentrate on learning the material, and about the effectiveness of their study strategies. Examples of the prompts questions include, "Do I need to continue to review to ensure I will remember the material after I finish the course?" and "Are the study strategies I am using effective for learning the training material?" By answering these questions, trainees may become aware of gaps in their understanding of the training material and deficiencies in their learning strategies. Subsequently, trainees should improve their self-regulatory activity, which should ultimately increase learning.

ADL's Research and Evaluation Team conducted three empirical investigations of the effect of prompting self-regulation on learning and attrition. In each study, trainees were randomly assigned to two experimental conditions: *continuous prompts*—trainees were prompted to self-regulate throughout the entire course and *delayed prompts*— trainees were prompted to self-regulate in the latter half of the course. The researchers compared each of these conditions against a control group in which trainees did not receive the intervention. Learning was assessed with a multiple choice exam in the first study and by participating in a simulation in the second study. In the first two studies, data from 263 trainees revealed that trainees who received the intervention learned more over time than trainees in the control condition (see Figure 6-2; Sitzmann, Bell, Kraiger, & Kanar, 2009).

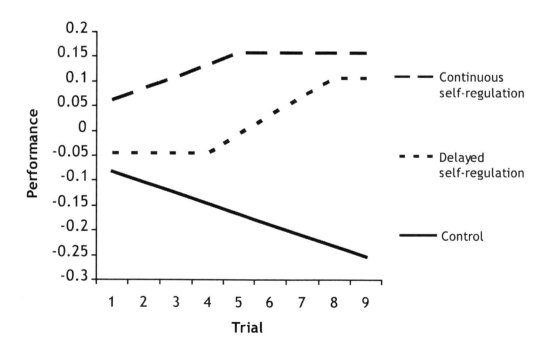

Figure 6-2. The effect of prompting self-regulation on learning across nine online training trials. This figure compares the relative effectiveness of continuous self-regulation and delayed self-regulation.

In the continuous prompts condition, trainees' performance gradually improved across the first four trials and then leveled off until the end of the course, relative to the other conditions. In the delayed prompts condition, trainees performed below average in the first half of the course. However, after the intervention was implemented mid-training, trainees' performance began to gradually improve over time. Finally, relative to the other conditions, the control group's performance gradually declined over time. By the end of the course, trainees who received the intervention were outperforming the control group by between 10 percent and 20 percent.

Reducing Attrition

The third study examined the extent to which prompting self-regulation reduced attrition from voluntary online training among 479 adult learners (Sitzmann & Ely, 2010). Attrition was 17 percentage points lower for trainees who were continuously prompted to self-regulate, relative to the control. Moreover, continuously prompting self-regulation provided a buffer against physically and mentally withdrawing from training following poor performance. When trainees did not receive the intervention, they concentrated less, were less motivated to learn, and were more likely to drop out following poor performance. Trainees who received the intervention stayed motivated, continued concentrating, and remained in the course, regardless of their performance. This suggests that adults have the skills necessary to succeed in e-learning environments, and simply reminding them to be good learners motivates them to employ the skills necessary to succeed.

Self-regulatory prompts are a no-cost intervention that can be incorporated in e-learning as SCOs. Moreover, they can be reused across courses in order to increase learning and reduce attrition. Hill Air Force Base in Ogden, Utah has taken the lead within the DoD community by implementing the prompts in a software training course called EXPRESS that teaches inventory management specialists to track aircraft parts. Designed to comply with SCORM standards, this intervention is included in the ADL Registry so that members of the DoD community can implement it for their e-learning courses. Members of the DoD community of practice may register learning assets in the ADL Registry to enable their discovery and reuse by other members of the community. For more information on the ADL Registry, see Lannom (this volume).

Interpreting Evaluation Data

The final mission of the Research and Evaluation Team is to ensure that members of the ADL community have tools to evaluate their courses and to correctly interpret their training evaluation data. End-of-course surveys are the most popular tool for collecting training evaluation data (Paradise, 2008). These surveys typically ask trainees whether they enjoyed the course and increased their understanding of the course material. Polls of members of the ADL community revealed that survey data is often the only form of evaluation data collected, and the data is usually used to infer whether trainees learned the course material.

Correct interpretation of evaluation data is essential to making informed decisions about training effectiveness. The Research and Evaluation Team undertook two large-scale meta-analyses—each with data from more than 25,000 trainees—in order to decipher the meaning of survey evaluation data (Sitzmann, Brown, Casper, Ely, & Zimmerman, 2008; Sitzmann, Ely, Brown, & Bauer, in press). Specifically, the team hoped to answer three research questions: 1) Do satisfied trainees learn more than dissatisfied trainees? 2) Can students accurately report how much they learned from training? and, 3) How should survey evaluation data be interpreted and how can it be used to improve the quality of training?

The studies produced overwhelming evidence that trainee reactions and self-assessments of knowledge cannot be used to evaluate whether trainees learned the course content—course satisfaction was not related to learning, and trainees were not accurate when they self-assessed their knowledge. Nevertheless, surveys that measure trainees' satisfaction with their instructional experience do have an essential role in evaluating some training courses. Trainee satisfaction is a strong predictor of attitude change in training. In training programs such as diversity, ethics, safety, and employee orientation courses, the goal of the course is to get trainees to embrace an attitude rather than to teach them new information. For example, the objective of diversity training is to ensure that trainees have an appreciation for diversity and are willing to work as part of a team with employees from different cultures and ethnicities. Trainees who enjoy these courses are receptive to attitude change, whereas trainees who do not enjoy a course are less likely to embrace the attitude advanced in the training program.

Use of Evaluations

Organizations need to plan how their evaluation data will be used before deciding what types of evaluation data should be collected (Kraiger, 2002). If they want to provide feedback to instructors or to market the course to potential trainees, surveys can provide an invaluable source of data. However, learning data—in the form of exams, instructor ratings of performance, or demonstrating the skills that were learned in training—must be collected if the goal is to understand whether trainees' knowledge and skills improved as a result of training. The Center for Research, Evaluation, Standards, and Student Testing (CRESST) has several state-of-the-art tools to evaluate learning outcomes. One example is the Cognitive Process Mapper, which is a tool for evaluating whether trainees' decision making skills improved as a result of training (Wainess, 2008). Trainees receive a problem to solve and the data they should evaluate to make the decision. This explicates decision making biases and permits instructors to observe whether trainees have the knowledge and skills to make correct decisions. Additionally, instructors can detect and correct trainees' misconceptions that lead to incorrect decisions.

Training Effectiveness Versus Efficiency

There is often a tradeoff between training effectiveness and efficiency. In general, investing more time and energy in developing quality courses and increasing trainees' instructional time inflates training expenses. The payoff for this investment is increased training effectiveness—changes in trainee attitudes, increased job knowledge, improved job performance, and, ideally, increased return-on-investment. Some recommendations for improving the effectiveness of e-learning courses will increase learning but may simultaneously increase training time.

Course Design Considerations

The ADL Research and Evaluation Team recommends that course designers incorporate a variety of instructional methods into courses, utilize practice, provide trainees with feedback on their performance, and include synchronous human interaction in training—even though following these recommendations may increase the amount of time required to develop and complete the course. For example, participating in synchronous communication requires all trainees to set aside time in their schedules to participate in chat discussions, and organizations may need to pay an instructor to lead the discussion. This may take trainees' time away from performing their job duties and increase the number of hours the organization needs to invest in instructional support, but it will also improve trainee satisfaction with the course and enhance trainees' knowledge of the course material. Moreover, trainees who use a variety of instructional methods in e-learning courses may require extended training time, and it can be expensive to develop a course with thought-provoking and informative lectures, discussions, assignments, and tutorials. However, the payoff should mitigate the cost. Effective training enhances job performance and reduces the need for retraining.

Self-Regulation

The analyses also demonstrate the substantial benefits of prompting trainees to self-regulate—learning was 10 percent to 20 percent better by the end of training than the control, and attrition was reduced by 17 percentage points. Once again these training efficiencies are accompanied by the cost of increased instructional time. Trainees who were prompted to self-regulate throughout training took an average of 5 minutes to respond to the prompts questions during a 5 hour course and spent 25 more minutes reviewing the training material than trainees in the control condition. The additional 30 minutes of training time may be justified by the learning gains, but organizations must be aware of this tradeoff.

Learner Control

One recommendation—providing trainees with control over their learning experience—may be the exception. Learner control reduces training time because trainees can skip over material they are already know. The research results also demonstrate that learner control has a positive effect on trainees' memory of factual information taught in training. Thus, providing trainees with control over the content, sequence, and pace of instruction may assist organizations in ensuring their employees get the most out of their training experience while minimizing the time they spend away from their jobs.

Conclusion

Training evaluation and metrics are essential for demonstrating the value and increasing the impact of training. Evaluation metrics keep organizations from perpetually investing in programs that drain valuable resources without producing meaningful results. ADL's Research and Evaluation Team helps ADL constituents to increase the impact of their training and ensure they have the data required to measure training effectiveness. This research suggests that when designed properly, e-learning can provide organizations with training that is more effective and efficient than classroom instruction. Additionally, the research highlights the importance of correctly designing training evaluations to capture critical data, and correctly interpreting evaluation data in order to make informed decisions about training programs. It is only through evaluation metrics and continuous improvements that the full value of e-learning technologies can be realized.

References

Brown, K. G., & Ford, J. K. (2002). Using computer technology in training: Building an infrastructure for active learning. In K. Kraiger (Ed.), *Creating, implementing, and maintaining effective training and development: State-of-the-art lessons for practice* (pp. 192-233). San Francisco: Jossey-Bass.

Clark, R. E. (1983). Reconsidering research on learning from media. *Review of Educational Research, 53,* 445-460.

Clark, R. E. (1994). Media will never influence learning. *Educational Technology Research and Development, 42,* 21-29.

Ely, K., Sitzmann, T., & Falkiewicz, C. (2009). The influence of goal orientation dimensions on time to train in a self-paced training environment. *Learning and Individual Differences, 19,* 146-150.

Kraiger, K. (2002). Decision-based evaluation. In K. Kraiger (Ed.), *Creating, implementing, and maintaining effective training and development: State-of-the-art lessons for practice* (pp. 331-375). San Francisco: Jossey-Bass.

Paradise, A. (2008). *State of the industry report 2008.* Alexandria, VA: American Society for Training & Development.

Sitzmann, T., Bell, B. S., Kraiger, K., & Kanar, A. M. (2009). A multilevel analysis of the effect of prompting self-regulation in technology-delivered instruction. *Personnel Psychology, 62,* 697-734.

Sitzmann, T., Brown, K. G., Casper, W. J., Ely, K., & Zimmerman, R. (2008). A review and meta-analysis of the nomological network of trainee reactions. *Journal of Applied Psychology*, *93,* 280-295.

Sitzmann, T., & Ely, K. (2010). Sometimes you need a reminder: The effects of prompting self-regulation on regulatory processes, learning, and attrition. *Journal of Applied Psychology, 95*, 132-144.

Sitzmann, T., Ely, K., Brown, K. G., & Bauer, K. (in press). The construct validity of self-assessments of knowledge: Meta-analytic evidence. *Academy of Management Learning and Education.*

Sitzmann, T., Kraiger, K., Stewart, D., & Wisher, R. (2006). The comparative effectiveness of Web-based and classroom instruction: A meta-analysis. *Personnel Psychology, 59,* 623-664.

Wainess, R. A. (2008). *Development and evaluation of a Cognitive Process Mapper.* Presented at the National Center for Research on Evaluation Standards and Student Testing, Los Angeles, CA.

The Authors

Traci Sitzmann, PhD, is a member of the faculty at the University of Colorado, Denver. She was formerly a research scientist at the Advanced Distributed Learning Co-Laboratory and a member of the Research and Evaluation Team.

Katherine Ely, PhD, is a research scientist at the Advanced Distributed Learning Co-Laboratory and a member of the Research and Evaluation Team.

Chapter 7

Challenges to SCORM
Eric Roberts and Patrick Shane Gallagher

Developing the Sharable Content Object Reference Model (SCORM) has been as much about managing expectations as it has been about harmonizing specifications and standards. In particular, SCORM's effect on instructional design has been of concern to researchers, designers, and content providers. The purpose of this chapter is to describe the goals and capabilities of SCORM, particularly with regard to what it was (and was not) intended to accomplish.

In the context of the ADL business paradigm (Wisher, this volume), this chapter addresses instructional design and pedagogical features that were assumed in the development of SCORM—and those about which SCORM currently remains silent. Future versions of SCORM may of course add capabilities that contribute towards achieving the ADL Initiative's long-term vision of quality training and education delivered on demand. How ADL intends to expand SCORM's capabilities is described by Panar, Rehak, & Thropp (this volume). This chapter outlines some capabilities and limitations of SCORM, described first in pedagogical terms and then in technical terms.

Initially, the C in SCORM stood for *Courseware*. This was changed early, as suggested at the first Plugfest in June 2000 by Mr. Philip Dodds. He questioned whether it might make more sense and might be more encompassing to imagine a sharable *Content* object reference model. Philip reasoned that "content objects" could be, of course, courseware objects, but they also could be seen as performance objects, documentation objects, or reference objects. The rationale was to think of learning as including performance support (Gafford & Heller, this volume) and to regard learning in more constructivist terms (Duffy & Cunningham, 1997; Fletcher, 2001; von Glaserfeld, 1989, 1997), in which learners actively engage in building internal models based on prior knowledge and learning strategies. Although ADL still refers to content objects, current thinking in ADL is that SCORM can apply to any digital object.

SCORM was based in part on the original Aviation Industry CBT Committee Computer Managed Instruction (CMI) design for e-learning (Robson & Richards, this volume). The original AICC design focus was on managed instruction using interoperable content. The primary use cases, described below, were based on delivery using a local area network of individual self-paced learning in a formal classroom context. SCORM extended and improved the basic CMI approach, enabling its adoption in true distributed learning available in classrooms, on local area networks, wide-area networks, and stand-alone systems—anytime and anywhere.

SCORM Current Capacity

SCORM integrates a set of e-learning standards and specifications to enable interoperable development and delivery of a tracked learning experience via the Web (Gallagher, this volume). Built on mature technology, SCORM systems primarily operate on sets of coupled content objects (Sharable Content Objects and assets) associated through a static structure (a content package) that includes explicitly defined branching logic (sequencing). SCORM accomplishes what traditional computer-based training was designed to accomplish, but in a way that is interoperable across learning management systems and compatible with delivery on the Web.

The instructional design and architectural assumptions on which SCORM was based arose from a careful survey of "use cases"—instructional strategies that were being used in designing most technology-based instruction at the time of SCORM's development. These strategies featured a hierarchy of three techniques.

First, the instructional materials were separated into a progressive series of modules, each concerned with a single instructional objective. Second, a procedure based on Keller's (1968) Personalized System of Instruction (PSI) was frequently found in the use cases. PSI requires modularization and then a pre-test before each module to allow learners who already know the material to skip over the module. Learners who enter and complete a module are given a post-test to determine if they have met its learning objective(s)—if not they are sent back through the module and post-tested again.

Third, Crowder's (1959) Intrinsic Programming was frequently found as an instructional strategy inside instructional modules. In Intrinsic Programming, instructional material—typically a short paragraph of text but also short audio presentations, brief videos, diagrams, etc. might be used—is presented and followed by a multiple choice question. A learner who answers correctly is moved along to the next instructional presentation in the module. Unlike most multiple choice test questions each distracter—wrong answer choice—is linked to specific remedial instruction intended to correct the misconception that would cause a learner to choose it.

Put together, these use case strategies were found either alone or combined as illustrated in Figure 7-1. The example of an Intrinsic Programming Item, adapted from Crowder (1959), would, of course, be one of many presented in the instructional module.

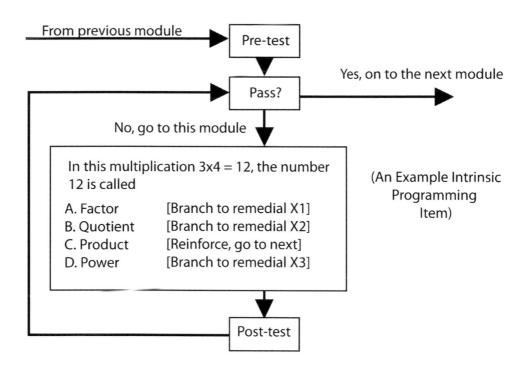

Figure 7-1. Illustration of the Instructional Strategies Found in Use Cases Underlying the Development of SCORM. A branching sequence is shown with movement to the next module or one of three remedial modules based on an incorrect response.

Based on its underlying assumptions of instructional strategies, SCORM increased the interoperability and accessibility of distributed learning, but at the cost of restricting broad adoption of new technologies. Further, many systems outside of middleware architectural assumptions employing learning management systems (LMS) and learning content management systems (LCMS) have evolved to incorporate training and learning activities independent of these middleware assumptions. Examples include email to instructors or chat functions between students. Advances in distributed technologies and architectures have outpaced those currently leveraged by the current version of SCORM.

Consensus building on specifications and standards to increase SCORM's capacity, however, can be protracted and contentious (Robson & Richards, this volume). Tradeoffs between the needs of learners, investments of vendors, and emerging capabilities of instructional design must be cautiously weighed.

Pedagogical Issues

As with any rapidly evolving technology, areas of improvement exist within SCORM. These areas may exist in its architecture but will affect instructional design and pedagogical outcomes. For example, the SCORM architecture is seen as confining learning content to implicit declarative knowledge, implying an inability to accommodate more advanced pedagogical models. Within the educational community, SCORM is considered an established framework with ubiquitous conformant content that does not easily allow learning to occur beyond the simple acquisition of declarative knowledge. It is thought to fall short in terms of cognitive and psychomotor skill acquisition (Jonassen & Churchill, 2004).

Applying other pedagogical models, such as simulations or games, within this framework may require careful analysis to determine whether they can be integrated into the existing SCORM or whether the existing SCORM needs to be extended to enable this type of training. For example, Xu (this volume) examines the relationships between SCORM and online game architectures, noting differences and similarities from the server side, the client side, and the communications component.

Users have tried to apply SCORM to use cases beyond its original assumptions but have found it difficult to do in a principled and consistent way. The current SCORM model constrains instructional designers, content developers, and tool vendors by assuming a fixed model for content and instructional design while at the same time providing only a limited framework for content reuse and repurposing. Limits to the current SCORM model that have been identified at various meetings over the past decade include:

- Support is restricted to single learners only

- Authors require advance knowledge of where content resides

- Successful content delivery is dependent on the specifics of network infrastructure

- Sequencing logic is tightly coupled to content structure

- There is limited flexibility for personalization and adaptability

- There is limited ability to contextually reuse content, especially smaller chunks

- Sharable Content Objects have a constrained definition that limits tracking of non-traditional SCORM content (e.g., simulations, games, collaborative experiences)

The Design Problem

ADL never set out to solve the "design problem" in instruction. One could assert that it is impossible to solve the "design problem." On asking whether some piece of instruction is "good," it is immediately necessary to extend the query: good for whom, good in what context, good under what conditions? ADL has a long term vision (Fletcher, 2006), but was indefinite about what could be accomplished in the short term to accommodate evolving and more robust designs.

What ADL *did* do was to try to figure out how to make Department of Defense (DoD) instructional materials accessible, interoperable, durable, and reusable. As described earlier, ADL focused its efforts for defining standards for interoperability and sharability on use cases of instructional scenarios that were deemed to represent a substantial portion of the instructional material being delivered to DoD learners. Much of this concerned declarative or procedural knowledge. The use cases described traditional, didactic computer-based instruction for individual learners without the (necessary) benefit of a live instructor. Field and laboratory exercises, traditional residential classroom-based instruction, physical skills instruction, attitude development, mentoring, socialization, and device-based training were purposely left un-addressed. It was judged that the task of corralling a significant portion of the vendor community that was developing most of DoD training would be challenging enough. It was a decision consciously made at the time as a starting point.

SCORM and Instructional Design

The issue of SCORM conformance is essentially unrelated to instructional design quality issues. SCORM is an availing technology. By agreeing to use SCORM as a standard for, primarily, interoperability and reusability, it is possible to realize desirable ends—if one puts in all of the necessary work to achieve those ends. SCORM neither ensures nor precludes good instruction. To get good technology-based instruction, you have to go through the rigor of building good instruction (Deibler & Berking, this volume).

SCORM—Software v. Standards

A minority criticism of SCORM is that SCORM is an inelegant architecture. This criticism misses an essential point. SCORM is not about software. It is about establishing a standard that allows for the creation and continued support of a community dedicated to training programs that scale, that inter-operate, that support sharing and collaboration, and that avail these benefits to those who will invest the effort to craft quality products.

Some argue that ADL's prescription of standards puts a stranglehold on the creativity of instructional designers. However, others in the academic community claim they cannot identify what cannot be done in a SCORM-conforming fashion (Wiley, 2000). There certainly are a host of learner behaviors that cannot be captured and assessed to inform instructional decision-making in current generation learning management systems.

Consequently, many of the complaints about SCORM arise from issues on which it is, simply, silent. SCORM is to instructional design as plain, brown wrapping paper is to Christmas presents. It is a standards-based wrapper; what is inside could be diamonds or it could be coal. SCORM nevertheless has availed so many indirect benefits that it is understandable that many would hope that it could have achieved more, that it could have achieved all sorts of oughtness, that it could achieve serendipity.

Technical Limitations

Gallagher (2007) also has looked at what it might take to allow SCORM to address virtual environments. In prior research, SCORM has been assessed against eight requirements describing functionality necessary to support a simulation-based learning environment. The functionality represented by these requirements supports learner introduction and initial setup; tracking learner profile changes, status and progress; furnishing and receiving simulation input and output data to other systems; providing simulation state feedback to the learner; providing contextual decision-making information to the learner; providing contextual decision-coaching to the learner; and providing end-of-period reflection input and storage capability per learner.

Providing contextual- and decision-dependent functionality requires the broadcasting of status data by some systems and the ability to make sense and act on that data by others. In this case, a specific system would be contained black-box fashion within a Sharable Content Object (SCO). Implicit within the implementation of these requirements is the need to communicate data between SCOs. Also implicit is the need for SCOs to persist (co-exist during runtime)—currently not allowed in SCORM.

Data Model
The argument could be made that SCORM (all versions) allows this communication now through the Run-time Environment using the existing application interface and data model. While this may be true to some extent, the CMI data model is a pre-defined, somewhat limited model designed to communicate data to an LMS about events occurring within a SCO. For example, it can communicate a learner's score compared to a preset mastery level indicating whether or not a learner has "passed," or it could communicate whether or not a learner has "finished" the SCO. It can also communicate other types of SCO-related event data including the learner's location within the SCO (i.e., bookmark). The *cmi.location* object which can do this has historically been used for multiple communication purposes and has been suggested by developers as a communication solution.

Another capability that could be considered in this context may be the CMI data model's ability to communicate a stream of interaction data using the *cmi.n.interaction* data object. A specific class of interaction called a performance interaction can track and communicate up to 125 specified and ordered Boolean events. This has the potential of assessing and scoring a learner in a simulation contained within a specific SCO. However, with only 125 Boolean pre-assigned and pre-ordered events, this method may not be robust enough for communicating rich state data snapshots produced by a simulation engine. Other potential CMI objects for storing and retrieving state data are the cmi.launch_data and cim.suspend_data objects. However these and the previous CMI objects, besides being limited in capacity, produce data that can only be read by the SCO producing it. In other words, there is no SCO-to-SCO communication.

As the goals of many SCORM users or developers include not only interoperability but reusability, the above solution may have another serious flaw. In using the CMI model for communication, data would have to be pre-defined either as strings or as arrays of Boolean data hard coded as read-only material within the content package and/or stored by the Run-Time Environment. Even if the data could be communicated to other SCOs, this process might couple the SCOs so tightly as to severely reduce reusability.

SCO-to-SCO Communications

SCO-to-SCO data sharing has been discussed in other contexts as complex arbitrary data sharing between learning objects. The ability to allow SCO-to-SCO data sharing could greatly facilitate reuse by encouraging the development of functional SCOs as components in a loosely coupled manner much like that of a Service Oriented Architecture (SOA). Also, the need for SCO-to-SCO data sharing was identified by SCORM researchers to be highly relevant to integrating SCORM with advanced pedagogical models such as simulations.

Gaps in sequencing have also been identified. These gaps encompass support for management and tracking, data values, and global variables as well as inclusion of if-then logic. The SCORM Sequencing and Navigation book discusses the inclusion of global objective variables with both Boolean or numerical data value storage and tracking capability. It also discusses the if-then model used to determine sequencing rules. However, as a programming language, it is very limited. Conditions are relegated to True or False with the exception of the Objective Measure (-1 - +1 values) and types are limited. Resulting actions are also limited in type allowing essentially only navigation decisions. Also, conditions are evaluated from either pre-set flags hard coded in the content package or by values contained within the Objective variable. Perceptions exist that coding and implementing these sequencing rules are difficult and are too low-level, similar to the difference between an assembly language and higher-level languages in computer programming.

Content Aggregation

With the current relationship sequencing has with content aggregation in SCORM, some would argue that what has been missing is a more robust mechanism for defining sequencing rules and relationships with content to allow for a strong reusability of content within SCORM. If one could truly separate content and its sequencing rules, then reusing content would become easier. Sequencing strategies that cannot be implemented today would be enabled. More intelligent environments (e.g., LMS, LCMS, and Intelligent Tutors) could be developed to take advantage of these changes and would ultimately assist in leading ADL towards its mission and vision.

Communication Standard

One of the recurring themes ADL has heard over the years, along with a theme heard during the SCORM 2.0 requirements-gathering process, was that a new communication standard is needed to support other non-Web browser-based delivery modes. Over the years, several in the simulation community have tried to harmonize the High-Level Architecture (HLA) standards with SCORM to support the ability to launch and track HLA-based simulations within SCORM environments. One of the barriers to allowing this to happen easily and cost effectively was the lack of support in SCORM for a robust communication protocol. There were several technical and developmental issues with integrating the two standards at the application level. This problem could have been resolved if SCORM had another approach to a communication protocol. More recently, ADL has heard the same issues from the Serious Gaming industry and game developers. This was also apparent at the 2008 Interservice/Industry Training, Simulation and Education Conference (I/ITSEC) where several organizations and individuals approached ADL about similar requirements and needs.

Stealth SCORM—Improving the Assessment Process

In one proposed architecture (Ellaway, 2008), presented as a response to the LETSI call for suggestions for next-generation ADL/(SCORM), content and context are specified independently, making it possible to move beyond static content to embrace newer pedagogies, which must be ADL's next step. Gleaning meaning from student experiences is a difficult task, however. Unlike selected-response assessments where correct and incorrect responses are explicit, judging students' constructed responses requires inference. How to make that practicable is the subject of another excellent paper (Shute & Spector, 2008), from the same call for white papers, that envisions a "stealth assessment engine" that would collect on-going information in games, simulations, and other virtual environments without disrupting the learning activities.

New directions in psychometrics allow more accurate estimations of learners' competencies. New technologies permit us to administer formative assessments during the learning process, extract on-going, multi-faceted information from a learner, and react in immediate and helpful ways. This capability is important given large individual differences among learners, and reflects the use of adaptive technologies described above. When embedded assessments are seamlessly woven into the fabric of the learning environment so that they are virtually invisible or unnoticed by the learner, this is *stealth assessment*. Stealth assessment can be accomplished via automated scoring and machine-based reasoning techniques to perform assessments of student progress that would be too hard for humans (e.g., estimating values of evidence-based competencies across a network of skills). A key issue involves not the collection or analysis of the data, but making sense of what can potentially become a deluge of information.

Conclusion

Jaron Lanier, often called the father of virtual reality, makes the point that it is impossible to engage in technology development without having some social-engineering effects (Lanier, 2010). That is true in the case of SCORM as it has been elsewhere. Design decisions always have direct consequences and indirect implications. Some of those decisions, as addressed here, meant restricting a focus to forms of instruction that are less dynamically interesting than many currently available. Others resulted in architectures that, arguably, can be labeled "inelegant." We might argue, however, that ADL's vision was less on technology and more on the social-engineering effects, it is about interoperability as well as sector relationships (Wisher, this volume). SCORM has become an international *de facto* standard in large measure because the goal was the establishment of a consensually negotiated foundation for a community to come together to address community goals: accessible, interoperable, durable, reusable content for learning and performance aiding. The starting point was the answer; the question was the challenge: how shall we do this thing?

References

Crowder, N. A. (1959). Automatic teaching by means of intrinsic programming. In E. Galanter (Ed.), *Automatic Teaching: The State of the Art* (pp.109-116). New York, NY: John Wiley & Sons.

Duffy, T. M., & Cunningham, D. J. (1996). Constructivism: Implications for the design and delivery of instruction. In D. H. Jonassen & P. Harris (Eds.), *Handbook of research on educational communications and technology* (AECT) (pp. 170–198). Mahwah, NJ: Lawrence Erlbaum.

Ellaway, Rachel A. (2008, October). *SCORM 2: Redefining Reusable Educational Activities.* Paper presented at the LETSI Conference, SCORM 2.0, Pensacola, FL..

Fletcher, J. D. (2001). What Do Sharable Instructional Objects Have to do with Intelligent Tutoring Systems, and Vice Versa? *International Journal of Cognitive Ergonomics,* 5, 317-333.

Fletcher, J. D. (2006). The ADL Vision. In, H. F. O'Neill and R. Perez. (Eds.) Web-Based *Learning: Theory, Research and Practice* (pp. 31-53). Mahwah, NJ: Lawrence Erlbaum.

Gallagher, P.S. (2007). *Assessing SCORM 2004 for its affordances in facilitating a simulation as a pedagogical model*. Doctoral Dissertation, George Mason University, Fairfax, VA.

Jonassen, D., & Churchill, D. (2004). Is there a learning orientation in learning objects? International Journal on E-Learning, 3(2), 32-41.

Keller, F.S. (1968). Goodbye, teacher ... . *Journal of Applied Behavior Analysis,* 1, 79-89.

Lanier, J. (2010). *You Are Not a Gadget: A Manifesto.* New York, NY:Alfred A Knopf.

Shute, Valerie J. & Spector, J. Michael (2008, October). Stealth Assessment in Virtual Worlds. Paper presented at the LETSI Conference, SCORM 2.0, Pensacola, FL.

Von Glasersfeld, E. (1989). Cognition, construction of knowledge, and teaching. *Synthese, 801*, 121–140.

Von Glasersfeld, E. (1997). Homage to Jean Piaget. *Irish Journal of Psychology,* 18, 293–306.

Wiley, D. (Ed.) (2000). *The instructional use of learning objects.* Online at http://www. reusability.org/read.

The Authors

Eric Roberts is the Chief Learning Scientist of the ADL Initiative.

Patrick Shane Gallagher, PhD, is currently the program director for the Advanced Distributed Learning (ADL) Technical PMO and is employed by Serco Learning and Human Capital Business Unit as a SCORM researcher.

Section II

ADL—POLICIES AND TOOLS

Chapter 8

The Path to ADL Policy
Michael W. Freeman

The Advanced Distributed Learning (ADL) Initiative's vision is to provide access to the highest quality education and training that can be tailored to individual needs and delivered cost effectively, anywhere and anytime. ADL's goal was to institutionalize and enable sharing of training content and information as well as to encourage adoption of innovative learning technologies and systems. To achieve these goals, ADL needed to set standards for products, processes, and systems so they were accessible, interoperable, durable, and reusable.

The purpose of this chapter is to describe the formulation of policy within the U.S. Department of Defense (DoD) that confirmed the ADL approach for internal adoption. This chapter, then, accounts for the methodology of ADL endorsement within the DoD and other military organizations. This policy stemmed initially from an Executive Order in 1999 that assigned the governmental lead in devising standards for distributed learning to the DoD (Bardack et al., this volume). Within the context of the ADL business paradigm, this chapter illustrates how a policy-directed, broad scale adoption creates a marketplace for ADL systems (Wisher, this volume). The DoD is indeed a large training organization, with forces numbering in the millions dispersed to 50 countries, with continuous training and career growth needs (Fletcher, this volume). Specific examples of the adoption of ADL in the form of the implementation guidelines, procedures, and practices within DoD are covered in Murray and Marvin (this volume).

Importance of Policy

Technology may be the relatively easier, and for many the more interesting, part of implementing a distributed learning program. Deciding how to apply distributed learning technologies and setting the necessary policies to drive a scalable implementation depend on authority, persistence, and timing. For this chapter, policy is considered to be a generalization about organizational behavior at a level which has structural implications for the organization (Katz & Kahn, 1978). Moreover, policy-making is an exercise in leadership and organizational change.

The larger the organization, the more important formal policies are to its effective and efficient operation. Policies are the primary methods for leadership to ensure the organization follows their philosophy and intent. They are also the primary mechanism for ensuring organizational compliance with laws, regulations, and other requirements. Policies can be developed and implemented by any or all of the layers of oversight for the organization. This includes governing boards and executive management. Within the DoD scheme, regulations by the military Services generally follow overarching policy issued by the Office of the Secretary of Defense, the legal authority.

The Timing of Policy

When dealing with policies that implement ever-changing technology, the decision-making takes on an added dimension. Until a technology is sufficiently mature, it is problematic that all related policy options are fully understood. The decision to proceed with a policy is based on a judgment that the technical work has sufficiently mitigated technical risk. This is not unlike decisions in the information technology industry on determining when to launch a particular product in the marketplace. In the case of ADL, a judgment was made that the Sharable Content Object Reference Model (SCORM) had progressed to the point that it could be firmly implemented, even though certain technical issues were not yet fully resolved (Roberts & Gallagher, this volume)—thus the importance of timing in issuing the ADL policy.

Policy Balance

It is important that organizational leaders carefully balance the need for clear policy with the need for freedom of action and initiative at the lower levels. If every detail is fixed in policy, and lower level managers and staff are not allowed some degree of flexibility, they may find it difficult to further the purposes of the organization. Therefore, it is useful to have a way to request exceptions to policy or some latitude in how it is implemented based on specific circumstances. In the case of ADL, SCORM is an enabling requirement, but the users, or DoD components, can procure any SCORM-conformant system that best suits their needs. Social media tools, for example, can be worked into SCORM environments if they are required (Fowler, this volume). This choice encourages competition amongst providers, which leads to better products at lower costs. A marketplace has formed.

Policy that is appropriate at a national level of government, such as the DoD, may be only marginally relevant to the needs of those at a regional level of government, and vice versa. There are certain policy issues that are common in distance education, particularly within regional planning organizations (Dirr, 2005). These issues may not all necessarily apply to distributed learning at a national governmental level, but it is useful to check them for possible inclusion. From the regional perspectives on education, the common threads of policy issues concern intellectual property, ownership of courses, faculty issues (e.g., teaching load, class size), student issues (e.g., privacy, disabled students), limiting insurance liability, commercialization (e.g., royalties or licenses), and teaching beyond regional, state, or international borders (American Council of Education, 2000).

E-Learning in Europe

The European Union has identified progressive education policies as a way to develop the most competitive and dynamic knowledge-based economy in the world, and information and communications technology are expected to play a vital role. The development of e-learning in Europe, however, has not yet had the expected impact despite broad political and social endorsements (Commission of the European Communities, 2008). Although large European companies report encouraging results from e-learning in the workplace, it is still under-exploited in adult education. This parallels the path of e-learning in the United States. The DoD, in 1999, responded to this situation by creating the ADL Initiative (Wisher, this volume). The DoD had determined that the lack of interoperability reduced the impact of technology on learning, education, and training and developed a program to address the issue.

DoD Policy Model

Within the U.S. Department of Defense, *Directives* establish policy and *Instructions* implement the policy. In other words, *Instructions* establish responsibilities, processes, and procedures for doing what the *Directives* say is important. The relevant Directive on military training stipulates that the office that oversees the ADL Initiative can exercise authority over the development, management, and delivery of advanced distributed learning, as well as issue direction for implementation (Department of Defense, 2009).

Although the DoD may seem very monolithic, the policy system is based on gaining the approval or acquiescence of the sub-organizations, known as the DoD components, that would be subject to the policies. This requires detailed coordination with the components, who formally comment on a draft policy issuance and may offer minor wording adjustments or outright non-concurrence. This leads at times to adjustments and sometimes to concessions, but ultimately a policy is issued. While the coordination and comment period can take a while, it improves the quality of the mandates and the likelihood that the components will not hesitate to comply with the final policy. It also improves the audit trail delineating who decided what and why.

DoD Instruction on Development, Management, and Delivery of Distributed Learning

This policy represents thousands of hours of effort in carefully writing and aligning policy with the organizational objectives for ADL. There were multiple meetings with the chief stakeholders over a period of several years; monthly meetings of the Total Force ADL Action Team kept the components informed (Murray & Marvin, this volume). The timing of the policy issuance depended on the maturity of SCORM (Gallagher, this volume) and the availability of the ADL Registry (Lannom, this volume). In late 2005, the ADL office in the Office of the Secretary of Defense issued a draft Instruction for formal coordination, resulting in DoD Instruction 1322.26, dated June 2006.

The highlights of this policy are:

- Embedded training and distributed learning shall be considered as the first option to meet training requirements of defense technology projects and acquisition programs.

- The DoD components shall share training resources to the maximum extent possible. A joint architecture and common standards for training technology shall be developed.

- Information is shared as broadly as possible except where limited by law, policy, or security classification. Data assets produced as a result of the assigned responsibilities are visible, accessible, and understandable to the rest of the Department of Defense as appropriate.

The ADL Business Case

In order to understand the specific policy implementation sections, it is useful to appreciate what ADL seeks to accomplish. Content and systems must have specific qualities that are associated with the ADL functional requirements. These requirements specify what content and systems must be able to do to enable automated delivery systems and reuse of content.

The Functional Requirements

Accessibility. The ability to locate and access instructional components from multiple locations and deliver them to other locations. For example, a content author can search the ADL Registry and identify relevant content that has already been developed by another organization and deploy that content to learners anywhere in the world on any LMS that conforms to the same version of SCORM.

Interoperability. The ability to take instructional components developed in one system and use them in another system. For example, content packaged for delivery in one SCORM-conformant LMS could be loaded into another LMS that conforms to the same version of SCORM for delivery to learners.

Durability. The ability to withstand technology evolution and/or changes without costly redesign, reconfiguration, or recoding. For example, upgrading to a new computer operating system should have no impact on the delivery of content to learners.

Reusability. The flexibility to incorporate instructional components in multiple applications and contexts. For example, e-learning content designed for one organization can be redeployed, rearranged, repurposed, or rewritten by other organizations with similar learning needs.

ADL has defined an ordered sequence of steps that specify what DoD organizations must do to conform with requirements. The ADL Requirements Flow, illustrated in Figure 8-1, includes: requirement – analysis – search – reuse/repurpose/ develop – follow standards – store – register – maintain.

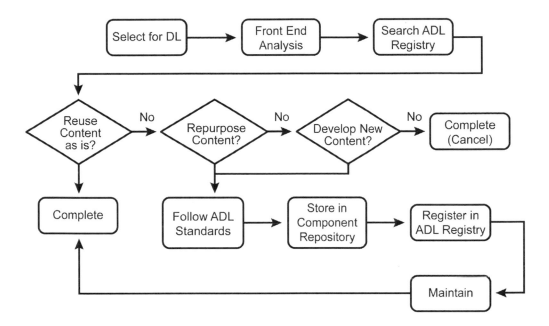

Figure 8-1. ADL Requirements Flow. ADL has defined an orderly sequence of steps that DoD organizations must follow to meet ADL requirements.

Select for Distributed Learning. The requirements flow begins with the identification of a training or education need and the selection of ADL as the method of delivery. Instructional designers often use a five-phased generic process called ADDIE to guide training design and development. ADDIE is an acronym for Analysis, Design, Development, Implementation, and Evaluation (Deibler & Berking, this volume).

Front End Analysis. Organizations are required to do a front end analysis of their learning requirement. While this seems self-evident and mundane, it is fundamental to the sharing of content. The policy also requires that the analysis consider cost, target audience, content, learning objectives, and delivery methods. Defining these information elements is the first step towards formally seeking off-the-shelf or learning content that can be repurposed (Shanley et al., this volume). The analysis is also the first step toward building useful metadata for identifying available content.

Search the ADL Registry. After identifying their requirements, DoD organizations are mandated to search for content that meets their needs that is available off-the-shelf or that can be repurposed. This requires using the central ADL Registry to search for matches using the metadata of existing content (Lannom, this volume). It also requires coordinating with the organizations that own the existing content, to obtain access. In a perfect world, this would be negotiated electronically between registries and repositories, but barriers presented by firewalls and differing security policies may make it necessary to contact content managers to enable movement.

Reuse Content As Is. If the identified content meets the needs of the organization as is, the content may be moved into the new organization's repositories, and the learning management system configured to load that content at the appropriate point in the course or performance support situation. Alternatively, the new user's systems could load the content directly from the original owner's site. To ensure that the content can be loaded and is reusable directly, the content must meet the basic software interoperability standards provided by being SCORM-conformant. Policy also requires that the content have organizational use rights (government use rights) and that the display/runtime software doesn't have limitations (e.g. royalties) to direct reuse. ADL also encourages packaging the original content in the smallest package that can be associated with a learning outcome.

Repurpose Content. If the content must be modified in order to meet the user's requirement, the user downloads the content, makes the necessary changes, and republishes it in their own repository as a new content object. This new object is required to have updated descriptive metadata that is registered to make it searchable for others. DoD agencies register content in a dedicated registry called the ADL Registry (Lannom, this volume).

Develop as New Content. If there is no existing content that meets the learning requirement, or if existing content can't be economically repurposed, the organization develops the content.

Follow ADL Standards. When a DoD or DoD-related organization develops new content, it must be developed to conform to ADL standards (SCORM).

Store in Component Repository. The developed content, or at least an official copy of it, must be stored in a repository that is accessible by others. That repository must be sanctioned by the repository component of the developing organization.

Register in the ADL Registry. The content must also be registered with the ADL Registry so other organizations can find it to determine its learning intent, audience, and other relevant information. Developing metadata begins with the analysis requirement.

Maintain. Finally, the organization that owns the content must maintain the content in the repository and update the registration when the content is changed. The owning organization is also responsible for determining when the content is no longer valid or useful and must either mark it as such in the registry or remove it.

The ADL Registry

The policy formally establishes the registry and assigns responsibility for operating it. It also defines the technical standards and general requirements. The registry enables organizations to find existing content for reuse or repurposing. It is important to note that the registry contains metadata describing content, and points to repositories where the content is maintained. It points to the right place, but doesn't contain the actual content.

Organizations acquiring or building new content must label the content with appropriate metadata that describes the original intended use and notes any limitations on use or repurposing by someone else.

Repositories

DoD policy requires organizations to store their content in repositories that can be accessed by others. They must also register their repositories in the ADL Registry, and include metadata describing the repository.

The policy also requires organizations to establish policies for their repositories in accordance with the parent organization's policies, and to identify a single contact who can approve repositories in their organization. This is intended to ensure that repositories are identified, and that they meet the technical and policy requirements of the member organization. It is also intended to empower member organizations with the capability to manage their own resources so that the parent organizations are not responsible for overseeing a myriad of systems and users. If there is a question about a repository, there is a designated person who can answer for the member organization.

Legacy Content Policy

Legacy content is that which already exists when the policy is approved. Since much legacy content was developed and maintained by organizations before the implementation of the DoD policy, there is no requirement for organizations to register legacy content, nor for the content to conform to ADL standards like SCORM. However, owning organizations are encouraged to register their legacy content, and ensure that it conforms to standards when it is effective and efficient to do so. However, there is no funding from the DoD for legacy content.

The policy was specifically defined to avoid problems and issues that could arise due to the potential costs of identifying and registering older content. Content owners were already required to register their content with a previous catalog or on a list of products prior to the establishment of the ADL Registry. Therefore, little additional effort is needed to search both the catalog and the registry.

Supporting Policy Enclosures

To support the main policy sections defined above, the Directive included four additional enclosures that expand on, and provide more detail to, the policy. These supporting enclosures are References, Definitions, ADL Registry Description, and Acquisition Guidelines.

References

The policy includes a reference section that provides complete identification of sources of other policies or information. This section is especially useful for identifying authoritative sources of information and requirements.

Definitions

The definition section provides precise definitions of important terms used in the policy. This is necessary to ensure that all involved understand specifically what is meant by terms, and what the policy applies to and doesn't apply to. Some of the critical terms are:

ADL Registry Description. This section describes the registry—how it's developed, and how it's used. The registry is absolutely critical to enabling reuse of content by clearly identifying the content with accurate metadata and allowing potential users to locate the content (Lannom, this volume).

Acquisition Guidelines for Systems and Content. Government contracting has many legal and administrative requirements when acquiring products and services. This enclosure provides sample or "boiler plate" wording for use in different parts of the acquisition documentation. The wording in statements of work and contracts must be very precise to ensure that the acquired products and services follow the established policies and procedures. For example, this enclosure provides a sample of wording on policy regarding standards conformance and certification (Panar, Brannon, & Poltrack, this volume):

Acceptance shall be based on one of the following:

Conformance. An error-free repeatable test log output for each content package, providing evidence that the CP SCORM-conformance label has been achieved, shall verify SCORM-conformance.

Certification. A certificate for each content package from an approved ADL Certification Testing Center, providing evidence that the CP SCORM (current version) Conformant conformance label has been achieved, shall verify SCORM conformance.

Conclusion

Providing access to the highest quality education and training that can be tailored to individual needs requires a solid policy foundation. The use of common standards for e-learning content and delivery systems that are accessible, interoperable, durable, and reusable is key to creating an e-learning environment that is cost effective. Within the U.S. Department of Defense, the ADL Initiative has institutionalized the implementation of its standards through a policy instruction. Others are welcome to follow this approach.

References

American Council on Education. (2000). *Developing a distance education policy for 21st century learning*. Washington, DC: American Council of Education.

Dirr, P. J. (2003). Distance education policy issues: towards 2010. In M.G. Moore & W.G. Anderson (Eds.), *Handbook of distance education* (pp. 461-479). Mahwah, NJ: Erlbaum.

Katz, D. & Kahn, R. (1978). *The social psychology of organizations*. New York: Wiley.

U.S. Department of Defense. (2009). *Military training* (Department of Defense Directive No. 1322.18). Retrieved from http://www.dtic.mil/whs/directives/corres/pdf/132218p.pdf

U.S. Department of Defense. (2006). *Development, management, and delivery of distributed learning* (DoDI No. 1322.26). Retrieved from http://www.dtic.mil/whs/directives/corres/pdf/132226p.pdf

U.S. Department of Defense. (1991). *Development and management of interactive courseware (ICW) for military training* (DoDI No. 1322.20). Retrieved from http://www.dtic.mil/whs/directives/corres/pdf/132220p.pdf

The Authors

Michael W. Freeman was the Deputy Director of the Advanced Distributed Learning Initiative from 2003-2006. He currently works in the e-learning industry in Fayetteville, North Carolina.

Chapter 9

Validating SCORM Conformance—Buyer Beware

Angelo Panar, Rovy Brannon, and Jonathan Poltrack

Conformance refers to the capability of software to meet technical requirements and work as expected. In the context of the Sharable Content Object Reference Model (SCORM), conformance relates to whether learning management systems (LMSs), content packages, and sharable content objects interoperate according to the specification of a particular edition of the model. The ADL business paradigm is predicated on an assurance that systems and content can interoperate, so that content developed for one SCORM-conformant LMS can be exchanged and used by another conforming LMS. Conformance is vital to the ADL marketplace.

How this is done is the subject of this chapter. In the context of the broad ADL business paradigm, this chapter addresses the quality assurance that underpins the interoperability line (Wisher, this volume). Quality assurance is fundamental to the successful creation of a fair marketplace for ADL products and services. This chapter also addresses the application of partnerships and collaborations in the evolution of SCORM conformance testing from its initial, bare bones rendering in Version 1.0 in January 2000 to the 4th Edition of SCORM 2004 in April 2009 (Chronology, this volume). A detailed introduction to SCORM is provided in Gallagher (this volume). It is important to note that just because a system or content conforms to SCORM, there is no guarantee of a quality learning outcome, as discussed in a general way by Clark (1994), and Sitzmann and Ely (this volume). Sound instructional design principles must be followed when using SCORM (Deibler & Berking, this volume).

Certification and Conformance

This chapter provides guidance on SCORM Certification. Certification refers to the process of validating that a product conforms to SCORM specifications. Certification, then, is the result of a series of steps that an organization takes, which, if successful, officially documents that a product or content is valid. Conformance refers to the actual testing of that product or content. Testing can uncover software defects that may violate SCORM, and thus result in the product being declared as non-conforming. The chapter begins with a discussion of conformance and a brief history of testing, followed by a discussion of the value proposition of certification. Later sections address the interests of those requiring a more in-depth knowledge of the procedures for certification and a consideration of potential challenges to certification.

Why is Conformance Important?

If the success of a standard is measured by the adoption rate of companies and products, the Sharable Content Object Reference Model (SCORM) has exceeded all expectations. Initially intended for use in the U.S. military and other government agencies, its adoption has reached far and wide as described in Section IV of this volume. Industry also offers cases of adoption.

The expansion of the use of digital content and the widespread adoption of SCORM standards to support instruction provides organizations and governments with the potential to share learning content and systems on a massive scale. This is not automatic, however. With this expansion of e-learning and the success of SCORM comes the reality that standards are of value only when they are consistently implemented. Sharing static digital content is not simple and straightforward for technical, organizational, and competitive reasons (Shanley et al., this volume). From a technical standpoint, it is possible that each system or tool developed could interpret portions of the reference model in slightly different ways, putting interoperability at risk. Moreover, as is the case in software testing in general, conformance testing can only establish that a product functions properly under specific conditions; it does not establish that it functions properly under every possible condition (Kaner, Falk, & Nguyen, 1999).

Beginning with the very early development work on SCORM, there was a keen recognition that there must be measures and methods for determining how well products conform to the model. As shortcomings in the measures were identified in implementing each edition of SCORM, the developers added clarifications and modifications to the model to mitigate the risk of reduced interoperability.

Creating interactive instructional content that can be tailored to individual needs, tracked, and shared across organizations is complex and differs across various development platforms. SCORM integrates a set of standards and specifications to support various high-level goals for instructional content known as the "ilities": accessibility, interoperability, durability, and reusability. Some add adaptability and maintainability to the list of "ilities" (Gallagher, this volume). The degree to which SCORM enables these "ilities" depends on how closely the delivery systems and instructional content follow the standard.

Most large organizations—government agencies, universities, and corporations—invest substantially in the development of learning, education, and training content. All seek to maximize the return on their investments by ensuring that their learning content is accessible, interoperable, durable, reusable, and maintainable. This goal influences many government agencies when seeking to purchase instructional technology infrastructure and content. Many products claim that they support or produce SCORM-conformant content. When purchasing decisions have significant impact, however, verifying claims of conformance is crucial. Those responsible for making purchasing decisions that involve investing significant capital in a system or content need a reliable way to validate product claims.

120

History of SCORM Conformance

ADL has made the process of verifying SCORM conformance very simple for consumers. Products that have been through an independent certification process provide assurance to purchasers that they support SCORM. All products verified by an independent test center as being SCORM-conformant are listed on the certified products page of the ADL Initiative Web site.

Evolution of the SCORM Testing Process

During early development of SCORM Version 1.0, ADL initiated a formal software development effort to create the SCORM Conformance Test Suite, now known as the SCORM Test Suite. It is important to note that SCORM Version 1.0 and Version 1.1 specifications were draft specifications, used as a test bed for interoperability. SCORM Version 1.2 was the first stable release of the specification, and it was the first to be released with an accompanying SCORM Conformance Test Suite. This software was freely available at the ADL Initiative Web site and was intended for use by the ADL community to test their content and LMSs. The Conformance Test Suite provided a means for content developers and LMS vendors to verify that they met the current, but changing, requirements of SCORM. In addition, ADL developed examples of SCORM-conformant systems such as the Sample LMS (now referred to as SCORM Sample Run-Time Environment (SRTE)) and the Maritime Navigation course as open-source examples of possible implementations of SCORM.

Plugfests

During this time, SCORM started gaining adoption in the learning community. To assist early adopters with SCORM, ADL planned events that focused on the technical aspects of SCORM, nicknamed "nuts and bolts," to promote interoperability between systems. In June 2000, ADL held the first of a series of these events, coining the term "Plugfest" to indicate their purpose. Plugfests brought together adopters of SCORM to create a forum for sharing their experiences with SCORM and to provide the ADL community with the opportunity to synchronize the evolution and convergence of commercial authoring tools, learning management systems, and Web-based courses with evolving open-architecture specifications. Attendees included learning software developers and content providers from various sectors of government, industry, and academia. Plugfest presentations and related materials are available for viewing or download at the ADL Initiative Web site. Plugfests included presentations on ADL and SCORM, but those were not the most interesting aspect. Plugfests included a "Plug n' Play" area that introduced the products of authoring tool, content, and LMS vendors through ad hoc, live interoperability tests. ADL provided a location, a network, and SCORM experts as mediators for the "Plug n' Play" area. Issues and ambiguities of the specification often came to light when real content was imported and executed in real-world LMS systems. Not only was this information valuable for the participants, but it served as a main driver for refining SCORM Version 1.2 and led to many of the requirements of SCORM 2004.

Incentives to Certify

Several incentives have been built in to the SCORM certification process since it was launched. Low certification costs encourage all organizations, regardless of size, to certify. In addition, the conformance requirements started with a limited common baseline to minimize initial implementation costs associated with SCORM adoption; these requirements have broadened and have become more specific over time. For example, the SCORM 2004 1st Edition contained approximately 50 LMS test packages, the 2nd Edition contained approximately 85 LMS test packages, the 3rd Edition contained approximately 120 LMS test packages, and the 4th Edition contains approximately 185 test packages. This approach to refining requirements eases content and LMS vendors into conformance and certification over a period of time, allowing them to implement fewer requirements at the beginning, but requiring more detail as time goes on.

Access to certification is convenient due to distribution of testing centers. Certification is available through three ADL Certification Testing Centers: the Wisconsin Testing Organization, located at the Academic ADL Co-Lab, Madison, Wisconsin; the Naval Undersea Warfare Center, located at Division Keyport; and the Korea ADL Test Center, in Seoul, Korea.

Setting Customer Expectations for SCORM Conformance

SCORM defines the mechanics by which content is imported into, and tracked by, an LMS. SCORM provides flexibility for the technologies used in the actual content and does not specify a specific instructional methodology. Content developers are free to use any technology that meets the requirements defined in SCORM. Similarly, LMS vendors are not bound to a specific technology or server environment.

Certification testing is performed by an independent third party. It provides consumers of distributed learning content and systems with the assurance that certified products have successfully implemented ADL SCORM specifications. Certification is concerned with technology, and not with instructional aspects of the content. It is also important to note that certification is not an endorsement by the ADL Initiative. It does not guarantee that a product has been tested for defects in functionality, nor does it guarantee that the product's content is instructionally sound.

Defining Certification

SCORM certification requires third party independent verification with the SCORM Test Suite. This process is often more thorough than first party verification and requires conformance tests not automated by the SCORM Test Suite. Over time, conformance and, consequently, certification have become more stringent due to additional testing of boundary conditions. There are two products that can be certified: learning management systems and content packages. The following sections detail the certification requirements for SCORM 2004 4th Edition.

Learning Management Systems Conformance Certification

An LMS that has received certification through an ADL approved testing center has met specific criteria. There are three LMS conformance categories: LMS Run-Time Environment Version 1.1 (LMS RTE 1.1); LMS Content Aggregation Model Version 1.1 (LMS CAM 1.1); and LMS Sequencing and Navigation Version 1.1 (LMS SN 1.1). In order to receive the label *LMS SCORM 4th Ed. Conformant*, LMSs must satisfy the requirements listed in Table 9-1.

Table 9-1

This table depicts SCORM conformance requirements for each of the three categories of LMS

SCORM 2004 LMS Conformance Matrix			
Requirements	LMS RTE 1.1	LMS CAM 1.1	LMS SN 1.1
Be able to launch an asset.	√		
Be able to launch a known SCORM 2004 4th Content Object (SCO).	√		
Provide and expose an API Instance as a Document Object Model (DOM) that correctly implements all API methods.	√		
Implement correct support for all SCORM 4th Ed. Run-Time Environment Data Model Elements.	√		
Implement correct support for all SCORM 2004 4th Ed. Navigation Data Model Elements.	√		
Be able to import and process a known conformant SCORM 2004 4th Ed. Content Aggregation Application Profile content package.		√	
Correctly initialize SCORM 2004 4th Ed. Run-Time Environment data model elements based on information supplied in a content package manifest.		√	
Implement correctly all of the sequencing behaviors defined by the pseudo-code included in the SCORM 2004 4th Ed. Sequencing and Navigation (SN) Version 1.1.			√
Support all SCORM 2004 4th Ed. Navigation Data Model Elements.			√
Support navigation user interface requirements.			√

Note that in SCORM Version 1.2 several conformance levels were available for LMS systems. This resulted in an inherent issue with interoperability due to the possibility of different levels of conformance between different systems. In SCORM 2004, the notion of differing levels of conformance has been removed. However, each edition of SCORM 2004 has included additional testing requirements to enhance interoperability.

Content packages must also meet specific criteria in order to be certified as SCORM-conformant. These requirements are defined in Table 9-2. To receive the *CP SCORM 2004 4ᵗʰ Ed. Conformant* label, the LMS shall adhere to the conformance requirements defined for each category of Content Package: Content Package Content Aggregation Model Version 1.1 (CP CAM 1.1); Content Package Run-Time Environment Version 1.1 (CP RTE 1.1); and LMS Content Sequencing and Navigation Version 1.1 (LMS SN 1.1).

Table 9-2

This table depicts the conformance requirements for each category of Content Package

SCORM 2004 Content Package Conformance Matrix		
Requirements	**CP CAM 1.1**	**CP RTE 1.1**
If the content package is a SCORM 2004 4th Ed. Content Aggregation Package Application Profile, the manifest shall comply with the Content Aggregation Package Application Profile Manifest requirements.	√	
If the content package is a SCORM 2004 4ᵗʰ Ed. Content Aggregation Package Application Profile and the manifest contains SCORM 2004 4ᵗʰ Ed. Sequencing information, then the sequencing extensions in the manifest shall comply with the SCORM 2004 4ᵗʰ Ed. sequencing extension requirements.	√	
If the content package is a SCORM 2004 4ᵗʰ Ed. Content Aggregation Package Application Profile and the manifest contains SCORM 2004 4ᵗʰ Ed. navigation or presentation information, then the navigation/presentation extensions in the manifest shall comply with SCORM 2004 4ᵗʰ Ed. Navigation/Presentation Extension requirements.	√	
If the content package is a SCORM 2004 4ᵗʰ Ed. Resource Content Package Application Profile, then the manifest shall comply with the Resource Package Application Profile Manifest requirements.	√	
If the content package manifest contains metadata, then the metadata shall be well-formed and valid according to the respective Controlling Document (e.g., XSD, DTD.)	√	
The content package shall contain at least one Sharable Content Object (SCO) resource or asset resource.		√
All SCO resources identified in the manifest shall comply with the SCO Conformance.		√

Putting the Two Together: Conformant Systems and Conformant Content

When LMSs and content packages adhere to the requirements summarized above, interoperability results. There are two main categories of interoperability:

Content/LMS Run-Time functionality. This category refers to interoperability of content and LMSs during content execution. SCORM defines a minimum set of requirements that the content must perform when launched. The LMS expects this communication along with additional optional "Gets" and "Sets" of data model elements. In addition, SCORM 2004 defines sequencing rules that are used to provide a predefined flow through content based on the learner's interactions with the content. SCORM-conformant systems will always present the content in the same manner due to standardized sequencing rules.

Content packaging. The SCORM Content Aggregation Model defines the means to package content in a single distributable file. This file contains the description of the content contained in the package including the course organization, sequencing rules, and some default data model values. When a content package and LMS are conformant, the package can be "imported" into the LMS. Reuse of content across multiple conformant learning management systems is enabled via content packaging requirements defined in SCORM.

Other Considerations: What SCORM Does Not Guarantee

SCORM does not test or enforce community-specific application profiles. This includes metadata usage and syntax requirements. It includes requiring specific data model elements, and requirements that all SCOs set scores or "bookmark" progress for future reentry.

SCORM does not test or require any specific functionality from the LMS provided client, other than basic navigation devices. Vendors are given a lot of flexibility to provide value-added features as a way to differentiate their products in the market.

SCORM does not test or restrict utilization of any external systems that support learning, such as simulations, games, or assessment engines. If content or LMSs leverage these types of features, their content will generally not work on other LMSs. This is not necessarily bad, but doing so needs to be disclosed up front and consumers need to know that such content will not be portable.

SCORM does not define requirements for authoring tools, nor does it test them. There are many ways to build SCORM content and also many ways to "add" interesting features. Numerous Web technologies, such as HTML, Flash, AIR, Silverlight, and others, bring additional implementation requirements to the table. Only the end product—the SCO or the SCORM Content Package—can be unambiguously tested.

SCORM does not define requirements for, or test, content development or instructional design processes. SCORM does not define the size of SCOs, the size of content packages, the structure of content, how the data model elements are reported, or other processes that are defined by the instructional designer. These concerns should be addressed within community of practice-specific developer guidelines. The ADL Guidelines, available at the Web site of the ADL Initiative, address a general set of concerns and recommendations that span several communities of practice.

SCORM Certification Process

The process for SCORM conformance certification is simple and inexpensive. The three independent certification centers provide rapid turnaround to customers by having a unified, efficient process. The simplified process is shown in Figure 9-1. At the time of this book's publication, the process was under review and may be modified. It is important to refer to the ADL Initiative Web site and the Web site of the Wisconsin Testing Organization for updates to the process.

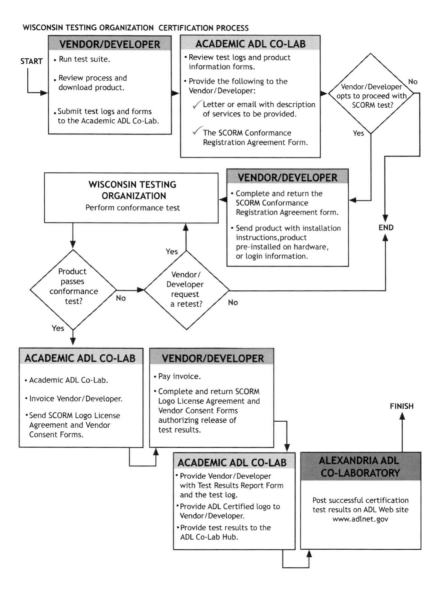

Figure 9-1. Conformance testing process. This figure depicts the steps vendors and developers must follow to receive SCORM certification. Courtesy of the Wisconsin Testing Organization.

Summary of the Process

Figure 9-1 shows the entire process flow and key decision points. The certification process can, however, be summarized in four steps. The Wisconsin Testing Organization Web site lists the following key steps in certification:

1. Complete a successful first party test with the ADL Test Suite and provide the test logs. It is important to follow the instructions carefully. Take note of how you log out of the SCORM course and include any special instructions with your application if necessary.

2. Fill out FORM 001, the SCORM Conformance Registration Agreement, and Form 002a, the LMS Conformance Testing Information Form. Applications can be sent by email, fax, or postal mail.

3. Submit both forms along with the Test logs (Summary and Detail) to the Testing Center. Please submit a manual that includes instructions on how to add users, import SCORM packages, enroll users, and launch courses.

4. Ship your product to the Testing Center, or if you are approved for remote testing, send access instructions.

The first step in the process is the most critical. Conducting a first party test with the freely available SCORM Test Suite provides immediate feedback on whether there are significant SCORM conformance issues. The test centers use the same software suite to conduct conformance tests, and a successful first party test eliminates most problems. The SCORM Test Suite software can be downloaded for free at the Web site of the ADL Initiative.

The administrative components of certification are simple, but a couple of key points can expedite the process. Testing cannot begin until the testing center has both forms, completed and signed (where applicable). Testing centers often have a queue of products awaiting certification, and submitting the applicable documentation allows the centers to begin certification work as soon as the product is ready. SCORM versions change, and some testing of earlier versions might be available. Indicating the correct SCORM version is an often overlooked detail that can save considerable time. Even though the test centers will generate their own test logs, it is essential to send self-test logs. The self-test logs are especially helpful if a problem is found at the test center. Auditors are able to compare official logs to the self-test suite and determine whether the problem is inherent to the product or whether some other technical issue exists.

Finally, the test centers must have access to the product in order to run the test. Providing access to content packages is generally simply a matter of sending files via an email attachment or supplying information to the auditor about where the files can be accessed. LMS validation, however, can be more complex. Given the flexibility of SCORM, systems can be built on many platforms and be fully conformant. Auditors need access to the version of the LMS platform the vendor wants certified in a working environment. This is accomplished by giving the auditor access to a fully functional version online or, in a more complex configuration, a server containing the software can be physically shipped to the testing center. It is not necessary for anyone from the submitting company to travel to the testing centers.

Upon successful completion of a test and payment of all required service fees, the testing center submits final approval to ADL. A letter signifying independent third-party testing is sent to the submitting organization, and the name of the product is made available on the ADL Web site. Appearance on the ADL Web site is the only officially sanctioned recognition of approval.

Testing Centers

There are currently three independent SCORM Certification centers. Two of the centers are located in the United States and one is in South Korea. The testing center in Madison, Wisconsin provides testing for civilian and non-classified military systems and content from North America and Europe. The testing center at the Naval Undersea Warfare Center (NUWC) Keyport provides SCORM conformance testing services for classified content and systems of the U.S. Department of Defense. The certification center in South Korea provides certification services to organizations throughout Asia.

In addition to conformance testing services, all of the testing centers provide some level of feedback and remediation to clients whose software does not pass the conformance test suite. If the amount of technical assistance needed exceeds a reasonable amount of time, the centers may provide hourly consulting at the developer's request. Auditors at each center undergo regular training and certification to maintain their expertise in the latest version of SCORM and provide helpful, independent advice on achieving conformance. The level of consulting services and remediation time provided vary depending on the policies of the testing center. Readers should consult the Web site of each center to determine the level of remediation support available.

Conclusion

Adoption of SCORM is growing across systems and content as the model becomes the accepted standard for e-learning development. As market demand for SCORM-conformant products grows, companies increasingly seek to market their learning management systems and content by emphasizing adherence to SCORM. The history and philosophy of SCORM conformance testing ensure a low cost and time commitment by product developers. Conformance certification benefits product developers of systems and consumers by ensuring proper implementation of the model. As with any claim about a product, purchasers of these products should verify conformance claims by consulting the ADL Initiative's Web site.

References

Clark, R. E. (1994). Media will never influence learning. *Educational Technology Research and Development, 42*, 21-29.

Kaner, C., Falk, J. & Nguyen, H. (1999). *Testing computer software*, (2nd Ed) New York: John Wiley and Sons.

Web Resources

Academic ADL Co-Lab. http://www.academiccolab.org/

Wisconsin Testing Center. http://www.academiccolab.org/certification

ADL Initiative. http://www.adlnet.gov

Korea Testing Center. http://www.adlkorea.or.kr/pslab/business/cnc.jsp

Naval Undersea Warfare Center Testing Center.
http://www-keyport.kpt.nuwc.navy.mil/ADL.htm.

The Authors

Rovy Brannon is the Director of the Academic ADL Co-Lab in Madison, Wisconsin.

Angelo Panar is ADL Enterprise Strategist at the ADL Co-Lab Hub in Alexandria, Virginia.

Jonathan Poltrack is a member of the ADL Technical Team at the ADL Co-Lab Hub in Alexandria, Virginia.

Chapter 10

The ADL Registry: A Technology for Finding and Reusing e-Learning Content
Larry Lannom

Standardization and reuse have been keys to technological advances from the industrial revolution to the proliferation of interoperable applications and services on the Internet. The ability to do the same in the e-learning field, in part by integrating and reusing existing learning objects, illustrations, videos, tests, games, and so on, depends not only on platform and content interoperability but on the ability to find the material and understand the terms and conditions associated with its reuse.

The solution to this problem within ADL is found in the concept of creating a registry that helps users find existing content through the use of searchable tags. Registries do not contain learning content, but instead point users to the location of specific learning content. In simple terms, a learning object is coded with structured descriptors termed metadata tags. In ADL, learning objects are also known as Sharable Content Objects or SCOs. The learning object, together with its metadata, resides in an independent content repository. The metadata also reside in a central registry, so a searcher need only consult the central registry to discover relevant content rather than each individual repository (see Figure 10-1). If the full content is needed, its location is known and it can be retrieved. The ADL Registry is the first instance of such an architecture for learning objects, now in use by the U.S. Department of Defense (DoD).

This chapter refers to the ongoing effort to expand the notion of the ADL Registry and develop open-source standards and specifications to allow reuse of content on a broad, global scale (Shanley et al., this volume). Other compatible registries can be created, such as with other government agencies, academic institutions, and the publishing industry. A federation of these registries offers a powerful tool for learning on demand. From the perspective of the ADL business paradigm, this chapter concerns enhancing the market and scaling mechanisms for locating interoperable, reusable learning content (Wisher, this volume). It provides a detailed and rather technical look at the first implementation of the registry model (Jerez, Manepalli, Blanchi, & Lannom, 2006).

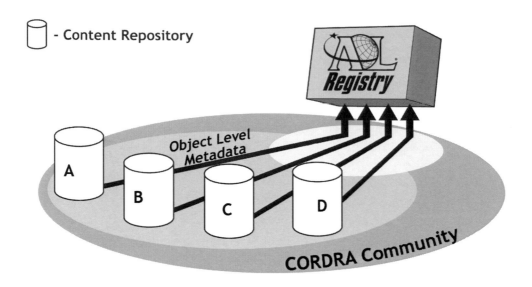

- Content Repository

Figure 10-1. The ADL Registry and associated repositories. This figure shows metadata from content repositories coded into a central registry.

The ADL Registry

The ADL Registry (ADL-R) is the first instance of a larger architecture that is described later in this chapter. It was built as part of the effort to fill a specific gap in the ADL business paradigm. SCORM and related activities go a long way towards providing interoperability across e-learning platforms and the many possible sources of learning content (Gallagher, this volume). Realizing the potential of these advances, however, depends on the interoperable content being found and acquired. Among other obvious advantages, this promotes reusability of learning content, such that courses and lessons can be at least partially built out of reusable pieces instead of being made out of whole cloth each time.

Just as SCORM provides specifications and standards for creating and delivering instruction to ensure interoperability and reusability, the leaders of the ADL Initiative collaboration saw a need to create specifications for registering content to facilitate the same end. The result was an effort to develop a Content Object Repository Discovery and Registration/Resolution Architecture (CORDRA). CORDRA is intended to be an open, standards-based model. It furthers the advances obtained through global adoption of the SCORM standards by providing specifications for designing and implementing information systems, including repositories and registries, so that proponents of widely distributed digital information may register the existence of that information and so enable others to find and use it.

In the natural world, the term ecosystem describes the complex relationships that exist among plants, animals, water, soil, and other elements of the natural environment. In technology, the same term may describe the relationships among hardware, software, people, and organizations that interact to deliver specific services. The ADL Registry was planned and built to help create an ecosystem of reusable learning content. It accomplished this through the recording of metadata describing learning content, serving as a showcase and providing a reference implementation of the CORDRA specification.

Technical Formation

Meetings with representatives from ADL, the Corporation for National Research Initiatives (CNRI), the Learning Systems Architecture Lab, then hosted at Carnegie Mellon University in Pittsburgh, Pennsylvania, and various government agencies, contractors, and ADL Co-Labs on the topic of creating a registry of e-learning material began in late 2003. They were initiated and led by Philip Dodds, the Chief Architect for SCORM, who continued to lead the overall effort until his untimely death in late 2007.

The challenge was simply stated: SCORM provided a solution to enabling the interoperability of e-learning content and platforms, but did not address the next key issue—managing that content in a network environment. The important questions are:

- How do users find content?

- How do course developers find content to incorporate into their work or to save them from re-inventing the wheel?

- How do government agencies know whether or not they need to commission specific types of content when it may already exist and perhaps even be readily available to them under some existing arrangement?

- Is it possible to update content automatically, so that a change in some standard method or practice or some background information on a given topic is always reflected in e-learning material?

The Challenges of Content Management

Two obvious potential solutions to these content management challenges were rejected from the start. The first was to manage the content by collecting it all into a single location or repository. This was a non-starter for both practical and technical reasons. Advertising the existence and availability of learning content is a more palatable option for organizations than ceding control of that same content. A distributed solution, in which content is kept under local control, is much more likely to generate cooperation among those who have the content. It is also more scalable, allowing for large increases in the amount of content to be spread across many systems and locations instead of straining the resources of a single organization, local system, or location.

A second approach, relying on existing Internet search engines, of which Google is the standard example, was also easily rejected. Not every repository is open to harvesting by search engines. For example, secure military and corporate intranets are not necessarily exposed to harvesting engines. Even if they were, the search process for specific pieces of learning content requires more precision than is available in standard search engines. It also requires sophisticated update management that tracks content status, indicating, for example, if content is new, if it has changed, or who can use it. We chose to solve the problem through the registration of metadata. The content would stay in the distributed collection of original-source repositories and those repositories would be virtually combined through the standardized registration of metadata describing the distributed content, a process known as federating.

Design Principles and Guidelines

ADL realized early in the process that persistent identification of content items would be key to managing them on networks (Kahn & Wilensky, 2006). This, among other reasons, led them to CNRI, which had pioneered the use of persistent identifiers on the Internet through its Handle System®, better known in some communities as the identifier resolution technology used in Digital Object Identifiers technology. CNRI, with funding from ADL, led the design of the registry that would become the ADL Registry.

A few design principles and guidelines emerged early during the technical planning:

Registry content. The Registry holds metadata only, with all content remaining in the existing set of distributed repositories. The content remains under the control of those who currently have it and who are using the Registry to record its existence.

Access to content. Registration of an item of learning content does not imply universal access to that content. The owner/manager of the relevant repository is the sole arbiter of access.

Access to metadata. All metadata in the ADL Registry is public. In the future, there may be restricted registries, or registries in which search results would be filtered by ability to access the registered content, but the early simplifying assumption was that all information in the registry would be public. That is still the case today.

DoD registries. Registration in a United States DoD-sponsored registry must be controlled. Only approved organizations, or those operating on their behalf, should be allowed to register learning content. This is articulated in DoD policy (Freeman, this volume).

Permissions. Within an organization, more than one level of registration permissions may be required, e.g., an organization may permit more individuals to register content than are allowed to delete those registration records.

Additional metadata. Multiple parties should be able to register metadata about a single content item, e.g., annotations or reviews of existing registered material. This would be restricted to approved organizations.

Persistent identifiers. All registered content objects should be tagged with persistent identifiers, specifically using a general purpose system called the "Handle System" to identify content and manage internal metadata.

Federating registries. A single registry, no matter how successful or large, will not be sufficient to support, in the long term, the technical infrastructure needed for the desired e-learning economy or ecosystem of reuse. Federating is a process that optimizes technology information resources, essentially enabling users to connect multiple resources and treat them as one.

Federated Repositories

A federation of multiple databases, or content repositories, can be accessed through a single user interface. Directories and registries may also be federated. The registry technology should be both as widely used and as widely useful as possible, and federating them is one way to accomplish this. This requirement yielded two additional design goals: 1) the ADL Registry should be the first instance of a set of registries in use across multiple communities, and 2) just as the registries federate sets of repositories, there must be a way to federate multiple registries into a registry of registries. Note that this was initially seen as a single master registry of registries. That concept is reflected in some early illustrations, but later consideration showed this to be much less likely than the formation of multiple federations, some of which could be overlapping.

An Approach to Content Management Architecture

The approach outlined above was called the Content Object Repository Discovery and Registration/Resolution Architecture (CORDRA). CORDRA was first announced at ADL's First International Plugfest in Zurich in March 2004, defined as:

> *...an effort to define a framework for the federation of digital collections. The framework, also known as "CORDRA specification" is intended to be an open, standards-based model for designing and implementing information systems including registries and repositories for the purposes of discovery, sharing and reuse of information. The CORDRA specification will describe how owners or managers of widely distributed information expressed in digital form may register the existence of that information and so enable others to find and use that information.*

Planning for future enhancements of the specifications underlying CORDRA was postponed while the ADL Registry was being developed and initially deployed. There were practical lessons to be learned, and enhancements remain a goal of the joint

ADL and CNRI effort. As the first instance of CORDRA, the development of the ADL Registry will help shape the global specifications.

The Advanced Distributed Learning Registry — CORDRA Applied

Development work on the ADL Registry began in 2004 and continued through 2005. In addition to defining requirements and developing the basic registry technology, this work included the always difficult task of agreeing on the metadata elements, both mandatory and optional, that would be used in the content registration. This was based on the Learning Object Metadata standard developed by the Institute of Electrical and Electronics Engineers (IEEE) Standards Association, and a component of SCORM (Gallagher, this volume), to describe learning objects and other digital resources used to support learning in order to support reusability, to aid discoverability, and to facilitate interoperability. The first operational instance of the ADL Registry was released on the Internet in December 2005.

Administrative infrastructure and policy work proceeded concurrently with the technology development. A policy issuance by DoD required the use of the ADL Registry by DoD components acquiring or commissioning e-learning content. The instruction, entitled "Development, Management, and Delivery of Distributed Learning," was released in June of 2006 (Freeman, this volume).

Operational Registry

Information and extensive documentation on both technical and administrative matters is found at the Web site of the ADL Initiative, which also links to the ADL Registry. Anyone may search the ADL Registry, but content registration is limited to approved parties. Those who wish to use the registry in any way should begin at the ADL Registry Web site.

ADL supports use of the ADL Registry through the ADL Registry Help Desk. This service is available to all for questions, comments, and recommendations. Contact details can be found at the ADL Registry Web site.

Practice Registry

ADL also supports a practice registry, which can be used by those planning to register, or even those currently registering, metadata in the ADL Registry. The practice registry is maintained as a clone of the operational ADL Registry, but it is not intended for operational purposes; data in the practice registry is routinely erased. The purpose is to allow registrants to conduct trials of registration, and may be used by the ADL-R Registrar to verify that potential registrants understand the registration process before they are given access to the operational registry. It may also be used for the development of registration applications, e.g., an extension to a repository that automatically registers any content that is uploaded into that repository. This allows developers to build applications in a realistic environment without worrying about interfering with production service or exposing mistakes due to lack of experience in metadata submission.

Open-Source Registry Technology

The basic technology underlying the ADL Registry is available for use by other organizations and other communities. One of the goals of the ADL Registry project is to enable wider usage of the technology, which would yield a larger developer base and the increased robustness resulting from a larger user base. One long-term benefit from an ADL perspective is that a vast quantity of interoperable learning content is possible. A short-term benefit is that the more a specific software product or system is used, the more likely it is that problems will be found and fixed, and the more likely it is that others will develop useful applications. To further this end, ADL and CNRI agreed that CNRI would create and make available a generic version of the ADL Registry, one that could be configured for other uses by other communities. This software is freely available at the CNRI Digital Object Registry Web site.

ADL Technology

Registry Data Model

The ADL Registry holds metadata describing learning material accessible from repositories external to the registry. Each registered item is represented in the Registry by one or more metadata records. The first of those records must be submitted by the organization that controls access to the learning object. Once the first record has been submitted, other organizations can submit metadata describing that same entity, e.g., reviews of the registered material. Multiple metadata records describing the same e-learning material are grouped together so that finding one record automatically reveals the others to those searching for learning content.

Registry Architecture

The ADL Registry is modular in design, in keeping with good software and system development practice. Architecturally, the Registry is best envisioned as a set of modules that interact with each other to provide the overall registration service. These modules are described below. See Figure 10-2 for a graphical representation of the ADL Registry architecture.

Registry Interface Mechanism. The initial registry work provided a stable HTTP interface sufficient for simple services, but that simple interface required that much of the desired functionality of the Registry be built on the client side. This required each client application developer to implement needed functions from scratch even if others had already implemented such functions. The Registry Interface Mechanism (RIM) was developed to both provide the simple interface to those whose requirements could be met through this interface alone, but also, and primarily, to supply an additional set of commonly needed operations and attributes for use by third-party developers and application builders. By providing a standard set of commonly needed functions and attributes, RIM ensures that multiple applications will yield common results when executing the same tasks, e.g., rendering HTML from XML or grouping and formatting large result sets. The 2009 version is referred to as RIM-Lite, indicating that additional interfaces, such as community-specific presentation profiles, are envisioned, although that functionality has not yet been specified.

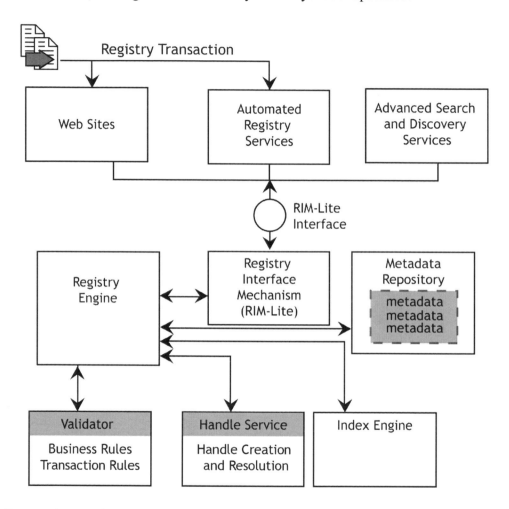

Figure 10-2. Registration Interface Mechanism (RIM). This figure shows the transaction flow for automating certain content registration functions.

Registry Engine. The Registry Engine module functions as the central registry coordination module, responsible for implementing, enforcing, and keeping track of all operations inside the Registry. This module also performs all authentication and authorization tasks for the system.

Validator Module. The Validator module examines and validates all input into the Registry using the relevant XML schema and business rules. XML is a general-purpose language used for the representation of structured data. Any given application of XML requires the creation of an abstract schema that defines the rules for a particular application, such as defining which data elements may be present, which elements must be present, and so on. Those rules are referred to as *transaction rules*. Some rules, however, cannot be defined in XML schema (e.g., acceptable date ranges), and so must be enforced using custom validation code. These rules are referred to as *business rules*. The validation module is responsible for both types. The ADL Registry has a defined schema and set of rules, and incoming data is automatically checked against both.

Metadata Repository. Metadata records submitted to the ADL Registry are held in a repository that is internal to the Registry. The repository technology used in the ADL Registry, as well as in the generic form of the Registry referenced above, is CNRI's Digital Object Repository. This is a general-purpose digital object repository and a core component in CNRI's Digital Object Architecture. A description of the repository and its role in Digital Object Architecture is beyond the scope of this chapter, but details are available at the CNRI Digital Object Registry Web site.

Index/Search Module. This module indexes and provides search functionality across the entire collection of metadata in the metadata repository. The indexing is performed according to business rules specific to the ADL Registry but could be adapted to other registries in other communities. These rules define which fields are indexed, how those fields are tokenized (i.e., split into indexed words or terms), whether to allow partial matches, stemming rules for different languages, and so on. This process is independent of the specific search engine that performs searches across the indexed records. This modularity enables other registry implementations to use different index engine technology if needed. The ADL Registry currently uses the Lucene search engine, one of the Apache projects. The Apache projects are a community of open-source software projects.

Handle Service. The Handle System is a general-purpose identifier system that identifies content objects, manages internal metadata objects, holds registry configuration information, enables locating and connecting to related registries (in the case of federation), and both authorizes and authenticates users. The ADL Registry uses this system to identify all e-learning material in the registry. Each approved organization is assigned a handle prefix and each item that they register is assigned a handle under that prefix. From that point forward the handle serves as the persistent identifier of the learning content item. The item can be referenced using that identifier, and if the content moves the handle can be updated and the references will continue to work. Registrants can choose to manage the handle themselves, or may opt for the ADL Registry to manage it for them. In either case, search results from the ADL Registry use handles to link to the e-learning objects. The handle service module is responsible for all interaction with the Handle System, both in creating handles and in resolving handles.

The configurable registry software available at the CNRI Digital Object Registry Web site makes similar use of handles. Detailed information on the Handle System can be found at the Handle System Web site.

Federation and Network Architecture

To describe networked information services as federated implies that they are autonomous at some level yet can be treated as a single collection at some other level. The ADL Registry federates autonomous collections of learning material by providing a single search point across the combined collections. The only requirement for this level of federation is that the individually managed repositories contribute standardized metadata to the ADL Registry. All other issues, such as access policies, funding, software platform, locations, and so on, remain entirely under the control of the repository managers. This level of federation is illustrated in Figure 10-2.

A further level of federation could occur across a given set of registries, of which ADL Registry would be a single instance. A set of registries would contribute metadata about their collections to a registry of registries, providing a single starting point for searching an even larger federation of e-learning repositories. This higher level of federation is the primary focus of the evolving CORDRA architecture. The ADL Registry can thus be described as the "first instance of CORDRA," as illustrated in the outer boundary of Figure 10-1.

Summary

Federation of heterogeneous data has been a technical challenge in information management for many years. Different approaches to organizing data, describing it, using different subject vocabularies, and so on can lead to a "Tower of Babel" effect when combining or even just using, data from multiple sources. In registry work, this issue manifests itself in the use of varying metadata standards and in varying vocabularies in different domains and communities of practice.

While some terminology distinctions, e.g., using different terms for the same concepts, can simply be mapped to one another without losing any precision, many differences in metadata standards and terminologies cannot be simply bridged, and mapping them to one another will result in loss of precision or meaning, e.g., what one group calls "creator" another group may subdivide into "author," "editor," "illustrator," and so on. When combined, a precise search for "editor" is no longer possible.

The ADL Registry and CORDRA do not currently provide solutions to these sorts of problems. However, the development work for the ADL Registry and CORDRA has created a framework and a set of tools for providing coherent approaches to the problem within given domains. Registries can pre-process metadata before indexing to provide varying levels of normalization, depending on the standards applied to submitting repositories. Also different levels of metadata can be used at the different federation levels, e.g., a registry can collect individual object-level metadata from its constituent repositories while a registry of registries could collect only community-level metadata as a starting point for a distributed search across multiple levels of practice, using queries specific to those communities.

Together, standardized approaches to registering metadata and persistent identification of e-learning and related material provide a common framework within which multiple communities of practice can optimize their own procedures. The ADL Registry is one such community. The ability that this technology affords is accessibility to high quality education and training content, a critical function of the ADL Initiative.

References

Kahn, R., & Wilensky, R. (2006). A framework for distributed digital object services. *International Journal on Digital Libraries*, *6*(2), 115-123.

Jerez, H., Manepalli, G., Blanchi, C., & Lannom, L. (2006). ADL-R: The first instance of a CORDRA registry. *D-Lib Magazine*, *2*(3), 1-18.

Manepalli, G., Jerez, H., & Nelson, M. L. (2006). FeDCOR: An institutional CORDRA registry. *D-Lib Magazine*, *12*(2).

Web Resources

Corporation for National Research Initiatives (CNRI). www.cnri.reston.va.us

CNRI Digital Object Registry. http://doregistry.org

Handle System. http://handle.net

Lucene. http://lucene.apache.org

The Author

Larry Lannom is a designer of search architectures for the Corporation for National Research Initiatives, Reston, Virginia.

Chapter 11

Reuse of Learning Content

Michael G. Shanley, Susan G. Straus, Matthew W. Lewis, Jeff Rothenberg, and Kristin J. Leuschner

The life-cycle costs of developing and maintaining materials have been factors limiting more widespread implementation of e-learning, despite evidence for greater training effectiveness and efficiencies (Fletcher, this volume). One strategy to mitigate the burden of content costs is to reuse existing e-learning content; that is, to repurpose existing digital content to produce new content for a different context, audience, or setting. However, the inability to easily exchange and reuse the same e-learning content, an impetus to creating the ADL Initiative in 1997, remains an enduring issue (Wisher, this volume). The costs of moving courses from the classroom to e-learning are caused, at least in part, by the need to redevelop content independently for each course and for different learning management systems. ADL is examining solutions to these issues (Camacho, West, & Vozzo, this volume). Development costs for e-learning can be reduced significantly by a strategy of reuse if digital content can be successfully reused on a large enough scale.

A reuse analogy might be the use of existing textbooks on a subject as a starting point for designing a new textbook, as opposed to designing the textbook from scratch. However, in the digital world, reuse would typically focus not on an entire book, but on reusable learning objects—chunks or modules of digital learning material that can be stored in searchable databases, known as learning object repositories, and then accessed by third parties to create new course content (Lannom, this volume). Just as libraries and bookstores provide a distribution mechanism in the non-digital world, widespread digital reuse will require a mechanism to bring together reuse "buyers" (e.g., trainers, end users) and "sellers" (e.g., training development organizations, authors). Large-scale reuse of learning objects, if achieved, would produce significant cost savings for e-learning and large gains for organizations.

The purpose of this chapter is to review a recent RAND study that addressed how the ADL Initiative might encourage the development of a broader learning object economy that cuts across organizations and establishes incentives for participation (see Shanley et al., 2009 for the full report). The study focused on training development organizations, a number of which have attempted to implement a reuse strategy internally. The study included interviews with personnel from 23 large training development organizations that had seriously pursued a reuse strategy. The study also examined the literature on knowledge management and on reuse in the domains of software and material development. The term "reusable learning object" (RLO) from the original study is termed "learning object" in the present chapter since reuse is a key functional requirement for ADL. In the context of the ADL business paradigm (Wisher, this volume), this chapter addresses the market and scalability component.

Markets for Learning Objects

To date, reuse of learning objects in e-learning has not been widespread. This is not surprising, given that public repositories and markets for learning objects are just emerging. Early attempts, including Apple Computers work in the "Educational Object Economy" project met with early enthusiasm but faced significant challenges to implementation.

Figure 11-1 shows an example of what a functioning distribution mechanism for learning objects might look like. On the demand side are training delivery organizations, trainers, and end users, all of whom could potentially benefit from the content of the repository. On the supply side are training development organizations, authors, publishers, market makers, and others who bring learning objects into a repository. Use of the repository is facilitated by key enablers, including standards, authoring tools, policies, and the perceived value of reuse. The repository itself might be provided as a service by some government body or association or be a marketplace where items are bought and sold.

Such mechanisms for exchange exist only in limited forms today. The number of organizations engaging in learning object-based reuse has not yet reached the critical mass needed for viable markets to form, and repositories are typically internal to a particular organization. While these internal repositories can be useful, they do not allow for reuse across a wide range of organizations, and they typically leave out independent actors, such as authors and publishers.

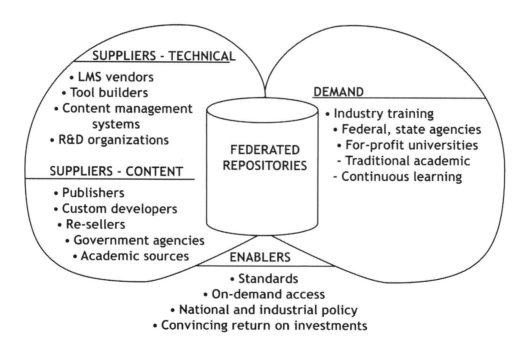

Figure 11-1. Reuse of learning objects. This figure depicts an example of a distribution mechanism for reuse of learning objects.

A key area explored in this research, and which is the focus of this chapter, is the importance of effective planning and implementation in order for training development organizations to realize genuine gains from reuse. We also consider ways in which other stakeholders in a learning object economy, including policymakers, educational organizations, and industry groups, can help support the development of a large-scale learning object economy.

How Widespread Is Reuse?

While reuse of learning objects has gained the most attention, this is only one of several existing reuse strategies. Other approaches to reuse differ in terms of the *granularity*, or grain size, of what is being reused (e.g., course content, structural assets such as templates, digital assets such as images), and the existence and maturity of markets using a specific approach as well as ways of implementing the approach (e.g., number and type of personnel involved, level of collaboration required, technologies employed). We identified four approaches in addition to learning object reuse.

Top-down Content Development
Under this strategy, multiple organizations collaborate on course design or coordinate in other ways (from the "top down") so that the resulting content can reach wider audiences. Top-down reuse includes the intentional reuse of content in so-called "multiple-use cases" (e.g., when digital content is designed for more purposes than just training, such as technical documentation or use within a help system) and the reuse of content in multiple forms of delivery (e.g., when content is designed for presentation on both a laptop and personal digital assistant). Examples of this approach were found in commercial training development companies working for large clients. (Another example is the cooperative development teams creating SCORM content in Europe; see Synysta & Staub, this volume).

Structural Reuse
Structural reuse refers to computer code that is designed to make the development environment more cost-effective in producing content. This type of reuse might be termed a "top-down computing environment" approach. In this type of reuse, the organization adopts some type of development structure, be it as simple as a template or style sheet or as complex as a content management system that allows users to create and reuse digital learning assets and content within a common authoring environment. Structural reuse also involves sharing processes (including Web services) to streamline procedures. Examples of this approach were found in commercial and some military schools' training organizations.

Bottom-Up (Asset-Driven) Reuse
In a bottom-up approach, the organization reuses basic digital assets in multiple learning contexts. These assets can include images, audio, video, animations,

or other digital material (e.g., presentation slides). In addition to efforts within organizations, there are highly developed commercial markets for digital assets in some areas, including photography, music, sound effects, and three-dimensional models. Examples of this approach were found widely in commercial, non-profit, and some military training organizations.

Concept Reuse

Concept reuse refers to reusing pedagogical approaches, including instructional methods, task decomposition approaches, assessment methods, and training interventions (Sitzmann & Ely, this volume). This reuse strategy is similar to a researcher's use of papers on related research as models for the design of a new study or the inspection and analysis of existing Web sites as model for the structure and content of new Web sites.

Our interviews revealed that at the time of the study (2006-2007), the learning object approach to reuse was considerably less prevalent than the top-down or bottom-up approaches. Roughly 20 percent of the organizations interviewed reported successful reuse. This number seems particularly low, given that the organizations interviewed had been chosen because they had relatively more experience with reuse than other organizations. However, other forms of reuse were more common. Seventy percent of the organizations interviewed reported using the bottom-up (asset-driven) approach, and 85 percent used some form of the top-down content development approach. Although some reuse approaches involved sophisticated collaboration, the most prevalent form overall was simple redeployment of entire courses (top-down reuse).

Understanding the full range of reuse options is important because these less-discussed options can serve as enabling approaches to facilitate implementation of learning object reuse over time (i.e., by building capacities necessary to reuse). For example, concept reuse requires the ability to quickly locate target content and explore it for possible emulation or partial structural replication. Understanding the ways in which the content is reused can then provide data to support the design of large-scale repositories that improve users' abilities to quickly search for and access content.

Challenges Associated with Learning Object Reuse

Since learning object-based reuse is in an early part of its development (before the existence of a learning object economy), there are several challenges associated with large-scale reuse of this sort. Six are identified here.

Technology for Reuse is Still Developing

Although basic technical standards for sharing content are well established, adoption of these standards is not ubiquitous. As shown in Figure 11-2, learning object reuse is at an early stage of the technology adoption life cycle (Moore, 2002). In this life cycle, new technologies generally have a small group of initial "innovators," i.e.,

146

people who try them out and/or experiment with them. If a technology shows promise and provides results, "early adopters" then take it on while its viability is still being assessed. However, between the phase of the early adopters and the next group—the "early majority"—there is a "chasm" that must be filled with a critical mass of less technologically savvy users who are willing to commit to using the new technology. Crossing this chasm places a large burden on developers to ensure usability and provide technical support for the technology.

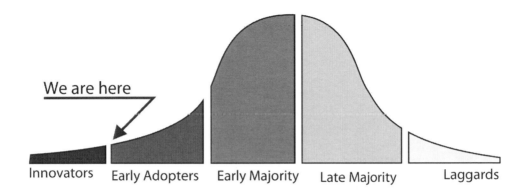

Figure 11-2. The revised technology adoption life cycle. This figure represents the typical pattern for adoption of new technologies.

Participants in about half of the organizations we interviewed felt that technologies pose a current obstacle to reuse. One issue is a lack of interoperability across learning management systems, which are needed to run e-learning software. Organizations reported that in nearly every attempt to develop reusable content, a course required technical adjustments to run on a system other than the one for which it was created, even if both systems were tested as being SCORM-conformant (Panar, Brannon, & Poltrack, this volume). In addition, authoring technologies for customizing content and CMSs are evolving, but are not yet to the point of being cost-effective for a wide range of potential users.

Return on Investment in Reuse

Implementation of a reuse initiative based on learning objects requires significant upfront investment and organizational change. The experiences of early adopters suggest that returns could be years away and are by no means guaranteed. Few of the organizations interviewed consider their return on investment from reuse to be anything more than modest, even after several years of pursuing a learning object-based reuse approach. Only 25 percent of the organizations we interviewed estimated that they had achieved a positive return in line with their expectations, and these organizations typically used either the top-down or the bottom-up approach to reuse, or both. The majority of organizations estimated that they had achieved lower than expected returns from reuse, and 35 percent reported no savings at all or a net loss. For many organizations, the decision to bypass a reuse strategy based on learning objects thus appears to make sense economically, at least in this early adoption phase of technological development.

Reuse and Complexity of Courseware Design

The reusable learning-object approach raises instructional design issues because an object's reusability will depend on the extent to which its content can stand alone and be kept separate from context, pedagogy, structure, and presentation. Thus, a reuse approach typically requires fundamental changes in how courseware is designed. Moreover, successful design for reuse must take into account the multiple ways in which content can be organized, or factored, in achieving a given goal (Page-Jones, 1980; Yourdon & Constantine, 1979). Having compatible factorization is important for reuse, because changing the factorization of otherwise appropriate content often makes the prospect of reuse cost-prohibitive. For example, software content might be factored by order of execution (phases), type of data, type of operation, or tier. Because e-learning involves much more than just functionality (e.g., terminology, pedagogy, disciplinary context), determining a commonly acceptable factorization becomes an important challenge.

Reuse—"Sweet Spots" Rather Than Widespread Success

Reuse requires careful selection of content that is suitable for "encoding" as learning objects. Reusable content needs to be general enough to have a wide market for reuse, while at the same time requiring minimal customization to be reusable. In the commercial software industry, content areas that have both wide reuse potential and that are easily customizable are known as "sweet spots." Sweet spots are determined by numerous attributes of the content, context, granularity, and functionality of the software in question; however, it has proven difficult to predict where sweet spots will occur and time consuming to identify suitable sweet spots.

Organizational Incentives Must be Aligned to Foster Large-scale Reuse

Interview participants suggested that disincentives to sharing content or reusing the content of others could become an obstacle to the rapid diffusion of reuse strategies. Research in knowledge management (i.e., the processes that organizations use to manage their intellectual assets) shows that individuals and organizations are sometimes reluctant to share their work or use work produced by others. For example, stakeholders might be concerned that the effort required to make content sharable is greater than the benefit received (especially when designing for a particular application and client), or they may be concerned about losing credit for ideas, losing status as experts, or becoming expendable.

Impediments to a Reuse Strategy

Participants in half of the organizations we interviewed noted that their organizations do not engage in formal strategic planning for reuse. In addition, a significant number of interview participants cited obstacles in creating metadata and repositories, and establishing effective collaborations among stakeholders, and many noted that the culture of their organization does not support reuse. Some interview participants cited issues concerning the creation of new organizational processes and procedures, obtaining sufficient staff training, and dealing with copyright issues or permissions.

How to Determine an Appropriate Reuse Strategy for Your Organization

There are four categories of questions organizational leaders should ask when considering how to develop a reuse strategy. These questions can provide guidance for determining the feasibility of developing an internal reuse market, or assessing the value of getting involved in large-scale reuse efforts involving multiple organizations. The basis of these questions is our interviews with 23 organizations from the U.S. government, foreign defense organizations, the commercial sector, academia, and other organizations associated with reuse, such as digital rights management.

1. What are our company's goals for reuse?

2. What approaches will serve as a starting point in our organization's reuse strategy?

3. In what ways is your organization capable of changing the way it develops content?

4. Is our organization willing to invest what is necessary to become an early adopter of reuse technology?

Planning and Implementing a Comprehensive Reuse Strategy

Developing and implementing a learning object reuse strategy poses perhaps the greatest challenge to an organization or consortium of organizations, as it generally requires members of organizations to operate in new ways. Achieving effective reuse is likely to involve the adoption or modification of resources and organizational practices pertaining to standards, tools, roles, work processes, and policies. Our interviews and review of the literature revealed a number of promising practices that support movement to a learning object reuse strategy. We first address implementing reuse within an organization. Next, we describe how to facilitate learning object reuse across multiple organizations.

Fostering an Internal Learning Object-Reuse Strategy
Goals and objectives. As the phrase "reuse strategy" implies, reuse doesn't happen in an *ad hoc* manner; it requires strategic planning. Strategic planning for reuse can be described as a deliberate effort to formulate and make fundamental decisions about how to define and implement a policy of reuse. If reuse is not the norm in

an organization, initiating a reuse strategy is likely to require comprehensive change management and development of an organizational culture that values reuse.

The organization should begin the strategic planning process by identifying its objectives in implementing a reuse strategy. This step entails determining what the organization expects to accomplish via learning object reuse and what return on investment it can expect to achieve. Addressing these objectives will help the organization to determine when to invest in reuse and to identify the kinds of material or training content that has a high likelihood of reuse. Answers to these questions should be used, in turn, to formulate realistic, specific, and measurable goals for reuse, along with metrics to evaluate progress toward goal accomplishment and a plan for monitoring and evaluating success.

Design Processes. Successful reuse via large public repositories requires a fundamental change in how digital learning is developed. Essentially, the course-centered approach must be replaced with an approach centered on a learning object or a sharable content object (SCO), a type of learning object (Gallagher, this volume). While SCOs can be large in scope, they are often associated with individual lessons or single learning objectives that are independent of the course context, structure, presentation, and pedagogy.

Thus, a key design issue is to establish the appropriate size of learning objects. Several interview participants in our study noted challenges in finding the right balance between the increased reusability of smaller objects and the higher design cost of dividing learning into ever smaller chunks. There is an inherent tradeoff between making learning objects large enough to be easily identified and discoverable through a database search versus small enough to maximize potential use. Thus, an organization embarking on a reuse strategy should establish a set of standards specifying the grain size for instructional content—e.g., will each SCO be a course, a lesson, or a learning objective? Other interview participants in our study emphasized the importance of making appropriate granularity decisions, which do not always remain constant across an organization.

In addition to defining standards for the size of learning objects, the organization should determine procedures for reusable learning object design. For example, organizations need to match types of learning content with preferred types of media. The organization may need to re-engineer internal processes to foster reuse, including establishing metadata schemes to capture the organization's training content.

The organization should also ensure that the technical infrastructure, including both hardware and software, supports production of reusable content. A successful reuse strategy requires investment in tools, such as an a learning content management system and appropriate authoring tools, as well as in integrating these technologies with work processes.

Staff roles. Staff roles are another important factor that can foster reuse. One component of successful adoption of innovations in organizations is the presence of a champion for the effort. Staff members are more likely to value reuse if a respected member or members of the organization promote its benefits rather than if senior managers merely mandate reuse. Typically, a champion is someone in a leadership position who can help ensure that the organizational context facilitates reuse by providing sufficient resources, effective training, and relevant policies.

An important lesson that emerged from our interviews was the importance of having personnel to facilitate collaboration between subject matter experts (SMEs) and technical staff to foster reuse within training organizations. For example, members of one organization in our study emphasized the importance of creating internal "boundary-spanner" or "synthesizer" roles within their staff as a means to enable reuse. Others noted the importance of finding technical staff who can collaborate successfully with educational experts, which is facilitated, in part, when technical and educational staff have some understanding of one another's functional areas.

Training. Implementing a reuse strategy, like any major organizational or cultural change, requires training. Some participants in our interviews noted a need for training on the potential for, or benefits of, reuse. This type of education can help set expectations about what a reuse strategy can accomplish. Members of the organization will likely need technical training regarding how to design for reuse, including instruction on standards for developing learning objects, metadata tagging, and use of new authoring tools or other systems. Staff may also benefit from training in teamwork skills when moving from an independent contributor to collaborative approach.

Incentives. Creating incentive mechanisms is a critical factor in addressing many of the challenges to implementing a reuse strategy. Both tangible and intangible rewards can be effective in motivating organizational members to effectively participate in reuse activities. For example, performance evaluations should include criteria associated with designing for reuse and reusing existing training content. Rewards, in the form of merit increases and/or bonuses, should be contingent on meeting these criteria. Examples of specific behaviors or outcomes that could be rewarded include contributing content to shared repositories, ensuring that content meets standards that facilitate reuse, reusing existing content, demonstrating decreased development time due to reuse, and contributing to other organizational efforts that support reuse (e.g., training others, contributing to reuse guidelines, establishing social networks that lead to reuse).

One potential informal or intangible incentive is reputation enhancement for employees who make important contributions to content management systems (repositories) or networks (Evangelou & Karacapilidis, 2005). For example, experts in at least one training development organization said that attaching the author's name to his or her output resulted in greater willingness to share knowledge. Respondents in two other organizations provided employee incentives by showcasing reuse successes.

The elements of a strategy described above can help the organization develop a culture that values reuse. Practices such as leader support, role assignments, training, and incentives can help cultivate a sense of shared purpose and identity among employees. These attitudes, in turn, can increase organizational members' feeling of belonging to a community and thereby enhance knowledge-sharing—a fundamental aspect of reuse (Dyer & Nobeoka, 2000; Evangelou & Karacapilidis, 2005).

Fostering LO-Reuse Across Organizations

Successfully implementing a broad-based reuse strategy involving multiple organizations may well require a level of collaboration and new associations with outside training organizations that most training development professionals have not experienced. For learning object and asset reuse, a successful reuse strategy may require interorganizational collaboration on such activities as metadata standards and repository design (Lannom, this volume). For top-down reuse and structural reuse, investments are needed in upfront collaboration to ensure proper design of learning content and the computing environment.

We identified several strategies that can facilitate interorganizational collaboration supporting broad-based reuse. (The ADL business paradigm offers additional information concerning how collaboration across organizations and sectors can be accomplished). First, entire organizations may need incentives to collaborate in reuse activities with other organizations. Managers of some organizations may fear that sharing training content will weaken their market advantage; however, Dyer and Hatch (2006) suggest that it is possible for an organization to achieve a competitive advantage even when sharing proprietary information in a knowledge-sharing network of competitors. A lead organization may need to set an example by heavily subsidizing content during the initial stages of network formation. For example, as Dyer and Nobeoka (2000) describe, Toyota supplied proprietary information on its entire production process and offered free assistance to its network of suppliers. In return, the suppliers were required to offer knowledge of their operations to the network or risk losing Toyota as a customer. In addition, Toyota did not demand a price decrease when a transfer of knowledge resulted in a productivity increase for a supplier; instead, Toyota recognized that such improvements would benefit the company in the long run and allowed the suppliers to collect the short-term gains.

Second is the formation of communities of potential reusers across organizations. Members of such a community can work together to ensure that procedures and business rules regarding reuse are established that meet the preponderance of members' requirements. Communities might strive to formulate subject-specific standards and guidelines for reuse processes that can apply across organizations, along with a common language for metadata and metrics to measure success. Communities may need ground rules that communicate expectations for participation, including policies that address the "free-rider" problem (i.e., member organizations that use the group's resources but do not contribution to the collective efforts). Finally, such a community might enhance its success by trying to reach agreements that add infrastructure capable of supporting the collective development environment of all participating organizations.

Third is the use of technologies for collaboration. Cross-organizational activities such as building repository communities and co-producing courses involve a number of steps and can entail significant transaction costs for participants. Collaboration can be aided by tools that facilitate communication and information sharing such as websites that support shared workspaces, document storage and editing, wikis, blogs, listservs, and the like.

Fourth is the use of strategies to foster interorganizational trust. Numerous studies of alliances between organizations have documented the importance of trust in creating and maintaining collaborative efforts (Faerman, McCaffrey, & Van Slyke, 2001; Kumar & van Dissel, 1996). Trust emerges through interpersonal interactions, and establishing trust can take a substantial amount of effort and time. Research (e.g., Moss-Kanter, 1994) has identified a variety of other organizational and interpersonal mechanisms to help develop interorganizational alliances, such as ensuring contact among organizational leaders to develop strategic goals and objectives, promoting interaction at mid-management levels, and using a neutral third-party for oversight of the collaboration.

How Market Makers Can Support a Reuse Strategy

The results from organizations' early experiences with reuse of training content suggest that the success of an effective distribution system for learning objects will depend on the extent to which training organizations are convinced of the value of learning object reuse. These expectations, in turn, will be heavily influenced by the degree to which early adopters of reuse are able to demonstrate positive returns. And, while there is much that organizations can do to improve the success of their own reuse strategies, the development of a mature learning object marketplace will require collaboration among a wide range of organizations in the private, public, and nonprofit sectors (see Figure 11-1). By working together, policy leaders in the government, the military, industry, trade associations, educational organizations, and other stakeholder groups can facilitate widespread reuse by (1) creating communities that build the business case for reuse and assist organizations in reuse efforts, (2) providing education, and (3) supporting research on reuse.

First, policy leaders can help to build a reuse market by taking the lead in facilitating the creation of new reuse communities. To build the economic case for reuse, these stakeholders would seek to establish consensus on a broader definition of reuse. This would mean supporting all five reuse approaches identified in our study, including concept reuse and structural reuse, as defined earlier. Members of such communities could also serve as consultants or trusted advisors to organizations that need assistance in developing a reuse strategy.

Second, stakeholder organizations should collaborate to sponsor and produce seminars, workshops, conferences, courses, and publications about critical reuse topics.

For example, educational efforts could focus on strategic planning, learning object design, training approaches, incentive design, achieving and measuring cost savings, identifying reuse "sweet spots," and other topics addressed in this chapter.

Finally, policy leaders should document the success of reuse activities and identify best practices in reuse by sponsoring research. For example, stakeholder organizations could invest in high-profile pilots that identify opportunities for different types of reuse or illustrate the critical factors for achieving a positive return on investment for learning object reuse.

Conclusion

This chapter set out to communicate the results of a study sponsored by ADL on reuse of training content to a broad audience of stakeholders in the training development community. Some organizations have demonstrated the value of internal reuse of content, and our findings identify best practices to foster such reuse. Reuse of training content across organizations has enjoyed much less success, yet we believe that development of a large-scale learning object economy holds promise for improving productivity and reducing training development costs. Collaboration among policy leaders across a range of organizations and sectors is needed to develop this economy.

References

Dyer, J. H., & Hatch, N. (2006). Relation-specific capabilities and barriers to knowledge transfers: Creating advantage through network relationships *Strategic Management Journal, 27*, 701-719.

Dyer, J. H., & Nobeoka, K. (2000). Creating and managing a high performance knowledge-sharing network: The Toyota case [Special issue: Strategic Networks]. *Strategic Management Journal, 21*(3), 345-367.

Evangelou, C., & Karacapilidis, N. (2005). On the interaction between humans and knowledge management systems: A framework of knowledge sharing catalysts. *Knowledge Management Research and Practice, 3*, 253-261.

Faerman, S. R., McCaffrey, D. P., & Van Slyke, D. M. (2001). Understanding interorganizational cooperation: Public-private collaboration in regulating financial market innovation. *Organizational Science, 12*(3), 372-388.

Kumar, K., & van Dissel, H. G. (1996). Sustainable collaboration: Managing conflict and cooperation in interorganizational systems. *MIS Quarterly, 20*(3), 279-300.

Moore, G. (2002). *Crossing the chasm: Marketing and selling high-tech products to mainstream customers* (2nd ed.). New York: Harper Business Essentials.

Moss-Kanter, R. (1994). Collaborative advantage: The art of alliances. *Harvard Business Review*, *72*, 96-108.

Page-Jones, M. (1980). *The practical guide to structured systems design*. New Jersey: Yourdon Press.

Shanley, M. G., Lewis, M. W., Straus, S. G., Rothenberg, J., & Daugherty, L. (2009). *The prospects for increasing the reuse of digital training content* (MG-732-OSD). Santa Monica, CA: RAND Corporation.

Yourdon, E., & Constantine, L. (1979). *Structured design: Fundamentals of a discipline of computer programming and design*. New York: Prentice Hall,

The Authors

Michael G. Shanley is a Senior Policy Researcher at the RAND Corporation, Santa Monica, California, specializing in training and emerging training technologies.

Susan Straus is a Behavioral Scientist at RAND. She studies the social impacts of information and communication technology in groups and organizations.

Matthew W. Lewis is a Senior Behavioral Scientist at RAND. His work explores how to apply and evaluate technologies that support learning and decision making.

Jeff Rothenberg is a Senior Computer Scientist at the RAND, specializing in software architecture and interoperability.

Kristin Leuschner is a Senior Communications Analyst at the RAND Corporation.

Section III

ADL AND NEW
TECHNOLOGIES

Chapter 12

Social Media Tools and ADL
Daniel Fowler

The Advanced Distributed Learning (ADL) Initiative is concerned with learning, education, and training delivered on demand; this depends on building systems and services that harness computer and communications technologies (Fletcher, this volume). It goes without saying that the technological environment has changed rapidly since ADL's formation in 1997 and it will continue to change in unforeseeable ways. With comparatively few barriers to their use, new online services are at times rapidly adopted by both educators and students with little regard to their efficacy and/ or interoperability. The particular technologies that we shall focus on in this chapter are social media tools, also known as *Web 2.0 platforms*.

Fundamental to these tools is the capability for learner-initiated interactions. Interactions are central to technology-based learning, with a prevalent belief that "the perceived quality of a learning experience is directly proportional to and positively correlated with the degree to which that experience is seen as interactive" (Wagner, 2006, p.47). Social media tools support a range of interactions: interactions for participation, interactions for communications, interactions for elaboration, and interactions for team building (Wagner, 1999). There is reason to expect, then, that the proper application of social media tools can enhance learning.

Specific social media tools include *blogs*, which generally are written by individuals to give commentary, news, and opinion; wikis which provide a collaborative, Web-based means for writing and editing text-based documents; and *social networks*, which provide a forum for communicating within concentric layers of one's personal network. These are Web-based systems that provide facilities for the reciprocal exchange of information (a key "interaction"); as such they provide the means for all users to both consume and produce content. In learning environments, social media tools promise to address gaps in student interaction and collaboration.

In this chapter, we shall discuss the various models for integrating traditional asynchronous learning management systems (LMSs) with social media tools. We will also describe some of the research that has been conducted on these tools. Similarly, we will describe how social networks are being created and used by the U.S. Department of Defense for knowledge management and informal learning. Finally, we shall also consider how the SCORM standards, which are oriented toward individual instruction, could be expanded to accommodate instruction that applies to social media tools.

What are Social Media Tools?

All Web-based social media tools have, at a minimum, a server where content resides, an easy-to-use Web user interface, and an application programming interface, or API, to enable integration with other programs. The most prevalent social media tools are blogs, wikis, and social networks. Sharing tools (e.g. photos, bookmarks) are also considered social media tools, but are used less specifically in education, and so are not addressed in this chapter.

Types of Social Media Tools

Blogs are designed for the publication of self-penned articles and normally provide a capability for publishing reader comment. Recently, microblogs, (e.g., Twitter) which limit the length of posts have become popular; these let users broadcast their thoughts in the form of alerts that are then sent to their "followers" (subscribers). Wikis were designed for open, collaborative article authoring; the most famous example of a wiki is the global encyclopedia, *Wikipedia*. In social networks (e.g., Facebook and MySpace), each user's content is found on their profile page, which also lists their "friends," whom they may or may not know in real life.

None of these technologies were specifically designed for education. However, as they were free (and fun), they became popular with instructors, particularly those in higher education and K-12. These instructors started using social media tools as experimental supplements to regular classroom interactions. LMS vendors, who have generally adopted ADL's Sharable Content Object Reference Model (SCORM), picked up on this trend, and started incorporating these technologies into their products. Features include email, student profiles, class announcements, online chat, discussion forums, and assignment submission/grading (see Table 12-1). Using these tools, instructors can assign content to their classes, and interact with their students, as well as provide a way for their students to interact among themselves. For completeness, examples of class-based tools, such as testing, are also presented.

Table 12-1

Interaction Tools in LMSs (as of July, 2009)

	ILIAS 3	Moodle 1.9	Blackboard Learn 9	Saba LS	Atlas Pro 2
SCORM 2004 capabilities					
Run-time environment	●	●	●	●	●
Content aggregation model	●	●	●	●	●
Sequencing and navigation	●	●	●	●	●
Social media tools					
Discussion forums	●	●	●	●	
Chat	●	●	●	●	
Blogs		Optional	●	●	
Wikis		●	●	●	
Community		●	●	●	
Conference		Optional	Optional	●	
Class-based tools					
Enrollment	●	●	●	●	
Announcements	●	●	●	●	
Testing	●	●	●	●	●
Surveys		●	●	●	●

A survey of online learning practitioners (e-Learning Guild, 2008) indicated the relative popularity of various instructional modalities in different sectors. The results are depicted in Figure 12-1. While traditional instruction and asynchronous e-learning are dominant, blogs and wikis are also strong, especially in the higher education and consultancy sectors.

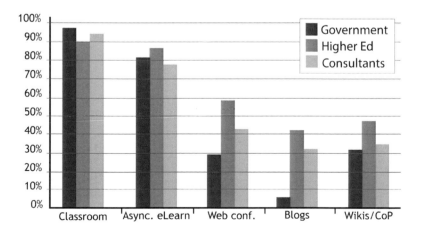

Figure 12-1. Popularity of instructional modalities. This figure depicts the use of different instructional modalities by sector.

159

What are the Benefits of Social Media Tools?

Why are social media tools popular? According to the constructivist approach in learning theory, learning is a self-governed, social/collaborative process (Vygotsky, 1978; Brown, Collins & Duguid 1989; Gamor, this volume) that can be facilitated by social media tools. For example, they afford learners the opportunity to reflect upon course content, and to discuss their thoughts with others. In addition, constructivist pedagogy suggests that students should be allowed to solve problems themselves, and social media can provide additional resources, such as media or people to support that effort. Furthermore, by incorporating competitive features (e.g., peer-to-peer grading), social media tools can increase class members' motivation and accountability, without necessarily requiring the active intervention of an instructor. Belanich, Orvis, and Wisher (2004) demonstrated a learning advantage to having small groups of students collaborate on writing test questions for other students. In contrast, traditional distance learning relies upon unsupervised assessment of superficial knowledge, typically by using multiple-choice tests; students can easily cheat on this form of assessment (Trenholm, 2007).

Table 12-2

Social media tools features and applications

Knowledge exchange	Open authoring tools can improve the accuracy and coverage of learning content	Basic
Community building	Social network tools allow novices to learn and interact within an established community of practice	
Communication	Social media tools provide various means for communicating with trainees/instructors	
Team building	Collaborative work strengthens team cohesion	
Assistance	Communication tools make classmates and instructors more available	
Assessment	Human grading allows for accurate assessment without sophisticated technology	
Active learning	More demanding assignments require deeper processing, which fosters trainee engagement	Derived
Competition	Metrics (e.g., number of contributions, peer rating) can spur competition between trainees.	
Instructional sequencing	Instructors can sequence learning activities manually, taking advantage of assessment results.	

A final benefit of social media, for classes that don't meet face-to-face, is that they help students get to know one another. Social network tools can be especially useful in this regard, as students can peruse their virtual classmates' profiles and build relationships in a low-risk manner. This can increase team cohesion and reduce feelings of isolation, a common cause of attrition in distance learning classes (Tyler-Smith, 2006).

Integrating Social Media in Instruction

Given that social media tools have many potential benefits, how can they best be integrated into the existing e-learning infrastructure? We have identified several models, current and future: self-managed, LMS integrated, embedded, and linked.

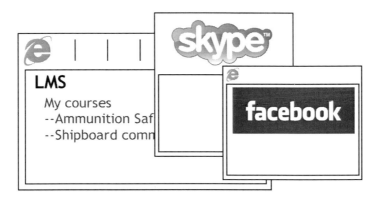

Figure 12-2. "Self-managed" model. This model allows students to use social media tools alongside an LMS-hosted course.

In the self-managed model (Figure 12-2), students use brand-name social media tools, such as Twitter and Facebook, alongside their LMS-hosted course. The advantage of using these well-established platforms is that they have the broadest range of features and the widest user networks, thus allowing access to new perspectives and reference material (Dalsgaard, 2009). However, the tools must be manually installed and configured. For instance, an instructor typically must create a group/area/tag for each class, and each student must join it. Research studies have shown that without the structure provided by an instructor (e.g., assignments, grading, and credits), social tools have little educational benefit.

Figure 12-3. "Built-in" integration model. In this model, the LMS provides social media tools for use.

The built-in model uses the social media tools supplied with LMSs (see Table 12-1). These may be for general use (e.g., a social network) or may be configurable for a specific class (e.g., a discussion forum or resource list). The advantage of using these features is that there is no extra software to install, and setup can be easier. Usability is also improved by using the same user interface/navigation components. However, as with the "self-managed" model, instructor guidance is typically required to make real educational gains. In addition, one is limited to the tools provided by the LMS, and tool use is not automatically synchronized with lesson content.

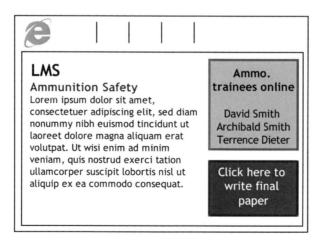

Figure 12-4. "Embedded" integration model. This model integrates social media tools as a standard part of the course.

In the embedded model (Figure 12-4), the LMS's built-in social media tools are integrated with course presentation. For instance, an instant messenger box may be used to see which fellow learners are currently online and available to help. In addition, some LMSs allow an instructor to sequence social learning into the flow of instruction. Several LMSs are beginning to follow this approach, including Moodle, a popular, free, and open source e-learning software platform.

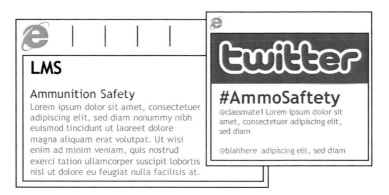

Figure 12-5. "Linked" integration model. This model integrates social media tools into instruction by automatically linking to stand-alone tools.

The final linked model (Figure 12-5) merges aspects of the self-directed and embedded models. As with the latter, social media tools are integrated into instruction, but instead of relying upon its own tools, the LMS instead links/embeds, and automatically configures, stand-alone tools.

In both the embedded and linked models, it would be desirable to have a standard means for developers to integrate social activities into courseware. This would allow them to develop interactive courses that work with every supported LMS. Having a standardized deployment environment could also open the door to (semi-automated) peer-to-peer assessment, instead of being reliant upon an instructor to monitor learners' activities. We discuss this later, in the "Integrating Social Media in SCORM" section.

Research Results

Only a few research studies have been performed, and the results on the comparative effectiveness of social media tools are still scant. Shailey Minocha and Dave Roberts (2008), of the UK's Open University (a distance learning university with more than 200,000 students) conducted a year-long trial of blog and wiki use within an instructor-led online course. Learners were told they could use the tools to reflect upon what they were learning, but they were not given specific assignments or credit for their use. In follow-up interviews, the researchers found that while most students liked using blogs, some lacked the confidence to reflect "in public," and others were unsure of the purpose of the exercise. Similar findings emerged in an MBA course taught at the University of Brisbane, Australia (Williams & Jacobs, 2004). There, many students were ambivalent about the value of blogs—roughly half opted not to use them, and of those that did, a third were not convinced that they aided learning.

In contrast, Rose Goldman, Amy Cohen, and Fred Sheahan (2008) of Harvard University's School of Public Health made blog use mandatory. They divided students into small groups, and asked each to create a seminar blog, which contained reflections on what they were learning. Group members took turns posting assignments each week, as well as commenting on the work of students. In post-course evaluation of native English speakers, 57 percent thought that using blogs helped them learn core material, while 36 percent found they helped with non-core material. Of the non-English native speakers (21 percent of the class), an even greater proportion (78 percent) reported that blogs helped with core and non-core material. This may indicate that blog postings, using "everyday" language, can help to reinforce academic concepts.

Ma and Yuen (2008) examined the impact of including wiki use in a graduate journalism class; their results indicate that wikis can (in collaboration with a tutor) improve performance. Students were required to prepare a news article using a wiki, which was then graded by an instructor. Students could elect to revise and resubmit their article, which some 75 percent of students did do. Ultimately, 22.6 percent of the variance in their final grade was due to the number of edits they made, illustrating the value of the collaborative authoring process made possible by using a wiki.

Military Adoption of Social Media Tools

How has the U.S. Department of Defense, a big user of online learning, taken to social media? The DoD's various online instruction programs are almost exclusively taken on an individual, self-paced basis, without reliance upon an instructor. This allows for low cost and flexible delivery, and given that social media typically requires a class, it is rarely used in DoD training currently. One example is the use of chat functions during a Web-based synchronous delivery of an advanced course for Army officers, as reported in Orvis, Wisher, Bonk, & Olson (2002). In that study, an analysis of more than 6,000 text messages indicated that more than 30 percent were social in nature during group problem solving in a "virtual tactical operations center."

In recent years Communities of Interest (COIs), also known as Communities of Practice, have become popular. They can be accessed from the Services' "knowledge portals": Army Knowledge Online, Joint Knowledge Online, (Camacho, West, & Vozzo, this volume), Navy Knowledge Online, and Air Force Knowledge Now. Each COI is built around shared interests, goals, missions or business processes, and contains a mix of announcements, resource links, member directories/profiles, and discussion forums. Within COIs, members help one another by exchanging ideas, sharing knowledge, and posting resources. In addition, a COI may have active facilitators who keep content fresh, recruit new members, and moderate other members' contributions.

COIs are oriented towards knowledge management, not learning a specific course. COI members are not required to make contributions to the network. Instead, COIs are more like super discussion forums, with additional elements that make social resources more visible. With the many different LMSs in the DoD, instructionally-integrated social media are unlikely to take off until a standard platform is developed to accommodate them.

Is Social Media Compatible with SCORM 2004?

How might SCORM and the related ADL technologies be updated to provide a standard platform for the integration of social media tools? SCORM has its roots in CD-ROM computer-based training standards, and, as such, embodies a traditional model of production and usage (Gallagher, this volume). The basic SCORM implementation has no intrinsic social or class-administration features. SCORM courses are typically created by a team of developers comprised of subject matter experts, instructional designers, and content Web developers (programmers and graphic designers). Individual learners access courses on a LMS.

Accommodating social media tools in this framework is difficult, but there are workarounds. Two of SCORM's central tenets are *reusability* and *accessibility*. To achieve reusability in practice, each course's Sharable Content Objects (SCOs) must be self-contained; thus, they cannot comprise much more than a set of media files. Furthermore, due to network security restrictions, access to Web services (e.g., social media tools) from within SCOs is blocked in SCORM-conformant courses.

Secondly, SCORM strives to enhance *accessibility* so that instruction can be accessed anytime, anyplace, and on a self-paced basis. This principle clashes with synchronous delivery, which requires access to an instructor or classmates.

A Model for Integrating Social Media in SCORM

There are good arguments for accommodating social media in SCORM. We have already discussed the various benefits of social learning activities. Currently, these must be coordinated by an instructor, using whatever tools he or she has in her LMS or that he or she has installed. An advanced SCORM would allow instructional designers to integrate social activities into courseware, as they do with "teaching guides" for textbooks. While these may still require an instructor's involvement (e.g., for grading students' work), it would lay the foundation for automation of social activities.

An example application would be to interweave blogging with lesson content (see Figure 12-6). Having completed Lesson 1 on his "LMS," a student, Sam, can't proceed until he has written a short essay and posted it to his blog on the Blog Platform. Once that's done, Pete (his partner) is alerted that he has a post to read and comment on. When Pete has done that, Sam is then alerted that he can proceed to Lesson 2.

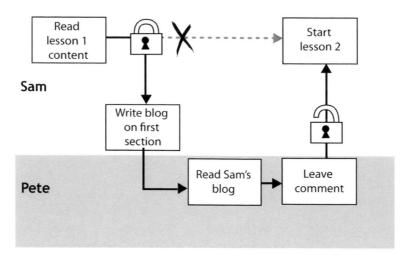

Figure 12-6. Blog-integrated workflow. This is an example of how a traditional course can integrate independent student activities into the course workflow.

The designer could also provide guidance on how to grade blog entries. This use case provides one example of how structured social activities can be used with traditional SCORM content to engage and motivate learners.

A further use of standardized social media tools would be to aid collaborative authoring. Consider a course that covers the politics of Afghanistan. The core material could be written by subject matter experts, but it is likely to become rapidly outdated. Using an advanced SCORM, instructors could take advantage of collaborative authoring. Instructional designers would code the content with editing permissions, including the approval path for making changes permanent. Learners with experience in the field could then update the course using a wiki interface. Thus, by taking advantage of the embedded or linked integration models, these features would by be available regardless of where the course was hosted.

Both of these examples illustrate the potential of a Web 2.0-integrated SCORM to harness learners' active participation, with or without an instructor's help.

Conclusion

In this chapter, we've examined the ongoing integration of social media tools and online learning. LMSs have always supported collaborative features, such as discussion forums and class email, and these are now being supplemented with new capabilities such as micro-blogs and social networks. All of these features provide a means for learners to reflect, demonstrate collaborative problem solving, and gain credit for their accomplishments. As these tools gain traction in e-learning and their effects on learning are better understood, particularly from a training perspective, they must work in harmony with ADL's requirements for accessibility, reuse, and interoperability.

The catch, currently, is that they require an instructor-and-class configuration to provide structure for instructional activities. Given this, it's not surprising that social media tools have gained the most traction in higher education, and the least in the government and manufacturing sectors. However, there is an opportunity to advance SCORM so that social activities can be programmed into instruction, regardless of whether a supervisor is available. In doing so, organizations such as the U.S. Department of Defense can obtain the maximum educational effect from social media, while taking advantage of their existing investments in distance learning infrastructure.

References

Belanich, J., Orvis, K. L., & Wisher, R. A. (2004). A question-collaboration approach to web-based learning. *The American Journal of Distance Education*, *18*(3), 169-185.

Brown, J. S., Collins, A., & Duguid, P. (1989). Situated cognition and the culture of learning. *Educational Researcher*, *18*(1), 32-42. Retrieved July 31, 2009 from http://www2.parc.com/ops/members/brown/papers/situatedlearning.html

Dalsgaard, C. (2006). Social software: E-learning beyond Learning Management Systems. *European Journal of Open, Distance and E-Learning*.2006:2. Retrieved July 31, 2009 from http://www.eurodl.org/materials/contrib/2006/Christian_Dalsgaard.htm

e-learning Guild (2008). The e-Learning Guild Snapshot Report on Learning Modalities. Retrieved from http://www.e-learningguild.com/research/archives/index.cfm?id=129&action=viewonly

Goldman, R., Cohen, A., & Sheanan, F. (2008). Using seminar blogs to enhance student participation and learning in public health school classes. *American Journal of Public Health*, *28*, 1658-1663.

Ma, W. W. K., & Yuen, A. H. K. (2008). News writing using wiki: impacts on learning experience of student journalists. *Educational Media Internatinal*, *45*(4), 295-309.

Minocha, S., & Roberts, D. (2008). Social, usability, and pedagogical factors influencing students' learning experiences with wikis and blogs. *Pragmatics & Cognition*, *16*, 272-306.

Orvis, K. L., Wisher, R. A., Bonk, C. J., & Olson, T. M. (2002). Communication patterns during synchronous web-based military training in problem solving. *Computers in Human Behavior*, *18*, 783-795.

Trenholm, S. (2007). A review of cheating in fully asynchronous online courses: A math or fact-based course perspective. *Journal of Educational Technology Systems*, *35*(3), 281-300.

Tyler-Smith, K. (2006). Early attrition among first time elearners: A review of factors that contribute to drop out, withdrawn and non-completion rates of adult learners undertaking e-learning programmes. *Journal of Online Learning and Teaching*, *2*(2). Retrieved from http://jolt.merlot.org/vol2no2/tyler-smith.htm

Vygotsky, L. S. (1978). *Mind in society*. Cambridge, MA: Harvard University Press.

Wagner, E. D. (2006). On designing interaction experiences for the next generation of blended learning. In. C. J. Bonk & C. R. Graham (Eds.), *The handbook of blended learning* (pp. 41-55). San Francisco: Pfieffer.

Wagner, E. D. (1999). Beyond distance education: Distributed learning systems. In H. Stolovich & E. Keeps (Eds.), *Handbook of human performance technology* (2nd ed.). San Francisco: Jossey-Bass.

Williams, J. B., & Jacobs, J. (2004). Exploring the use of blogs as learning spaces in the higher education sector. *Australasian Journal of Educational Technology*, *20*, 232-247.

Web Resources

Communities of Interest, Defense Link. http://www.defenselink.mil/cio-nii/sites/coi/coi.shtml.htm

The Author

Daniel Fowler leads the Research and Evaluation Team at the Advanced Distributed Learning (ADL) Initiative. At ADL, his team is responsible for evaluating the impact of online training systems, and for determining the cost-effectiveness of new learning technology.

Chapter 13

ADL and Intelligent Tutoring Systems

Xiangen Hu, Arthur Graesser, and Daniel Fowler

This chapter describes Intelligent Tutoring Systems (ITS) and the extent to which these computationally sophisticated learning environments can be accommodated in the ADL technical element of interoperability. ITSs have some distinctive characteristics that are difficult to mesh with online learning management systems. However, the ADL framework has progressed to the point where it can handle the key architectural components of ITSs. An important next step is for the ADL community to move forward with developing ITSs for diverse training needs.

In the context of the ADL business paradigm, intelligent tutoring is a case of making a proven instructional technique accessible to designers through interoperability (Wisher, this volume). Within the business paradigm, it is an example of the Instruction and Pedagogy line pulling the Interoperability line. Robust sector relationships with academic laboratories are in place, and the ADL Initiative has previously funded academia and industry to develop prototype models (Murray & Marvin, this volume). Much remains to be done in determining a best technical approach to advance ADL with this technology, consistent with the needs for interoperability, accessibility, and reuse.

The purpose of this chapter is to contrast a conventional approach to designing instruction for delivery by computer to an approach that mimics the role of a human tutor during one-on-one instruction. The fundamental characteristics of an intelligent tutor are described and leading examples are presented. Also described are the challenges facing the ADL community in incorporating intelligent tutoring into the Sharable Content Object Reference Model (SCORM).

Traditional Computer-Based Training

Computer-based learning platforms have evolved rapidly; they encompass conventional computer-based training (CBT), interactive simulation, interactive multimedia instruction, hypertext/hypermedia, question-based information retrieval, animated conversational agents, virtual environments, serious games, and computer-supported collaborative learning amongst other instructional formats.

What we call "online learning" or "Web-based training" generally follows the first format, CBT. CBT was first widely deployed in the 1980s, and embodies a form of mastery learning. In CBT, the learner (1) reads material presented on screen, (2) performs a multiple choice, order, or fill-the-gap type test, (3) gets automated feedback, and then (4) branches either to a new topic of instruction, or to review material for the current topic.

The sequencing of topics and testing differs depending upon the system's pedagogical model, such as: sequencing topics by prerequisites (Gagne, 1985), structuring topics into a top-down hierarchy (Ausubel, Novak, & Hanesian, 1978), or dynamic sequencing of topics (O'Neil & Perez, 2003). CBT systems are typically used individually in a self-paced manner, with text content that is sometimes supplemented with figures/pictures, tables, and diagrams. More advanced CBT systems include multimedia components such as animations, video, or interactive games.

CBT generally requires little custom programming, resulting in low development costs. As CBT does not require a human instructor, deployment costs are also low. While CBT systems that use dynamic sequencing are responsive to student performance, they respond infrequently, at a coarse grain level. As a result, for students, the CBT experience is like learning from a textbook. Therefore, CBT systems are best suited to courses where the content is mostly factual or procedural, and to learners that are motivated to learn. When equivalent content and pedagogies are used in online and in classroom settings, learning is equivalent (Sitzmann, Kraiger, Stewart, & Wisher, 2006).

Intelligent Tutoring Systems

Intelligent Tutoring Systems focus on applying well-understood human learning principles to a target knowledge domain. Successful ITSs have been developed for mathematically and semantically well-formed topics including algebra, geometry, programming languages (*Cognitive Tutors*, Anderson, Corbett, Koedinger, & Pelletier, 1995), physics (*Andes*, Atlas, and Why/Atlas, VanLehn et al., 2002; VanLehn et al., 2007), electronics (*Sherlock*, Lesgold, Lajoie, Bunzo, & Eggan, 1992), information technology (*SQL-Tutor*, Mitrovic, Suraweera, Martin, & Weerasinghe, 2004), and military training (*Virtual Sand Table*, Wisher, Macpherson, Abramson, Thornton, & Dees, 2001).

Some recent ITSs handle knowledge domains that are not mathematically precise and well-formed. The *Intelligent Essay Assessor* (Landauer, Laham, & Foltz, 2003) uses natural language processing to grade students' essays on a range of (pre-selected) topics in science and history, performing as reliably as experts of English composition. *AutoTutor* (Graesser, Chipman, Haynes, & Olney, 2005; VanLehn et al., 2007) helps college students learn about computer literacy, physics, and critical thinking skills by holding conversations in natural language. *AutoTutor* results in learning gains of approximately 0.8 standard deviation units, or sigma, above average, which translates to a 29 percent improvement compared with reading a textbook for an equivalent amount of time (Graesser et al., 2004; VanLehn et al., 2007).

Intelligent Tutoring System Architecture
ITSs draw on theories and frameworks from the cognitive and learning sciences. Most ITSs have a pedagogical model, student model, and expert model as well as a

domain knowledge model. These models are created using a formal (programming) language so that the ITS can make inferences with them.

The student model allows ITSs to infer the current state of the student's knowledge, including gaps and misconceptions. The pedagogical model includes the techniques used to teach the domain knowledge, making inferences and decisions based on the changing state of the student model and the prescriptions of an expert model. The ultimate goal of an ITS is to use the pedagogical model to move the student towards an expert understanding of the domain.

Intelligent Tutoring Systems in Operation

Intelligent tutors use frequent student interaction to build a model of the student's knowledge and learning strategies in finer detail. ITSs use this model to determine how to respond next (Woolf, Aimeur, Nkambou, & Lajoie, 2008). Commonly used responses include feedback on the student's last move, correcting student errors, providing content hints, suggesting learning techniques, and selecting a new problem. The student modeling and adaptive response processes are derived from cognitive science theories, and are often embodied in artificial intelligence algorithms within the ITS.

A prototypical ITS operates as follows. At its highest level it is a model of interaction between learner and machine using a turn-altering stimulus-response dynamic. A tutoring session is comprised of a dialog with two possible modes of interaction: tutor-initiated dialogs and learner-initiated dialogs.

In each dialog, the tutor has a collection of *items* that can be presented to the learner. They can require different types of responses from the learner, such as to provide an acknowledgment (read and click next button), select a response to a test/ quiz, or enter a response to a question in natural language.

In tutor-initiated dialogs the following steps occur:

1. The tutor selects the first item and presents it to the learner. A learner response is solicited.

2. The tutor interprets the learner response. The learner response may be constrained by the format, but not necessarily by content. For example, it can be a multiple-choice response from a fixed set of alternatives, or it can be an expression in natural language, such as a short verbal response or essay.

3. The tutor assigns a value to each stimulus-response pair. The assignment can take into account the history between the tutor and learner.

4. The tutor selects the next item based on student performance (present and past).

5. The tutor decides how the selected item is to be delivered.

Most ITSs follow the above five basic behavior assumptions, with differences arising in steps three, four, and five.

In learner-initiated dialogs, the learner may ask a question, then:

1. The tutor evaluates the proposal.

2. The tutor selects the appropriate item, such as a problem or a step in a problem.

3. The tutor decides how the selected item is to be delivered and delivers the item.

The above basic assumptions are completely theory-neutral and merely describe the tutoring session behaviorally.

Other ITS features

In addition to this core method, other ITSs have the following features:

Generative capability. Instead of relying on "canned" responses, the system can generate appropriate live feedback.

Mixed initiative conversation. The capability to initiate interactions with the student as well as to interpret and respond to their input. The interaction is sometimes in the form of natural language.

Interactivity. Appropriately contextualized, domain-relevant, and engaging learning activities.

Self-improvement. The capabilities to monitor, evaluate, and improve the ITS's own performance, by learning from how students use the system.

Simulation. Simulations of systems, devices, or processes used to contextualize instruction about the simulated systems, devices, or processes.

Advantages and Disadvantages of Intelligent Tutors

Intelligent Tutoring Systems differ from CBTs in a number of ways, although we resist the temptation to draw sharp boundaries between the two classes of systems. ITSs yield more substantial learning gains, are more responsive to the learner, are designed according to empirically validated learning theories, and attempt to provide an optimal alignment between the content/skills to be acquired and the computational architecture. In the lab, ITSs typically show results of an approximate 1.0 standard deviation (sigma), or 34 percent improvement in learning compared to classroom teaching (Dodds & Fletcher, 2004; VanLehn et al., 2007). In the field, some ITSs have been widely deployed to great effect; for example, Carnegie Learning's math and algebra tutors are in use in thousands of schools throughout the United States.

These benefits are offset by some obvious limitations. For example, ITSs require custom programming of their domain knowledge, reasoning rules, student model rules, and user interface. This level of complexity makes it difficult to build

172

authoring tools for use by instructional designers instead of programmers. The cost and time it takes to build a new ITS are, therefore, high and hard to predict. Furthermore, ITSs' content and processing modules are generally not interoperable, shareable, or easily modifiable.

Intelligent Tutors and SCORM

SCORM content is standardized as self-contained SCOs that can be used in any SCORM-conformant LMS (Gallagher, this volume). Once content is created in such a fashion, it can be extensively reused; this can yield substantial cost savings.

Although SCORM was originally designed with ITSs in mind (Dodds & Fletcher, 2004), most ITSs are not SCORM-conformant. The most recent major version of SCORM (SCORM 2004), contains a Sequencing & Navigation model (henceforth SN model) that is designed to support adaptive branching between SCOs. Could this be used to support ITS features in SCORM?

SCORM's Sequencing and Navigation Model

The SN model of SCORM allows course designers to sequence "learning activities" according to the learner's progress. Within the model, learning activities are arranged in a hierarchical organization called the activity tree. A SCORM-conformant learning management system selects the next learning activity based on the learner's progress and performance in assessment activities. Once the learner has completed all of the activities on the current branch of the activity tree, he or she moves across or up a level, until the tree is complete. The following is a comparison between ITSs and the SCORM Sequencing and Navigation model:

Representation of knowledge. Domain knowledge in ITSs is structured (e.g., as concepts, propositions, if-then rules, principles, and/or other data structures). In contrast, domain knowledge in SCOs is unstructured.

Evaluation of learner's input. The student model in ITSs can be based on a wide range of inputs, and input evaluation mechanisms can be tailored to the domain of knowledge and the system pedagogy. Some ITSs accept natural language responses and employ facilities in computational linguistics to assign values to these responses. The SN model of SCORM accepts learner evaluation data as a basis to select the next SCO, but it does not support user interaction at a fine-grain (within lesson) level.

Selection of next learning activity. Selection in an ITS uses a pedagogical model and a student model, and is conditional on the learner's performance. In the SN model of SCORM, selection is dependent upon a set of rules defined in the activity tree, which is less flexible—they rarely considering anything more than the student's performance.

Delivery model. A delivery model specifies how the selected item is presented. ITSs are typically standalone applications, so content presentation is tailored to the system's teaching strategies. In SCORM, content presentation is constrained by being browser-based, which limits the scope of user interaction.

Expanding SCORM to Support Intelligent Tutors

As we have discussed, despite the capabilities of the SN model, there are still fundamental barriers to the support of ITSs in SCORM. How can SCORM be extended to accommodate ITSs, as well as other interactive learning architectures? We propose a research and development program to break these limitations, culminating in a new version of SCORM.

First, we propose that SCORM be extended to support server-based processing. This capability is necessary for complex inputs such as natural language, and for complex assessment. Future ITS applications may also accept non-verbal inputs from learners (such as emotions, facial expressions, and intonation).

Second, we propose that SCORM implement probabilistic rules, to mimic the selection mechanisms in ITSs. The rules should be sensitive to a complex set of constraints in the student profile.

Third, we propose that SCORM include a standard delivery model. This would allow SCOs to access external Web services. Thus, SCOs would no longer be packages of static raw media files with metadata, and could support the advanced features required by ITSs.

Conclusion

Intelligent Tutoring Systems have been in development since the 1970s. They represent a more theoretically-driven, interactive approach to delivering individual instruction than today's computer-based training. While the learning outcomes can be impressively higher than CBT, their cost and complexity has proven to be an impediment to widespread success.

While it was originally hoped that SCORM could form the foundation of a new range of reusable ITSs, its interoperability and security constraints have limited it as a platform for immediate applicability of ITSs. Similarly, while SCORM can store some student data using its tracking model, its current format is too restrictive for ITSs.

Although the SCORM Sequencing and Navigation model made a promising step towards addressing these problems, the harmonization of SCORM and ITSs is likely to be a long journey. An assessment of services and architectures that can add functions to the core SCORM capabilities is needed (Panar, Rehak, & Thropp, this volume). We concluded this chapter with proposals for the next steps along that journey.

References

Anderson, J. R., Corbett, A. T., Koedinger, K. R., & Pelletier, R. (1995). Cognitive tutors: Lessons learned. *The Journal of Learning Sciences*, *4*(2), 167-207.

Ausubel, D., Novak, J., & Hanesian, H. (1978). *Educational psychology: A cognitive view* (2nd ed.). New York: Holt, Rinehart, & Winston.

Dodds, P., & Fletcher, J. D. (2004). Opportunities for new "smart" learning environments enabled by next-generation web capabilities. *Journal of Educational Multimedia and Hypermedia*, *13*(4), 391-404.

Gagne, R. M. (1985). *The conditions of learning and theory of instruction* (4th ed.) New York: Holt, Rinehart, & Winston.

Graesser, A. C., Chipman, P., Haynes, B. C., & Olney, A. (2005). AutoTutor: An intelligent tutoring system with mixed-initiative dialogue. *IEEE Transactions in Education*, *48*, 612-618.

Graesser, A. C., Lu, S., Jackson, G. T., Mitchell, H., Ventura, M., Olney, A., & Louwerse, M. M. (2004). AutoTutor: A tutor with dialogue in natural language. *Behavioral Research Methods, Instruments, and Computers*, *36*, 180-193.

Landauer, T. K., Laham, D., & Foltz, P. W. (2003). Automated scoring and annotation of essays with the Intelligent Essay Assessor. In M. D. Shermis & J. Burstein (Eds.), *Automated essay scoring: A cross-disciplinary perspective* (pp. 87-112). Mahwah, NJ: Lawrence Erlbaum Associates, Inc.

Lesgold, A., Lajoie, S. P., Bunzo, M., & Eggan, G. (1992). SHERLOCK: A coached practice environment for an electronics trouble-shooting job. In J. H. Larkin & R. W. Chabay (Eds.), *Computer assisted instruction and intelligent tutoring systems: Shared goals and complementary approaches* (pp. 201–238). Hillsdale, NJ: Erlbaum.

Mitrovic, Suraweera, Martin, & Weerasinghe (2004). DB-suite: Experiences with Three Intelligent, Web-based Database Tutors. *Journal of Interactive Learning Research (JILR)*, *15*(4), 409-432.

O'Neil, H. F., & Perez, R. (Eds.) (2003). *Technology applications in education: A learning view*. Hillsdale, NJ.: Erlbaum.

Sitzmann, T., Kraiger, K., Stewart, D. and Wisher, R. (2006). The comparative effectiveness of Web-based and classroom instruction: A meta-analysis. *Personnel Psychology*, *59*(3), 623-664.

VanLehn, K., Graesser, A. C., Jackson, G. T., Jordan, P., Olney, A., & Rose, C. P. (2007). When are tutorial dialogues more effective than reading? *Cognitive Science*, *31*, 3-62.

VanLehn, K., Lynch, C., Taylor, L., Weinstein, A., Shelby, R. H., Schulze, K. G., et al. (2002). Minimally invasive tutoring of complex physics problem solving. In S. A. Cerri, G. Gouarderes, & F. Paraguacu (Eds.), *Intelligent Tutoring Systems 6th International Conference* (pp. 367-376). Berlin: Springer.

Wisher, R. A, Macpherson, D. H., Abramson, L. J., Thornton, D. M., & Dees, J. J. (2001). *The virtual sand table: Intelligent tutoring for field artillery training* (Research Report 1768). Alexandria, VA: U.S. Army Research Institute for the Behavioral and Social Sciences.

Woolf, B. P., Aimeur, E., Nkambou, R., & Lajoie, S. (Eds.) (2008). Proceedings from ITS 2008: *Intelligent Tutoring Systems: 9th International Conference on Intelligent Tutoring Systems*. Montreal, Canada: Springer.

The Authors

Xiangen Hu, PhD, is a professor in cognitive psychology at the University of Memphis and is a faculty member of the Institute of Intelligent Systems. Dr. Hu is also the director of the ADL Memphis Intelligent Tutoring Systems Center at the University of Memphis.

Arthur Graesser, PhD, is a professor in the Department of Psychology, an adjunct professor in Computer Science, and co-director of the Institute of Intelligent Systems at the University of Memphis.

Daniel Fowler leads the Training Evaluation Team at the Advanced Distributed Learning Initiative Co-Lab Hub in Alexandria, VA.

Chapter 14

Adopting Virtual Worlds in ADL: The Criticality of Analysis
Keysha I. Gamor

The ADL Initiative develops and implements e-learning technologies across the U.S. Department of Defense (DoD) and federal government. In collaboration with government, industry, and academia, ADL promotes international specifications, standards, and best practices for designing and delivering learning content that leads to effective, meaningful training. In doing so, ADL uses technology to bridge the gaps created by distance, time, and space.

As with e-learning, ADL has a responsibility to assist DoD and the federal government with identifying technologies to address current and future training or educational challenges. DoD and other agencies throughout the federal government seek to employ technologies to deliver sound content efficiently and economically and increase access to DoD and federal resources.

Given the broad goals of ADL and its vision for high quality, on demand learning, it is understandable that DoD, the federal government, and thus ADL, all have a keen interest in immersive e-learning environments, such as the computer-based simulated environments called virtual worlds (VW) and the capabilities they may afford the training and education industry. Hype aside, there are good reasons to be interested in virtual worlds. The E-Learning Guild (Whiteside, 2002) offers three main justifications for considering immersive learning environments: to increase learner motivation; to support high-level, performance based learning outcomes; and to increase transfer of training to the job environment.

This chapter discusses the characteristics of virtual world technology, the hype around virtual worlds, and some critical considerations to take into account before purchasing a virtual world platform. In the context of the ADL business paradigm, the chapter illustrates the pull of the Instruction and Pedagogy line on the requirements for interoperability (Wisher, this volume). In particular, this chapter addresses the careful analysis needed before embedding virtual worlds in a learning environment consistent with SCORM requirements (Gallagher, this volume). In view of the tremendous creativity in the virtual world community, it is impractical to expect developers to abide by a "standard" for virtual worlds just as is the case for game developers (Xu, this volume). Other means, such as, for example, service oriented architectures or data models to communicate between a virtual world and a learning management system could be used. From an ADL perspective, the learning experiences with virtual worlds must be consistent with the needs for accessibility, interoperability, and reuse.

What are Virtual Worlds?

There is no single, agreed upon definition of "virtual world." However, all definitions acknowledge that a virtual world is an online simulation of either a real or fantasy world environment populated by avatars, which are pictorial or graphical representations of the human participants. A virtual world can also be described as "a synchronous, persistent network of people, represented as avatars, facilitated by networked computers" (Bell, 2008). EDUCAUSE, a non-profit association concerned with leveraging technology to improve higher education, defines a virtual world simply as an "online environment whose 'residents' are avatars representing individuals participating online." (The EDUCAUSE Learning Initiative, 2006). Still, other definitions which address the specific affordances of this modality help us understand the potential of the technology as well. Examining popular virtual world applications can help frame an understanding of virtual worlds as "online 3-D virtual worlds ... within which residents are able to establish identities (avatars), explore, create and communicate. [Further, a virtual world may] lend itself well to social networking, collaboration and learning" (Institute of Electrical and Electronics Engineers, 2009).

Avatars

The Association of Virtual World's Blue Book helps novices get started in virtual worlds by first explaining what an avatar is: "'Avatar' comes from Hindu mythology and means the incarnation of a divine being. But in the virtual world an avatar is an icon or representation of a user (Association of Virtual Worlds, 2008)."

In a virtual world, however, the avatar is also both a navigational and experiential tool. With the avatar being a representation of self, learners ascribe a personal connection that enables them to engage in the virtual space as an extension, alternative, or augmentation of the real world. Thus, we see the adherence to social norms and behaviors, such as observance of personal space, "eye" contact, attention to appearance, emotions, gesturing, etc., typically seen in face-to-face interaction.

While the use of avatars in virtual worlds is the standard method of navigation and interaction, there is currently no standard definition of virtual worlds in general. Therefore, it is important to examine the commonalities among the available virtual world platforms to help frame a conceptual understanding of what virtual worlds offer beyond what our current instructional design toolkit provides.

The Evolution of the Virtual Worlds Industry

The concept of virtual worlds as a collaborative learning tool is not new. In fact, three-dimensional (3D) virtual worlds have been around since 1995, with one precursor, Multi User Domains (MUDs), dating back to 1978 (Jackson, 2007). The pace of development began to accelerate in the mid-1990s on multiple fronts. Since 1995, there has been a series of new launches of virtual worlds, ranging from virtual worlds prototypes on through the first release of Second Life, currently the most used virtual world, in 2003. Second Life is used for many different purposes, including community-building and games, but also for business collaboration and for educational purposes.

Early on, the concept of virtual worlds was also explored in science fiction novels such as *The Three Stigmata of Palmer Eldritch* (1965), *Neuromancer* (1984), and *Snow Crash* (1992), and in popular films which led to film sequels and launching a mini-industry of movie-themed comics, video games, and animations as well. The launch of AlphaWorld (1995) signaled the beginning of a new era in virtual worlds by providing a Web-based, collaborative virtual environment. Mega hits like EverQuest (1999) and World of Warcraft (2004) continued to popularize virtual worlds into mainstream entertainment vernacular and culture. The video game industry also began offering virtual world and role-playing games both for dedicated video game hardware, as well as for online play.

This is, by far, just a look in the past. With augmented reality, mixed reality, improved mobile technologies (Brown, this volume), and other emerging technologies, virtual worlds will continue to morph in years to come.

The Virtual Worlds "Hype" Cycle

As the Gartner Hype Cycle for Social Virtual Worlds shows (Figure 14-1), interest in virtual worlds has fluctuated since their debut in 1987. Over the last several years, however, there has been a marked increase in awareness and attention in the virtual worlds industry, summarily followed by a leveling off of priority focus and investment. A leading technology consulting and research group contends that "public virtual worlds are [now] suffering from disillusionment after their peak of hype in 2007" (Gartner Inc., 2008a) and growth in the industry will continue to level off until optimal ways to use the technology become apparent. Perhaps an increase of successful implementations will spark the new surge in interest and investment (Gartner Inc., 2008a) to sustain the market until there is a new breakthrough.

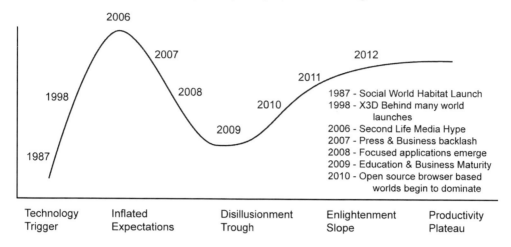

GARTNER HYPE CYCLE For Social Virtual Worlds
Temporal Perspective by Gary Hayes muvedesign.com 2009 Jan

Figure 14-1. Gartner Hype Cycle for Social Virtual Worlds. The hype cycle depicts the cycle of fluctuations of interest and investment in the technology of virtual worlds. http://www.muvedesign.com/the-virtual-worlds-hype-cycle-for-2009/

Although Gartner's Hype Cycle shows a steep decline from 2006-2009, those in the education and training industry recognize that this is not a true decline. It is not a matter of interest waning or the hype being dispelled. The matter is simply this: now that there is significant improvement in the technology and in its available features, what can the industry really accomplish with virtual worlds? Many pilot tests, projects, and programs are underway to explore just that.

While this application of virtual worlds is not new, the wider adoption of virtual world environments for training and learning raises the risk of repeating the mistakes made when the industry was trying to figure out how to adapt content from the classroom to the e-learning environment. This is the challenge: industry is faced with determining how to both design and develop new content, or adapt classroom and/or e-learning content, for use in virtual worlds.

Implementation Success

A Gartner Inc. press release indicating that 9 out of 10 virtual worlds programs fail within 18 months of launch (2008b) highlights the need for the industry to identify concrete requirements and discover useful applications that will lead to an increase in successful implementations and, ultimately, more quickly to the next evolutionary node along the immersive learning continuum. Failing to do so may result in a continuous series of failed pilots, sustained waning of the adoption cycle, and persistent risks of serious disappointment—possibly to the point of participants in virtual world projects eschewing the technology altogether.

The Virtual Worlds Investment Cycle

A significant drop in investments in virtual worlds from 2007 to 2008, underscores the need for continued research; according to Gartner Inc. (2007), more than $1 billion was invested in virtual worlds in 2007 whereas that amount fell to $885 million in 2008 (Jackson, 2007). While there are likely many factors contributing to this decline in investment, including a serious global recession, it is important to note that even though 9 out of 10 business experiments with virtual worlds fail within 18 months, there are estimates that by 2012, 70 percent of organizations will have established their own private virtual worlds (Gartner Inc., 2007). With continued interest, and despite mounting failures, there have been some successes. It is clear that many see the potential that virtual worlds offer. Now, it is up to the training, education, and entertainment industries to determine the best ways to methodically and effectively exploit the unique capabilities and affordances of virtual worlds in order to fully integrate this technology into our instructional and gaming design toolkits and culture.

One solution to the problem of what to do with virtual worlds is evident in the education and training industry, specifically. Crafting meaningful learning experiences has, historically, been a great challenge in situations where context is as important as content. Role playing scenarios, case studies, and discussions are a few of the instructional strategies used to provide a rich, experiential aspect to traditional classroom and e-learning courses. These same strategies can still be used in a virtual world; however, the approaches now have the added benefit of a group dynamic in a persistent, graphically rich space that is real, rather than imagined; that is co-created rather than dictated; that is simultaneously shared by many for the purpose of collaboration, rather than accessible to a few. Indeed, virtual worlds have also given way to new instructional strategies not possible in traditional learning environments.

There are, undoubtedly, fringe experiments being conducted with the specific goal of shifting learning paradigms with this tool. While contributing to the overall failure rates of virtual reality implementations, these "way out" and often failure prone projects are a necessary part of the process of discovering new ways to use virtual worlds.

Thus, instead of jumping on the virtual world bandwagon "for the cool factor" or "because competitors are doing it," a clear understanding of the features that most virtual worlds share helps decision-makers identify the unique attributes that may address specific training, education, or performance improvement needs, which will also inform purchase decisions. There are six features most virtual worlds have in common (Federation of American Scientists, 2009; Virtual World Review, 2009). A brief examination of the benefits of these affordances, as shown in Table 14-1, for the individual and the community in which individuals operate, illustrates virtual worlds' value as a teaching and learning medium.

Table 14-1

Virtual World Affordances and Their Benefits for Individuals and Groups

Affordances of virtual worlds	Individual-focused benefit	Group-focused benefit
Co-creation	Fosters peer-to-peer support and tutoring	Fosters multi-user content development or modification
Co-existence	Enlivens communication and interaction; blurs the line of distance	Enables multi-user simultaneous interaction in a shared environment
Collaboration	Enables users to self-select groups based upon goals or needs	Encourages users to develop peer, affinity, skill, interest, and/or groups
Graphical User Interface	Offers visual context of environment and other inhabitants	Offers visual context of environment and other inhabitants
Persistence	Maintains 24/7 existence; provides convenient access	Enables progress and change to take place regardless of individual log-in status; helps close the distance/time gap
Presence	Defies distance; provides situated context	Minimizes feelings of 'disconnectedness'

In addition to the basic affordances of virtual worlds, most applications either boast other attributes aimed at a specific audience or offer enhanced capabilities for one or more of these six common features. Determining the most appropriate tool for one's needs requires knowing what, if any, additional features are needed beyond the six basic common features that may help in reaching the intended instructional goals of the virtual worlds initiative (Sitzmann & Ely, this volume). This step, along with an analysis of organizational and technical considerations, helps to narrow the list of potential applications that address the concrete requirements identified during the requirements analysis phase of an education, training, or performance improvement project.

There is little definitive guidance in performing requirements analysis for virtual worlds, and there is a need for further research in this area. However, an examination of fundamentals of instructional design may provide a framework to guide the requirements analysis phase.

Designing for Learning in Virtual Worlds

The remainder of this chapter is based upon the premise that designing for learning in virtual worlds should be grounded in three basic tenets of sound instructional design. These stipulate that instruction and knowledge construction have a better chance at being successful if 1) they are based upon a learning environment and content resulting from requirements-driven design, 2) have clear objectives, and 3) target the appropriate audience. Sound instructional design methodologies will help instructional designers create successful learning experiences for this modality, which can ultimately be linked into systems that also support SCORM (Panar, Rehak, & Thropp, this volume).

In order to move toward a better understanding of designing learning experiences for virtual worlds, it is necessary to examine the fundamentals of instructional design. Such an examination will, at a minimum, help designers avoid making mistakes that could jeopardize their virtual learning curricula and programs. Part of the Advanced Distributed Learning Initiative's mission is to develop best practices that reduce risk and increase the opportunities for success. The analysis phase is an important first step in ensuring sound design for virtual worlds instead of a "buy it, build it, they will come" ideology.

Virtual World Design and Learning Frameworks

The tenets of a traditional instructional design model apply to designing learning opportunities for virtual worlds—with some modifications. Certainly, there is a need to conduct all five phases of the Analysis, Design, Development, Implementation, Evaluation (ADDIE), or similar, instructional design process model (Deibler & Berking, this volume). For the purposes of this chapter, the ADDIE model will serve as a foundational model for the virtual worlds learning framework. While it is often referred to as a "production process," ADDIE offers much more to the instructional designer than production—which is the end result. ADDIE is a substantial framework (known by a variety of names) that has been proven in many industries (architecture, software, engineering, training design, etc.). One approach for designing learning experiences for virtual worlds is not only to follow, but to augment ADDIE, and to leverage lessons learned and best practices obtained through research and experience. The analysis phase of the ADDIE model may be applied to determine needs and uses of virtual worlds as a potential teaching and learning tool.

As a potential teaching and learning tool, the power that virtual world platforms offer is especially important "when learners need to gain high-level skills (e.g., in Bloom's taxonomy: application, analysis, synthesis, and evaluation) in order to perform critical job functions (e.g., develop sales strategies to meet clients' unique requirements)...." (Whiteside, 2002, p.9). By their very nature, virtual worlds provide an immersive learning experience that learners identify with as being realistic, authentic, meaningful, challenging, and motivating (Affiliated Computer Services,

2009; Calongne, 2008; Dede, 2007; Gamor, 2001; Gao, Noh, & Koehler, 2008). As shown in Table 14-2, the concept of immersion in virtual worlds is achieved through the six common characteristics which have different in-world representations.

Table 14-2

Affordances of Virtual Worlds and Their Representation In-world

Affordances of virtual worlds	Representation of affordances in virtual worlds
Co-creation	Materializes through building concepts, objects, and other creations together
Co-existence	Emerges through occupying space with other participants at the same time
Collaboration	Exists through sharing ideas, thoughts, and work products synchronously and asynchronously, constructing a potentially endless feedback/interaction loop
Graphical User Interface (GUI)	Appears through a representation that illustrates the key elements of the authentic context(s) necessary to create a feeling of "thereness"
Persistence	Manifests through preservation of ideas, thoughts, work products, and other objects
Presence	Appears as the capability to engage in real-time interaction with others who are in world

Understanding these characteristics helps the instructional designer to identify relevant learning theories and models that could apply to teaching and learning in virtual worlds.

While the education and training industry has not yet agreed on an approach for designing learning for virtual worlds, standardizing a learning framework should not be quite as difficult a task, since virtual worlds as multimedia learning tools, embody the elements of constructivist learning environments. Constructivist learning environments enable "[l]earners [to] build personal interpretation of the world based on experiences and interactions" (Dabbagh, 2008; Dede, Clark, Ketelhut, Nelson, & Bowman, 2005; Nelson, Ketelhut, Clarke, Bowman, & Dede, 2005; Delwiche, 2003; Walker, 2009). Experiences and interactions are embedded within authentic contexts which provide learners the opportunity to construct knowledge from multiple perspectives and situations (Dabbagh, 2008; Jonassen, Grabinger, Harris, 1991; Rheingold, 1991). David Jonassen and colleagues (1994), leaders in constructivist theory and methods, point out that there social and cognitive constructivism has significant implications for instructional design that can be applied to virtual worlds as constructivist learning environments. Table 14-3 sheds light on VW affordances through mapping principles of constructivism for instructional design against affordances of virtual worlds.

Table 14-3

Principles of Constructivism for Instructional Design Mapped Against Virtual World Affordances

Principles of constructivism for instructional design (Jonassen, Campbell, & Davidson, 1994)	Affordances of virtual worlds
Offer multiple representations of reality	GUI Collaboration Presence
Represent the inherent complexity of the real world	Persistence Coexistence
Emphasize knowledge construction, rather than reproduction	Co-creation
Present authentic tasks (instruction in context rather than out of context)	Coexistence GUI
Provide real-world, case-based or problem-based learning opportunities, rather than pre-determined, prescriptive instructional sequences	Persistence
Encourage reflection on experience	Collaboration Persistence
Enable context-and content-dependent knowledge construction	Presence GUI
Support "collaborative construction of knowledge through social negotiation, not competition among learners for recognition"	Collaboration Presence

There is much research to build upon here, but the space limitations of this chapter allow only brief mention of a few key components.

In addition to constructivist theory, Kolb's experiential learning model provides a useful way of understanding the nature of learning that is context- and experience-based. According to Kolb (1984a), "learning is the process whereby knowledge is created through the transformation of experience. Knowledge results from the combination of grasping experience and transforming it." In other words, experience offers a way of knowing that is personal. Personal experience is memorable and meaningful in a way that is unique to the individual. Once an individual has an experience and constructs meaning from it, the knowledge gained is accessible for reflection, sharing or transfer to other situations, contexts, or experiences (Kolb, 1984b; Jonassen, Davidson, Collins, Campbell, & Haag, 1995).

Constructivist epistemology and experiential learning theory are just two of many constructs that can contribute to building a framework for optimizing the unique features that virtual worlds add to the instructional designer's toolkit.

Regardless of one's concept of *how* the tool may be used (e.g., as a course activity hub, course's sole delivery mode, or a course's preplanned, discrete event tool), there are characteristics inherent in the nature of virtual worlds themselves that shape the learning experience. That is, virtual worlds are by nature **constructivist** (knowledge and meaning are generated from experience), **experiential** (effective learning occurs when people directly create meaning by interacting with the learning environment, its contents, and its inhabitants), **constructionist** (effective learning happens when learners actively make things), and **compelling/motivating/ challenging** (for example, games—both serious and entertainment types, role plays, and immersive problem identification or solving activities). There is much research and experience in these areas, eliminating the need to take shots in the dark at or to start from scratch in the development of new instructional approaches.

Constructivist and/or experiential instructional principles, theories, and models are a logical place to start when determining how virtual worlds can facilitate a solution to an instructional or performance improvement challenge. In addition to considering these requisite principles, theories, and models during the analysis phase, instructional designers must also leverage the unique benefits of the 3D experience in order to exploit the best of virtual worlds to address a specific requirement, or set of requirements.

Focus on Analysis

The purpose of the analysis phase in the ADDIE process model is to consider requirements or other issues that may provide direction on what, if any, instructional solution is necessary. Assuming an instructional solution is necessary, and once a virtual world tool is identified as part of a solution, then it comes down to deciding on which tool to use. (Certainly, due diligence is required in order to arrive at the previously mentioned assumed solutions.)

To get started, however, designers may benefit from asking these questions from the partial checklist shown in Figure 14-2 to reassess their preliminary conclusions.

186

Analysis Checklist

√   What learning goals does my current learning design fail to address? Or, where might the unique affordances of virtual worlds enhance my existing curriculum?

√   What specific instructional strategies are optimal at addressing the failed learning goals?

√   Using my current toolset, how can I design an intervention to implement the required instructional strategies?

√   Is there a gap between my current toolset and the instructional strategies I need to implement? If no, then use the appropriate tool from the current toolset. If yes, then consider new tools, such as virtual worlds.

√   With what existing instructional interventions must new tools or platforms interface?

Figure 14-2. ADDIE Analysis Phase Checklist. A thorough analysis checklist may assist in procurement decisions.

Deepening the Analysis

Since ADDIE is not intended be a detailed, step-by-step process model, the requirements analysis must also recognize the other considerations to take into account. Completing an IT infrastructure analysis, audience analysis, and a job/task/learning experience analysis are a few of the considerations that must be made. Each of these analyses will help to further identify and refine needs that will influence learning intervention solution and procurement decisions. Augmenting the ADDIE process model with Khan's e-learning framework may help identify most of the critical questions that should be addressed since ADDIE, in general, is neither detailed nor prescriptive.

Khan's e-learning framework is applicable to virtual worlds and augments the ADDIE process model by providing more detailed phases and specific steps than the ADDIE model. The eight dimensions of Khan's framework (Khan, 2005) represent areas requiring consideration early in the e-learning development process and revisited throughout the project's lifecycle as part of a continuous improvement strategy. These dimensions are critical to establishing a successful virtual world learning experience—whether it be an event or entire curriculum of events: institutional, pedagogical, technological, interface design, evaluation, management, resources support, and ethics. Each of the areas delineated in the framework must be examined before selecting a virtual world application (Voorhees & Dawley, 2008). The analysis phase must identify all limitations and restrictions in order to avoid acquiring a tool that cannot be used.

The ADDIE process model frames the method for identifying the performance problem; ensuring that the problem is, in fact, education or training related, and illuminating the various aspects of an organization that need to be factored into the overall learning strategy. Khan's framework, on the other hand, augments ADDIE by providing specific guidance on ADDIE vis-à-vis his eight dimensions. These eight dimensions help avoid missing any critical success factors when designing a learning project. Solution sets resulting from these analyses can be assessed only after the identified weaknesses in the training program are thoroughly identified.

Neglecting the analysis phase poses the same risks inherent in any solutions-based project, regardless of the anticipated outcome or desired solution. Requirements must drive solutions definition and tool adoption, and not the other way around. Virtual worlds, like any other tool, should be analyzed as an "enabler" for the specific solution, not as an end unto itself. In addition, affordances and potential uses of virtual worlds and other tools should be factored into the examination of prospective solution sets in order to select the solution with the highest probability of success.

Potential Uses

Starting with what we already know about course development and sequencing content may help instructional designers use virtual worlds to augment existing curricula and discover unique, meaningful uses of virtual worlds. The Virtual World Implementation Continuum shown in Figure 14-3 illustrates how virtual worlds can be used to support various components of a learning curriculum.

Virtual World Implementation Continuum

Figure 14-3. Virtual World Implementation Continuum. This figure illustrates the range of uses of virtual worlds in a learning program.

The Virtual World Implementation Continuum illustrates that there are multiple possibilities for how virtual worlds may be used in a learning environment. Whether applied in traditional, face-to-face classroom or e-learning settings, the unique affordances of virtual worlds can enrich almost any learning experience. Using virtual worlds in a learning context does not have to be an "all or nothing" proposition. Indeed, there is a risk of losing some of the inherent benefits of virtual worlds (persistence and community-building through co-existence and collaboration) when applied in an ad hoc manner; however, when the decision to use this implementation approach is confirmed, it should have little impact on the overall experience since the requirement did not underscore these specific affordances (persistence and long-term community-building) as critical for goals set forth in the needs analysis. A closer examination and understanding of each implementation option will help to refine the requirements even further.

Activity

Through the use of Immersive Activity Objects (also thought of as Discrete Learning Events), virtual worlds provide a platform for experiential activities that illustrate, for example, a concept that can be applied in a real-world scenario *in-world* or in context. This use of virtual worlds is supplemental and would be suitable for augmenting instructor-led or e-learning courses. Using virtual worlds in this manner adds another dimension to a blended-learning solution that gives learners the opportunity to conduct several higher-order thinking skills at once by using practice, replay, multiple perspectives, role playing, metacognitive analysis, review/dialog, and feedback. This use of virtual worlds could be compared to a simulation with the added dimensions of co-existence and persistence. A virtual world environment enables many participants serving in different roles as many times as they would like. The world remains as the group leaves it, facilitating review, analysis, and reflection. Imagine recording sessions and using them with different classes, offering participants the opportunity to consider multiple perspectives other than those presented in their immediate learning event. Imagine the benefit of having the opportunity to discover and/or solve another problem that resulted from the decisions made in the previously experienced event. In this sense, learning is not disjointed, but fluid—just like real life.

Module

Some content may benefit from having an entire immersive module. In these cases, the content is such that reading about it and discussing it alone doesn't provide a meaningful, memorable, personal understanding of it. For instance, experiencing a module on *Interacting with the Press* would have much more meaning than just reading one. What does it mean to: "Be careful about your choice of words when speaking to members of the press" or "Can seemingly innocent comments put people or a country at risk?" These concepts are not easy to express in words only. Crafting a realistic scenario wherein students can participate in and examine an interview from multiple perspectives would enable them to understand the complexities of both monitoring one's own words and behavior, and also being aware of the words and behavior of those surrounding them. Such a design requirement would also necessitate an opportunity for practice. Role-playing, in addition to observation, would be a useful exercise. Participants could be divided into teams to design a scenario. Afterwards, they could present their scenario, asking the observers to predict behaviors and outcomes as they go along. Learning facilitators could contribute by sharing real interviews from the Internet and discussing the salient issues. There are many options when there is an instructional need to provide first-hand experience in order to understand and construct personal knowledge about a given topic.

Lesson

Facilitating a lesson in a virtual world could be valuable if, for example, the main goal of the lesson is based on situated cognition. For instance, in a course on harassment (while students could read about the harassment laws, scenarios, and anecdotes) constructing a personal understanding would best come from experience. Build consequences into the scenario and the student motivation will likely peak as focus grows more intent. Sound like a game? This is no game, for in real-life, consequences result from our actions. It's better to learn how to analyze a scenario, identify a problem, and solve the problem in an environment where the cost of failure is lower than to experience them in real life where the cost is generally exponentially higher and more difficult to correct. In the case of experiencing the world of harassment within a virtual environment, on the other hand, failure simply provides more learning opportunities and increased knowledge transfer to the real world (Kolb, 1984, 1984b).

Course

A course or an extended learning experience is defined as a set of immersive events centered on an overall course goal and a specific set of learning objectives. Under what circumstances would it be useful to facilitate an entire course or extended learning experience in a virtual world? Virtual worlds would significantly benefit a course or learning experience whose objectives are bound to higher order thinking skills that require analysis, synthesis, and evaluation opportunities. A good example is viewing a "course" as an evolving group of learning experiences designed to help learners gain first-hand experience in analyzing defect detection; predicting outcomes of accurate and inaccurate detection skills; and testing alternate actions. Further, incorporating a knowledge support network in an extended learning experience by inviting subject matter experts, former learners, or participants representing multiple perspectives may build a community that could continue well after the formal "course" construct has come to an end rather than simply as a discrete set of learning experiences.

The group dynamic should not be underestimated (Johnson & Johnson, 1996), especially in virtual worlds, for it is a prime environment for many learners to come together simultaneously in a graphically rich, interactive context. In this case, learners continue to have access to an environment that could serve as an environment wherein they can refresh skills, volunteer as a mentor, and share real-life experiences. In addition, such a learning experience can provide instructors and learners more context and performance-specific feedback during the experience, rather than simply the didactic responses typically seen at the end of online instruction events. Since the feedback occurs during the learning process, rather than after, learners can analyze the feedback and make necessary modifications as they go through the experience. These are powerful benefits of immersive learning in virtual worlds.

Offering a course entirely in a virtual world brings with it many opportunities to challenge the way we teach and learn in order to work smarter. Given the technologies designed to improve productivity, access, and communication, it is time that the affordances of these technologies drive the way they are applied.

Program

An entire learning program is normally comprised of a variety of media and resources applied within a set of learning experiences designed to address multiple, related subjects. The main thrust of a program can benefit from having a virtual world as its central platform if higher order thinking skills, context, and/or access to experts are critical. Consider a "town hall, student union, cohort, or conference hall" metaphor. The virtual world could serve as a meeting place, learning platform, or a place organized around themes, which facilitators and participants generate, develop, and maintain. David Jonassen and colleagues (1995), leaders in constructivist learning theory and methods maintain that "constructivist environments engage learners in knowledge construction through collaborative activities that embed learning in meaningful context and through reflection on what has been learned through conversation with other learners" (p. 13). With this model, the interactions may be directly and indirectly evaluated within the community to understand a learner's individual performance. Instead, perhaps these interactions will be evident from the performance observed during the specific learning events or experiences comprising the overall course or program.

Conclusion

Virtual worlds promise to usher in new ways of teaching and learning. Building upon what we already know about teaching and learning in online environments is an important first-step when designing future studies to explore virtual worlds as learning environments. As societal expectations about learning and learning experiences continue to develop, meaningful, carefully designed applications of virtual worlds in formal training settings can help pave the way for the new ways of teaching, learning, communicating, interacting, and socializing. To get there, a good start is to begin with elements that are tried and true. What we know for sure is that if requirements are clearly defined and options are clearly understood, the chosen solution, at a minimum, stands a greater chance for success at its intended purpose. A thorough requirements analysis as a prerequisite may even yield results beyond our expectation, and that's a good thing

As is the case with other emerging technologies, such as social media (Fowler, this volume), intelligent tutoring systems (Hu, Graesser, & Fowler, this volume), mobile devices (Brown, this volume), and games (Xu, this volume), ADL must maintain an awareness of the power of these technologies, and of course virtual worlds, to enhance learning outcomes or increasing training efficiencies. This awareness must feed into future specifications, standards, models, services and architectures to achieve the ADL vision of the highest quality training and education delivered on demand. This is the future of e-learning.

References

Affiliated Computer Services. (2009). *3D learning and virtual worlds*. Dallas, TX: Author.

Association of Virtual Worlds. (2008). *The blue book: A consumer guide to virtual worlds* (4th ed.). Retrieved April 12, 2009 from http://www.associationofvirtu-alworlds.com/pdf/Blue%20Book%204th%20Edition%20August%202008.pdf

Bell, M. (2008). Toward a definition of "virtual worlds." *Journal of Virtual Worlds Research*, *1*(1), 2-5.

Calongne, C. (2008). Educational frontiers: Learning in a virtual world. *EDUCAUSE Review*, *43*(5). Retrieved April 2, 2009 from http://www.educause. edu/EDUCAUSE+Review/EDUCAUSEReviewMagazineVolume43/ EducationalFrontiersLearningin/163163

Dabbagh, N. (2008). *Select instructional models/theories to develop instructional prototypes*. Fairfax, VA: Instructional Design Knowledge Base, Graduate School of Education, George Mason University. Retrieved December 3, 2008 from http://classweb.gmu.edu/ndabbagh/Resources/IDKB/models_theories.htm

Dede, C. (2007). Reinventing the role of information and communications technologies in education. *Yearbook of the National Society for the Study of Education*, *106*, 11 – 38.

Dede, C., Clark, J., Ketelhut, D., Nelson, B., & Bowman, C. (2005). *Fostering motivation, learning, and transfer in multi-user virtual environments*. Cambridge, MA: Harvard Graduate School of Education. Retrieved July 12, 2009 from http:// muve.gse.harvard.edu/muvees2003/documents/Dede_Games_Symposium_ AERA_2005.pdf

Delwiche, A. (2003). *MMORPG's in the college classroom. The state of play: Law, games and virtual worlds*. New York, NY: New York Law School. Retrieved November 2, 2009 from http://www.nyls.edu/user_files/1/3/4/17/49/ Delwiche.pdf

Federation of American Scientists. (nd). *FAS virtual worlds whitepaper*. Retrieved March 20, 2009 from http://vworld.fas.org/wiki/FAS_Virtual_Worlds_ Whitepaper

Gamor, K. I. (2001). *Moving virtuality into reality: A comparison study of the effectiveness of traditional and alternative assessments of learning in a multisensory, fully immersive VR physics program*. Unpublished doctoral dissertation, George Mason University, Fairfax, VA.

Gao, F., Noh, J., & Koehler, M. (2008). Comparing student interactions in Second Life and face-to-face role-playing activities. In K. McFerrin, R. Weber, R. Carlsen, & D. A. Willis (Eds.), *Proceedings of Society for Information Technology and Teacher Education International Conference* (pp. 2033-2035). Chesapeake, VA: AACE.

Gartner Inc. (2007, April 24). *Press release: Gartner says 80 percent of active internet users will have a "Second Life" in the virtual world by the end of 2011*. Retrieved March 20, 2009 from http://www.gartner.com/it/page.jsp?id=503861%20

Gartner Inc. (2008a). *Press release: Gartner highlights 27 technologies in the 2008 Hype Cycle for Emerging Technologies*. Retrieved March 20, 2009 from http://www.gartner.com/it/page.jsp?id=739613

Gartner Inc. (2008b). Press release: Gartner says 90 per cent of corporate virtual world projects fail within 18 months. Retrieved March 20, 2009 from http://www.gartner.com/it/page.jsp?id=670507

The EDUCAUSE Learning Initiative. (2006, June). *7 things you should know about virtual worlds*. Retrieved June 2, 2009 from http://www.educause.edu/ELI/7ThingsYouShouldKnowAboutVirtu/156818

Institute of Electrical and Electronics Engineers. (nd). *IEEE islands in Second Life*. Retrieved May 3, 2009 from http://www.ieee.org/web/volunteers/tab/secondlife/index.html

Jackson, P. (2007, March 23). *The real business of virtual worlds: Firms creating new virtual worlds must balance real revenues with high risks*. Cambridge, MA: Forrester Research. Retrieved May 3, 2009 from http://www.forrester.com/Research/PDF/0,,44748,00.pdf

Johnson, D. W., & Johnson, F. P. (1996). *Joining together: Group theory and group skills* (6th ed.). Boston, MA: Allyn and Bacon.

Jonassen, D., Campbell, J., & Davidson, M. (1994). Learning with media: Restructuring the debate. *Educational Technology Research and Development*, *42*, 31-39.

Jonassen, D., Davidson, M., Collins, M., Campbell, J., & Haag, B. B. (1995). Constructivism and computer-mediated communication in distance education. *The American Journal of Distance Education*, *9*, 7-26.

Jonassen, D. H., Grabinger, R. S., & Harris, N. D. C. (1991). Instructional strategies and tactics. *Performance Improvement Quarterly*, *3*, 29-47.

Khan, B. H. (2005). *Managing e-learning: Design, delivery, implementation and evaluation*. London, UK: Information Science Publishing.

Khan, B. H. (2007). Flexible learning in an open and distributed environment. In B. H. Khan (Ed.), *Flexible learning in an information society* (pp. 1-17). Hershey, PA: Information Science Publishing.

Kolb, D. A. (1984a). *Experiential learning: Experience as the source of learning and development*. Englewood Cliffs, NJ: Prentice Hall. Retrieved April 29, 2009 from http://www.learningfromexperience.com/images/uploads/process-of-experiential-learning.pdf!(31.05.2006)

Kolb, D. A. (1984b). *Experiential learning*. Englewood Cliffs, NJ: Prentice Hall.

Nelson, B., Ketelhut, D., Clarke, J., Bowman, C., Dede, C. (2005). Design-based research strategies for developing a scientific inquiry curriculum in a multi-user virtual environment. *Educational Technology*, *45*(1), 21-27.

Rheingold, H. (1991). *Virtual reality*. New York, NY: Summit Books.

Virtual Worlds Review. (nd). What is a virtual world? Retrieved April 6, 2009 from http://www.virtualworldsreview.com/info/whatis.shtml

Voorhees, A., & Dawley, L. (2008, November). *Evaluating SL course experience: A learner's evaluation and faculty response*. Paper presented at the Annual Conference of Association for Educational Communications and Technology, Orlando, Florida.

Walker, V. (2009). 3D virtual learning in counselor education: Using Second Life in counselor skill development. *Journal of Virtual Worlds Research*, *2*, 13-14. Retrieved June 2, 2009, from http://jvwresearch.org/index.php?cms=1248927995.

Whiteside, A. (2002, September 4). Beyond interactivity: Immersive web-based learning experiences. *The eLearning Developers' Journal*, *3*. Retrieved April 6, 2009 from http://www.elearningguild.com/pdf/2/090402des-h.pdf

The Author

Keysha Gamor, PhD, is an Instructional Systems Designer (ISD) and Research Scientist at the Advanced Distributed Learning Initiative (ADL) for the Office of the Secretary of Defense. In this role, Dr. Gamor is responsible for developing ISD guidelines for emerging technologies, such as Web 2.0, 3DI, virtual worlds, and virtual reality.

Chapter 15

Why ADL Is Serious About Games
James Xu

The learning, education, and training communities are facing challenges, and opportunities, not seen before. The young adults entering the workforce were raised in environments surrounded by an arsenal of consumer electronics ranging from cell phones to gaming consoles and much in between. Not only were they constantly learning how to use and interconnect these devices, they were also figuring out how to apply these technologies for personal entertainment, communications, and everyday activities (Prensky, 2001). These digital natives bring with them expectations of learning that incorporate advanced interactive and immersive technologies with learning experiences that were at times self-centered and at other times socially contagious.

In order to meet the expectations of these digital natives, those responsible for providing learning, education, and training must determine how to infuse the techniques, structures, and formats of new technologies into training and education practices. In order to take advantage of their digital upbringing, we need to merge interactive technologies, such as games and simulations, with a learner-centered pedagogy in which learners are given more control over learning goals, methods, and resources (Garris, Alhers, & Driskell, 2002). The purpose of this chapter is to discuss the application of serious games within the Advanced Distributed Learning (ADL) Initiative. The overarching aim is to take advantage of the power of serious games in a manner that is consistent with the functional requirements of ADL—accessibility, interoperability, durability, and reusability. In the context of the ADL business paradigm (Wisher, this volume), this chapter concerns first the pedagogical influence of games on future instructional designs and second its affect on future models of interoperability.

The Realm of Serious Games

ADL focuses on advancing technologies in learning, education, and training primarily through a continual cycle of understanding what others are learning, researching, developing, and disseminating. The technology known as serious games is among several immersive technologies that ADL is focusing on; others are discussed elsewhere (Gamor, this volume; Fowler, this volume; Hu, Graesser, & Fowler, this volume). This chapter discusses how game and simulation technologies, especially serious games, may be used effectively in learning and training environments. It further discusses the options for integrating serious games into the ADL scheme for interoperability.

To understand serious games, we must first take into account the entire spectrum of interactive media that range from games to simulations, as depicted in Figure 15-1.

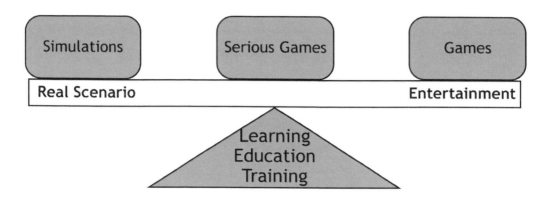

Figure 15-1. Spectrum of interactive media. This figure depicts the wide range of interactive media.

On the right end of the spectrum, there are games built for the purpose of entertainment. Players can fly strange looking spaceships that are beyond imagination, fire powerful weapons that don't exist in reality, soar through the sky on the backs of creatures that could only belong to another planet, and possess super-human abilities that no man could ever dream of. A child with a physical disability can compete in a 100-meter sprint with other children in game worlds, an experience not possible in real life.

The main goal of these games is to let users step out of the real world and immerse themselves in the game world to have fun and to make their fantasies come true. Games, then, are simulations that emphasize entertainment that is engaging and immersive, but often at the expense of realism. As Gee (2003) argues, playing such games helps learners grasp meaning, learn to follow commands, and develop a sense of identity.

Simulations

On the opposite end of the spectrum, there are simulations built to closely resemble specific aspects of the real world for the purpose of training and rehearsal. In contrast to games, simulations emphasize realism at the expense of entertainment. Users can simulate the take-off and landing of a Boeing 747 jumbo-jet anywhere in the world by operating realistic looking on-screen controls, the performance of a medical procedures on critically injured soldiers in combat zones, and the management of chaotic evacuations caused by natural or man-made disasters. While learning and practicing real world operations and procedures in a virtual space may not be as entertaining as playing games, it could be the best thing trainees can do to prepare themselves for the workplace.

Serious games reside in the middle of the spectrum and share the characteristics of both ends of the spectrum. Unlike games meant for entertainment alone, they are designed for the purpose of learning, education, and training. The "game" in serious games indicates that serious games use game design principles and methodologies to offer immersive environments and engaging interactivities. The "serious" in serious games indicates that serious games are built not just for fun and entertainment. Their goal is to use the game as a vehicle to deliver a message, content, or experience that can be applied in the real world. Thus serious games are interactive media that teach a lesson, provide an experience, or deliver a message through an engaging immersive environment.

In comparison to traditional learning activities addressing comparable learning objectives, game players exhibit higher levels of effort and motivation (Tennyson & Jorczak, 2008). When learners are engaged in the learning process, they learn better and retain knowledge longer. Serious games offer the best of both worlds— learning through engagement! Conferences, such as the Games, Learning and Society Conference co-sponsored annually by the Academic ADL Co-Lab, are devoted to the scholarly underpinnings of serious games and how game technologies can enhance learning, culture, and education. Significant investments are being made in bringing gaming to the education and training enterprise.

Serious Games for Learning, Education, and Training

Why should serious games be considered as a learning tool? To answer this question, let us first examine the characteristics of the digital-native learners for whom video games are part of life. According to a Pew study of American teenagers (Pew Internet & American Life Project, 2008b),

- 99 percent of boys and 94 percent of girls play video games

- 80 percent of teens play five or more different game genres, and 40 percent play eight or more types of games

- 65 percent of game-playing teens play with other people who are in the room with them

- 27 percent of game-playing teens play games with people with whom they connect through the Internet

The Pew study supports the popular belief that most teenage boys play video games. At the same time, the numbers indicate that teenage girls are almost equally active in playing games. Another very important aspect of this study is that, contrary to the popular belief that teen game players are less social, teenage gamers treat gaming as social experiences. These numbers confirm that most teen learners today are fully aware of, well prepared for, and very comfortable with immersive technologies, and that serious games can be an effective tool for learning.

But teens are only a part of the total audience in the learning, education, and training space. In corporate training and continuing education, adult learners seek new knowledge and skills, better career opportunities, or higher work productivity. Compared to teens, are adults ready to use new technologies such as serious games in their learning process? Another study showed that 81 percent of adults aged 18 to 29 years played games, and 23 percent of adults aged 65 years or older played games (Pew Internet & American Life Project, 2008a). These numbers confirm that interest in interactive media, such as serious games, is strong across generations. Advances in integrating serious games into education and training practices can be beneficial to learners of all ages.

Fitting Serious Games in the Learning, Education, and Training Space

To answer the question of "Do serious games fit in the space of learning, education and training?" we need to think about the characteristics of both learning and games to determine if game design principles can be effectively melded with pedagogy. As children, we learn how to play games; as we grow up, we learn through playing games, even though the "play" doesn't feel like "play" sometimes. Even serious events like wars have some characteristics of game play. Education has many traits of game play as well. We play out world events in classrooms, for example. Using game design principles, game designers seem to have found a way of getting people to learn by making learning engaging and enjoyable.

Most adult learners bring life-long experiences they can apply, problems they want to solve, and motivations and commitments that drive them forward. They learn best with a hands-on, problem-solving approach that enables them to apply the new skills and knowledge immediately. As an interactive media, serious games reflect the principles of engagement, goals, rules, and challenges. The challenges in serious games could represent problems learners want to solve and the competition they face during the process; the rules could provide directions and guidance to learners; the engagements could allow learners to immerse themselves in the learning process; and the goals could show learners the values and achievements of learning. Clearly, a well designed serious game can offer learners enjoyable learning experiences through game play.

These principles parallel many principles of adult learning theory. For example, Knowles (1970) has established that adults learn experientially, want relevancy, learn best when learning is of immediate value, tend to be self directed, and approach learning as problem solving. But this is just one side of the equation. What about the messages that serious games are meant to deliver, or the lessons that serious games are designed to teach? Are serious games a suitable media for delivering good learning from the instructional design point of view?

Models of Motivation

In Keller's ARCS model of motivational design (Keller, 1987), there are four components for promoting and sustaining motivation in learning: attention, relevance, confidence, and satisfaction.

Attention. The first step in the learning process is to get learners' attention. Without this step, learning cannot take place. Additionally, their attention must be maintained throughout the learning process.

Relevance. In order to maintain learners' motivation, learning content must be relevant to learners' past experiences and future needs.

Confidence. Learners gain confidence when they experience success through a series of challenging tasks.

Satisfaction. Learners are rewarded by reaching goals of the learning process.

Keller's ARCS model has been taught and/or applied in 17 different countries, and has been used both to enhance existing instructional materials and to develop new materials. The model has been proven to work well across delivery systems and across cultures (Shellnut, 1996). Serious game design principles resemble many of the features of Keller's ARCS model in promoting learner motivation.

Motivation in Traditional Online Instruction

Unfortunately, the high level of motivation engendered by games is not always present in traditional online instruction, thus the interest by ADL in incorporating gaming features. The ADL Co-Lab has conducted baseline research that tracked changes in motivation across modules of a course.

Instruction that includes a gaming component to enhance motivation has clear advantages over traditional online instructional methods. There are many things to consider during the instructional design process, but serious games are well positioned as a vehicle to engage and motivate learners, and that's what we were looking for on the other side of the equation. Do serious games fit in the space of learning, education, and training? The answer is yes.

Do Serious Games Work in the Space of Learning, Education, and Training?

For years, serious games have been designed for, and used by, various industries and organizations and include military games, government games, educational games, business games, healthcare games, political games, religious games, art games, and others (Bergeron, 2006; Michael & Chen, 2006). The *Taxonomy of Serious Games* (Sawyer & Smith, 2008) gives us a great overview of the serious game landscape as presented in Table 15-1.

Table 15-1

A Taxonomy of Serious Games

	Games for Health	Advergames	Games for Training	Games for Education	Games for Science and Research	Production	Games as Work
Government & NGO	Public Health Education & Mass Casualty Response	Political Games	Employee Training	Inform Public	Data Collection / Planning	Strategic & Policy Planning	Public Diplomacy, Opinion Research
Defense	Rehabilitation & Wellness	Recruitment & Propaganda	Soldier/ Support Training	School House Education	Wargames / Planning	War Planning & Weapons Research	Command & Control
Healthcare	Cybertherapy / Exergaming	Public Health Policy & Social Awareness Campaigns	Training Games for Health Professionals	Games for Patient Education and Disease Management	Visualization & Epidemiology	Biotech Manufacturing & Design	Public Health Response Planning & Logistics
Marketing & Communications	Advertising Treatment	Advertising, Marketing with Games, Product Placement	Product Use	Product Information	Opinion Research	Machinima	Opinion Research
Education	Inform about Diseases/Risks	Social Issue Games	Train teachers / Train Workforce Skills	Learning	Computer Science & Recruitment	P2P Learning Constructivism Documentary?	Teaching Distance Learning
Corporate	Employee Health Information & Wellness	Customer Education & Awareness	Employee Training	Continuing Education & Certification	Advertising / Visualization	Strategic Planning	Command & Control
Industry	Occupational Safety	Sales & Recruitment	Employee Training	Workforce Education	Process Optimization Simulation	Nano/Bio-tech Design	Command & Control

With roots in the Department of Defense and military services, ADL has a keen interest in the development of military games. Here are some of the examples:

U.S. Army. America's Army is one of the most well known and successful military games. It was designed and developed originally for recruiting purposes and was later on used for training.

U.S. Air Force. MyBase was initially designed for public awareness, recruiting, educational gaming, and to share learning across the Air Force. Its expansion plans include medical and technical training (Gardner, 2009).

U.S. Navy. Battle Stations 21 uses a trainer that is a ¾ scale mock-up of a naval ship, housed in a building. It is used to provide new recruits with a series of highly realistic naval ship simulations over a 12 hour period. Recruits are tested on their teamwork and on the basic skills they need when reporting to their first ship (Gardner, 2009).

U.S. Marine Corps. The Deployable Virtual Training Environment (DVTE) is composed of a computer hardware suite and 17 software applications that leverage computer gaming, simulation, and visualization that enable Marines to focus on developing their tactical decision making skills while refining their tactics, techniques, and procedures (Gardner, 2009).

All have received positive feedback from servicemen and women and the general public.

Outside the DoD and based on more than 2,000 data points from three college level business, economics, and management classes, Blunt (2006) demonstrated that serious games not only work well in education, they have profound impacts on the learning process by engaging learners through an enjoyable learning experience, resulting in superior learning outcomes.

Serious Games Design Considerations

Although there is evidence that serious games are effective, merging learning and playing is not an easy task. It presents challenges to both instructional designers and game designers. Instructional designers and game designers usually approach their specialties from different perspectives, presenting challenges to collaborating on creating learning content. Instructional designers are often perceived to take a boring approach to the delivery of content. Game designers are, on the other hand, sometimes accused of being more concerned about fun than serious about learning. To a certain degree, these observations may be true and the cause may be found in the different focuses inherent in instructional design and game design. Instructional design is outcome driven. Learners reach their objectives though understanding and memorization, and are measured by a set of test scores. Game design is interaction centric. Learners reach their objectives through game play, storytelling, and are measured by their achievement levels. Even though instructional designers and game designers use different design approaches, their goal is the same—to deliver the content and knowledge to learners. So, how can they work together? When serious games are used to deliver certain topics and enhance learning experiences, they have to be designed for and contribute to the overall learning requirements. Instructional designers should focus on defining those requirements while game designers should be focusing on designing the most suitable game plays and mechanics to meet those requirements. Instructional designers should think of serious games as a new media selection—an interactive and engaging media—in addition to graphics and videos, when designing learning instructions.

Unlike big title entertainment games which target hardcore gamers, the target audiences of serious games are learners. Serious game designers should not assume that learners all have the most advanced gaming hardware; the design focus should be on the message that is to be delivered in the games, not on special effects. Bigger is not necessarily better in the world of serious games. Many serious games are designed as mini-games that deliver very specific content.

Most importantly, serious games are designed for learning, while making learning engaging and enjoyable. If learners simply have fun while missing the messages that serious games are designed to deliver, the design has failed!

Fitting Serious Games into ADL

ADL has always been in the forefront in finding, defining, developing, adopting, applying, and advancing standards, specifications and cutting-edge technologies in learning, education, and training. ADL's process includes discovery, learning, research & development, and dissemination. Its goal is to enable effective and efficient training that is available anywhere and anytime. It constantly seeks new ways to improve the quality of training, shorten the time to train, and reduce the cost in training operations. Serious games are among several immersive technologies that ADL is studying to determine their potential as learning technologies. ADL is especially concerned with instructional design considerations using immersive technologies, interoperability among multiple learning environments, and performance/competency-based assessments. It is likely that complex learning scenarios may integrate multiple types of delivery methods.

To examine the potential of integrating games into learning, we have to understand the differences and similarities of both systems technically. At a high level, Learning Management Systems (LMSs) and Massive Multi-player Online Games (MMOGs) are similar in terms of system architecture. Both systems contain three main components:

The Server-Side Component
This component stores content and user profile information, manages content delivery mechanisms, and processes complex logic for user progression. Server-side functions between LMSs and MMOGs are very similar. Table 15-2 shows a comparison of one key server-side function between SCORM-compliant LMSs and MMOGs.

Table 15-2

Comparison of Server-Side Functions Between SCORM and Game Design

SCORM Sequencing	Game Level Design
Launch content to learner	Deliver a level to player
Track learner progress	Track skills and scores
Determine next in sequence	Determine next challenge
Locate and launch next content	Load and deliver next level
until all objectives are reached	until highest level is reached

The Client-Side Component

  This component has a straightforward function—to interact with the user—but it has also has a direct impact on the user. Designs of effective learning content and designs of an engaging game for learning are manifested in the client-side. Table 15-3 provides a comparison of key functions between SCORM content and game design.

Table 15-3

Comparison of Client-Side Functions Between SCORM and Game Design

SCORM Content Design Considerations	Game Design Considerations
Learners	Players
Objectives	Goals
Assessments	Scoring
Media types & navigations	Game play & AI
Colors & layouts	Scene rendering

The Communication Component

  The functions of the communication component are similar between SCORM-conformant LMSs and MMOGs, but the way they are implemented is different. The differences are presented in the table below.

Table 15-4

Comparison of Communication Functions between SCORM and Game Design

SCORM Communication	MMOG Communication
Browser based	Proprietary clients
API defined	Whichever way we like
Data model defined	Whatever the game needs
Client-side activities	Both client-side & server-side

As we can see, the major difference between a SCORM-conformant LMS and a typical MMOG is in the implementation of communication between the client and its server. In order to be SCORM-conformant, the client has to be Web browser-based, the data transfer has to use a SCORM defined API (application programming interface), and only the SCORM-conformant data elements are allowed in the communication. These requirements set some limitations on what type of client we can build. But on the other hand, as long as we act within the SCORM requirements, we can do anything we like to serve the learning needs. There are several ways to integrate game and simulation components in a SCORM-conformant LMS environment.

Develop games that run in a Web browser. All game play activities have to happen inside the browser. Any data element that is sent to the server has to go through SCORM API calls. Since games run in a browser, there is no difference to the communication and server components than when processing a regular Web page. Today, the most common platform for building games using this methodology is Adobe Flash. A game built with Adobe Flash can be delivered from the server as if it were a regular Web page; all activities are executed inside the browser, and the Adobe ActionScript can interface with SCORM API easily. LibSCORM, a JavaScript library developed by the Academic ADL Co-Lab, makes the communications between Adobe ActionScript and the SCORM API even easier (Academic ADL Co-Lab, 2009).

Develop games that open a Web browser within them. These can be stand-alone games running outside a browser. During certain game plays, when learning content is needed, a browser session or multiple browser sessions can be launched within the game and learning content is delivered to those browser sessions. Since learning content is still delivered to Web browsers, even though running inside a game, there is no difference to LMSs that deliver the learning content. The development considerations should be given to interactions between the game and the browser sessions within it so the correct learning content can be delivered at the right time.

Develop games that communicate with SCORM LMS servers without using a Web browser. Since no browser is used, this implementation breaks the LMS limits set by SCORM. In order to make this to work, a special component has to be set up between the game client and LMS server to handle the communication so the game will operate without a browser and the LMS server will receive SCORM-conformant API calls and data elements. Sponsored by ADL, BBN Technologies developed a prototype to demonstrate such integration of a military simulation with SCORM. In this prototype, a pair of Web services was used to handle the communications (BBN Technologies, 2007). This research work removed certain limitations in SCORM and opened doors for broader integration of games and simulations with SCORM.

Conclusion

Through the "growing up" of the game industry, serious games have defined themselves with real purposes and have shown potential in delivering real meaning while offering engaging and enjoyable experiences. They may not replace teachers in classrooms and trainers in the field, but they will be effective tools for learning, education, and training. Serious games bring us challenges as well. To unleash the potential of serious games, a new set of technical skills and infrastructures should be planned and acquired. Even though learners are ready for the change, additional resources need to be put in place in order to develop learning materials that can take advantage of serious game technologies. Subject matter experts who understand the design of serious games are the key to success. Finally, it will take an attitude and culture shift in society to realize the full value of this emerging technology.

At ADL, serious games are one of the several immersive learning technologies that we are focusing on as learning technologies of the future. Today's young learners are the driving force of the future. To teach them, you have to understand them. They will not change for the world, so, the world has to change for them. Because, it's their world!

References

Academic ADL Co-Lab. (2009). *LibSCORM*. Retrieved December 10, 2009, from http://www.academiccolab.org/libscorm

Blunt, R. (2006). *A causal-comparative exploration of the relationship between game-based learning and academic achievement: Teaching management with video games.* Unpublished doctoral dissertation, Walden University, Minneapolis, Minnesota.

Gardner, D. (2009, March). *Immersive training for DoD today and in the future.* Paper presented at the Defense User's GameTech Conference, Orlando, FL.

Garris, R., Alhers, R., & Driskell, J. E. (2002). Games, motivation, and learning: A research and practice model. *Simulation & Gaming, 33*(4), 441-467.

Knowles, M. S. (1970). *The modern practice of adult education: From pedagogy to andragogy.* Englewood Cliffs, NJ: Prentice Hall.

Michael, D., & Chen, S. (2006). *Serious games – Games that educate, train, and inform.* Boston, MA: Thomson Course Technology PTR.

Pew Internet & American Life Project. (2008a). *Adults and video games.* Retrieved August 9, 2009, from *http://www.pewinternet.org/~/media//Files/Reports/2008/PIP_Adult_gaming_memo.pdf.pdf*

Pew Internet & American Life Project (2008b). *Teens, video games, and civics*. Retrieved August 9, 2009, from *http://pewinternet.org/~/media//Files/Reports/2008/PIP_Teens_Games_and_Civics_Report_FINAL.pdf.pdf*

Prensky, M. (2001). *Digital game based learning*. New York: McGraw-Hill.

Sawyer, B. & Smith, P. (2008, February). *Taxonomy of serious games*. Paper presented at the Games Developers Conference, San Francisco, CA. Retrieved August 9, 2009, from http://api.ning.com/files/jq93AYyGqPSBsMNqAVB08HNSYjwv4yvwE8gwXh6yiD0_/seriousgamestaxonomy2008.pdf

Shellnut, B. (1996). *John Keller: A motivating influence in the field of instructional systems design*. Detroit, MI: Wayne State University.

Tennyson, R. D., & Jorczak, R. L. (2008). A conceptual framework for the empirical study of instructional games. In H. F. O'Neil & R. S. Perez (Eds.), *Computer games and team and individual training* (pp. 3-20). Amsterdam, the Netherlands: Elsevier.

The Author

James Xu is a member of the Immersive Learning Technologies team at the ADL Co-Lab Hub in Alexandria, Virginia.

Chapter 16

ADL and Mobile Learning Opportunities
Judy Brown

One of the early graphics used by the ADL Initiative in 2000 depicted a collection of Sharable Content Objects being assembled in real-time and on-demand to meet the needs of a learner, who may be situated anywhere. A worker is seen grasping a personal digital assistant device, being trained, seemingly just in time. ADL anticipated a world where learning materials would someday be available anytime and anywhere. The technology for such access was not quite ready in 2000, and the necessary infrastructure was not yet in place. Today, however, the possibilities are much more tangible because the systems are in place and are largely operational, making the opportunities all very exciting. Indeed, the original mobile paradigm of *anywhere, any time* has changed to *everywhere, all the time* – or on-demand.

Mobile devices have become ubiquitous, with more than four billion devices in everyday use around the globe at the end of 2009, and use of them is certain to continue to grow. Connectivity is available almost everywhere—even in very remote areas—and new learning and performance support initiatives using mobile devices are being implemented worldwide. There is a digital revolution taking place today—in our hands. The number of mobile phone users has overtaken the number of non-users, according to the United Nations telecommunications agency. That means more than half the people on the planet now have cell phones, versus 12 percent in 2000.

Institutions and businesses that built durable modular learning content that conforms to SCORM (Gallagher, this volume), as recommended by ADL, can often reuse relevant modules on mobile devices for reach-back or recall at critical learning moments, such as during job performance. Since small, highly granular learning chunks work well on mobile devices, much existing modular content can easily be used today using a mobile browser.

The purpose of this chapter is to examine the opportunities for learning on demand that mobile devices make possible. In the context of the ADL business paradigm (Wisher, this volume), this chapter describes the push of pedagogy and instructional design made possible by the mobile learning impetus. Secondly, this chapter concerns the external marketplace that has already formed and discusses how ADL can play a role in furthering the quest for on-demand learning.

Mobile Learning Defined

E-learning is generally referred to as distributed learning in the military services of the United States. This definition includes distance learning other than pure correspondence, computer-based training delivered over a network, and Web-based training. The instruction can be synchronous, asynchronous, instructor-led, computer-based, or a blended combination.

Mobile learning, or m-learning, is learning that happens when the learner is not at a fixed, predetermined location, or learning that happens when the learner takes advantage of the learning opportunities offered by mobile technologies. Some marketing firms define mobile learning as "knowledge transfer events, content, tools, and applications, built using mobile information architecture and accessed on handheld computing devices" (Ambient Insight, 2009, p. 16).

A learning management system (LMS) is software for delivering, tracking, and managing training or education. LMSs include a wide range of systems. LMSs can manage training and educational records, distribute courses over the Internet, and offer features for online collaboration. With the improvement in mobile browsers, many LMS courses are already available through mobile devices, and it is unlikely that there will be mobile LMSs anytime soon. Rather, LMSs will be accessible through mobile browsers, connected to content through a back end. Within SCORM 2004 4th Edition, a mobile device can gain access to shared information about a Sharable Content Object, allowing a learner to continue progress on a mobile device with Internet access to the LMS even when unable to use more conventional devices such as laptop computers.

Why is Mobile Learning Important?

The importance of mobile learning is growing for several reasons, including cost and its unmatched capability of reaching a significant portion of the world's population. It is inexpensive when compared to traditional learning, and even some forms of e-learning, so its potential for return on investment is tremendous. Furthermore, it is as far-reaching as there are people with mobile devices. Mobile devices are also becoming more personal, with the capability of recognizing the user, the location, and the user's preferences. Leaders in the field, such as Seymour Papert, founding faculty member of the Massachusetts Institute of Technology Media Lab, recognize that it is not possible to teach people everything you know. Rather, it is better to position them where they can access what they need to know when they need to know it.

Effective use of mobile learning technologies can bring us closer to improved personalized learning—delivering the right materials, to the right person at the right time and in the right place. The trends, as seen in late 2009 when this chapter was prepared, indicate increased and growing usage. According to some analysts, the global market for mobile Web 2.0 technologies may quadruple from 2009 levels to exceed $22 billion in 2013. Some estimate that one out of every seven minutes of media consumption today takes place via mobile devices with 19 million mobile Web users in the U.S accessing the Internet on a weekly basis. Industry researchers expect mobile usage to grow by 60 percent over the next two years and that nearly 75 percent of workers will be mobile by 2012. These estimates demonstrate the enormous potential of m-learning for workforce training and education. A recent survey by the Pew Internet & American Life Project predicts that by the year 2020, most people across the world will use a mobile device as their primary means for connecting to the Internet (Rainie & Anderson, 2008). Mobile technology is also being integrated into traditional educational environments.

Experts increasingly view training in terms of being continuous, ongoing, and flexible, and the trend is towards using a cell phone for "prosthetic knowledge."

Dr. Conrad Gottfredson, an industry consultant, has identified what he refers to as the "Five Moments of Learning Needs," which mobile devices are perfectly suited to meet. These moments are:

- When learning for the first time.

- When wanting to learn more.

- When trying to remember.

- When things change.

- When something goes wrong.

The effectiveness of mobile learning in terms of learner satisfaction is another positive sign for the future of m-learning. Dana Koch, a learning architect, notes that overall user satisfaction ratings on their mobile courses averaged 4.4 on a 5.0 scale—compared to a 4.0 learner satisfaction rating, on average, for the computer-based versions of the same compliance courses (Boehle, 2009). It is yet to be determined whether these ratings will continue long-term, or if this satisfaction is a result of the learners appreciating the easy access to the materials when it is convenient for them.

Mobile Devices for Learning

There are numerous choices for mobile devices already being carried by the majority of the population; however, the focus should be on the capabilities and increased opportunities for mobile learning and job performance support as the devices continue to evolve and improve.

Whatever devices learners carry today, they will most certainly be different tomorrow. Clearly it is easiest to implement mobile learning in environments where all users have the same type of device, but mobile browsers have improved enough to be very useful for delivering learning materials, regardless of the device's make and model. The most common devices currently in use include:

BlackBerry devices. These have been the most common DoD devices deployed to date. These are also very common in corporate learning. Kristofor Swanson, global human resource mobile strategy lead at Merrill Lynch claimed: "Using BlackBerry smartphones to deliver learning has been so effective that participants now take their courses in about 45% less time, saving about four to six hours in lost productivity per annum. These employees have also scored higher on competency exams than their colleagues studying in a traditional online format" (Intuition, press release, 2008).

The iPhone. This device has also been widely adopted. The iPod Touch is also a viable option and offers most of the capabilities of the iPhone, but without the monthly charges for cellular coverage. It is amazing to realize that the processing power of the iPhone and similar devices today equal or exceed enterprise systems of the 1960s.

Other mobile devices. Other mobile devices that are used in the U.S. include Windows Mobile, Google Android, and Palm devices. Most offer many of the same features of the BlackBerry and iPhone. Although Nokia makes the most widely used devices in the world, these devices have yet to create a significant market in the U.S.

Amazon's Kindle and the Sony Reader Digital Book. These are e-book readers that are options for textbooks and manuals, but they do not support interactivity at the same level as BlackBerry, iPhone, and similar devices. Game and music-related mobile devices such as those made by Sony and Nintendo are also used for learning.

These different, though related, devices often include capabilities such as voice recorders, cameras, scanners, readers, and Global Positioning Systems (GPSs) that may not be available on computers currently used for e-learning. It is interesting to think about the possible increases in learning opportunities and in learning engagement if all learners had access to the capabilities of mobile devices such as these. The opportunities for learning and engagement are increased significantly when learners have mobile devices in their pockets for use whenever there is time available for learning, or when specific needs arise. Mobile devices offer the processing and connectivity of a computer, the audio and video features of media players, and the communication capabilities of a telephone or computer.

Mobile Learning Experiences

The bottom line when it comes to m-learning is that ultimately it is about capabilities, not devices; about the learning experience, not the technology itself. Mobile devices afford new opportunities for learning, and do so at a cost that is a fraction of the costs of devices such as laptop computers. As noted m-learning expert Ken Carroll observed, "But perhaps even more fundamental is the nature of online or mobile learning themselves. I'm seeing a lot of people trying to stuff old educational habits into new Web 2.0 clothes, but it tends not to work. In the same way you would not film a newspaper and put the contents on TV, learning objects for new media have to be designed for the purpose. I don't see many start ups who are getting this part right" (Carroll, 2008).

Table 16-1 *Types of Mobile Learning Activities.*

Assessment	Content	Mobile Options	Performance
Quiz	Review/remember	On demand	Job aid
Alerts	Audio recordings	Location specific	Checklist/procedures
Survey	Video recordings	Simulation	Decision support
Test	On-demand access	Game-based	Coaching/mentoring
Poll	Field guide	Augmented reality	Conferencing
Feedback	Reference	Capture/share	Reminders
Point-in-time check	Presentations Assignments Updates	Geo exploration Reporting Note taking	Translation Transcription

When people first discover m-learning, they tend to think in terms of miniaturized e-learning. However, m-learning offers a great deal more than simply a miniaturized form of e-learning. The advantages of m-learning include:

e-Learning (Lite). M-learning is the best choice for short learning content for initial learning or reach back.

Performance support. Mobile devices are the best choice for serving as job performance aids for use when and where needed. This includes on-the-job support, access to information, education and reference, podcasts, updates, alerts and checklists, and collaboration. Mobile devices provide access to experts when and where needed for coaching, mentoring, and social networking.

Assessment. Mobile devices can easily be used for study aids; flash cards for materials that must be mastered, and used for assessment through quizzes, tests; surveys and polls; and certification

Innovation. There is a continuous process for identifying and exploring new opportunities afforded by mobile devices. Among these are games and simulations, location-based learning, augmented reality, and personalization.

User generated content. Users generate content that may include collection of data, notation of changes, and feedback.

e-Books. Mobile devices make e-books, texts, and reference materials immediately available.

Sami M. Leppänen, former Head of Learning Solutions at Nokia, notes that mobile learning should positively differ from e-learning by being more personal, more networked, and more fun, as well as offering interactivity, and spontaneity.

Pocket SCORM

The earliest initiative combining SCORM standards with mobile learning came from m-learning experts at Tamking University in Taiwan (Lin et al., 2004). Lin and colleagues created a system for early versions of SCORM 1.2 and made it freely available for Pocket PC devices, calling it Pocket SCORM.

The experts at Tamking University, which hosted ADL's second International Plugfest in 2006, understood the potential for growth of mobile devices in delivering distance education courses. They focused on the issues of transferring PC-based SCORM to a Pocket PC-based system. Pocket SCORM Architecture is able to operate even when the mobile device is physically disconnected from the network, without losing any student's learning record. Collected records are retained and then sent back to the LMS, which runs at the sever side, after the device is back on online.

Taiwan's TransAsia Airways is among the corporate adopters of Pocket SCORM. It implemented Pocket SCORM to provide on-demand training to their pilots during wait times between flights. The technology enabled the pilots to study for their required monthly licensing tests during their downtime while awaiting airline schedules.

Implementing m-Learning

Currently, the most common usage of mobile devices and learning is providing medical and language content in the private, civil, and military sectors.

Medical Training

Several military medical schools in the United States have adopted mobile devices for learning, most using podcasts and references. Sheppard Air Force Base in Texas is the Air Force's largest training facility. The Base has transferred its medical training regimen from the multiple textbooks used by students to one small, portable device. Each corpsman can now use a mobile device to access any needed information during training, as with textbooks, but more quickly and efficiently, and can carry it with them into the field, which they cannot do with textbooks. Retaining continuously updated references with the most current treatment guidelines, even when deep in the field away from other hard-wired technology, is invaluable for helping them succeed in providing top medical care.

Air Force training experts also note that using this technology has decreased the course attrition rate from 26 percent to 9 percent and that the use of the devices decreases medical errors by providing easy access to references for medications. The healthcare industry has been a leader in finding applications for mobile devices. According to Sam Adkins (2008), "The most sophisticated innovations in mobile learning are emerging from the healthcare industry, which will have a significant impact on mobile learning in the U.S. and across the globe, particularly in the area of patient education." In the future, mobile devices may be used for electronic prescriptions, and for patient education.

Language Acquisition
　　Mobile devices that are used as language translators have proven to be a valuable tool. An early translator program was used years ago to teach sign language to students. Today, mobile devices help U.S. soldiers serving in the Middle East as well as United Nations peacekeepers in the Horn of Africa. One provider emphasizes a "declarative first" approach to language learning, and provides a suite of language tools in both audio and video formats on iPod Touch, and iPhone devices. Recently, mobile devices have provided users with the option to "see" live usages of a word or phrase in a specific language via Twitter comments.

　　In addition to medical and language applications, the U.S. Defense Ammunition Center has created a mobile version of their *Ammunition Multimedia Encyclopedia: The Complete Munitions Tool*, which enables users to explore image details, shipping information, and other related materials. This mobile version ensures that the most up-to-date munitions information is always at hand.

　　The United Kingdom's Royal Army has also successfully implemented mobile technology in delivering language materials to soldiers in Iraq and Afghanistan using iPods. Soldiers often prefer loading the materials onto their own devices, so CDs were deployed to theater for transfer. Learners should be given access to training, resources, and learning in a format that they will use and digest willingly. The Royal Army also deployed Nintendo DS devices with much success. Initially, they were used to provide courses in basic math skills and incorporate "brain-training" concepts. The U.K. Royal Army is also creating materials that incorporate soldiers' input in combination with familiar military topics to provide examples and questions.

　　The Royal Army has also deployed materials for vehicle maintenance and electronic performance support systems for vehicle electricians, which enabled them to work on equipment in the field even when they had not seen the equipment before. Content was loaded on to digital cards and sent for insertion into the Nintendo devices.

　　The Canada ADL Partnership Lab is also exploring mobile learning and performance support. They partnered with the Royal Canadian Mounted Police to successfully mobilize their "Investigator's Toolbox," which gives them online access to warrant templates, instructions, policies, relevant laws, and additional resources they need to collect data in the field.

Future Capabilities

　　There are several technology capabilities that have great promise for increasing learning opportunities. Some have already been implemented in academic labs and by groups outside the United States. These include two dimensional (2D) codes, biometrics, context awareness, Femtocells/Picocells, Long Term Evolution, Machine-to-Machine, Near Field Communication, projection chipsets, sensors, and spacing learning. Cloud computing also lessens complex processing requirements.

2D Code. A QR Code is a matrix code (or two-dimensional bar code) created by a Japanese corporation in 1994. The QR is derived from "Quick Response," as the creator intended the code to allow its contents to be decoded at high speed. QR Codes are common in Japan, where they are currently the most popular type of two-dimensional codes. Moreover, most current Japanese mobile phones can read this code with their camera.

Biometrics. Security applications that verify a person's identity based on their physical attributes, such as fingerprint readers or iris scanners, have been in use for some time. Recently, biometric security has started to appear in mobile phones, personal digital assistants, and notebook computers where the need for miniaturization represents a technological challenge.

Context aware. In computer science this refers to the idea that computers can both sense and react based on their environment. Devices may have information about the circumstances under which they are able to operate and, based on rules or an intelligent stimulus, react accordingly. For example, a context-aware mobile phone may "know" that it is currently in the meeting room, and that the user has sat down. The phone may conclude that the user is currently in a meeting and reject any unimportant calls.

Femtocells/Picocells. These are small, indoor base stations that are not intended for public access, but are used for wireless communications within small areas such as a home or an airplane (femtocell) or in slightly larger areas such as one floor of an office building or airport terminal (picocell). Analysts predict that these small base stations for wireless communications will be one of the fastest growing areas of mobile communications in the next few years, and that there will be more than 100 million users worldwide, with Europe being among the strongest markets

Long Term Evolution (LTE or 4G). Long Term Evolution is the last step toward the 4th generation of radio technologies designed to increase the capacity and speed of mobile telephone networks. The current generation of mobile telecommunication networks is collectively known as 3G (third generation).

Machine-to-Machine (M2M). M2M refers to data communications between machines. M2M is most commonly translated as Machine-to-Machine but has sometimes been translated as Man-to-Machine, Machine-to-Man, Machine-to-Mobile, and Mobile-to-Machine. Among cellular telephone service providers, M2M means Mobile-to-Mobile, and describes calls that do not involve landlines. Like all evolving technologies, its definition also continues to evolve, but it generally refers to telemetry or telematics that is accomplished using networks, especially public wireless networks.

Projection chipsets. This capability enables mobile devices to integrate tiny, onboard projectors, so that viewing is no longer confined to a tiny screen, but enables content to be easily viewed on a wall.

Sensors. Sensors provide the capability for noting and recording nearly any bit of datum (or giant sets of data). Mobile devices can act as sensors in a larger system, for nearly any desired goal.

Spacing learning. Academic researchers have long been aware of the phenomenon that delivering learning over time generally improves retention—the "spacing effect." Mobile tools can reinforce important knowledge with the use of spaced testing or reminders. Several vendors are currently exploring the potential for this application for mobile learning devices.

Benefits and Caveats

Mobile learning can offer continuous, ongoing, flexible learning opportunities that are relevant as well as readily available. In addition, it has the potential to enable reflection, can provide both informal and formal learning, offers personalization capabilities, and may also support optimum spacing of learning for retention.

At the same time there are some concerns that do need to be addressed, including issues related to connectivity, cost, data charges, device ownership, security, and changing technology.

Prevailing definitions of mobile learning will continue to evolve. The Mobile Learning Network (MoLeNET), the U.K.'s largest mobile learning project, defines mobile learning as "*the exploitation of ubiquitous handheld technologies, together with wireless and mobile phone networks, to facilitate, support, enhance, and extend the reach of teaching and learning. Learners involved may or may not be mobile. Learning can take place in any location, and at any time, including traditional learning environments, such as classrooms, as well as other locations including the workplace, at home, community locations and in transit*" (MoLeNET, 2010).

Currently, there is a tendency to think of m-learning in terms of e-learning, but there are many other types of mobile learning. Today some e-learning is already being accessed through mobile computer browsers through LMSs using SCORM, but not all content is available. The most common issue concerns Flash-based content that is not supported on most U.S. mobile devices today.

Going forward, the global ADL community must address the mobile learning needs as the industry moves more towards the dynamic and often virtual environments of cloud computing. Some questions to be addressed include tracking, content registry, and security:

Tracking. Does all mobile learning material need to be tracked? If not, what does?

Content registry. Should mobile content be registered in a repository if it is already available as a full course?

Security. Although mobile learning has been in the background since the early days of the ADL Initiative and the development of SCORM, it is only now being implemented seriously in military pilot projects. These implementations highlight questions related to security, ownership of devices, and appropriate usage.

Mobile Learning and Standards

Mobile options are a part of the learning architecture and there is a compelling need to address standards for mobile learning. As ADL moves forward with efforts to harness the potential of the next generation of technology-based learning, it is certain that mobile learning will play an increasingly large role in the broad world of distributed learning.

References

Adkins, S. S. (2008). *The US market for mobile learning products and services: 2008-2013 forecast and analysis*. Monroe, WA: Ambient Insight. Retrieved from http://ambientinsight.com/Resources/Documents/AmbientInsight_2008-2013_US_MobileLearning_Forecast_ExecutiveOverview.pdf

Ambient Insight Research (2009). *Ambient Insight's 2009 Learning and Performance Technology Research Taxonomy*. Monroe, WA: Ambient Insight Research, LLC.

Boehle, S. (2009, September). Don't leave home without it. *Training Magazine*. Retrieved from http://www.nxtbook.com/nxtbooks/nielsen/training0909/#/32

Carroll, K. (2008, August 20). Please, sir, where are the education start-ups? Message posted to http://eu.techcrunch.com/2008/08/20/please-sir-where-are-the-education-start-ups/

International Association for Distance Learning (n.d.). Glossary of distance learning terms. Retrieved from http://www.iadl.org.uk/glossary.htm

Intuition (2008, May 29). Intuition and Merrill Lynch recognized for mobile learning innovation. *PRZOOM*. Retrieved from http://www.przoom.com/news/34917/

Lin, N. H., Shih, T. K., Hui-huang Hsu, H., Hsuan-Pu, C., Han-Bin, C., Wen Chieh, K., & Lin, L. J. (2004). Pocket SCORM. Distributed computing systems workshops, 2004. In *Proceedings of the 24th International Conference* (pp. 274-279).

mobiThinking (2009). Mobile web: Latest facts and stats forecast a rosy outlook | mobiThinking. Retrieved from http://mobithinking.com/blog/latest-mobile-stats

Mobile Learning Network (2010). What is mobile learning? Retrieved from http://www.molenet.org.uk/

Rainie, L., & Anderson, J. (2008, December 14). *The future of the internet III.* Washington, DC: Pew Research Center. Retrieved from http://www.pewinternet.org/Reports/2008/The-Future-of-the-Internet-III.aspx

Savill-Smith, C., Attewell, J., & Stead, G. (2006). *Mobile learning in practice.* Retrieved from http://www.lsneducation.org.uk/user/order.aspx?code=062526

Shih, T. K., Lin, N. H., Hsuan-Pu, C., & Kuan-Hao, H. (2004). *Adaptive Pocket SCORM Reader. Proceedings of the IEEE 2004 International Conference on Multimedia and Expo, ICME 2004.*

Additional Reference Resources

Ally, M. (2009). *Mobile learning transforming the delivery of education and training.* Retrieved from http://www.aupress.ca/books/120155/ebook/99Z_Mohamed_Ally_2009-MobileLearning.pdf

Brown, J., & Metcalf, D. (with Christian, R.). (2008). Mobile learning update. *Elliott Masie's Learning Consortium Update.* Retrieved from http://www.masieweb.com/p7/MobileLearningUpdate.pdf

Burnett, R. (2009, July 22). Vcom3D's iPod translator device is a valuable tool for U.S. soldiers. Retrieved from http://www.physorg.com/news167499348.html

EDUCAUSE. *2009 Horizon Report.* Retrieved from http://www.educause.edu/ELI/2009HorizonReport/163616

Garreau, J. (2008). Get smart. *The Wilson Quarterly.* Retrieved from http://www.wilsoncenter.org/index.cfm?fuseaction=wq.essay&essay_id=497267

ILearn No. 2, iPods in the Classroom, Spring 2009. Retrieved from http://issuu.com/ktenkely/docs/ilearn_2?mode=embed&layout=http%3A%2F%2Fskin.issuu.com%2Fv%2Flight%2Flayout.xml&showFlipBtn=true

Mobilize, don't miniaturize. (2008). Retrieved from http://patterns.littlespringsdesign.com/index.php/Mobilize_Don%27t_Miniaturize

Mobile-Barcodes.com (n.d.). *QR-Code readers.* Retrieved from http://www.mobile-barcodes.com/qr-code-software/ *Conference, 1,* 325-326.

Thalheimer, W. (2007, June). *Spacing learning over time: A research-based secret.* Paper presented at ASTD Annual Conference, San Diego, CA. Retrieved from http://astd2007.astd.org/PDFs/Handouts for Web/M105.pdf

Web Resources

Ambient Insight Research. http://ambientinsight.com

Mobile web: Facts and statistics. http://mobithinking.com/blog/latest-mobile-stats

Mobile Learning Blog Content Community. http://cc.mlearnopedia.com

Mobile Learning News and Resources. http://mlearnopedia.com

The Author

Judy Brown is an education technology consultant and a member of the ADL Initiative's Immersive Learning Technologies team. Previously she was Director of the ADL Academic Co-Lab in Madison, Wisconsin.

Section IV

IMPLEMENTATION STRATEGIES

Chapter 17

ADL Implementation – U.S. Department of Defense

Kristy Murray and Dean Marvin

The U.S. Department of Defense (DoD) is a leading implementer of the ADL Initiative. The ADL Initiative was created to remedy a specific challenge within DoD, the lack of interoperability of distributed learning content that inhibited the sharing of that content within and between the military Services. The advantages of using technology, in terms of learning efficiencies and outcomes, were not being realized, and the benefits of reusing what others had developed were being lost. The implementation of ADL within the DoD, however, required more than just the right interoperable technology. The challenges went beyond the technical, encompassing cultural and policy issues, as noted by the Government Accountability Office in a report that examined the early phases of ADL (GAO, 2003).

The purpose of this chapter is to describe the challenges of implementing ADL within the DoD and the specific activities and programs undertaken to meet these challenges. Hopefully, the description can aid other agencies, organizations, and governments facing a similar circumstance. Within the context of the ADL business paradigm, this chapter addresses sector relationships and the creation of a market demand (Wisher, this volume). On the technical side, it explains the development of prototypes that exemplify applications of ADL technologies not available in the marketplace.

The perspective on implementation is that of the Joint ADL Co-Lab in Orlando, Florida, which has prime responsibility for realizing the ADL vision within the DoD components. Why Orlando? Orlando is home to the four major Services, plus the Coast Guard, formed into an inter-Service military body that supports acquisition and technical excellence in modeling and simulation, distributed learning, training systems, and human performance, referred to collectively as Team Orlando. Team Orlando provides senior-level guidance and direction to the joint modeling and simulation requirements and prioritization process, senior-level guidance, and interaction to facilitate cross-pollination of technologies, and integration and processing of lessons learned as they relate to training and instrumentation issues in support of Service requirements and initiatives.

Culture and Policy

In 2002, the Government Accountability Office (GAO) initiated a review to understand the expectations of DoD for the ADL Initiative, its implementation status, and major challenges affecting program implementation. The GAO is an independent agency that works for the U.S. Congress, and is tasked with investigating how the federal government spends taxpayers' dollars, although this particular review was conducted as an internal study. The technical challenges and issues discussed in the GAO report are addressed elsewhere in this volume, such as the development of SCORM (Gallagher, this volume) and its limitations, the ADL Registry of learning content (Lannom, this volume), and fielding military skills content (Camacho, West, & Vozzo, this volume).

An important cultural issue specified in the report relates to organizational resistance to changing individual training from delivery in traditional, instructor-led classroom training to delivery by technology. Those administering the schoolhouses that provided traditional classroom training were reluctant to change to ADL delivery since funding and infrastructure were tied to counts of students in those classrooms. At the time, 2002, the commitment of senior leadership to implementing new training delivery technologies across the military Services varied, but there was an overall preference for the traditional schoolhouse training. Overarching policy that specifically addressed the use of ADL was in the early stages of formulation, with the consequence that the military Services did not then have high-level direction on which to base their internal regulations.

That lack of direction began to change in 2006 when the DoD issued an official instruction requiring the use of ADL technologies throughout the Department of Defense. The instruction, DODI 1322.26, entitled "Development, Management, and Delivery of Distributed Learning," was a major turning point in the implementation of ADL technologies (Freeman, this volume).

Change Agents

The implementation of SCORM and other ADL Initiative projects within the DoD required, in addition to policy, the use of change agents. The change agents took several actions along four lines to foster efforts leading to widespread adoption of ADL technologies. These change agents included providing training in SCORM, funding the prototype program, providing collaborative environments for testing and refining the technologies, and establishing technical "tiger teams" within the DoD to solve technical issues which appeared to restrain interoperability. The change agents were formally organized through an ADL action team. The ADL Initiative also supported programs and policies that encourage those in the federal government, academic, and private sectors to collaborate with the ADL Initiative in developing and advancing the technologies.

Training in SCORM

Training in SCORM is collaboratively provided by the ADL Co-Labs. SCORM training for DoD organizations has been a part of sector relationships and the efforts of tiger teams. Training takes multiple forms including conference tutorials, online courses and examples, onsite or hosted tutorials, helpdesk services, and guidelines and best practices.

Conference tutorials. Members of the ADL team have provided SCORM training at conferences. These usually take the form of tutorials on the first day of the conferences where in-depth discussion can occur.

Online courses. Online courses have been created and shared as SCORM courses to serve as both training and examples. Courses are available for those new to ADL as well as for those implementing advanced features. The Academic ADL Co-Lab has been a critical source of SCORM training and includes online courses in its curriculum.

Onsite and hosted tutorials. In addition to conference tutorials, members of the ADL team provide tutorials in the offices of DoD organizations. ADL has also hosted DoD organizations for SCORM training in ADL labs.

Help desk services. A significant source of training for those implementing SCORM has been the help desk services of the ADL Web site. Access to the ADL Help Desk is available via email or phone. Upon receiving a request for help, the ADL Help Desk personnel will triage the request. They may be able to respond to an easy question promptly, while a difficult question that requires coordination, and in-depth research may take longer. All requests are tracked to ensure timely responses. Responses typically include examples, documentation, references, step-by-step processes, and/or expert dialogue directly with the requestor.

Guidelines and best practices. ADL publishes Guidelines and Best Practices periodically to enhance the development of interactive and engaging, Web-based instruction. Examples include:

- The original *ADL Development Guidelines*, published in 2002.

- The *Instructional Planning Guide for Content Developers and Project Managers*, published in 2002. This Guide provided the community with templates and samples of instructional, multi-media, Web page, and graphics design and development processes.

- The *ADL Guidelines for Creating Reusable Content with SCORM 2004*, published in 2008, is the latest version of evolving "assistive" products produced by the ADL Initiative. This version was provided in CD format to all those registered for ImplementationFest 2008, and is accessible for download on the ADL Web site (Deibler & Berking, this volume).

Software libraries. The Open Platform for e-Learning (OPEL), depicted in Figure 17-1, is a by-product of the prototype program. OPEL is a collection of libraries, tools, and services for building distributed, cross-platform, SCORM-conformant software. It can provide the basic building blocks of any software designed to work with the SCORM standard. Employing a highly modular design, tools written using OPEL can work cooperatively and simultaneously on the same underlying data. OPEL provides integrated services such as a content repository, a run-time environment, an ADL Registry client, and a "Unified Object Model," and supports versions of SCORM back to Version 1.2.

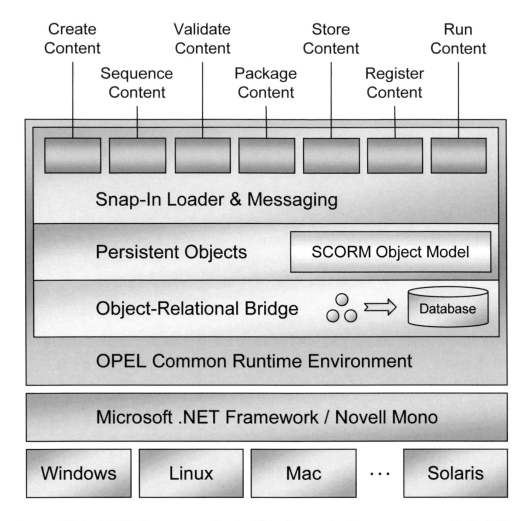

Figure 17-1. OPEL Component Stack. This figure depicts components for building SCORM-conformant software.

ADL Prototype Program

Another change agent for facilitating SCORM implementation was a program to develop and test prototypes. The ADL Initiative launched a formal prototype program in 2000, with the inception of the Joint ADL Co-Lab in Orlando, Florida. JADL contracted and managed a research and development program from 2000-2007 that produced several prototypes to integrate ADL technologies and further the mission of the ADL Initiative. The intention of the prototype program was to spur the interest of industry in building systems and tools compatible with the specifications and standards promoted by the ADL Initiative. In addition to being compatible with ADL specifications and standards, prototypes needed to address Service-specific issues and requirements.

The JADL highlighted the majority of completed prototypes during select conferences and continually seeks sponsors who will further the research efforts in order to develop marketable applications and products.

The prototypes from this seven-year program generally fall into one of three categories. Each of the categories represents a time period associated with a particular focus:

- 2000-2003. Provide incentives to promote SCORM development within the Services.

- 2003-2005. Investigate advanced capabilities such as repository/registry mechanisms, SCORM sequencing, and simulations.

- 2005-2007. Focus on integrating capabilities into a system-of-systems architecture.

Initial Incentives

During the first few years of the prototype program, prior to 2003, the process focused on ensuring funding across the Services. The program did not clearly define prototype topics, and some awards were granted simply to meet the requirement to ensure the participation of each Service. A later evaluation of this process showed that it caused several problems. The program produced several proprietary products that did not have any real potential for transition, and there was redundancy in some of the work—without any real success or value-added to ADL research and development. Furthermore, although the selected prototype efforts each had a military sponsor, in many cases the sponsor failed to carry the research forward.

Advanced Capabilities

Several successful prototypes focused on advanced capabilities to extend or fully use the ADL specifications and standards. These prototypes focused on simulations, the ADL Registry system, estimating the costs of developing SCORM content, and providing language and culture training with animated mentors.

The Civil Support Team Trainer (CSTT), a collaborative, distance learning system used by the National Guard, helps developers create interactive courseware and simulations. In 2003, the JADL Prototype Program funded further development of the CSTT, to research the possibility of launching a multi-user simulation from a SCORM-conformant learning management system (LMS), while tracking and assessing student performance and communicating those results through SCORM. This effort succeeded in launching CSTT from a sharable content object (SCO). It tracked student performance by aggregating events within the CSTT simulation and communicating with SCORM global objectives.

The ADL Registry Client application was a 2005 prototype that received additional funding in 2007. The focus of this effort was to develop an open source tool to monitor changes of learning content objects that are formally registered with ADL

Registry (Lindsey, Pisel, & Pike, 2006). The product has since transitioned directly to the ADL Registry work (Lannom, this volume).

The Content Complexity Measurement Tool, COCOMO-SCORM (Garnsey, Edwards, Ward, & Marvin, 2006) is another prototype that is still creating interest. The research question for this effort was, *"How much does it cost to develop a SCORM course?"* The developed prototype is a distributed learning cost estimation tool to estimate the development efforts and associated costs for developing SCORM-based content. The Software Technology Support Center at Hill Air Force Base in Utah, the Submarine Learning Center in Groton, Connecticut, and the Naval Air Systems Command, Orlando, Florida, have used this tool and have expressed interest in taking over sponsorship for government use.

The Online Mentors for Cultural Familiarization and Language Training Organization was another successful 2003 project. The Naval Postgraduate School and the Defense Language Institute in Monterey, California, worked with industry to develop this capability. This project addressed the potential for ADL to provide online cultural training and sought to determine the effectiveness of animated mentors for language and cultural training. A paper on this research was presented at the International Training and Education Conference (ITEC) in 2005, and the effort has transitioned to another government program sponsored by the Defense Advanced Research Projects Agency. ITEC is Europe's largest and most established defense training and simulation conference and exhibition. Industry has now developed a proprietary tool to enhance this training application, a language trainer that is down-loadable via an i-Pod, used successfully by the U.S. Army.

System-of-Systems Integration
The JADL developed the JADL 2012 Integrated Prototype Architecture (IPA) to provide an abstract framework focusing on systems integration. The IPA is a "system-of-systems" architecture that addresses the issues of integrating the SCORM and other ADL technologies at the enterprise level within and among organizations throughout the world. The IPA is not a prototype, but it evolved from the prototype effort as a preliminary model designed to help guide the prototype process. Furthermore, the IPA is NOT a representation of what future policies or revisions to the SCORM may require of learning management systems or other SCORM-conformant tools, systems, and content. The JADL 2012 IPA simply represents one possible problem space that can be used as a sounding board for the types of research that occur within the JADL Prototype Program.

Many of the prototypes during this time period focused on integrating capabilities. A key focus was integrating didactic and experiential training. Weil, Marvin, and Travers (2007) developed a series of workflows (or templates) that illustrate the variety of instructional possibilities inherent in integrated didactic/ experiential training. A technical implementation of such integrated didactic and experiential training using SCORM was the focus of a prototype by Travers, Roberts, and Marks (2007). This prototype used the World Wide Web Consortium (W3C) Web services standards (including XML, SOAP, and Web Services Description Language) to provide communications among the SCORM Run-Time Environment, the new Distributed Training Event Coordination Service, and training systems.

One of the goals of the Integrated Prototype Architecture was to support the development of independent components that could easily be integrated to form a capability through Web services. The training systems used in these prototypes represent one kind of independent component. An independent assessment engine is another example. A 2007 prototype by Smith, DuBuc, and Marvin (2007) developed an assessment data model to capture complex assessment data across multiple learning and training systems for analysis and processing by an independent assessment engine.

Plug & Play Research Environments

The JADL offers multiple research and testing environments. It established its first ADL Plug & Play lab in September 2002. While the focus of the lab has evolved over time, the intent to give our partners an environment for testing distributed learning tools and processes in an open laboratory setting remains. These test environments offer a variety of learning management systems, games, development/authoring tools, and tools such as the Open Platform for E-Learning (OPEL) and the Sample Run-Time Environment; some developed via the JADL prototype program. The labs providing these capabilities include the Learning Technology Lab, the Joint ADL Developers Environment, and the Training Technology Center.

Learning Technology Lab

The ADL Co-Lab Hub in Virginia hosts the Learning Technology Lab. The Lab enables developers to test course content in a closed-network. This environment includes a variety of learning management systems that are currently used by the U.S. Military Services as well as academia and industry. The Lab provides the opportunity to test for compliance and/or functionality of SCORM content. This is a capability accessible virtually from any location.

The Learning Technology Lab welcomes government and contractors who are developing content for use by the government, and permits developers to use government-owned and other exemplar authoring tools to help in the development of cutting-edge content, assessments, graphics, etc.

Training Technology Center

The JADL Co-Lab hosts the Training Technology Center, which is a central location for testing, developing, and showcasing the newest innovations in Gaming and Virtual Worlds (Xu, this volume; Gamor, this volume). The Center makes it possible to easily explore ways to integrate immersive technologies with the current field of LMS technologies. The Center has two main focus areas, the Game-based Training Testbed and the Virtual World Testbed.

Game-based Training Testbed. This testbed houses both high-end computers and the newest console systems, providing a perfect environment for testing and experimenting with the newest game applications and development tools. The Testbed has a full suite of game software, including examples of current generation game-based training applications, commercial products that have been modified to build Serious Games, and modifiable games that could potentially be used in the development of future Game-based Training applications.

The Virtual World Testbed. This testbed houses Virtual World technologies and platforms. The Virtual World Testbed is fully networked and capable of running any Virtual World software or servers for applications from low-fidelity browser-based solutions to fully immersive augmented reality-based applications of virtual worlds. The Virtual World Testbed also supports ADL's Second Life Island and JADL's installation on the Team Orlando Island as part of the Military Coalition in Second Life. Second Life is a popular virtual world accessible through the Internet, used by individuals and organizations that include corporate, academic, government, and a spectrum of private entities. Second Life users have the option to buy a private island, or islands, which are used for a variety of purposes that include business, politics, education, and special projects. Users may buy their own island, or may join with others to buy an island together for collaborative projects. The JADL is also working with Joint Forces Command, Defense Acquisition University, and the developer of Nexus to move toward a browser-based implementation of Nexus. Nexus has been adopted by several government agencies for developing virtual world environments for a variety of government training scenarios.

Sector Relationships and Tiger Teams

From its inception in 1997, the ADL Initiative worked in close coordination with DoD organizations. Implementation could not be assumed but must rather be planned in a collaborative manner. This section describes the key activities underpinning the planning, beginning with an ADL action team established to represent Service interests. The ADL action team played a vital role in establishing current ADL policy. To help carry out policy and promote ADL, the Joint ADL Co-Lab formed numerous agreements with various DoD organizations for a myriad of uses. These include Memoranda of Understanding, Memoranda of Agreement, and Cooperative Research and Development Agreements. These agreements are the basis for mutual sharing of information, sharing usage of the Co-Lab spaces, sharing research efforts, and other forms of collaboration. On occasion, these agreements led to the formation of tiger teams that provided focused assistance to DoD organizations. Two of these tiger team efforts are described below.

Defense Nuclear Weapons School

ADL entered into an agreement with the Defense Nuclear Weapons School to help the school transform their training from exclusively instructor-led to a blended program using ADL technology. The school faced increased demand, which greatly exceeded their classroom capacity—with some courses having a three-year waiting list of potential students. The tiger team provided an analysis of content, made strategic recommendations, and assisted in the initial transformation efforts.

Joint Strike Fighter Program Office

To help carry out the DoD Instruction 1322.26, ADL provided tiger teams to work with DoD Acquisition Categories I and II programs. ADL collaborated with the Joint Strike Fighter program, a large acquisition program, to provide SCORM training, instructional design assistance, access to plug & play research environments, and assistance with selecting system software.

Defense ADL Action Team

The Defense ADL Action Team (DADLAT) advises and assists the DoD with the goal of ensuring that DoD personnel have access to cost-effective, high-quality education and training, tailored to individual needs, whenever and wherever required. The Action Team is chartered by and responsible to the Office of the Deputy Under Secretary of Defense for Readiness. The DADLAT was formerly known as the Total Force ADL Action Team. While the format is similar, the membership of the DADLAT is more closely aligned to the policy and implementation partners from each of the Services. Furthermore, the DADLAT scope is much broader and encompasses all aspects of ADL.

Historically, the Action Team has served as a means to convene distributed learning agencies and organizations to discuss ADL issues. Action Team meetings allow participants to share problems and discuss possible solutions in an open forum, providing a continual collaborative process as ADL was adopted across DoD. The current membership and set of responsibilities are described below.

Membership

The participating members are representatives of DoD entities with interests in distributed learning. There are at least two representatives from each Service. One representative is from a Military Service Headquarters and provides input at the policy level. A second member from each Service focuses on implementing ADL technologies and/or training development products. Membership consists of representatives from the Military Services (with Reserve Components), the National Guard, the Joint Forces Command, and the Joint Forces Staff College.

Responsibilities

The primary responsibilities of DADLAT include:

- Serving as Service focal point for distributed learning policy, practices, and procedures.

- Providing a forum for discussion and resolution of practical issues in implementing ADL technologies.

- Serving as a forum for discussion and resolution of policy and practical issues in ADL implementation.

- Promoting Service collaboration on ADL efforts.

- Recommending DoD and ADL research and development priorities.

- Assisting in identifying metrics for evaluating ADL use.

- Promoting the use of ADL in education and training programs.

Conferences

Hosting and participating in select conferences are critical to providing SCORM training. Conferences bring together implementers of ADL, and assist other groups in formulating a strategy for implementing ADL and e-learning approaches to training and education. In addition to hosting ADL Plugfests, ADL hosts an annual ImplementationFest and regularly participates in the Interservice/Industry Training Simulation and Education Conference and the International Training and Education Conference. Each of these conferences serves a different purpose, as described below.

ImplementationFest

Each year, the JADL hosts a conference called ImplementationFest. ImplementationFest convenes a unique gathering of military, industry, and academic education/training professionals who focus on learning about and discussing new distributed learning capabilities that support the U.S. military forces. The hands-on experiences of the conference participants combined with the opportunities for networking, learning military insights, learning about the future of ADL, and meeting informally make this conference the premier event for the Department of Defense distributed learning community.

Networking. Providing opportunities for informal networking may be ImplementationFest's greatest value—a venue to establish and strengthen networks of people and ideas in the DoD distributed learning community. ImplementationFest facilitates a rich environment for face-to-face meetings with interdisciplinary teams of professionals that facilitate collaboration of efforts.

Military insights. ImplementationFest is a great opportunity to share and explore knowledge about what the Services are doing, and to learn what perspectives they share on where they are heading in the future in such areas as distributed learning technologies, research, methodologies, and organization. Attendees appreciate the informative military presentations and find much value in the Services providing distributed learning challenges.

The future of ADL. Attendees also appreciate the opportunity to hear leaders discuss their respective fields of modeling and simulation and instructional technology, and to learn of current and future efforts that are pushing the frontier of distributed learning.

ImplementationFest is an ideal venue for bringing together the ADL community for the purpose of educating, discussing, and, in general, furthering the overall goals of the ADL Initiative and Training Transformation. The ImplementationFests began in 2002 and have been a big part of the ADL implementation plan. The first year, ImplementationFest included approximately 40 people, and most participants were local. ImplementationFest expanded each year and now attracts an international audience of more than 300 participants.

Interservice/Industry Training Simulation and Education Conference (I/ITSEC)

I/ITSEC is an annual conference that, "…promotes cooperation among the Armed Services, Industry, Academia, and various Government agencies in pursuit of improved training and education programs, identification of common training issues, and development of multiservice programs." (I/ITSEC, 2010). Initiated in 1966 as the Naval Training Device Center/Industry Conference, the conference has evolved and expanded through increased participation by the Army, Air Force, Marine Corps, Coast Guard, and Industry. In 2009, I/ITSEC included 607 exhibiting companies and approximately 20,000 visitors, registered attendees, and exhibitors. Approximately 50 percent of the registrants were from government.

I/ITSEC is an important part of the ADL Initiative's annual efforts. Not only has the ADL Initiative hosted numerous booths during past conferences, but more importantly, I/ITSEC has provided a platform for presenting research papers, information updates, tutorials on SCORM and the ADL Registry, and other topics of interest to the Initiative. ADL Initiative team members who attend I/ITSEC learn what other organizations are doing in the realm of distributed learning/training, and forge relationships with key military and industry partners.

International Training and Education Conference (ITEC)

ITEC is Europe's largest and most established Defence Training and Simulation Conference and Exhibition. It is essentially the European equivalent of the I/ITSEC conference. ADL has provided tutorials and sessions at ITEC focused on discussing the current status of SCORM, the ADL Registry, and the Content Object Repository Discovery and Registration/Resolution Architecture. ITEC provides an opportunity to collaborate with European colleagues on ADL implementation.

Summary

Implementation of ADL throughout DoD has been at the forefront of the ADL Initiative's vision of providing access to the highest quality education and training, tailored to individual needs, delivered cost effectively, anywhere and anytime. The organizational resistance to shifting individual training from the classroom to delivery by technology in the early phases of ADL, noted in the Government Accountability Office report (GAO, 2003), has largely been overcome as evidenced by more than ten million course completions in a single year (Wisher, this volume). The training in SCORM, the ADL prototype program, the Learning Technology Lab, the Implementation Fests, and the Defense ADL Action Team have all contributed to mitigating the resistance to change.

The Joint ADL Co-Lab, working closely with the other U.S. and Partnership Co-Labs, has been instrumental in moving the DoD closer to success in achieving the ADL vision. Its ability to respond to technical issues through specialized tiger teams and to host specialized seminars has provided essential skills and knowledge to those at the front edge of implementation. The ADL Initiative deals beyond the technical aspects of interoperability and instructional design, realizing the importance of supporting its user base.

References

Garnsey, M., Edwards, L., Ward, K., & Marvin, D. (2006). COCOMO and SCORM: Cost estimation model for Web-based training. *Proceedings of the Interservice/ Industry, Training, Simulation & Education Conference (I/ITSEC) 2006.*

Interservice/Industry, Training, Simulation & Education Conference (2010). Retrieved February 23, 2010 from http://www.iitsec.org/

Lindsey, A. M., Pisel, K., & Pike, W. Y. (2006). The ADL Registry Client: Solving the currency issue of content reuse. *Proceedings of the Interservice/Industry, Training, Simulation & Education Conference (I/ITSEC) 2006.*

Office of the Deputy Under Secretary of Defense (Readiness) (2000). *Department of Defense implementation plan for Advanced Distributed Learning.* Washington, DC: Author. Retrieved from http://prhome.defense.gov/docs/ adl_implementplan.pdf

Smith, B., DuBuc, C., & Marvin, D. (2007). Learner assessment data models for standardizing assessment across live, virtual, and constructive domains. *Proceedings of the Interservice/Industry, Training, Simulation & Education Conference (I/ITSEC) 2007.*

Travers, V., Roberts, R. B., & Marks, J. (2007). A Web service architecture for integrating didactic and experiential learning. *Proceedings of the Interservice/ Industry, Training, Simulation & Education Conference (I/ITSEC) 2007.*

U.S. Government Accountability Office (2003). *Military transformation: Progress and challenges for DOD's Advanced Distributed Learning programs* (GAO Publication No. GAO-03-393). Washington, DC: Author. Retrieved from http://www.gao.gov/new.items/d03393.pdf

Weil, S. A., Marvin, D., & Travers, V. (2007). Integrating didactic and experiential training: Round pegs in square holes? *Proceedings of the Interservice/Industry, Training, Simulation & Education Conference (I/ITSEC) 2007.*

Web Resources

Interservice/Industry, Training, Simulation & Education Conference (I/ITSEC). http:// www.iitsec.org/

Team Orlando. http://www.teamorlando.org

The Authors

Dr. Kristy Murray is the Director of Advanced Distributed Learning (ADL) Co-Laboratories. Based at the Joint ADL Co-Lab in Orlando, Florida, Dr. Murray oversees operations of both the ADL Co-Lab Hub in Alexandria, Virginia, and the Joint ADL Co-Lab.

Dean Marvin is a retired Marine Lieutenant Colonel who works as a Senior Military Analyst at the Joint Advanced Distributed Learning Co-Lab, in Orlando, Florida, where he leads Research and Development efforts.

Chapter 18

ADL and Federal Agencies

Paul Roitman Bardack, George Koch, and Reggie Smith III

Distance learning has the power to move a country from the industrial age to the information and knowledge age for a brighter future for all. It has the power to better prepare members of the armed forces, the government workforce, students, consumers, and life long learners for the challenges ahead. Although earlier forms of distance learning, such as correspondence courses, have existed in the United States for more than 120 years, the Internet has brought distance learning to a new phase. To many in the profession it is a phenomenon with incredible potential.

The Internet produced an explosion in online learning that was quickly embraced throughout the learning, education, and training communities. Governments at the federal and regional, and provincial or state levels have been leading users (Holden & Westfall, 2006). How a nation implements online learning varies at the different levels of governance. Academia and industry have their own internal policies and practices. The government can play an important role in fostering partnerships and collaborations across sectors that can ultimately lead to wide use at a lower cost.

Research studies have been quite consistent in reporting the no-significant-difference phenomenon (Russell, 1999). That is, general use across all forms of distance learning in which the human instructor is not physically present leads to learning outcomes between the distance learning treatment and a classroom control group that are at least equivalent. When using computers or the Web in well-designed, self-paced instruction, the Rule of Thirds applies—learning outcomes can increase by one-third or training time can be reduced by one-third (Fletcher, this volume).

In higher education, distance learning is providing undergraduate and advanced degree programs to students in offices, at community colleges, and at various receive sites. The corporate world is using distance learning, both internally and externally, for all aspects of training, saving millions of dollars each year (USDLA, 2009). Government is providing efficient, online regulatory training, skill development, professional development, and many other forms of workforce training and education, reducing the need to send employees to classrooms near and far.

This chapter describes the course of efforts that extended the impact of the work of the Advanced Distributed Learning (ADL) Initiative from the U.S. Department of Defense (DoD) to other agencies of the federal government, and eventually to those who are not part of the government of the United States. This widening occurred initially through the stimulus of public policy, and later because it simply made sense. In the context of the ADL business paradigm, this chapter concerns the strategic development of partnerships and collaborations to further understanding of the value of interoperability of online learning systems and content, and extend the acceptance

233

of standards (Wisher, this volume). In terms of the ADL experience, this chapter highlights some of the critical steps and activities involved in extending the payoff from an initial DoD investment.

Policy as an ADL Foundation

Policy is a mechanism that establishes a set of goals and objectives, and then, through a system of resources, activities, and content, brings about a set of intended and observed outputs (Pacey & Keough, 2003). Policy enables one to gather and document research that leads to specific goals based on support and consensus building. The United States is recognized for a pluralistic form of governance that receives and processes input from a broad range of government and non-government agencies, as well as from the private sector and influential advocacy groups. All played a role in the early success of ADL.

In November 1997, the U.S. DoD and the White House Office of Science and Technology Policy (OSTP) launched the ADL Initiative as a response to the findings of the Quadrennial Defense Review (Wisher, this volume). From this, the SCORM standard emerged (Gallagher, this volume), and implementation within DoD followed (Murray & Marvin, this volume).

Federal Training Technology Initiative
In 1998, motivated by the progress made in employing advanced distributed learning by the Army National Guard and other interested federal agencies, notably the Department of Labor, the OSTP moved to consolidate federal efforts via a Federal Training Technology Initiative. The learning technology vision of this initiative encompassed a number of national electronic learning initiatives. All were focused on using the power of learning technologies to broaden the reach of educators and trainers faced with the daunting challenge of moving America's workforce into the information age and the emerging knowledge economy. These efforts resulted in a gathering of public and private sector education, training, and technology leaders at the Lifelong Learning Summit hosted by then Vice President Gore on January 12, 1999. Following this meeting, President William J. Clinton signed Executive Order 13111, which, among other things, directed the Department of Defense to take the federal lead in developing learning technology standards in collaboration with academia, industry, and other government agencies. Thus, a sequence of policies from the White House down solidified the platform and core political base for the ADL Initiative.

The ADL Initiative was, and still is, an overarching effort that focuses on leveraging net-based technologies to provide distributing learning anywhere, anytime. The ADL Co-Laboratory (Co-Lab) Hub, located in Alexandria, Virginia, near Washington, DC, has become a leading center of collaborative thinking on the application of the learning sciences. Together with the Joint ADL Co-Lab in Orlando, Florida, it is also the primary center for development and application of future ADL technologies and systems (Murray & Marvin, this volume). Its strategic location enables a range of organizations to demonstrate technology and collaborate on policy-related issues, with ready access to decision makers in the federal sector.

ADL partnerships among the federal government, private-sector technology suppliers, and the broader education and training community are the means for formulating voluntary guidelines that meet common needs. By making software for e-learning accessible, interoperable, durable, and reusable. The ADL Initiative ensures that academic, business, and government users of learning software obtain the best possible value from their investments in learning technology.

The success of the ADL Initiative is measured by several results. These include the extent to which: (a) organizations are able to purchase high-quality learning software less expensively in the future than they do today; (b) the size of the learning software market increases; (c) producers of learning software achieve a higher return on their investments; and (d) standards promoted by ADL are adopted.

The Office of the Secretary of Defense, the Department of Labor (DoL) and the National Guard Bureau established the ADL Co-Lab as a forum for cooperative research, development, and assessment of new learning technology prototypes, guidelines, and specifications. Potential customers included all other U.S. federal agencies that engage in training activities in a distributed learning environment. In addition, non-federal-government persons or entities that meet criteria for participation may also be customers of this effort. The range of potential participants is shown in Figure 18-1.

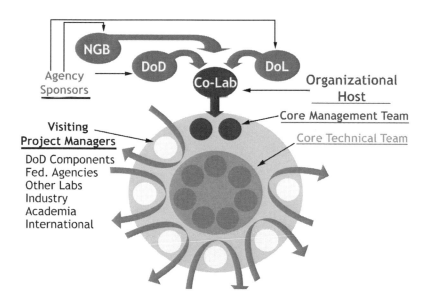

Figure 18-1. Concept of operations for collaboration. This figure depicts the range of organizations participating in ADL's collaborative efforts.

Each of the three initial partners offered a unique set of resources and capabilities to the ADL Co-Lab. The partners committed resources either by direct funding or as "in kind" assistance. First, DoD provided expertise in integrating advanced research and development of learning technologies as well as standardization of learning content and reusable object development.

Second, the Employment and Training Administration (ETA) within the Department of Labor sought to increase opportunities for accessible lifelong learning anywhere, anytime through collaboration and coordination regarding learning technologies among stakeholders and partners, such as Federal agencies, vendors, private sector groups, state and local government, non-profit, and other entities. In addition, the ETA wished to continue the growth and development of the Federal Learning Exchange to provide support for e-Government activities managed by the Office of Technology and Information Systems within the Department of Labor.

Finally, the National Guard Bureau (NGB) provided expertise in demonstrating the integration of ADL technology and philosophy into business culture, policies, and practices. From the policy side, this also enabled ADL to see how changes in directives and instructions would impact the military, particularly a shared usage model the Guard implemented to support both the Department of Defense and the civilian agencies. The NGB has a dual mission: providing the states and territories with units trained and equipped to protect life and property, and also providing units trained and ready to support national requirements.

The Structure of Partnerships

Creating partnerships has been a very important second step in advancing the work of the ADL Initiative. To expand collaboration and develop partnerships in both the public and private sectors, ADL held a series of events called "Plugfests" to bring together early adopters of the SCORM. The purpose of the ADL Plugfests was to establish a common test bed for experimenting with new object technologies designed with specific qualities using previously established guidelines (Wisher, this volume). The Plugfests gave early adopters of ADL standards and specifications a chance to create and demonstrate prototypical object components designed to be launched and tracked from multiple learning management systems (LMSs). Representatives from numerous federal agencies participated in the Plugfests, gaining first-hand knowledge of the standards promoted by ADL and the opportunity to gauge the depth of the interest. They also enabled ADL to expand its collaborative partnerships, as shown in Figure 18-2.

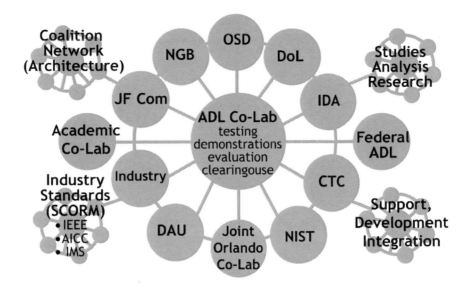

Figure 18-2. ADL Co-Lab Partnerships. This figure depicts the range of partnerships that the ADL Initiative has developed to support e-learning standards and specifications.

The National Guard Bureau did a study in the 1990s that indicated that a leading cause of death and injury to National Guard members was commuting to and from their homes to training locales. As a result, motivated by a desire to reduce training-related travel, the National Guard Bureau embraced distributed learning through an effort called the Distributive Training Technology Project (DTTP). The goal was to assure that the vast majority of Guard members would be within easy driving distance of a Guard-supported classroom, generally located within an Armory. There, through secured and unsecured networks, the Guard members would receive the instruction needed for both their professional training and personal development.

The National Guard Network

The National Guard possesses a complex internet protocol telecommunications network that delivers data and video services to users in 54 U.S. states and territories. The network consolidates video and data communications functions to support readiness, mobilization, command and control, and computer emergency response, in addition to the various missions assigned to the National Guard. These include: command, control and communications, and distance learning via the distributed network; disaster assistance; incident response; information operations; and changing missions involving new state, local, and national-level responsibilities.

The Distributed Training Technology Project is a state-of-the-art communications and learning-delivery system designed to support National Guard members and the communities in which they serve. There are hundreds of multimedia classrooms and mobile assets throughout the country, linked by an internal, secure intranet. These sites support such varied activities as military and terrorism-preparedness training, simulation training, first-responder instruction, foreign language-sustainment training, emergency operations support, and communications support. The system is readily adaptable to the military's growing and evolving missions to safeguard Americans and their interests, both at home and abroad.

Working with a combination of private contractors from industry, and organized through the office of the Chief Information Officer of the National Guard Bureau, a network of more than 330 distance learning classrooms was developed by 2000. Multi-point audio conferencing and video teleconferencing equipment was a standard feature of the classrooms, permitting one-to-one and multi-party communications to take place. In most instances, moreover, a teacher's podium and control panel were set aside toward the front or side of each classroom to permit greater individual control of the learning environment.

National Guard Shared Use Program

Prior to the terrorist attacks on September 11, 2001, Guard training was usually provided on the weekends; Armory classrooms throughout the United States were filled with men and women obtaining skills training needed to help them master current requirements or to receive training for promotions. Outside the weekends, however, the expensive classrooms were almost always underutilized.

As a result, the Guard embarked upon a policy of "shared use" of its networked classrooms. Memoranda of Understanding or Agreement were actively sought with a host of other institutions—federal agencies, neighborhood schools, trade associations, and others—allowing the members of those organizations to use the classrooms.

For example, personnel from the Mine Safety Health Administration drove to selected classrooms and received common training together; staff of the Minority Business Development Administration saved meeting costs by gathering in multiple classrooms and conferring virtually; United States Marine Corps personnel could access training securely from behind a firewalled ".mil" domain; the Defense Acquisition University expanded the reach of its programming by permitting its students to receive training at Guard classrooms; and so on. Sometimes a fee was charged, sometimes not; but in all instances the National Guard received extraordinary public relations, community relations, and political benefits.

National Guard-NASA Partnership

Dozens of shared use partnerships were established with the National Guard. The most visible of all, from a public relations standpoint, was one established with the National Aeronautics and Space Administration (NASA). Urban, suburban, and inner city schoolchildren—some of whom had never before even seen a computer in person—were brought to National Guard classrooms in Virginia, Texas, and elsewhere to learn the rudiments of science from one another's teachers, from one another, and from NASA scientists based at the Johnson Space Center in Houston, Texas. Indeed, one component of the NASA partnership enabled schoolchildren across the United States to travel to nearby DTTP classrooms to communicate with astronauts orbiting the earth in the Space Shuttle. This program was spotlighted by a national television network in its nightly newscast.

Given the tremendous reach of the DTTP program, it was only natural that ADL would want to work closely with it to help achieve its own goals of creating learning content and platform interoperability among and between various Federal agencies. As a result, the National Guard maintained DTTP classrooms and equipment at the Alexandria, Virginia ADL Co-Lab Hub for several years. During this time, the Co-Lab hosted significant numbers of National Guard Bureau and contractor personnel. This gave the ADL Co-Lab Hub the daily atmosphere of a lively facility regularly visited by men, women, and children representing a wide variety of government, nonprofit, trade association, scholastic, and other institutions.

Outreach for National Security

The ADL Initiative also has a close working relationship with the North Atlantic Treaty Organization (NATO) Working Group on Individual Training and Education Developments. It is supported by functional experts from NATO and the NATO/Partnership for Peace (PfP).

Convoy Training. The most effective way to prepare for an ambush in hostile territory is to train for it. For NGB leaders, training has been a key factor in transforming the National Guard from a strategic reserve to a relevant operational force that supports emerging missions at home and abroad. The NGB has used game-based education and training software as one tool to achieve the required level of training. In collaboration with the ADL Initiative and the Defense Advanced Projects Research Agency (DARPA), the NGB explored the potential for delivering DARPA's "DARWARS Ambush!" training software over its DTTP distance-learning assets.

"DARWARS Ambush!" is a game-based training module that prepares soldiers for the types of ambushes they will likely experience during deployment. Rather than teaching specific driving or shooting skills, DARWARS Ambush! seeks to prepare soldiers mentally for hostile encounters through interactive role-play exercises.

The Army currently uses a variety of convoy trainers, but most are costly, cumbersome, and inflexible. Ambush!, on the other hand, can be used with standard desktop or laptop computers, in stand-alone or networked modes, and can be modified quickly by trainers to match the ever-changing mission-rehearsal and battlefield environments. The tests were extremely successful, and the partners, in cooperation with the Texas Army National Guard, are now looking to expand their efforts by piloting the software to help train soldiers being deployed to Iraq and Afghanistan.

In the spirit of the original policy document, Executive Order 13111, ADL actively engages with federal agencies seeking support in understanding ADL standards and how best to implement them. Some, such as the National Institute of Standards and Technology (NIST) under the U.S. Department of Commerce, have hosted Plugfests. Others, such as the Department of Labor, have placed their employees in work assignments at an ADL facility. The majority of outreach, however, has been conducted with specific groups trying to solve specific problems.

Department of the Treasury

The mission of the Department of Treasury is to serve the American people and strengthen national security by effectively managing the U.S. Government's finances, promoting economic growth and stability, and ensuring the safety, soundness, and security of the U.S. and international financial systems. The Department's mission highlights its role as the steward of U.S. economic and financial systems, and as an influential participant in the global economy. The various operating bureaus make up 98 percent of the Treasury workforce of 116,000.

Internal Revenue Service (IRS). The IRS is the largest of Treasury's bureaus. It is responsible for determining, assessing, and collecting internal revenue in the United States. The IRS Bureau was an early adopter of online learning with a focus on training its workers each year to address the yearly changes in the U.S. tax code. The IRS Bureau worked directly with the ADL Co-Lab Hub, which hosted briefings and workshops for the IRS Bureau as it moved to implement its advanced distributed learning strategy. Technical staff at the Bureau also participated in the ADL Technical Working Group, adding valuable insight on implementation issues and benchmarks in their process for selecting a learning management system.

Department of Labor

The Department of Labor fosters and promotes the welfare of the job seekers, wage earners, and retirees of the United States by improving their working conditions, advancing their opportunities for profitable employment, protecting their retirement and health care benefits, helping employers find workers, and tracking changes in employment, prices, and other national economic measurements. In carrying out this mission, the Department administers a variety of Federal labor laws including those that guarantee workers' rights to safe and healthful working conditions. The size of the workforce is 17,000.

Mine Safety and Health Administration (MSHA). The MSHA reflects a culture of prevention which embeds safety and health as core values. Inspectors are trained to direct their efforts to areas or activities that are most likely to place miners at risk. Education and training for the mining industry is essential to reducing the number of accidents and illnesses. The MSHA ensures that its training specialists and technical support personnel are readily accessible to the mining industry.

ADL assisted the Department of Labor in the selection of an enterprise-wide learning management system to cover all eight Agencies of the Department. ADL also assisted the MSHA in identifying vendors to create online learning content that addressed the training needs of the mining industry, with a focus on mitigating mining accidents and illnesses.

Department of Transportation

The mission of the Department of Transportation is to serve the United States by ensuring a fast, safe, efficient, accessible, and convenient transportation system that meets our vital national interests and enhances the quality of life of the American people, today and into the future. The Department has a workforce of 59,000.

Federal Aviation Administration (FAA). Within the Department of Transportation, the FAA oversees the safety of civil aviation. The safety mission of the FAA is its highest priority. The FAA, which operates a network of airport towers, air route traffic control centers, and flight service stations, develops air traffic rules, allocates the use of airspace, and provides for the security control of air traffic to meet national defense requirements.

The FAA sought the assistance of the ADL Co-Lab Hub to help a nationwide team understand the current status of authoring tools for online learning. The training platform to train air traffic controllers needed to be updated to the new enterprise-wide leaning management system. The company which produced the authoring tools used to create the current content had gone out of business, and the content lacked interoperability. ADL conducted an analysis of current authoring tools and prepared a paper outlining the features of vendor-developed and open-source authoring tools for the FAA, with an emphasis on interoperability. ADL hosted a review of vendors and participated in the FAA user group.

Department of Health and Human Services

The Department of Health And Human Services (HHS) is the United States government's principal agency for protecting the health of all Americans and for providing essential human services, especially for those who are least able to help themselves. The Department administers more grant dollars than all other federal agencies combined. HHS' Medicare program is the nation's largest health insurer, handling more than one billion claims per year. HHS has a workforce of 64,000.

Centers for Disease Control and Prevention (CDC). The CDC works with states and other partners, providing a system of health surveillance to monitor and prevent disease outbreaks (including bioterrorism), implement disease prevention strategies, and maintain national health statistics. The Center guards against international disease transmission, with personnel stationed in more than 25 foreign countries.

The CDC became a partner organization with ADL as the CDC moved to expand the development and delivery of online learning during the world wide SARS epidemic. At the time CDC delivered 70 percent of their learning content via video and 30 percent online. Their agenda was to expand online delivery to 70 percent. ADL presented at CDC conferences and workshops as they moved to change the delivery mix, and provided consultation as requested. The CDC participated in many of the ADL open working groups during the period.

Partnerships with Advocacy Groups

Another category of a partnership began in 2005, when the United States Distance Learning Association (USDLA) signed a Memorandum of Agreement with the Academic Advanced Distributed Learning (ADL) Co-Laboratory in Madison, Wisconsin.

This partnership allows the USDLA to support the development and implementation of standards for distributed learning (currently, SCORM 2004), as well as sharing research with other Academic ADL Co-Laboratory partners, participating in advisory meetings, and collaborating with the partners on projects that will enhance quality, reduce current costs, and promote the development of interoperable systems for the delivery of distributed learning. According to Dr. John G. Flores, Chief Executive Officer of the United States Distance Learning Association (2005):

"This new association partnership will bring increased and shared opportunities for both the Academic ADL Co-Lab and USDLA to further educate the distance learning community and USDLA membership with new and cutting edge technologies in the blended learning environment, increase participation in the NSU/USDLA Distance Learning Leaders Certificate Program with new sessions on SCORM, as well as provide the Academic ADL Co-Lab community, events locations for special higher education track sessions, conference keynotes, and ADL tutorials in co-operation with USDLA's official conference."

Overall, this relationship brings together the best of all worlds in support of distance education and training constituencies everywhere to include pre-K-12 education, higher and continuing education, and home schooling as well as business, corporate, military, government, and telehealth markets.

Partnership Center for Online Workforce Development
In November, 2009, ADL supported the founding of the Center for Online Workforce Development at George Mason University (GMU) in Fairfax, Virginia. Online learning has become commonplace at George Mason University and at many other of our nation's leading colleges and universities. Less common, however, is its use as a workplace tool for training and retraining America's workers. As a result, the opportunity for our nation's workforce to adapt to new and often rapidly changing economic challenges and opportunities is diminished.

Building upon the call by the President of George Mason University to "take the knowledge of the university into the workplace and the larger society," (GMU,

2009) the George Mason University Center for Online Workforce Development is the nation's first interdisciplinary academic research center designed comprehensively to promote online learning as a vehicle to produce a more globally competitive workforce. The Center engages all members of the GMU community in the implementation of its two-part mission:

- To undertake original research that becomes the foundation for more widespread and more effective use of distributed learning technologies to train and retrain America's workers.

- To develop courses which take the knowledge of the university into the workplace.

Center activities are to include sponsoring basic, methodological, and applied research studies; capturing and sharing best computer-based training practices; developing online training and retraining courses for those seeking jobs, or looking to advance their careers, in select industries; hosting academic and public meetings and conferences; and forging partnerships with community colleges, trade associations, and others throughout the United States, the Commonwealth of Virginia, and the greater Washington, DC region.

Conclusion

Implementing the program of the ADL Initiative requires collaboration within the DoD and the federal government at large as well as collaboration with industry, academia, and state and local entities. ADL works with standards and specification groups identified elsewhere (Robson & Richards, this volume) and learning industry advocacy groups such as the United States Distance Learning Association, the American Society for Training and Development, The Masie Center, the McdBiquitous Consortium, and others to gather input, feedback, and best practices in the use and adoption of SCORM.

The synergism promised by these partnerships will permit current and future partners and collaborative agencies to leverage their resources and capabilities in support of their current and future needs, the ADL vision, and other collaboration and initiatives resulting from Executive Order 13111. The convergence of customer demand, access to broadband networking technology, advances in distributed learning technologies and philosophies, and broad-based support by the federal government, industry and academia provide a unique opportunity to reap the benefits of the ADL vision. The ADL Co-Lab has become a major global center for distributed learning collaboration, testing, and assessments, and has succeeded in creating partnerships to support common goals.

Distance learning has the power to transform a country from the industrial age to the information age and onto the knowledge economy for a brighter future for all.

This chapter has described examples of the critical steps needed to create your online learning initiative. Collaboration with other organizations leverages what others already know and can help guide you in most effectively meeting your training needs.

References

Department of Defense (1999). *Strategic plan for Advanced Distributed Learning*, April 30, 1999.

George Mason University (2009). *The vision statement for George Mason University.* Retrieved April 5, 2010, from http://www.gmu.edu/resources/visitors/vision/vision.html.

Holden, J. T., & Westfall, P. J. (2006). *An instructional media selection guide for distance learning* (2nd ed.). Boston: United States Distance Learning Association.

Pacey, L., & Keough, E. (2003). Public policy, institutional structure, and strategic implementation. In M. Moore & W. Anderson (Eds.), *Handbook of distance education* (pp. 401-406). Mahwah, NJ: Lawrence Erlbaum Associates.

Presidential Executive Order 13111(E.O. 13111): *Using technology to improve training opportunities for Federal Government employees.*

United States Distance Learning Association (USDLA) (2009). *United States distance learning facts and figures.* Retrieved October 18, 2009, from http://www.usdla.org/index.php?cid=109

United States Distance Learning Association (USDLA1) (2009). *United States Distance Learning Association: Sponsor and affiliate profiles.* Retrieved October 18, 2009, from http://www.usdla.org/index.php?cid=145

The Authors

Paul Roitman Bardack is Director of the George Mason University Center for Online Workforce Development in Fairfax, Virginia. He served as Deputy Director of the ADL Initiative from 2008-2009, and is Chairman Emeritus of the United States Distance Learning Association.

George Koch is Director, Government Implementation at the ADL Initiative.

Reggie Smith, III is a training analyst at Booz, Allen, Hamilton, Inc. Mr. Smith is also President of the United States Distance Learning Association.

Chapter 19

ADL Implementation through Joint Knowledge Online
Joseph Camacho, Jerry West, and Marty Vozzo

The evolution of the Joint Knowledge Online (JKO) portal is a leading example of implementation of ADL technologies in the military services of the United States. JKO represents the realization of the Department of Defense's (DoD) vision for training individuals for joint operations (Department of Defense, 2004). It is designed to prepare future decision makers and leaders to employ joint operational art and to understand the common relevant operating picture rather than a service-specific view. From its inception in 2003, the emergence of this joint capability reflects the collaborative nature of the ADL business paradigm (Wisher, this volume). It further provides empirical testimony to the value and outcomes of scaling from an initial operating capability to an ever expanding learning portal used by members of the Services world wide.

Developed by the U.S. Joint Forces Command (USJFCOM), training and education content rendered through the JKO portal applies ADL standards, information technology, and strategic collaborations to provide a cost-effective virtual joint training and education environment. This is accomplished through continual collaboration with the ADL Initiative to accelerate the development and delivery of interoperable content in response to requirements from combatant commands, military services, and combat support activities. Metrics accounting for the success of the JKO portal are provided later in this chapter.

JKO is available to U.S services and DoD personnel through an internal DoD network. It is available to multinational and interagency partners within the U.S. government through a public portal on the Internet. A combination of several commercial off-the-shelf products support the various technical functions within the portal, and include a government off-the-shelf, SCORM-conformant learning management system, communities of interest supporting the organization, accessibility of content in a common area, and open source software.

Pre-JKO Implementation of ADL — August 2003 through May 2006

The 2003 DoD Training Transformation Strategic Plan introduced the concept of creating a global knowledge environment and joint learning portal for joint individual training and education. This initiative was incorporated in the 2007 *Vision for Joint Learning Continuum and Joint Officer Development*. The strategic plan identified the Joint Knowledge Development and Distribution Capability (JKDDC) as the organization responsible for establishing a global knowledge environment. Developing, facilitating access to, and distributing joint knowledge and information assets for individual joint training via existing and future networks are central to its mission.

In August 2003, the Secretary of Defense established the program's Joint Management Office, operating under the Joint Staff and co-located with the ADL Co-Laboratory Hub in Alexandria, Virginia. The Office led the adoption of the ADL Sharable Content Object Reference Model (SCORM) for joint individual training, the cornerstone of ADL capabilities and technical standards (Gallagher, this volume). However, DoD policy directives concerning SCORM implementation were not yet issued, and few military organizations were voluntarily converting legacy content and business processes to conform to SCORM standards in the absence of such policy (GAO, 2003).

JKDDC incorporated SCORM conformance standards as an early adopter. It was fully established by August 2005 as the DoD leader for ADL implementation. Officials formally announced the completion of its first SCORM-conformant courses, the standup of a web-portal hosted by the Joint Staff, and interim distribution and operational capabilities based on a federation of learning management systems in use across the military services. By May 2006, prior to migration from the Joint Staff to the USJFCOM, the Joint Knowledge Development and Distribution Capability had developed 19 SCORM-conformant courses related to joint training, with access through a Web site portal for online delivery.

JKO Implementation of ADL — April 2007 to October 2009

In May 2006, the Joint Knowledge and Distribution Capability was established as part of the USJFCOM J7/Joint Warfighting Center. A liaison office remained at the ADL Co-Lab Hub to fully promote use of ADL capabilities. In April, 2007, Joint Knowledge Online was officially launched as the DoD portal for joint individual training.

Building on the ADL strategic collaboration established during its start-up period, JKDDC developed Joint Knowledge Online (JKO) on a fast track, leveraging four important partnerships. The first partnership was with the U.S. Army Knowledge Online and Defense Knowledge Online capabilities for hosting military non-secret and secret network and intranet services. A partnering arrangement with the Defense Acquisition University led to collaborative development of Atlas Pro as a government off-the-shelf learning management system. An additional set of partnerships with multinational organizations addressed content development and conversion of Web-based courses for multinational interests. Finally, a partnership and collaborative working arrangement with the ADL Co-Labs focused on quality assurance and SCORM conformance testing (Panar, Brannon, & Poltrack, this volume). By mid-2009, JKO stocked more than 300 SCORM-conformant Web-based courses. Examples of these courses are *Fundamentals of NATO*, *Introduction to International Humanitarian Law*, and the *Combined Joint Task Force*.

Levels of Interactivity in Courses

JKO courses vary in terms of interactivity. Levels of interactivity describe the interaction between the learner and the computer, ranging from Level 1 to Level 4 (Betrancourt, 2005; Schwier & Misanchuk, 1993). Level 1 is used primarily for introducing an idea or concept. The learner has little or no control over the sequence and timed events of the lesson material. Minimal interactivity is provided by navigation icons. Stepping through a PowerPoint presentation is an example. Higher levels give the student more control over the lesson's scenario. Multiple software branches (two to three levels) based on responses are coded in the design; this is called sequencing and navigation in SCORM (Gallagher, this volume). Level 4 interactivity reveals extensive branching (four or more levels) and a level of sophistication approaching intelligent tutoring (Hu, Graesser, & Fowler, this volume). To date, JKO courses are predominantly Level 2; however at the time of this writing, the program is moving to higher levels of interactivity on a progressive basis.

Social Media

JKO also facilitates online chat rooms and discussions encompassing more than 50 communities of interest serving more than 1,000,000 JKO users spanning a wide range of military, interagency, and multinational organizations. These are examples of social media tools (Fowler, this volume). Communities of interest provide a way for individuals to keep one another current on developments of a shared topic and assist with better top-down communication for sharing information and ideas, generally within a joint functional topic area. Examples of these communities of interest are joint task force headquarters, joint electronic warfare training, and joint urban operations.

External bodies and associations have formally recognized JKO accomplishments with awards such as the 21st Century Best Practices Award granted by the United States Distance Learning Association. As noted in these awards and recognitions given to JKO, ADL implementation has played a significant role as an enabler and contributor to developing and sustaining JKO. It has been a true and effective, two-way collaboration.

Components of Joint Knowledge Online

The JKDDC business model incorporates ADL implementation within each of its five components:

Knowledge Development and Distribution Guidelines. JKDDC develops and publishes courseware content guidelines which govern JKO development and distribution as well as promote SCORM standards across the joint community as the *de facto* global standard for technology-based learning.

Advanced Concepts. Research is often oriented towards advanced concepts for future inclusion in JKO. For example, the incorporation of advanced intelligent tutoring prototypes under development by the ADL Co-Labs is a vital part of JKDDC's mid-term plans (Hu, Graesser, & Fowler, this volume). Long-term plans for advanced concepts will embrace more complex learning designs to include gaming, modeling, and simulation-based learning that will lead to more efficient and more effective training.

Repositories. The distribution architecture is built around adoption of ADL repository guidelines for registration of repositories and efficient discovery and reuse of courseware and sharable content objects (Lannom, this volume).

Certification and Tracking. Certification and tracking of training and education course content is enabled by collaborations with ADL adopters employing tools and other learning technology-based standards to automate the updating of military personnel training records.

Policy Compliance. As an early adopter of DoD policy to provide policy direction governing the adoption of SCORM and other learning technology-based standards (Freeman, this volume), JKDDC has developed tools to automate many of the compliancy processes encompassing SCORM-conformant content development, distribution, and registration of content and content repositories. For example, a tool known as ROCCE (Rapid Online Content Creation Environment) creates a collaborative online learning environment that enables virtual teams to function seamlessly to produce new distributed learning content—SCORM conformant content that integrates directly with the AtlasPro learning management system. Using ROCCE, subject matter experts, instructional designers, media specialists, and programmers can use automated processes to reduce development time and costs to produce SCORM-conformant learning content.

Course Offerings

The availability of distributed learning content has increased substantially since May 2006. Hundreds of joint and multinational courses, supplementary presentations, and instructional resource links are available via the JKO portal network system. Additions are made continually, and courses are periodically updated based on a pre-planned review cycle.

A taxonomy defines a coding scheme for JKO courses by nine functional areas, four levels of war (tactical, operational, strategic national, strategic theater), origin (U.S. or multinational), a course and course module numbering system, and network availability (non secure, secure, or public Internet). The nine functional areas are:

- J1: Joint Personnel

- J2: Joint Intelligence

- J3: Joint Operations

- J4: Joint Logistics

- J5: Joint Plans

- J6: Joint Communications

- J7: Joint Training

- J8: Joint Integration Level Information

- J9: Joint Experimentation

All content is registered in the ADL Registry (Lannom, this volume). Many courses are open to the public through the JKO Internet Public portal. This provides access to unclassified, releasable courses that are relevant to joint, integrated operations, and to multinational and interagency partners that do not otherwise have access to military networks and shareable joint courses.

JKO Metrics of Success

Figures 19-1 through 19-3 depict metrics spanning the migration and evolution of the JKO capability from inception as part of the Joint Staff to its maturation under USJFCOM. Historically, learning outcome metrics support the *Rule of Thirds* principle introduced by analysts from the Institute for Defense Analyses, based on analysis of the efficiencies and cost-effectiveness of computer-based instruction (Fletcher, 1997; Fletcher, this volume). Moreover, in comparison with the industry standard for Web-based development and distribution costs, JKO delivery of Web-based instruction has resulted in cost savings of 48 percent in comparison to schoolhouse delivery methods, as shown in Figures 19-1 through 19-3 below.

Cost Savings for Development

By providing development, conversion, and hosting services, the Joint Knowledge Development and Distribution Capability enables stakeholders to take advantage of ADL capabilities without paying for the overhead of installation, development, and maintenance of the courseware development infrastructure. This results in an additional savings for the stakeholders and the DoD overall. JKDDC development costs include all funds allocated through the Training Transformation program and spent on the following development activities:

- Instructional system design

- SCORM coding

- Community of interest design/development

- Subject matter expert support/reachback

- Media/content development

- Subject matter expert content validation and testing

- Course conversion

- Content maintenance

- Collaborative tool development/maintenance

Figure 19-1 illustrates the JKO value proposition in terms of the expectation of economies-of-scale as the number and demand for courses increase. Courseware development estimates for incorporating SCORM standards are currently between $10,000 and $12,000 per course-hour for Level I and Level II interactive multimedia instruction (IMI) courseware. This is significantly less than the benchmark of $20,000 that is used to estimate prospective Level I IMI courseware development costs.

By meeting the initial, relatively low demand of the stakeholders from combatant commands for "something" to address critical gaps in training joint knowledge, ADL enabled JKDDC to close the immediate gap with Level I courseware. Concurrently, a more mature training management process evolved which provides more refined requirements and priorities. It will be interesting to see if the economies-of-scale trend holds true after stakeholder demand is reset to a subsequently higher level on courseware interactivity. Understanding this relationship could be confounded if the sophistication of training requirements demands more costly development costs.

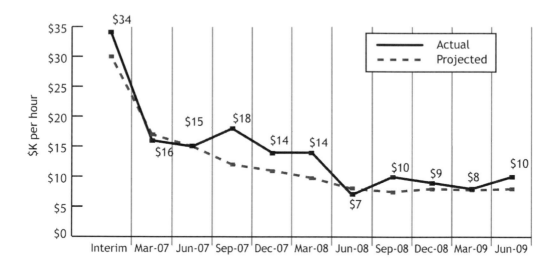

Figure 19-1. Course development costs. This figure depicts cost of developing one hour of training (in thousands of U.S. dollars).

Cost Savings for Distribution

The promise of JKO is largely associated with the use of distributed networks to provide individual training to a large, dispersed audience much more easily and at a lower cost than would be possible using traditional instructional techniques which depend on a central training facility or mobile training teams.

Distribution Cost accounts for the money spent on the following distribution activities:

- Portal development

- Portal maintenance

- Course hosting

- Enterprise information security

- Community of interest hosting

- User validation

- Infrastructure development/maintenance

- SCORM-conformant learning management system development and federation

Just as with development costs, the distribution costs have benefited from economies-of-scale. These costs are represented in Figure 19-2 by dividing the quarterly expenditures for the above activities by the total number of hours of training delivered to the individual.

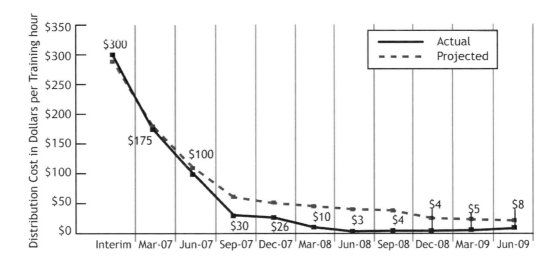

Figure 19-2. Training distribution costs. This graph shows the courseware distribution costs per hour of training delivery (in U.S. dollars).

We can see that the decreasing cost trend continues even through maturation of the requirements. From this, we can conclude that either this change in the requirement base did not have a significant impact on the requirements for the distribution infrastructure, or that the increase in individual demand for training is increasing faster than the maturation of the requirements, or both. For the future, we must keep a close eye on these costs as fundamentally different training modalities offered in the form of advanced technologies fielded into the architecture grow.

Return on Investment

Figure 19-3 summarizes JKO distribution cost avoidance for the period October 2007 through March 2009. Cost avoidance is often used as a measure of effectiveness by analysts to estimate return on investment (ROI). This particular figure illustrates what is termed first order ROI, total operational cost savings. The second order ROI related to development cost avoidance and the second order ROI related to distribution cost avoidance are presented in Table 19-1.

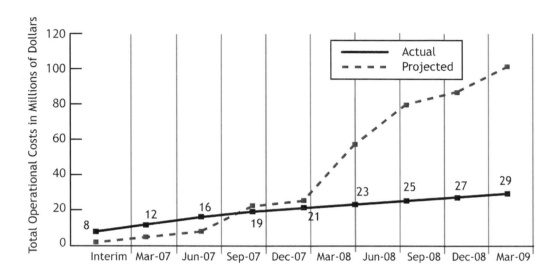

Figure 19-3. Operational costs. This figure depicts the first order return on investment as total operational cost savings (in millions of U.S. dollars).

Cost Avoidance

Table 19-1 suggests a cumulative estimate of $22M cost-avoidance realized by the DoD in 2009 by use of the Joint Knowledge Development and Distribution Capability processes to develop more than 1,100 hours of Web-based courseware. Based on an estimated annual budget of $8M for JKDDC, there is a demonstrated $250M of cost avoidance associated with centralized JKO distribution strategy. This is achieved by leveraging existing DoD information technology infrastructure and using a government off-the-shelf learning management system developed by the Defense Acquisition University and advanced by JKDDC.

Table 19-1

Comparison of JKDDC Development and Distribution Costs (in U.S. dollars)

	IDC Process Development	JKO Lean Development	Cost Avoidance	IDC Process Distribution	JKO Lean Distribution	Cost Avoidance
Mar 07	3,500	2,000	1,500	2,000	2,000	0
Jun 07	5,500	3,000	2,500	10,000	3,200	6,800
Sep 07	7,600	4,100	3,500	20,000	4,400	15,600
Dec 07	11,500	5,100	6,400	55,000	5,600	49,400
Mar 08	15,000	6,200	8,800	70,000	6,800	73,200
Jun 08	19,400	7,100	12,300	148,000	8,000	140,000
Sep 08	23,400	9,100	14,300	202,000	9,200	192,800
Dec 08	27,500	10,000	17,500	225,000	10,400	214,600
Mar 09	31,200	10,000	21,200	262,000	11,600	250,400
Jun 09	34,000	10,900	23,100	290,000	12,800	277,200

Interagency Collaborations and Outreach

Collaborations between the ADL Initiative and JKDDC have played a significant role in breaking information and knowledge-sharing barriers across the U.S. government. On April 11, 2007, a notable agreement was signed between the Department of Defense and the Department of State in support of National Security Presidential Directive 44 to enable the Foreign Services Institute (FSI) and the Joint Knowledge Development and Distribution Capability to collaborate in the development of an online individual training program for reconstruction and stabilization operations.

As a byproduct of the agreement, DoD and the Department of State developed an online course called *Interagency 101* as the first of a series of joint military and interagency culture-sharing courses, using ADL SCORM standards, JKO guidelines, and JKO authoring tools, and hosted on a SCORM-conformant LMS at the Department of State/FSI and JKO. In June 2009, *Interagency 101* was incorporated as a prerequisite to congressionally-mandated training for 2,000 Civilian Reserve Corps personnel recruited to support reconstruction and stabilization operations. As of the summer of 2009, approximately 1,000 personnel from across the interagency community have used JKO to receive cultural awareness training in support of stabilization and reconstruction operations.

Future ADL Implementation

The Joint Knowledge Online is an improving capability that will continue to mature in parallel with ADL capabilities to enable the development of distributed learning programs with interactive instruction and immersive training environments to enhance individual performance in joint assignments. As stated in the goals and objectives and program execution plan, the ADL Co-Laboratory network will continue to play a major role as a key enabler for advanced concepts initiatives and represent JKO interests in the broader science and technology community focusing on individual and small team training technologies research and development. In addition, ADL will play the synergistic role of an enabler of partnerships between JKDDC and interagency, multinational, and international organizations to promote knowledge sharing and interoperability.

The requirement for more advanced skills training to meet emerging requirements for contextual, experiential, and collaborative online learning strategies will automatically mean a greater reliance on collaborations across academia, government, and industry to offset the expected higher developmental and operational costs. In the near-term, JKO will continue to rely on SCORM standards to maximize the potential for content reuse and interoperability as part of a stream-lined business process. In the mid-term, to meet expanding joint military training requirements, JKDDC will leverage ADL development of the immersive learning environment systems such as small group training simulations, serious games (Xu, this volume), virtual worlds (Gamor, this volume), and social media tools (Fowler, this volume) as part of its future group training services.

References

Betrancourt, M. (2005). The animation and interactivity principles in multimedia learning. In R. E. Mayer (Ed.), *The Cambridge handbook of multimedia learning*, pp. 287-296. New York: Campbridge.

Department of Defense (2004, June 9). *Department of Defense training transformation implementation plan.* Washington DC: Pentagon, Office of the Under Secretary for Personnel and Readiness.

Fletcher, J.D. (1997). What have we learned about computer based instruction in military training? In R. J. Seidel and P. R. Chatelier (Eds.), *Virtual Reality, Training's Future?*, New York, NY: Plenum Publishing.

Schwier, R., & Misanchuk, E. (1993). *Interactive multimedia instruction.* Englewood Cliffs, NJ: Educational Technology Publications.

U.S. General Accountability Office (2003). *Military transformation: progress and challenges for DOD's advanced distributed learning programs* (Report No. GAO-03-393). Washington, DC: Author.

Web Resources

Internet Public Network. http://jko.cmil.org

The Authors

Joseph Camacho is the Government Program Director for the Joint Knowledge Development and Distribution Capability Joint Management Office in Suffolk, Virginia, and is the Chair of the NATO Training Group Working Group on Individual Training and Education Developments.

Dr. Jerry West represents the United States Joint Forces Command Joint Warfighting Center's interest in the Advanced Distributed Learning Co-Laboratory Hub in Alexandria, Virginia as the Joint Knowledge Development and Distribution Capability Liaison Officer.

Marty Vozzo is the Deputy Director responsible for managing day to day operations of the Joint Knowledge Development and Distribution Capability Joint Management Office in Suffolk, Virginia.

Chapter 20

ADL - A European Perspective
Geir Isaksen and Ion Roceanu

In the late 1990s, many military organizations across Europe were on the verge of implementing computer-based training (CBT) in their education systems. There was no in-house development capability, and courses purchased from vendors were based on very expensive "license per completed students" agreements. In all cases, none of the courses could be reused or even maintained by the armed forces. The armed forces had installed many different local systems using CBT courses, with no interoperability among these systems. Many of the e-learning courses were simply text on a screen, and the feedback from the students was not very positive. The armed forces of both Norway and Romania began exploring the technologies developed by the Advanced Distributed Learning (ADL) Initiative, sponsored by the U.S. Department of Defense in its own efforts to solve the same problems.

This chapter outlines the history of the early implementation of ADL technologies by the Norwegian and Romanian armed forces. It highlights the experiences, challenges, and benefits the two nations have experienced in the process of implementing an ADL capability in their respective armed forces. This chapter also describes how the leadership of the Norwegian Defense University and the Romanian "Carol I" National Defense University supported the establishment of advanced distributed learning (ADL) offices. A working partnership with the ADL Initiative has resulted in introducing advanced training technologies to the non-defense communities in their own nations and in the general region. This experience mirrors the impact that the work of the ADL Initiative in the United States has had outside the Department of Defense in the academic, civilian government, and commercial sectors throughout the U.S. and outside its borders.

The Norway ADL Partnership Lab

The Norwegian ADL Partnership Lab is located at the Norwegian Defense University College (NoDUC)/ADL office at the Akershus Fortress in the capitol city of Oslo. The NoDUC is responsible for all higher education within the Norwegian Department of Defense (NoD). This includes basic officers' training, the Military Academies for the three branches, and the Command and Staff College. NoDUC offers military Bachelor's and Master's degrees.

During the last part of the 1990s, the NoD started to buy computer-based education distributed on CD-ROMs or installed in so-called computer-based technology classrooms. Very often these off-the-shelf products were purchased during the procurement of new military equipment without a joint set of specifications and regulations. In most cases the courses had to be run on specific software or players. This made it very difficult to reuse the courses directly within the NoD, due to the lack of a joint computer system. Many of the courses had a license fee for the number of enlisted students per year. The NoD did not own the rights to the source code, and in some cases, access to source code vanished due to a vendor's bankruptcy.

The Implementation of Advanced Distributed Learning Technology

In 2001, the NoD established a joint computer system that provided individual computers to all employees, with all computers connected to an internal intranet. Now everybody within the NoD could communicate through email, as well as store and access files. The ADL Office was responsible for the newly acquired Defense learning management system (LMS), and for the first time the NoD was introduced to a specification called SCORM. The first courses installed on the Defense learning portal were application training modules for Word, Excel, Windows, and Internet Explorer. A single sign-on solution allowed a user to access the LMS when she or he has logged on to the computer system. Within months all employees had completed these mandatory courses, and thanks to the SCORM specification, students' progress and results were stored in the Defense LMS.

At that time, Dr. Robert Wisher, Director of the ADL Initiative, was the U.S. member of the NATO Training Group (NTG) Working Group for Individual Training and Education Development (WG IT&ED) together with the Director of the Norwegian ADL Office, LtCol Hans Sigurd Iversen. The first contact between the ADL Initiative and the Norwegian Defense ADL community was made in this group. It was through the meetings in the NTG WG IT&ED that the Norwegian Defense University College first learned about advanced distributed learning and the extensive role of the ADL Initiative as a champion of SCORM, although the ministry already had an interest in using SCORM.

Since 2004, the Norwegian ADL Office has used its experience with the technologies of the ADL Initiative to help other countries, including Estonia, Latvia, Lithuania, and the Ukraine, to establish an ADL capability. They have been introduced to SCORM, authoring tools, ADL regulations, and learning management systems.

Development of ADL

The NoD obtained the first detailed information about SCORM standards and specifications by downloading the SCORM books from the ADL Initiative's Web site. It was obvious that the potential benefits of using SCORM-conformant content, such as reusability and interoperability (Gallagher, this volume), were great for the NoD. The NoD recognized advanced distributed learning as a valid learning method that could reduce costs and contribute to more effective education of large student groups.

Early in 2003, a draft set of Norwegian Defense ADL guidelines mandating the use of SCORM 1.0 was included in tender processes to ensure that new custom-made e-learning courses were interoperable, durable, and reusable. At this point, most of the courses consisted of a single sharable content object (SCO), and the reusable part was actually the whole course itself. This, however, reduces the reusability of the content (Deibler & Berking, this volume).

In the period from 2003 to 2006, the market price within Norway of one hour of custom made e-learning unexpectedly decreased. The feedback from the vendors indicated that the use of clear technical standards that included a set of known specifications, SCORM, also reduced the vendor's production costs. At that time, vendors who were reluctant to use or develop SCORM-conformant tools were no longer considered by the NoD. This resulted in more vendors adopting SCORM standards. By 2009, nearly 100 percent of Norwegian e-learning vendors delivered SCORM-conformant content.

In 2004, the NoD portal was upgraded to a newer version of the LMS. This version of the LMS was SCORM 2004-conformant, with simple sequencing functionality. For the first time the NoD was able to implement SCORM-conformant courses that used simple sequencing. For example, a course developed for the Navy contained a pretest that, based on the score, allowed the student to skip certain SCOs if he or she already knew the material.

The Norwegian Department of Defense was the first organization to publish regulations that required the use of SCORM when buying or developing e-learning courses. The ADL policy instruction issued by the U.S. Department of Defense was translated and signed by Major General Tom Henry Knudsen, commanding officer of the Norwegian Defence Education Command, in April 2006. This instruction defines the use of training needs analysis as well as technical and pedagogical standards (Freeman, this volume).

Sharing Content

In 2006, courses in *Laws of Armed Conflict* were also translated into English, facilitating the sharing of the courses with the member countries in the NTG WG IT/ED. The NoD also reused a course developed by the United States called *Combating Trafficking in Persons*. Using the capabilities of SCORM and the SCORM Reload Editor, a SCO that is related to specific U.S. law was removed before implementation in the NoD Training Portal. The NoD has developed and translated several SCORM-conformant courses and made them available for reuse, and also has reused five courses developed elsewhere. In a report to the Ministry of Defense in 2009, the NoD ADL Office demonstrated that because the NoD has implemented SCORM as the mandatory standard, it has been able to reuse five e-learning courses developed by our partners, saving the NoD about $350,000 in development costs. SCORM's tracking capability documents that almost 5,000 NoD employees have completed the basic course called *Laws of Armed Conflict* at a cost of less than $2.00 per student.

ADL Challenges

The NoD is now facing the challenge of determining how to store content in a way that makes it possible to edit and reuse SCORM content in-house without relying on the original authoring tool to do so. The NoD has not yet built new courses based on existing SCOs from different courses.

ADL Cooperation

Since the establishment of the Norwegian ADL Partnership Lab in 2008, the Norwegian Defense ADL Office and the ADL Initiative have been cooperating in common projects such as the development of the Training and Education for Peace Support Operations (TEPSO) e-learning course and the Multinational Federated Search and Retrieval project.

Through annual meetings and participation in national ADL conferences, the European ADL partner labs continue to interface with the ADL Initiative, the ADL Co-Labs, and the Canadian ADL Partnership Lab. Representatives from the ADL Initiative have participated at all Norwegian ADL conferences since 2006.

Current ADL Projects

Training and Education for Peace Support Operations

Tasked by NATO through the NTG WG IT/ED, several of the ADL Partnership Labs are cooperating with other parties to develop e-learning courses that can be shared and used across the alliance, based on a manual created by the Working Group, *Training and Education for Peace Support Operations*. This manual identified more than forty tasks, most of which can be rendered in an ADL format.

Multinational Federated Search and Retrieval (MFASR)

The MFASR project is studying possible mechanisms to enable content-sharing automatically among the partners in the alliance. There is a need to be able to search, discover, preview, and download content from national content repositories. Since 2007, this has been a joint effort involving the ADL Initiative and the Canadian and Norwegian ADL Partnership Labs. The concept for the technical solution was proven in 2008, and will be further developed and incorporated with the ADL Registry (Lannom, this volume).

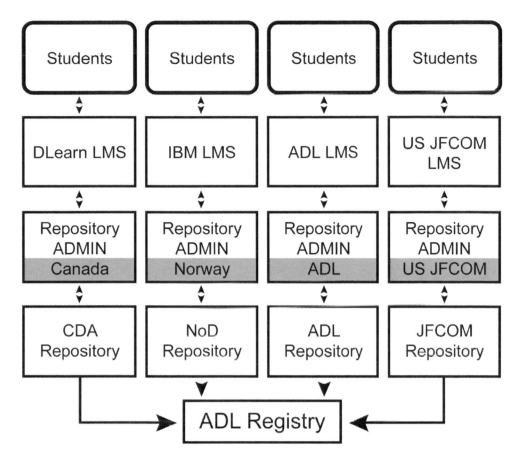

Figure 20-1. MFASR principal diagram. This diagram depicts the relationships between national respositories and the ADL Registry.

E-Bridge

There is also a need to more closely incorporate technical documentation in the development of SCORM-conformant e-learning, especially in training on technical equipment. The Norwegian ADL Partnership Lab contributes and participates in the E-Bridge project, a joint U.S. and European effort to develop a set of standard application programming interfaces that will allow any SCORM-conformant authoring tools to communicate with technical documentation in the S1000D format. S1000D is the international specification for technical publications (Gafford & Heller, this volume).

Future Projects

In the near future, the Norwegian ADL Partnership Lab will focus on three main content-related areas: content development, content management, and content delivery. There will also be a focus on emerging technologies and mobile learning.

Virtual Worlds and Serious Games

Together with NATO Allied Command Transformation, the NoD will start to explore the possibilities offered by virtual worlds such as Second Life (Gamor, this volume) and gaming (Xu, this volume). The NoD is beginning to implement gaming as a training method in the services and will need to be able to administer and track both gaming and simulation in an LMS in the future. It will also develop a capability to record a classroom session and publish it in SCORM format in the LMS in order to reach students who could not follow the session in real time.

Defense Portal on Internet

The NoD ADL office seeks to establish an unclassified learning capability on the Internet. This is fundamental to creating an environment for learning anytime, anywhere.

Mobile Learning

The NoD will seek to implement the capability to make content available on mobile platforms and to disconnected clients, in addition to the Internet or intranet. This application is termed Mobile Learning (Brown, this volume). The challenges will be to track student progress and obtain results. Platforms like mobile phones, Nintendo DSs, and iPods will be tested in cooperation with ADL partners in different research and development projects.

Norwegian ADL Partnership Lab and Industry

The NoD ADL Partnership Lab will work with Norwegian vendors to develop SCORM 2004-conformant authoring tools. The first Defense/Vendor R&D agreement was signed in June 2009.

ADL Perspective – the Romanian Experience

The Romania ADL Partnership Lab, through the "Carol I" National Defense University's (NDU) Romanian Advanced Distributed Learning Department (RoADL-D), collaborates with the ADL Initiative on developing technical frameworks and standards in national and international contexts, with participation from government, industry, and academia.

The RoADL-D vision has a "Network Based Education – Student Oriented" focus as part of its core mission to develop and manage multilevel, standardized, online learning curricula according to ADL principles. The RoADL-D promotes e-learning and e-training for civilian and military personnel for lifelong learning and military education. The department is involved in research projects developed at the national, European Union, and NATO levels, and offers expertise on creating SCORM 2004-conformant educational content, authoring tools, and integrated systems for education and training.

From the Beginning

In the autumn of 2004 the Senate of the "Carol I" National Defense University decided to research the possibility of adding e-learning technology to educational capabilities and services. The national research program initiated a project called the "e-Learning Pilot Centre for Security and Defense" inside the national research program and, a year later, in October 2005, the Advanced Distributed Learning Department was founded. The purpose of this project was to create an integrated system to improve the effectiveness of educational activities based on information technology and to generate, develop, and manage the distance learning curricula according to ADL principles.

In defining the e-learning environment components, we started from the general educational and training objectives in accordance with the NDU`s mission within the educational and training military and civilian systems. We also had to define a center of gravity for the enterprise for building the system. We considered that even if the main features of an e-learning system are technological, the most important element is represented by participants, learners, and tutors. The program had to establish a link between the technical and human dimensions through a focus on educational and training content. The ADL master plan was built around those three dimensions: technical, participants, and content. To reflect these dimensions, the Romanian ADL master plan was titled "Network-Based Education – Student Oriented," which is most appropriate to our ADL vision and expectations.

The Romanian Adventure

From that point on, the Romanian adventure began, in terms of developing real ADL capabilities. "Adventure" is the correct name for an enterprise in which nobody on the project had more than basic knowledge or experience of e-learning in general, or advanced distributed learning in particular. Few people were willing to support such a new idea and work to defeat the natural concerns about its viability. Furthermore, there was little support for budgeting for a project that initially seemed closer to science fiction than to reality. Fortunately, the Senate of the NDU gave RoADL a "blank check," trusting in the competencies of the team. Decision-makers from the Ministry of National Defense also approved the enterprise as a short-term research project. However, the ADL project in Romania would have not been implemented at all, or at least would have taken more time, if we had not had the support from the international ADL community: the NATO WG IT&ED; the ADL Initiative, especially from its Director, Dr. Robert Wisher; the Partnership for Peace (PfP) Consortium ADL Working Group (Synytsya & Staub, this volume); NATO Allied Command Transformation; and the U.S. Joint Forces Command.

Managing the Process of ADL Capabilities Development

Proceeding from the general educational objectives in full accordance with the military training requirements and the Bologna process documents, the team developed an initial three-year master plan based on five steps: 1) research and develop expertise on e-learning and advanced distributed learning, 2) select an ADL architecture framework, 3) develop required technical capabilities, 4) develop a distance learning educational curricula, and 5) develop a new didactical and content development approach.

The Bologna Process was established in 1999 to create a European higher education area by making academic degree standards and quality assurance standards more comparable and compatible throughout Europe.

E-Learning and ADL

The team developed a generic plan for studying the principal aspects needed to develop subject matter expertise that included:

Fundamental theories of e-learning. These include distance learning, advanced distributed learning, online learning, Web-based training, and related e-learning tools.

Teaching and learning processes based on information technology. These processes include instructional design knowledge, digital content development, pedagogical aspects, adult learning, etc.

Technical tools and e-learning systems. Tools and systems include learning management systems, learning content management systems, authoring tools in content development, and content standardization, especially SCORM specifications.

Best practices and case studies. Best practices and case studies are drawn from university virtual campus advanced distributed learning in NATO and the Partnership for Peace Consortium, e-learning in the military and civilian institutions, corporate and stakeholder experience, and others.

ADL Architecture Framework

The core of any master plan is the end-state of the project. The end-state is strongly related to the objectives, directions of effort, empirical studies and analysis, logistics and financial support, and others. The "Carol I" NDU e-learning project's end-state is *to create distributed network-based education—student-oriented in order to develop valuable digital standardization content and deliver knowledge where, when, and to whom it is needed.*

The direction of the project's efforts was guided by the role and mission of institutions in the military and national education systems. The specifics were mandated by the double educational objectives of both the military training requirements in accordance with NATO standards, and those of the national educational system, based on the Bologna documents. As a result, the efforts of the ADL department are two-fold, defined as being both e-education and e-training. E-education is based on the Bologna Process and focuses on developing the educational services support capabilities covered by the Bologna documents. Those define the national educational requirements to provide for: bachelor's, master's, and doctoral level studies; and post-graduate online courses (online master's degree). E-training focuses on NATO requirements and standards, and it has the long-term purpose of developing both individual and team military capabilities. E-training relies on the Advanced Distributed Learning technologies and, consequently, is based on SCORM standards.

RoADL has three different categories of online educational services related to didactic, online instruction in either a standalone or blended mode. Each is described below.

Full online courses. Many administrative and student activities are performed online. The courses are designed to conform to SCORM standards. The SCORM content used for supporting this set of courses is both imported from the ADL community developers and developed in-house. Putting into practice the ADL principle of reusability (Shanley et al., this volume), all content and SCOs are shareable among the ADL stakeholders of the NATO WG IT&ED. Participants also share their experiences in SCORM development, and the expertise of subject matter experts, further reducing costs. At this time, the NDU provides five online courses leading to a certificate, and fourteen other courses based on free-access without certificate recognition.

Blended learning. Some educational activities are accomplished on-site; others, at least 66 percent, are supported online. Consequently, the ADL environment provides the possibility to combine within one single curriculum both SCORM content courses and other content formats, such as: html, word, excel, ppt. file, pdf, pictures, video, and so on. It is more difficult to manage a blended curriculum than a fully online one, due to the complexity of the educational objectives and restrictive content sequencing. Ideally, for all courses there would be a way to have the same version of SCORM-conformant content supported in both synchronous and asynchronous modes of delivery. This is now the case for three courses.

Educational services support for master and doctoral level studies. The ADL system provides a very good virtual collaborative space for teachers and students. In addition to collaborative tools, it is necessary to offer real-time access to a knowledge and content repository to both learners and teachers.

The Big Picture

The Romania ADL environment reflects multiple facets, as shown in Figure 20-2. It comprises three different levels represented by participants, including learners and instructors, technical, and educational services. It supports multiple educational and training processes through a number of Web-based features: learning content management systems, a knowledge portal, collaborative tools, a digital library, and a SCORM-based repository. The ADL environment provides synchronous and asynchronous course delivery. To support synchronous ADL capabilities, the NDU designed an ADL laboratory with multiple work stations, and the capability to offer face-to-face didactical activities using SCORM content for those courses which cannot be delivered by Internet. This gives tutors the capability to tailor courses in accordance with both specific educational objectives and the learner's profile by reorganizing the sequencing of SCOs, and by adding, replacing, or modifying the content as desired.

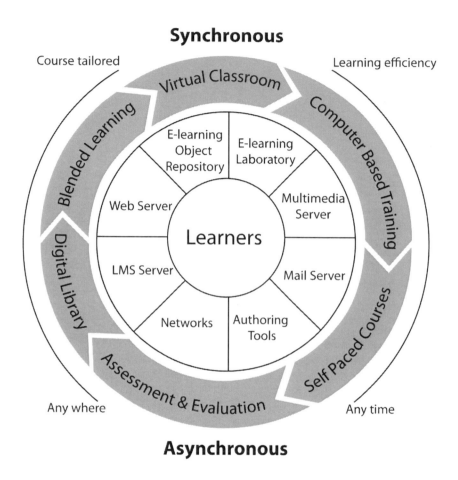

Figure 20-2. Development of the Project—Technical Capabilities. This figure depicts the framework for developing the distributed knowledge network.

RoADL's e-learning model (Figure 20-2) was the starting point, and the main interest was building the distributed knowledge network and capacity for creating the educational service support for both synchronous and asynchronous delivery. From our perspective, the technical issues of the e-learning project are: hardware and communications infrastructure, learning (content) management system, commercial on the shelf software, in-house developed software, and content development authoring tools.

Hardware and communications infrastructure. This consists of: e-learning laboratory, Internet, NDU`s intranet and MoD`s intranet connections capabilities, servers machine park, network storage attached equipment, and different types of peripherals.

The learning management system. The LMS is the heart of any e-learning system. The NDU uses two different LMSs for different purposes—one off-the-shelf and one open-source. The first LMS delivers synchronous digital content, as well as lab-synchronous and integrated curricula for courses. ILIAS, the open-source LMS, manages the online courses.

Digital content authoring tools. Authoring tools are specialized software that may be stand-alone or embedded into the LMS. This category includes the software for evaluation tests and for online or local testing sessions.

Development of the Project – Educational Curricula

The e-learning project is designed for learning and teaching while the technical aspects represent only the platform, comparable to a school building in the classical educational system. It is necessary to build the technical capabilities, but the main mission is still the educational processes, teachers, students, books, and knowledge. The educational capabilities cover the third level of our e-learning reference model, and focus on content, curricula, human resources, students, teachers and tutors, specific didactical and psycho-pedagogical aspects, educational objectives, and so on. From this perspective we believe that the digital content and its didactical aspects represent the key role in the e-learning enterprise.

Digital content is the most sensitive issue in the NDU's ADL project. If the LMS is the heart, content is the brain of any e-learning system and it plays the key role in achieving the educational objectives. It could be an easy or a very hard matter of any discussion! It is easy when speaking from the theoretical perspective, and it could be very hard when trying to develop content that is fully compliant with both the educational principles and the technical standards of development. It is well known that in the digital content development enterprise, there are three pillars: subject matter experts, instructional designers, and content developers (Deibler & Berking, this volume). No one of them is more important than others and, consequently, having proper digital content requires people who are well prepared for their jobs. To achieve this capability, the NDU has set up a training framework that includes best practices in e-learning, a short training session based on technical standards to provide information and to spread knowledge about instructional design principles, and so on.

The most challenging problems relate to the human resources, especially educators, not to technology. To solve these issues, we have instituted teacher teams who study the principles and teach them to others. Our concerns center on the question "Who can deliver this knowledge?" The link between educational objectives and e-learning objects has been debated for years. In designing and authoring the course, the course team must address a number of educational issues that arise as a direct result of adopting the learning object approach.

Didactical and Content Development Approach

One of the most important aspects to planning an e-learning system is the need to change the way one approaches educational content development and teaching methods. From our perspective, this is crucial, because no matter what technology is used, if the content is dull and the teaching method is not special, the system will fail. A new way of teaching means coordinating educational objectives with students' expectations as well as with teachers' and instructors' teaching abilities. Hence, we have developed a broad program to develop new teaching abilities for both the teachers in the NDU and the instructors in the lifelong learning system. We have developed and implemented four online courses with 100 percent of the educational content fully developed in-house, and a tutorial system for six additional courses using content provided by our NATO and PfP partners.

Lessons Learned

The RoADL-D has gained considerable expertise and knowledge through its efforts to develop and implement advanced distributed learning both within the Department of Defense and throughout the country. In the process it has developed a list of "lessons learned."

- Keep in mind: e-learning has 90 percent educational objectives and only 10 percent technology

- Attract the students; the teachers will join.

- Minimize words about e-learning; demonstrate by results.

- In the beginning, short, useful courses bring the best results.

- More freedom in learning means more progress for the students.

- Create the motivation for the students – and give them recognition.

- Provide tutoring support; the students appreciate it and they feel part of the learning environment.

- Do not assign more than 20-30 students per tutor. We started with 50 students per tutor, and now we work with 25.

Research, Publications, and Conferences

When developing Romania's ADL capabilities, one of our main interests was to connect to knowledge sources and high levels of the research and technology communities focused on e-learning in general and ADL in particular. Based on the principle "learn from the best and share the knowledge with those who want to know," we decided that undertaking research and connecting to the scientific community by participating in conferences and publications would play a principal role in our enterprise.

Research Activity

The first 12-month research project, called "e-learning Pilot Centre for Development and Delivering the Security and Crises Management Course Content," started in 2005 with a 100,000 Euro budget from the national research authority. The goal of this project was to create a basic ADL infrastructure, to explore the capabilities of developing and delivering SCORM content, and to highlight the benefits of the ADL system. In addition to the official scope, we had the undeclared purpose of connecting to the national and international e-learning and ADL scientific communities working within the boundaries of the ADL Initiative, as well as to the experience and work of universities and others. The results of our research were published both in Romania and abroad.

Additional research projects were funded by national research authorities in the field of e-learning and ADL, with different main focuses. The first was to secure citizen education against non-war threats, based on the virtual e-learning space. The second was to provide an educational portal for learning foreign languages and for teaching matters in foreign languages. The third was to research and develop a mobile learning-type virtual network with real-time access to knowledge and learning.

The Romanian ADL Partnership Lab also became involved with other international projects, including the "Multinational Virtual Learning Environment" sponsored by the Office of Naval Research Global. This project has the very ambitious goal of eliminating language barriers in learning by incorporating a real-time multi-language translation engine into the core of the LMS. This capability would enable access to learning resources to students from different countries even if the content and tutors work in other languages. This project has completed the first stage and will continue.

Conferences and Publications

Another area of interest of the Romanian ADL Department, of equal importance to the research activities, is sharing knowledge about advanced distributed learning through publications and conferences. Consequently, in the spring of 2005 RoADL-D launched the "e-Learning and Software for Education (eLSE)" conference. Since 2005, the purpose of the annual eLSE conference has been to "Promote e-learning related activities by providing a forum for the exchange of ideas, presentation of technical achievements, and discussion of future directions." The first conference gathered more than 70 researchers, professors, and e-learning stakeholders from national and international academic and corporate communities. Year after year, the value of the papers presented has demonstrated eLSE's contribution to the profession and its use as a tool both for participants who learn and those who communicate their presentations. Each conference has had a different central topic:

- Common and Specific Constructs Characteristics between e–Education and e–Training

- E-Learning Capabilities and Perspectives

- Educational and Technical Dimensions

- E-Learning Network-Based Education—Student Oriented

- Higher Education and Evolution of Advanced Distributed Learning

The five annual events to date have published more than 600 papers by authors from 21 countries, not only from Europe but also from Asia, North America, and Africa. The last three events were held in the English language, which opened the conference to the world and improved both quality and visibility. More than 400 participants were present at Bucharest in 2009, engaging in discussions of a very large range of subjects related to e-learning and ADL.

Summary

Norway and Romania are leading advocates of ADL within their military training structures. Through deliberate partnerships with the ADL Initiative, both nations have established ADL capabilities that incorporate SCORM and are pursuing the development of content repositories consistent with the ADL Registry. These national implementations have moved beyond the boundaries of military training and education. For example, the Romanian Ministry of Education is pursuing a much broader implementation of SCORM across the country.

Within the ADL business paradigm, the experiences within Norway and Romania demonstrate the value of formal partnerships in expanding the marketplace for interoperable systems, tools, and content (Wisher, this volume). Other applications within Europe are described by Synytsya and Staub (this volume). The activities described here can serve as a model for other nations who wish to pursue applying the benefits of ADL to satisfy national training and education goals.

Web Resources

Bologna Process. www.ond.vlaanderen.be/hogeronderwijs/bologna/

eLSE Conference (2009). http://adlunap.ro/else2009/

National Defense University Romanian Advanced Distributed Learning Department (RoADL-D). http://adl.unap.ro

Norwegian Defense ADL Centre. http://www.ffu.mil.no

The Authors

Commander Geir Isaksen is an ADL Adviser at the Norwegian Defense ADL Centre (NoDADLC), a part of the Norwegian Defense University College in Oslo. NoDADLC has oversight responsibility for all development, implementation, and acquisition of ADL within Norwegian Defense.

Dr. Professor Ion Roceanu has served as the Director of the Romanian Advanced Distributed Learning Department of the "Carol I" National Defense University since its founding in 2005. He assumed responsibilities for the Romania ADL Partnership Lab in 2009.

Chapter 21

e-Learning, SCORM, and the ADL Korea Partnership Laboratory from the Korea Perspective

Insub Park, Won Ho, and Jungsub Yun

Standardization is a key factor to consider in determining a future direction when fostering a new industrial sector. For the last decade, given the imperatives of a knowledge-driven economy and a learning society, e-learning has drawn attention from various sectors of Korea's social and political economy, with much attention given to its potential for education and training for skill formation. There has been a great deal of debate on standards, and on research and development activities for facilitating the e-learning industry. As a result, the Sharable Content Object Reference Model (SCORM) has attracted attention from the global perspective.

The work of the ADL Initiative has been highlighted in the e-learning industry, and developing a relationship with ADL has been a very significant factor in constructing a global e-learning society. The Republic of Korea, as a leading technology- and knowledge-driven economy, has been actively involved in this work, and, in recent years, the Korean e-learning market has grown by approximately 10 percent every year. The purpose of this chapter is to describe the background, approach, and outcomes of ADL implementation in Korea. In the context of the ADL business paradigm, this chapter addresses the development of partnerships and an e-learning marketplace (Wisher, this volume).

Policy and e-Learning Industry Development

Just after the boom in "dot.coms" in 2000-2001, the e-learning industry began to emerge in the Republic of Korea. It has been the focus of much attention by various ministries of the Korean government concerned with the development of the national economy. In 2004, this led to the enactment of the e-Learning Industry Development Act.

Nine ministries, including the Ministry of Education and Human Resource Development (MoE), the Ministry of Commerce, Industry and Energy (MoCIE), and the Ministry of Labor (MoL), were involved in writing the law and also had responsibility for organizing the Committee for e-Learning Industry Development in which the private sector also participates. Among the ministries, the MoCIE (now the Ministry of Knowledge Economy, MKE), has had primary responsibility for carrying out industry-specific policies and projects, and has also coordinated the generic policies. The MoE focuses on e-learning in the context of education, and the MoL oversees policies and projects related to skill formation training of workers.

The nine responsible ministries formulated and carried out a variety of policies and projects for development of the e-learning industry. These are categorized into six areas: establishment of standardization and certification system, technology development and capacity-building, manpower cultivation, support for start-ups and improvement of distribution systems, use of e-learning, and diffusion of a knowledge-based economy and society through e-learning.

The enactment of e-learning legislation and policies was a signal to the private sector that the government considers the industrial policy for development of the sector to be important and promising. It is against this background that the public-private Joint Committee for the Development of the e-Learning Industry, in which policymakers and specialists from the private sector participate, has been organized and operated.

The Korea ADL Partnership Laboratory

The Korea ADL Partnership Laboratory (hereafter Partnership Lab) was established in January 2007. The U.S. Department of Defense (DoD) and the Ministry of Commerce, Industry and Energy (MoCIE) of the Republic of Korea signed an Intent to Cooperate to support cooperative development of ADL capabilities. The Korea Institute for Electronic Commerce (KIEC), now the National IT Promotion Agency (NIPA), is the acting agency on the Korean side. In March 2007, as one of co-facilitators of the Partnership Lab, the KIEC also joined the International Federation for Learning, Education, and Training Systems Interoperability (LETSI) as a sponsor. The KIEC was a government funded agency under the MoCIE. It was founded in 1998, and was responsible for facilitating e-business and e-learning under the Law of Electronic Transactions and the e-Learning Industry Development Act. KIEC's name changed after it was integrated with two other government agencies, the Korea SW Industry Promotion Agency (KIPA) and the Institute for Information Technology Advancement, to become NIPA in August, 2009.

Internally, the KIEC has organized a cooperative system to conduct the work of the Partnership Lab such as implementing SCORM (Gallagher, this volume) and CORDRA (Lannom, this volume). Many organizations involved with e-learning in Korea have joined this system. They include the Korea Education and Research Information Service (KERIS), the Korea Research Institute for Vocational Education and Training (KRIVET), the Korea e-Learning Industry Association (KELIA), and the Korean Agency for Technology and Standards (KATS). This system of relationships is shown in Figure 21-1.

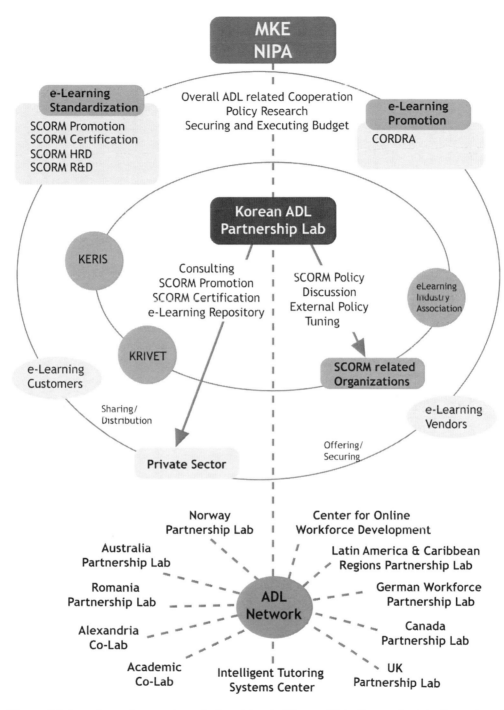

Figure 21-1. e-Learning sector relationships in Korea. This figure depicts the network of cooperative relationships of the Korea ADL Partnership-Lab.

SCORM Certification Capabilities

As an example of their efforts supporting SCORM standardization, especially as a follow-up activity of the Partnership Lab, the KIEC operates the SCORM Conformance Auditing Center which certifies SCORM content and LMSs produced by Korean vendors.

Providing SCORM and LMS certification was requested by Korean vendors for a long time. It was a priority because language differences between English and Korean created difficulties in the auditing process for SCORM certification, resulting in additional costs to the vendors. The KIEC sent personnel who would conduct the audits of content packages and LMSs for training, with full cooperation from the Academic ADL Co-Lab in Madison, Wisconsin (Panar, Brannon, & Poltrack, this volume). As a result, although only 13 products were SCORM-certified during the four year period from 2003-2006, 20 LMSs and courses were SCORM-certified by the Korea ADL Partnership Lab during the three year period from 2007-2009. This is a significant increase over the earlier rate of developing SCORM-certified content and LMSs.

Another cooperative activity is developing SCORM experts for the workforce. The KIEC conducts SCORM-specific education and training called SCORM School. By the end of 2008, it supplied 224 SCORM practitioners to government and industry. Most are employed as "knowledge workers." In addition, to support SCORM diffusion throughout the country, it published a *SCORM Handbook* as well as a series of SCORM documents that have been translated into Korean, and distributed them to universities and vendor associations. A local ADL mirror Web site enables Koreans to easily access ADL materials.

Implementation of SCORM

A major SCORM standard-based e-learning system in Korea is the Cyber Home Learning System (CHLS). CHLS has been a very successful e-learning pilot project. It has been carried out throughout the country, and represents a valuable case that demonstrates a SCORM application that has been implemented and tested in a national context.

The Cyber Home Learning System

The CHLS originated as a response to several educational, social, and political issues. It focuses on primary and secondary education with the intent of reducing the high additional education costs for families, incurred by sending children to private grammar schools or for private tutoring. At the same time, CHLS enhances and strengthens the quality of public education. It addresses a long-standing problem arising from the high motives and force of education in Korean society. Given the existence of the knowledge-driven and learning society, the alternative of e-learning drew the attention of policy-makers because it addresses a long-standing and challenging problem.

The CHLS was launched in two large cities and one province during the second half of 2004—the cities of Daegu and Gwangju, and the province of Gyongsangbuk-do, located in the south-eastern part of the Korean peninsula. In 2005, the program was implemented nation-wide, in 16 Metropolitan and Provincial Offices of Education (MPOE). The MoE establishes the master plan of the CHLS and coordinates related parties and projects. The CHLS center (or KERIS) conducts basic research, provides standards guidelines, and supports content/systems operation. The MPOE provides the services of the CHLS, and operates the systems. It is basically an organic central-regional cooperation system, as shown in Figure 21-2.

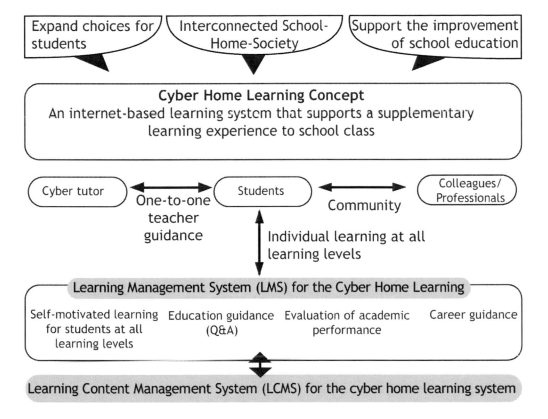

Figure 21-2. Conceptual diagram of the Cyber Home Learning System (Cho, 2006). This diagram depicts the structure and relationships of the CHLS.

CHLS's services include providing free learning content, online testing, and interacting with teachers to support students, as well as customizing the e-learning programs based on specific needs. The contents are developed in levels: complementary, standard, and advanced Korean language, sociology, mathematics, science, and English, for instance. Online tutorial services between teachers and students are available. This enables a student to obtain help from teachers on a one-to-one basis within the context of facilitating her/his learning progress, and on the basis of immediate convenience such as place, time, or even teaching-learning method. It is designed to gain as many benefits as possible from the use of the Internet. It also extends to areas of consultation, counseling on career paths for the future, and to the broader learning community. As a result, it has one-million participants, including 840,000 students. The workflow of CHLS services is shown below in Figure 21-3.

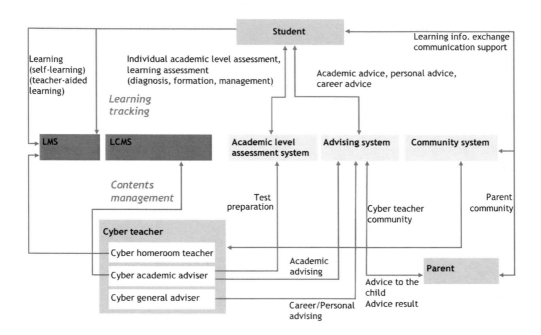

Figure 21-3. Cyber Home Learning System workflow. This figure diagrams the workflow of the service system (Cho, 2006).

In relation to the standardization of learning content and/or management systems, the CHLS project was centrally coordinated for interoperability and content reuse by the MoE and a government-funded institute, the KERIS, as an acting agent. There are 17 organizations in the project that operate their own separate servers and LMSs. Content is developed, in part, by each of the 16 MPOEs, although the project is under the control of the MoE. The content is shared and distributed among the MPOEs through their different learning management systems. To do this, content must be developed in a standardized manner in order to be more efficient and interoperable. To achieve this, content developers must follow guidelines, and SCORM 2004 has been applied. KERIS and the MoE coordinate and control this process.

SCORM and Workforce Training
From another perspective, the MoL also encourages adoption of SCORM standards. The MoL is responsible for vocational training for workers, as mentioned above. For the vocational training program, the MoL encourages enterprises to foster e-learning, and provides some financial resources for support, according to the employment insurance refund provision.

The market size of specific e-learning vocational training that is financially supported from the employment insurance was 10 percent of the total Korean e-learning market in 2007, approximately $1 billion U.S. (at 1,200 Korean won to the U.S. dollar). This implies that the MoL is a key player in inducing private capital investment in the e-learning industry, and the insurance can be an attractive incentive.

Then how is it related to standardization and SCORM? E-learning content for vocational training is evaluated and graded in terms of quality of the content. If the courses are evaluated at a higher level, then the costs are refunded at a higher rate from the employment insurance support. The evaluation process is based on a set of criteria. One of the criteria is whether the content was developed using standards for interoperability and/or re-use. More than 50 percent of clients request to apply SCORM standards and specifications. This work is conducted by a government funded institute under the MoL, the Korea Research Institute for Vocational Education and Training.

Implications and Summary

In parallel with the accumulation of knowledge and experience gained from the early adoptions described above, there are a few additional features that should be considered.

First, from the technological perspective, some claimed that SCORM seems to be "heavy" in some aspects. It would be more desirable to follow SCORM standards if it was easier or "lighter." In particular, sequencing of SCORM 2004 is reputed to be too difficult to implement perfectly in Korea. In order to overcome this problem, some suggest using templates. Even so, it is still difficult to understand and use them. Because of this, a specific, culture-oriented sequencing case study was conducted in order to collect internal and external sequencing templates and to develop desirable models. Implementation of SCORM may need to be flexible.

Second, a shortage of SCORM-skilled manpower can be a barrier in the process of fostering the SCORM standard. This is because the imbalance between the supply of SCORM specialists and the demand for SCORM-conformant content and systems brings about a tension. For instance, developing SCORM-conformant content and systems may increase development costs because of needing to hire SCORM-skilled manpower for additional work of SCORM-conformant instructional design. Because of this, small enterprises may not invest enough in implementing SCORM sequencing in content development. This may lead to producing content that is of reduced quality.

Third, balancing educational efficacy and price competitiveness is also a matter to be countered. Although an objective of developers is to enhance the educational effects of their content, another objective is to be more competitive in price than others. Then, the question is to identify an optimal point between both educational effect and price competitiveness in implementing SCORM. Therefore, fourth, this returns to the issue of improving the ease of learning and using the SCORM standard.

In sum, lastly and more importantly, without trial and error through employing SCORM, it is not easy to improve it. And at the moment it is difficult to expect to share e-learning content without SCORM to the current degree, and maybe in the future (Shanley ct al., this volume). Furthermore, in this sense, to build a global e-learning society, the role of the Korea ADL Partnership Lab should not remain bilateral, but should expand beyond it.

References

Cho, Y.-S. (2006, January). *Case of using SCORM in the Cyber Home Learning System*. Paper presented at the 2nd International Plugfest, Taipei, Taiwan.

Jesukiewicz, P. (2007). *SCORM and CORDRA*. Paper presented to the Korea-ADL Workshop, Seoul, Korea.

Web Resources

Korea ADL Partnership Lab mirror Web site: http://www.adlkorea.or.kr

The Authors

Insub Park is the Director of Specialized HRD Division, the National IT Promotion Agency, Korea.

Won Ho is a Professor at the Kongju National University, Gognju, Korea.

Jungsub Yun is Senior Researcher, e-Learning Division, the National IT Promotion Agency, Korea.

Chapter 22

ADL-ILCE Partnership Lab for Latin America and the Caribbean
Jose Cartas

The success of the ADL Initiative is predicated on a successful network of partnerships and collaborations. Originally directed to collaborate within the U.S. government through an Executive Order in 1999, ADL has served to foster a much broader marketplace for interoperable distributed learning systems and content. Interest in ADL technologies and an accompanying collaborative spirit have grown well beyond U.S. borders, not only in other nations but also in regional consortia. The purpose of this chapter is to describe the partnership between ADL and countries in Latin America and the Caribbean, implemented through a regional international organization. Within the ADL business paradigm, this chapter focuses directly on the collaboration and partnerships aspect (Wisher, this volume).

The Latin American Institute of Educational Communication (ILCE), headquartered in Mexico City, is an international organization comprising fourteen member States: Bolivia, Colombia, Costa Rica, Ecuador, El Salvador, Dominican Republic, Guatemala, Haiti, Honduras, Mexico, Nicaragua, Panama, Paraguay and Venezuela. Throughout its history, which dates to 1954, the ILCE has focused its efforts on the development, research, and dissemination of media and information technologies for distance education, training, production of educational material, and human resource development.

ILCE has broad experience in the development of vanguard educative models that encourage the use of virtual learning spaces, the use of satellite technology, videoconferencing, e-learning, and multimedia applications. It also promotes and uses innovative techniques and theories in the design of learning processes, taking into consideration users' context, capabilities, needs, motivation, and interests.

The ADL Initiative recognized ILCE as a well-qualified and well-positioned institution to create the Latin America and Caribbean Regions ADL Partnership Lab (ADL-ILCE Partnership Lab), given its history, purpose, experience, and influence in the region in the use of communicative technologies to support education (Department of Defense, 2007). The ADL-ILCE Partnership Lab is a natural extension of ILCE's existing network in Latin America and complements the bond with ADL's network of Co-Laboratories and global Partnership Labs.

Formal ADL Relationship

On March 26th 2007, ILCE and the ADL Initiative announced their partnership for Latin America and the Caribbean region. The objective was to maximize benefits from distance education technologies, as well as to optimize prevailing communicative technological capabilities of the countries in the region. The signed document, an Intent to Cooperate, was released in Washington, DC through an announcement specifying that this initiative was the result of discussions and meetings between the United States of America and several Latin American and Caribbean countries that realized a common technical interest in e-learning. These discussions led to ILCE becoming the fifth ADL Partnership Lab, along with the United Kingdom, Canada, Australia, and Korea.

Among the main tasks of the ADL-ILCE Partnership Lab is emphasizing the importance of promoting education and training for all, in any place and at any time. ILCE promotes these goals by sharing ILCE's technological resources, such as its repository, for the reusability of learning objects, and collaborating with multiple institutions to develop and operate online courses, using its own instructional design methodology and technological infrastructure for distance education. In this context, the ADL-ILCE Partnership Lab fosters the creation of an international and inter-institutional network, to promote SCORM implementation, especially throughout Latin America and the Caribbean.

This chapter highlights four projects: the adoption of SCORM in Latin America, the translation of selected ADL documents into Spanish, the creation of a regional training network on using SCORM for online courses, and the creation of a Latin American center for digital resources.

Supporting the Adoption of SCORM in Latin America

The ADL-ILCE Partnership Lab knew that there was a compelling need to develop a plan to introduce SCORM into the region. SCORM was a new idea and there were few materials for training and education. The initial requirement, then, was to offer courses on SCORM and make them available to a broad audience.

Basic Course on SCORM: A Solution for Educators
The objective of this project was to develop and operate an online SCORM 1.2 course in Spanish for Latin American educational institutions. The course would help these institutions understand strategies, standards, and characteristics of SCORM to facilitate creating and operating online courses based on Sharable Content Objects (SCOs). This is necessary to ensure the reusability and interoperability of certified learning management systems. (LMSs).

As part of this project, ILCE is pioneering the design and implementation of an online SCORM course in Spanish, based on the model's technical requirements. This project intends to make SCORM available to all the countries of the region.

Annual Training

The basic SCORM course was offered three times during 2008 and three more courses were programmed for 2009. The first course was carried out from November 12 – February 6, 2008, and lasted 60 hours. Course participants came from 30 educational and non-educational institutions from both the public and private sectors of several States in Mexico, as well as from the Hispanic community in the United States.

In the second course, given from January 12 – February 20, 2009, teachers and researchers from the main educational institutions from northern and central Mexico enrolled in the course. The third course took place from May 25 – July 7, 2009. Diverse national and international institutions participated. This course was also part of a training program on SCORM for ILCE staff. The fourth course started in August 2009, and enrolled more than 200 participants from Latin American countries and Mexico. The fifth course took place in the late fall, 2009.

A sample of institutions participating in the Basic Course on SCORM is presented in Table 22-1 below.

Table 22-1

Representative Sample of Institutions Participating in ADL-ILCE's Basic SCORM Course

Participating Institution	Country
National University of Salta	Argentina
Polytechnic Faculty of UNA	Paraguay
University of La Paz	Paraguay
Technological University of Panama	Panama
State Distance Education University	Costa Rica
State University of Bolivar	Ecuador
Experimental Pedagogic University "Libertador"	Venezuela
University of Veracruz	Mexico
University of Aguascalientes	Mexico

There has been a higher demand for every course than originally expected. Participation had to be limited because of constraints related to the technological infrastructure and availability of human resources at the ADL-ILCE Partnership Lab. Each course was fully enrolled, and more than 600 individuals, representing several dozen individual educational institutions and organizations, have completed the training.

Development of ILCE's Instructional Design Method

The ADL-ILCE Partnership Lab's instructional design group is composed of a multidisciplinary team of educators, media analysts, and psychologists. They have developed, through years of experience, an original instructional design method, based on psycho-pedagogical theories, for designing Sharable Content Objects from a learning perspective.

The ILCE's capability to convene regional interests has led to the establishment of an informal ADL working group, which has succeeded in promoting a positive response to our initial SCORM courses, and in creating new working relationships with a variety of national and international educational institutions. Thus, ADL-ILCE has created a valuable database of possible future partners that could contribute to advancing SCORM adoption and possibly forming future alliances with the ADL-ILCE Partnership Lab.

The first phase of the community consolidation around SCORM includes the creation of a national and international database containing more than 800 registrations from university deans, directors, managers, officials, professors, and researchers from 420 public and private institutions throughout the Latin American and Caribbean regions. A breakdown of total course registrations by country is shown in Table 22-2.

Table 22-2

Total Registrations in SCORM Course by Country (mid-2009)

Country	Participating Institutions
Mexico	377
Argentina	4
Bolivia	4
Panama	4
Guatemala	3
Peru	3
Colombia	3
Brazil	2
Costa Rica	2
Ecuador	2
El Salvador	2
Honduras	2
Nicaragua	2
Paraguay	2

Chile	2
Venezuela	2
Uruguay	2
Dominican Republic	1
Haiti	1
Total	**420**

Future Plans

During the next several years, the ADL-ILCE Partnership Lab will continue to promote the adoption of SCORM standards and specifications throughout the region, and, specifically, will:

- Offer the basic course on SCORM four times a year.

- Strengthen ILCE's staff participation in the Basic Course on SCORM.

- Increase dissemination and undertake a promotional campaign on SCORM, in order to acquire new interest groups.

- Design and operate an advanced course on SCORM (SCORM 2004).

- Register at least 100 university deans from Latin American institutions.

- Update the ADL-ILCE Partnership Lab database.

Translate into Spanish and Disseminate SCORM Related Materials

The objective of this project is to translate documents, handbooks, and articles related to SCORM, currently only available in English, into Spanish. They will be made available on the Web and as printed materials, in order to inform educators of the importance and characteristics of SCORM and promote its use.

Translation Projects

The ADL-ILCE Partnership Lab has translated into Spanish the official bulletin of the International Federation for Learning, Education, and Training Systems Interoperability and distributed it among all the sponsors and partners. In addition to translating handbooks and strategic documents into Spanish, the ADL-ILCE Partnership Lab has also translated the following course documents into Spanish:

- Best Practices for Content Developers of SCORM LSAL

- SCORM 2004 (Introduction to SCORM)

- Handbook of SCORM Content Aggregation Model

- Handbook of SCORM Run-time Environment

- Handbook of SCORM Sequencing and Navigation

- SCOURSE – a course about SCORM provided by the Academic ADL Co-Lab

- SCORM Course School 1.2

- SCORM 1.2 to 2004

- Information on standard ISO SC36, the entry point for SCORM as a global standard

Future Plans

The ADL-ILCE Partnership Lab will continue to promote SCORM materials and documents to facilitate the dissemination of standards among Latin American countries. This will provide strategic benefits for distance education development in these countries.

Regional and National Leadership Efforts

The ADL-ILCE Partnership Lab recognized a need to create greater visibility for SCORM, beyond occasional courses that are primarily introductory in nature. This led to the creation of a broader outreach effort. There is substantial interest in SCORM, so developing a forum to support the dialogue between ADL experts and other educational professionals on the needs and interests of researchers, implementers, and practitioners became a priority.

Create a Regional Inter-Institutional Training Network Based on SCORM

The ADL-ILCE Partnership Lab has implemented a project to create a regional, inter-institutional network for SCORM training.

Objective. Create an international and inter-institutional network to promote and introduce SCORM to Latin American and Caribbean universities and institutions, in order to develop e-learning technologies and promote the creation of SCOs in Spanish for interoperability and reusability throughout the region.

Presentation of experiences and results. An International Forum, e-Learning Perspectives Using ADL-SCORM Technologies, took place in Mexico City in May 2006. During this event, international experts from all over the world presented their SCORM applications, developments, and experiences. Discussion themes focused on the future of ADL technologies and on defining the steps needed to establish international cooperation.

The Forum attracted approximately 500 specialists representing 150 universities and educational institutions, with the majority coming from Mexico and other Latin American countries. Twenty-four papers were presented by world renowned specialists on ADL technologies and SCORM applications and development, including speakers from Korea, Taiwan, Australia, Chile, the United States, and Mexico.

The Forum facilitated the establishment of working relationships among different Latin American educational institutions interested in collaborating directly with the ADL-ILCE Partnership Lab on the dissemination, operation, and certification of content and LMSs using ADL's SCORM technologies. Among the most active institutions, the following stand out: the University of Sao Paulo, Brazil; the University of Arts, Sciences and Communication of Chile; the major National University of San Marcos, Lima, Peru; and the Central American Technological Institute of El Salvador.

Due to the large number of participating institutions, the ADL-ILCE Partnership Lab emphasized a proposal for establishing a Latin American Network for collaboration, made up of 76 public and private universities and organizations, as part of the ADL community. The Forum was a complete success and met its goals and participant expectations.

Creation of the ADL-ILCE Partnership Lab Web site. Considering the increasing demand and importance of SCORM in the region, the ADL-ILCE Partnership Lab updated its Web site in November 2008, to provide greater support to interest groups around SCORM. Currently, there are 270 registered members from more than 150 Latin American and Caribbean institutions who actively participate on our Web site.

Presentations on SCORM to different institutions. SCORM has been presented to many different public and private institutions in Mexico and Latin America that are interested in establishing joint projects to improve training systems and certification processes. Among these are nine National State Secretariats and six national educational institutions in Mexico, as well as major universities in Ecuador, Argentina, and Honduras, and the Electronic System of Public Hiring of Panama.

Presentation of the reference model to ILCE's personnel. This effort was conducted through meetings with all different departments of ILCE to introduce SCORM and demonstrate its advantages and benefits.

Attention to specific requests for courses. This effort developed a methodological proposal jointly with several groups from ILCE. It was focused specifically on training and human development, and on acquiring SCORM abilities, initiated at the request of the Federal Electricity Commission of Mexico.

Future Plans
The ADL-ILCE Partnership Lab will continue to work with educational, government, and commercial groups to further the adoption of SCORM standards and certified technologies within the region. These efforts will include:

- Exchanging knowledge on achievements in education and training based on SCORM.

- Establishing the link between standards, markets, and innovation.

- Gathering experiences and requirements to improve SCORM, including innovations such as games (Xu, this volume), social media tools (Fowler, this volume), mobile devices (Brown, this volume) and virtual worlds (Gamor, this volume).

- Implementing SCORM in Mexican and Latin American institutions to promote the exchange and reusability of SCOs.

Create a Latin American Center of Educational Virtual Collection

The objective of the proposed Center is to establish the necessary conditions for creating a virtual center to store and manage digital educational resources from Mexico and Latin America. This will support the creation and production of innovative materials and models in the region for using information and communication technologies.

The plans for this project were drafted in 2009, and much work has been done in the description of the different phases and the budget, taking advantage of the ADL work on registering learning content (Lannom, this volume).

Future Plans

As part of the Center's work, future plans include developing projects to take advantage of the CORDRA Project (Content Object Repository Discovery Registration/Resolution Architecture), which promotes the establishment of a central registry of a world-wide network of repositories. The Center also plans to contribute to the development and implementation of the "Multiple Screen Project." This project is being planned to establish an integrated (or comprehensive) satellite system, with radio and television channels, regional reception and content production centers, and an Internet educational portal for the establishment of knowledge networks.

The convergence of various media solutions, based on a flexible technological platforms, will enable the establishment of educational, training, and continuous education opportunities that will support parallel efforts to improve economic development in Latin American communities.

Outlook for Future Implementations and Recommendations

The ADL-ILCE will continue its leadership role in implementing SCORM standards and specifications in Latin America and the Caribbean through multiple initiatives. It has developed strategies to further the goals of SCORM-based advanced distributed learning throughout the region.

SCORM Implementation Strategies in Latin America

The ADL-ILCE Partnership Lab has developed a set of strategies for implementing SCORM in the Latin America and Caribbean regions.

Integrate awareness of cultural influences. SCORM implementation must consider issues related to the region's socio-cultural identity, including its languages, geography, and culture.

Collaborate on projects. Collaborate with educational services (and/or authorities), universities, and public and private organizations, on specific projects that will contribute to further knowledge and implementation of SCORM.

Develop specifications for content development. Collaborate with other ADL global partners and working groups to improve methodological specifications in didactical content development that are compatible with SCORM.

Collaborate on advancing educational technologies. Continue to work with educational technology and standard-based institutions that promote interoperability and sharing of knowledge, learning content, and e-learning tools.

Disseminate research and development results. Work with others to promote joint publication of research and development results in national and international academic forums.

Promote development of Spanish language SCOs. Continue to support the production of Sharable Content Objects (SCOs) in Spanish.

Provide access to technology tools. Share ILCE's technology tools and infrastructure, such as its repository for the reusability of SCOs.

Support consistent methodologies and standards for online course development. Collaborate with other institutions in the development and implementation of online courses, using ILCE's learning-content development methodology and its e-learning infrastructure.

Specific Implementation Activities

The general implementation goals will be achieved through several specific activities.

- Translate and write articles related to SCORM.

- Increase course offerings on SCORM in Spanish and implement the model through online services, workshops, and videoconferencing.

- Create new online courses based on SCORM guidelines, such as courses focused on Instructional Design and SCORM (Deibler & Berking, this volume) and Shared Content Objects.

- Consolidate a metadata model in Spanish based on SCORM in order to unify criteria for the reusability of learning objects (Shanley et al., this volume).

- Promote inter-institutional meetings among academics and experts to define common interests and cooperation for didactical methodologies applied to e-learning.

- Channel certification of contents designed according to SCORM standards from public and private educational institutions in Latin American and the Caribbean, through ILCE to the ADL Evaluation and Certification Centers.

- Exchange information and technical data through an ADL-ILCE inter-institutional collaboration network.

- Organize forums, congresses, and plugfests in different Latin American countries in order to exchange experiences on SCORM.

Summary

The excellent working relationship between ADL and ILCE has created a critical partnership for the Latin American and Caribbean region. In its role as an ADL Partnership Lab, ILCE has enabled the up-to-date implementation of SCORM and eventual technology advances in the area of content discovery and reuse. The response within the region has been tremendous concerning what SCORM offers and how ADL can facilitate the compatibility of interests between parties. SCORM has proven to be an equalizer across language boundaries as others share the vision to provide high quality education and training on demand.

Web Resources

Latin America and Caribbean Regions ADL Partnership Lab.
http://www.adl-ilce.org.mx/

Author Notes

The following organizations and universities in Latin America and the Caribbean have received presentations on SCORM.

Mexican National State Secretariats:

- Secretariat of Communication and Transport (Information and Knowledge Society Coordination)

- Secretariat of Labor

- Secretariat of Health

- Secretariat of Public Education for the State of Mexico

- Secretariat of Foreign Affairs

- Federal Commission for Electricity

- National Institute of Social Development

- Federal Judiciary Council

- National Population Council

National Educational Institutions:

- National School of Technical and Professional Education

- National Polytechnic Institute

- Technical Universities throughout Mexico

- Polytechnic University of the State of Mexico

- Ibero-American University

- General Directorate for Industrial and Technological Education

Other International Institutions:

- Catholic University of Santiago de Guayaquil (Ecuador)

- National University of Salta (Argentina)

- Zamorano University (Honduras)

- Electronic System of Public Hiring of Panama

The Author

Josè Cartas is the Director of the Latin American and Caribbean Regions ADL Partnership Lab. Mr. Cartas has also represented the Ministry of Education of Mexico for the World Bank in the area of technological education.

Chapter 23

Partnership for Peace Consortium and the ADL Working Group
Kateryna Synytsya and Timo Staub

The Advanced Distributed Learning (ADL) Initiative is open to collaborations and partnerships with those who share a common goal and vision for learning on demand. At the North Atlantic Treaty Organization (NATO) Summit in 1999 in Washington, which recognized 50 years of mutual support through the alliance, heads of state and governments endorsed the Partnership for Peace (PfP) Training and Education Enhancement Program, which encouraged the use of ADL to optimize and improve training (NATO, 2003). Re-endorsements of this program have been made at subsequent NATO summits, and numerous nations have endorsed ADL with enthusiasm (Isaksen & Roceanu, this volume).

The purpose of this chapter is to describe some leading ADL efforts by nations in the Partnership for Peace (PfP) program. This chapter describes the activities of the ADL Working Group (ADL WG) within the PfP Consortium of Defense Academies and Security Studies Institutes. It briefly outlines methods of collaboration, the adoption of ADL technologies, the creation of learning content, and the current challenges to the ADL WG. The ADL WG provides opportunities for people from different countries to collaborate together on specific projects, providing advice and support for one another, and using complementary knowledge and skills. Working together within the ADL WG in this way has contributed to better understanding among countries, and has been an integral part of the trust-building process that is part of the mission of the PfP. Within the context of the ADL business paradigm, this chapter describes activities that focus on collaboration and partnership aspects as well as the interoperability, pedagogy, and design aspects (Wisher, this volume).

The Partnership for Peace Program

The purpose of the PfP is to foster an atmosphere of cooperation to support stability in the European, Caucasian, and Central Asian regions, and to promote cooperation among non-NATO and NATO countries in Europe, Central Asia, and southern Caucasus. Another organization, the Euro-Atlantic Partnership Council (EAPC), was founded in 1997 as a forum for political consultation on various issues between NATO and Partner countries. Both EAPC and PfP are linked to the NATO structure. The basic principle for this cooperation is voluntary participation. Each Partner country commits to preserving democratic societies.

At the end of 2009, there were 22 members of the PfP, including six western European countries, four countries belonging to the former Yugoslavia, and twelve from the former Soviet Republics. Several of the earliest PfP member countries have joined NATO as full members. For countries that are not NATO members, PfP has been the prime instrument for defense collaboration, and for developing the military and civil interoperability that countries needed to be able to contribute to international crisis management and peace support operations.

At the end of 2009, there were 50 countries participating in EAPC/PfP. Besides primary goals, such as the building of defense institutions, Partner countries work together on issues such as civil emergency planning and cooperation with other international organizations, including the United Nations. In addition, NATO/PfP/ EAPC has adopted a policy on combating trafficking in human beings, has issued guidelines in this area for personnel in NATO-led operations, and has used advanced distributed learning technologies to provide education and training on this issue.

The PfP Consortium (PfPC) is a voluntary association of organizations in NATO and PfP countries responsible for learning, education, and training in defense and security policy. Currently, the Consortium consists of more than 350 organizations in almost four dozen countries. The PfPC is a "consortium of the willing," and its mission includes "strengthening defense and military education through enhanced national and institutional cooperation," which is being implemented by collaborative activities within working and study groups. The groups organize seminars and workshops, publish policy papers and research results, develop reference curricula, and share courses that contribute to the education of future leaders. The Consortium supports not only face-to-face activities but also virtual networking and the collaboration of experts through its portals.

The ADL Working Group

The PfP Consortium Advanced Distributed Learning Working Group (ADL WG) was established shortly after the founding of the Consortium, and focuses on the use of e-learning to foster educational collaboration, training transformation, interoperability, and education for reform. The group shares education and training solutions among organizations from Partner and NATO countries. Its activity focuses on several related tasks:

Creation and Exchange of Common Education and Training Content
The sharing of learning content builds a platform for common standards in training, as well as better understanding of approaches and solutions implemented within the EAPC. Special emphasis is given to issues that go beyond national defense training, such as training for peace support operations, language training, and security policy education.

Establishment of Common Education and Training Methods

The group offers white papers, guidelines, and training in instructional design. It identifies common quality criteria, and offers best practice examples. In their first production of courseware, new Cooperative Development Teams (CDTs) usually rely on the instructor's guide, which is a document that explains the basics of course planning, structuring, and development, referring to human-computer interfaces, and demonstrating proven instructional design samples. Together with intensive training workshops, this document facilitates the transfer of expertise within the group, and provides a simple framework for the creation of learning materials and assessments.

Support of Interoperable, Free, and Open-Source Technology

The interoperability of e-learning technology is fundamental to enabling organizations to choose a technology that fits their needs and resources at a given moment, with the additional assurance that they can move on to other vendors and providers without losing their learning content. Free and open source software systems and courses give additional security, providing all participants with equal access to internationally recognized learning content and software. This provides a foundation for the first steps when introducing e-learning in partner organizations.

Open-Source Learning Management System

The ADL WG offers its ILIAS learning management system (LMS), hosted by the International Relations and Security Network (ISN) based in Zurich, for course delivery on an individual and organizational basis. ISN is the world's leading open access information service for international relations and security professionals. ISN promotes greater knowledge sharing, learning, and collaboration through an array of free, high-quality information services, including e-learning consulting, content, and technology services and products.

ILIAS is a Web-based, open source LMS. It supports learning content management and tools for collaboration, communication, evaluation, and assessment. ILIAS was developed collaboratively with the University of Cologne (Germany) and others in November 1998. The team published ILIAS as open source software available to all in 2000. A new version of ILIAS was developed in 2004, called ILIAS 3; it was the first open source LMS that was SCORM 1.2-conformant. Upgrades have since made it SCORM 2004-conformant.

Courses

The ADL WG courses are used world-wide as a part of the curriculum, usually serving as pre-training for face-to-face courses and exercises, or as supportive and reference material. The ILIAS LMS also provides hosting for particular organizations to develop and run courses to save costs as they establish their own internal ADL capability. This is an excellent example of expanding the market for interoperability and scaling through an open source option, within the goals of the ADL business paradigm.

Enhancements of the ILIAS LMS are coordinated with stakeholders, with interoperability as a fundamental requirement. For example, a SCORM editor is under final development to simplify the instructional design processes. Although the group does not yet have a repository of separate reusable learning objects, e-learning courses may be obtained as SCORM packages to be delivered by an organization through its LMS.

The object-oriented vision of learning content first offered in SCORM at the level of sharable content objects (SCOs)—instructionally meaningful learning objects traceable in an LMS—was further extended towards generic content elements in the authoring tools: The learning content created by these tools can be exported and shared not only as a SCORM package, but also as structured content according to its XML schema. It is adaptable to the organizational templates, which define its appearance and behavior, thus smoothing integration of the imported content into the "native" courses developed by this organization.

Cooperative Development Teams

Course development within the ADL WG is supported by several Cooperative Development Teams consisting of professionals responsible for specific but interrelated functions.

Project management. This function includes communication with subject matter experts and stakeholders; pulling together resources; setting goals, deadlines, and priorities; and arranging for comments and feedback.

Instructional design. This function is responsible for the overall planning of the ADL course, defining learning objectives for particular modules and lessons, converting available material into learning experiences, storyboarding, and creating assessments (Deibler & Berking, this volume).

Technical implementation and support. The purpose of this activity is to cover all issues related to programming, use of various multimedia tools, incorporation of interactive exercises, and ensuring SCORM-conformance of the produced learning content.

The size of the team depends on the workload and competencies of the individuals. The clear identification of major tasks facilitates collaboration both within the CDT, and with other CDTs which may participate in the same project. The ADL approach adopted by the group enables the independent development of the SCOs by several authors using different tools. This not only increases the team's efficiency due to parallel tasking, but also provides greater flexibility in applying relevant development tools for specific learning assignments. For example, interactive exercises require very specific development skills; therefore these may be identified early to be completed in time for course assembly from particular SCOs.

ADL Challenges

Although e-learning solutions have proven to be a valid mechanism for world-wide education and training, there are a number of challenges for the ADL WG. Recent meetings have been held in Bucharest (Romania), Sofia (Bulgaria), Kiev (Ukraine), and Oberammergau (Germany). The Working Group meets twice a year to discuss topics of mutual concern, and to offer workshops to participants working at a more technical level. The meetings address the challenges facing the Working Group and consider the potential solutions. The recurring challenges relate to content, technology, and attitudes.

Content-Related Challenges

Defense and security issues are always subject to scrutiny when it comes to open publication. This poses an additional barrier to the free and open exchange of the learning material, in particular by requiring its delivery under controlled conditions. Moreover, national regulations and a lack of trust in network security not only complicate the availability of the courses through the Internet but also bring into question their development, due to high development costs and limited distribution. When it comes to using publicly available ADL courses, educational organizations face the challenge of differences in curriculum structure and priorities, non-native languages, as well as pedagogical acceptance by the staff. However, the ADL approach, based on interoperability, facilitates the adaptation of courses at the SCO level, the transfer of courses to local secured environments, and enables control of the student's learning progress, meeting the basic needs of national defense training.

Technology-Related Challenges

E-learning solutions cover a wide spectrum of environments, simulations, and courses. In military organizations, strict regulations of IT tools, services, and available file formats limit the choice of multimedia and communication support tools even while students' expectations of technology may be rather high (Xu, this volume; Fowler, this volume). A choice between high-tech and low-tech courses may also be dictated by the bandwidth, which is still an issue for many military organizations in partner countries.

SCORM enables easy migration of high-tech courses to the local LMS, accessible through the organizational intranet and thus saving on the connection, whereas other courses are accessible to students worldwide through the Internet. Standards conformance supports smooth progress along the path of technology innovations, allowing for the co-existence of legacy content together with the latest acquisitions.

Attitude-Related Challenges

Countries and institutions with a low e-readiness are often reluctant at the senior management level to accept or approve advanced distributed learning for education and training. E-readiness reflects not only the status of connectivity and technology infrastructure, government policy, and legislation, but also the general attitudes and everyday use of information and communications technology for business and leisure. To overcome this barrier, technology should come with some training, explanation, and tangible examples that show the added value of ADL in training and education. In this respect, the group focuses on grass-roots efforts to build ADL acceptance and adoption by training ADL users and developers, and by sharing and discussing use-cases and best practices.

To achieve the decision-makers' buy-in of the ADL approach, it is important to offer an opportunity to pilot the approach, to test its applicability, and to support an easy start-up without the significant investments typically needed for technology-rich solutions. This is one of the benefits of interoperability, enabling affordable e-learning solutions and scalability through a stepped growth of support for ADL within the organization, moving from simple courses and a limited number of users to large-scale use.

The ADL Initiative's functional requirements, sometimes called the "ilities," have been adopted by the ADL WG because they are crucial to meeting the challenges outlined above. In addition, the ADL WG has informally added *adaptability* and *affordability* to the core "ilities":

Accessibility of the learning content so that it can be discovered, and delivered on demand, anytime and anywhere through the Internet or other networks.

Interoperability among independently developed courses and various LMSs, enabling defense academies and security study institutes to take advantage of what others have developed.

Durability of legacy content so that it can be delivered on upgrades to systems together with the introduction of interactive multimedia and new technologies.

Reusability provides the flexibility to incorporate instructional components in multiple applications and contexts.

Adaptability of the ADL courses at the level of individual SCOs, allowing learning content to be sequenced in different ways for different learners. Furthermore, the visual appearance of learning content should also be adaptable, especially if it consists of interactive text.

Affordability of e-learning solutions due to the exchange of the courses and their *re-use* in particular organizations, as well as the use of free Internet hosting capabilities for those who are early in ADL implementation.

Use Cases and Statistics

Figure 23-1 illustrates the steady growth of the ADL users at the PfP LMS. About 70 courses are freely available to everyone, offering introduction to a variety of defense-related topics.

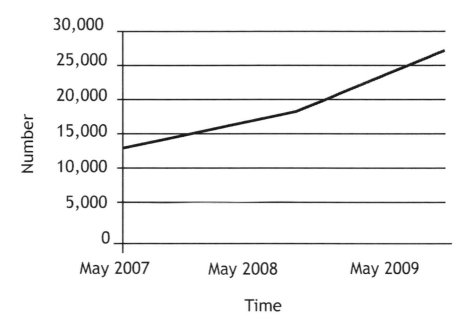

Figure 23-1. User accounts on PfP LMS 2007-2009. This graph shows an almost doubling in growth in the number of users accessing the PfP LMS during a two-year period.

The topics include courses on defense institution building, peace support operations, civil military co-operation, international law and security issues, NATO structure and activities, English courses for staff officers, etc. The English Language Training Enhancement Course is a typical example of an international collaboration in an ADL course development where distributed experts located in Sofia (Bulgaria), Garmisch-Partenkirchen (Germany), San Antonio (Texas, USA), and the Ukraine CDT (Kiev, Ukraine) could benefit from the assistance, review, and feedback provided by individuals and organizations participating in the ADL WG. Some of the ADL courses, such as the Introduction to NATO course, passed through several updates and restructuring, and have been amended, adjusted to national curriculum, and translated to other languages.

The increasing international use of ADL courses has led to an improved understanding of the ADL approach. Thus there is a growing experience in the re-use of assets in language courses, and the ADL course developers recognize the importance of reusability considerations at the planning and design stage. Hence, new interactive exercises in map reading will be designed as learning objects for multiple uses in introductory modules of courses on radio communication, medical evacuation, operational planning, and related subjects.

Conclusion

The ADL framework is still not fully exploited by the PfP community, but it has increasingly gained acceptance, and the user numbers are growing. In the future, issues of maintenance, update, and adaptation of the existing courses to particular learning groups will gain more weight within the course life cycle. Together with the need for rapid content production it will draw more attention to the learning objects repository as a source for ready-to-use course components. In this respect, the standardization of course interfaces is important for the natural integration of course components obtained from various sources.

The concept of creating a repository of learning objects has great potential for the PfP Consortium, which is tracking technical developments in the ADL Initiative (Lannom, this volume). The repository concept may be further extended to support the following tasks: 1) informing all those who uploaded a learning object (alone or within a package) from the repository that an updated version is available; 2) enhanced search capability based on content and competency taxonomies, similarities, and delivery modalities (audio/text version, mobile content version, etc.); and 3) "on-demand" assembly of the course version (low/high tech, test/browsing, delivery style/modality) for the organization or individual.

References

North Atlantic Treaty Organization. (2003). *NMA advice on the PfP Training and Education Enhancement Program (TEEP) – Advanced distributed learning (ADL) and simulation* (Military Committee Memorandum No. MCM-064-03). Brussels, Belgium: NATO.

Web Resources

North Atlantic Treaty Association (NATO).
http://www.nato.int/cps/en/natolive/index.htm

NATO issues. http://www.nato.int/issues/pfp/index.html

NATO PfP. http://www.aco.nato.int/page164915817.aspx

The PfP Consortium. https://consortium.pims.org/

The Authors

Dr. Kateryna Synytsya is a Deputy Director of the International Research and Training Center for Information Technologies and Systems (under National Academy of Sciences and Ministry of Education and Science of Ukraine) located in Kiev, Ukraine. She joined the ADL Working Group shortly after its establishment, and has been working both as a member and co-chair.

Mr. Timo Staub has been working as the head of e-learning and strategy officer of the International Relations and Security Network (ISN), located at the ETH Swiss Federal Institute of Technology in Zurich, Switzerland. He has been with the ADL Working Group since 2002, and chaired the group from 2006 to 2009.

Section V

ADL—THE WAY AHEAD

Chapter 24

Future Pathways for SCORM
Angelo Panar, Daniel Rehak, and Schawn Thropp

The Sharable Content Object Reference Model (SCORM) has accomplished the initial goals of the ADL Initiative in solving problems of interoperability, durability, and reusability. However, the steady advancement of information and communications technology, contributions from the learning sciences, and a growing interest in "Web 2.0" approaches to learning put into question the power of the original assumptions that were the basis for SCORM (Fletcher, this volume; Gallagher, this volume). The purpose of this chapter is to consider ways to evolve SCORM to better achieve ADL's vision of high quality training and education delivered on demand. In the context of the ADL business paradigm (Wisher, this volume), this chapter addresses the need to extend the interoperability line to embrace new instructional designs and pedagogical approaches that can lead to greater learning efficiencies and outcomes.

In their identification of challenges to SCORM, Roberts and Gallagher (this volume) reflected on limitations from both a technical and pedagogical perspective. SCORM accomplished its initial functional goals of accessibility, interoperability, durability, and reusability, but in ways that limited the flexibility of tailoring instruction to individual needs. This chapter discusses a set of themes on possible future directions for SCORM, beginning with a general view of transitioning training technologies. The chapter identifies a process for moving SCORM to a new level of capability, and further describes some specific examples of technical issues and opportunities. Ultimately, SCORM will be supplanted due to technological obsolescence, but there is no set timetable for that eventuality.

Transition of Training Technologies
Training technology relies on advances in computer-based instruction (CBI), which has assimilated many earlier forms of instructional media (Gibbons & Fairweather, 2000). CBI has transitioned from a stand-alone format to a format of networked delivered instruction. It has transitioned from procedural languages to authoring systems, incorporating steady advances in development tools and pedagogical designs. CBI, and e-learning in general, will continue to evolve as technology evolves.

Before SCORM, courses could not be moved from one LMS to another, and content pieces could not be reused across different courses. SCORM was built on proven work of relevant organizations, and has long been viewed as the first step on the path to a true learning architecture. Figure 24-1 depicts the transition of technologies for training, in the context of ADL as viewed shortly after the introduction of the initial SCORM 2004.

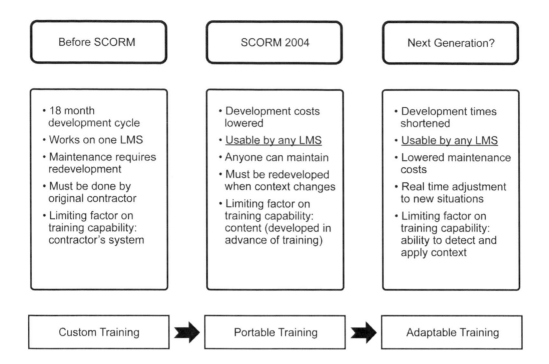

Figure 24-1. A transition of training technology benefits. A reduction in development cycles and increase in training capability is displayed over time, from before SCORM to the next generation.

Suggestions on how to move to the next generation arise from meetings and workshops sponsored by other organizations, from stakeholders and developers of SCORM-conformant products, and from the ADL staff. Collectively, they are referred to as the ADL community, a loosely related network of individuals and organizations who support SCORM and the ADL vision. Earlier work by one member of this community, the Learning Systems Architecture Lab at Carnegie Mellon University, identified missing capabilities, outstanding technical issues, and concepts important to the architectural evolution of SCORM (LSAL, 2003). For example, the LSAL report suggests a SCORM service model in which the instructional delivery system is decomposed into a collection of components, each with a defined service behavior and interface.

In 2008, an organization external to ADL, but part of the ADL community, conducted an independent requirements gathering process for the evolution of SCORM, the results of which were presented at the LETSI SCORM 2.0 workshop in Pensacola, Florida. During this process more than 100 white papers were submitted describing various needs and requirements to allow the learning, education, and training community to do more with SCORM. A broad range of ideas, needs, and requirements were presented. Some of the most frequently mentioned needs and concepts may be achievable by evolving current SCORM over a short period of time. Others depend on a sweeping change and a fundamental redirection of SCORM.

The pathway to the next generation SCORM may be viewed as a progression from experimental capabilities, based on research and development advances and single point implementations, to candidate capabilities, based on public specifications or draft standards where multiple independent, interoperable implementations are under development and publicly demonstrated. The candidate capabilities progress to a common capability which is supported by vendors and adopted within the community. The common capability is fully documented and supported by ADL, and is included in the test suite for SCORM conformance. Finally, a required baseline capability is part of all community profiles with widespread use and proven adoption. SCORM 2004 4th edition is the current baseline capability. This pathway may be viewed as a maturity-based approach as described in the next section.

As in the past, the success of ADL continues to be predicated on partnerships and collaborations with those who develop the technology, those who implement the technology, as well has those who rely on the technology for interoperable e-learning experiences. This discussion focuses on aspects that must be considered as technology continues to advance, and describes a possible course of activities. This is subject to change, and all updates are made available on the ADL Initiative Web site.

What's Next for SCORM

The Advanced Distributed Learning Initiative has embarked on a major update to SCORM that moves toward harmonizing current applied practice in e-learning with new capabilities. SCORM being a profile of a collection of standards, standards development, and evolution is critically important to ADL. As part of the SCORM "harmonization" effort—alignment with current standards and practices—ADL is interested in a model of how standards can be used in SCORM as well as in the process of developing those standards.

The ADL community regularly raises several conflicting issues regarding using and developing standards that drive ADL efforts. Examples of the give and take of these conflicts include:

- "Standards take too long to develop" versus "Standards groups need to spend unbounded time to reach near unanimity, not just consensus."

- "Commercial product developers want to wait until the standard is finalized" versus "Prototyping is important to validate standards before they are finalized."

- "Intellectual property rights governing standards are confusing; all work should be free and open" versus "Individual standards development organizations have inherent business models and processes."

- "Only internationally recognized *de jure* standards (i.e., only ISO/IEC standards) are acceptable" versus "Specifications or informal agreements are OK."

- "Standard (or component) X is essential" versus "X is optional or not of value; generally differentiated by subset of the community."

Maturity-Based Approach

Cognizant of these conflicting issues, ADL is proposing a maturity-based approach to define the standards to be included in SCORM. SCORM is based on capabilities, not standards. These capabilities are expressed in one or more technology components. Judgments are needed on the maturity and adoption of these capabilities or components within the ADL community. SCORM becomes a collection of capabilities—those widely adopted, with known maturity, each supported by one or more standards. Furthermore, each standard has its own level of maturity. This approach allows different communities to add capabilities to meet their needs, producing their own community-specific SCORM derivatives. For example, the MedBiquitous Consortium has developed a specific SCORM variant for professional medicine and healthcare education.

Maturity and adoption are measured along several dimensions, with a ranking on each dimension ("A" as most mature to "D" as least mature), as illustrated in Figure 24-2. Throughout their lifecycles, capabilities generally move forward along each dimension independently, reflecting increased maturity and adoption. One challenge is to develop measurable, repeatable metrics for each dimension and a means to combine the individual metrics into a single ranking for a component, i.e., SCORM becomes a collection of "A" level components and capabilities, supported by a set of underlying standards.

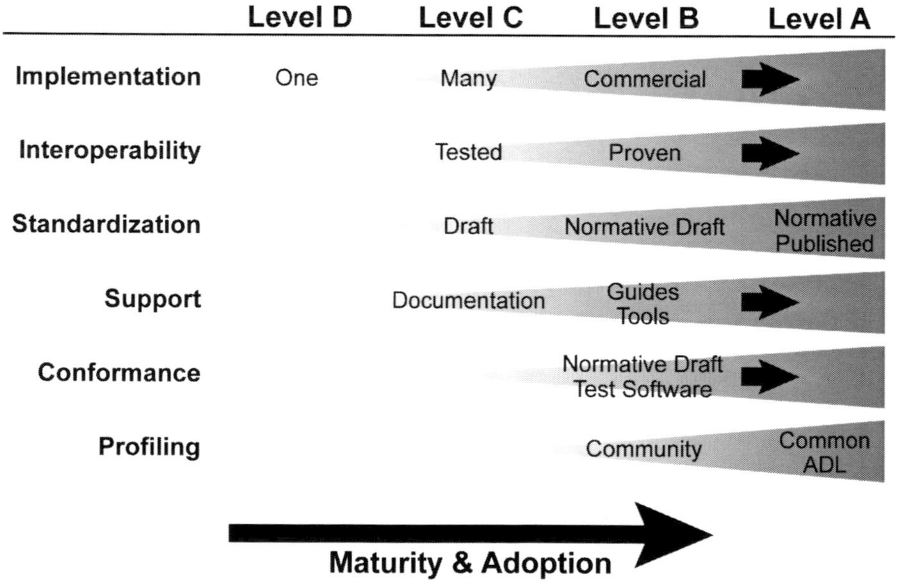

	Level D	Level C	Level B	Level A
Implementation	One	Many	Commercial	
Interoperability		Tested	Proven	
Standardization		Draft	Normative Draft	Normative Published
Support		Documentation	Guides Tools	
Conformance			Normative Draft Test Software	
Profiling			Community	Common ADL

Maturity & Adoption →

Figure 24-2. The SCORM Maturity Model. This figure depicts how various capabilities are measured in terms of maturity and adoption.

ADL recognizes the need for *de jure* standards that describe interoperability of components, and encourage their development. The maturity model measures only the existence of a normative process and normative wording, i.e., developing formally recognized standards by accredited standards development organizations or community-based specification development groups. These normative documents include not only the definition of the standard but also conformance requirements imposed on implementers. Understanding and trusting the provenance of those normative statements and their associated intellectual property rights is a significant challenge facing the ADL community. The legal authority of the authors or standards developers to assert their rights, their licenses and provenance, and to have a commensurate trust in their processes need to be understood. ADL believes that using open standards, developed in a transparent environment, enables the broadest community support, adoption, and flexible adaption within the SCORM Maturity Model.

ADL Activities

To move forward in updating SCORM, individual components and standards must be identified, potentially revised or updated, and their maturities measured. This work on individual components and standards fits within a broader "harmonization" framework. ADL's revised process for developing the next release of SCORM includes a schedule-driven release and update cycle advertised well in advance to allow vendors and developers to plan. For example, in the future ADL will identify full releases of SCORM components in a specified quarter of a stated year; these releases will often be accompanied with supporting prototype technology and testing framework. Capabilities are initially determined by maturity. Capabilities or updates may be dropped to meet schedule and integration requirements—official SCORM releases shall be internally consistent and well vetted. ADL will conduct its work with the following practices:

- Full, regular ongoing disclosure of work progress, e.g., weekly, including summary status reporting from contributing organizations on standardization work.

- Public documentation of ADL's decisions combined with open meetings.

- Ex-ante intellectual property disclosure and use of "open" licenses wherever feasible.

- Full support at release, e.g., documents, sample content and software, conformance, training, published with the underlying standards.

- Community involvement and feedback during all phases of the work.

Technical Refresh of Core Standards

The ADL community has previously identified issues with SCORM that could be addressed by progressive changes to SCORM 2004. Some of these incremental fixes focused on topics such as: refining sequencing; enabling communication among sharable content objects (SCOs) as well as with external systems supporting the learning (i.e., simulations, games, immersive environments); developing more robust data models; and enhancing security.

Most of these issues centered on obtaining more guidance and requirements for specific topics. Some of the topics that were identified were:

- Clarifying and fixing the scoping issues with objectives in sequencing rules.

- Permitting rollup of learning objective data within the sequencing model.

- Establishing a more general learning objective or competency model.

- Enabling SCOs to communicate with other SCOs.

- Providing assistance, guidance, and recommendations on a variety of user interface issues.

- Providing use cases and usage guidance for the cmi.mode and cmi.credit data model elements.

- Providing an interoperable approach to extending the data model.

- Addressing security issues within the current SCORM architectural model.

- Providing more guidance and assistance with cross domain issues.

- Providing support for distributed content delivery.

- Providing support for mobile and immersive delivery of SCORM content.

- Providing more guidance or requirements on data persistence and data reporting.

This is not an exhaustive list of community provided feature requests for SCORM. All of these features fit within the broader SCORM Maturity Model described above, i.e., the maturity of any proposed solution must be measurable, they must permit profiling of SCORM by communities of practice, and, most importantly, they must enable (or not restrict) future, possibly currently unknown, capabilities.

Potential Capabilities and Components

Web-Service API for Communication

Service orientation, as a means of separating things into independent and logical units, is a common concept in software engineering (Erl, 2006) and is the basis for reusing software functionality. Service oriented architecture (SOA) is a software structure or "…architecture for building applications that implement business processes or services by using a set of well-defined loosely coupled black-box components designed to deliver a well-defined level of service" (Hurwitz, Bloor, Baroudi, & Kaufman, 2007, p. 27). An ADL example is the SCORM service model proposed earlier by LSAL in which a collection of plug-and-play components, such as learner assessment, each have a defined service behavior and interface (LSAL, 2003), and further refined using more formal service-oriented modeling techniques (WFADL, 2007).

In a SOA, the software architecture defines which software components to use and how those components interact with each other (Hurwitz et al., 2007). This architecture is embodied in a course or other instructional unit as defined by an instructional designer. The design and implementation of sharable content objects face the same issues as that of designing and implementing services in a SOA. In fact, the distinction between the two is blurring. For example, the communication channels and functionality within the legacy SCORM-based Integrated Prototype Architecture (Murray & Marvin, this volume) was prototyped using Web services, a staple of SOA implementation (Travers, Roberts, Guin, Tomlinson, & Marks, 2007).

The ADL community has called for a new application programming interface (API) to communicate between content and learning systems. There are two main reasons why there is a need for a new communication model. One is to enable non-browser based content to communicate with a more robust and useful communications protocol. The current ECMAScript protocol is more suited to traditional Web browser environments. The other is to resolve specific security constraints within a browser, known as cross domain scripting. Moving toward a different, Web-service-enabled communication protocol would also take advantage of the newer service-oriented methodologies that are more suited for environments in which the learning, education, and training community works.

Content Aggregation/Content Markup
There are many descriptions of how content is aggregated to form larger units of instruction or information. As the underlying technologies (e.g., Internet, Web) continue to change, how do aggregation models change, if at all? Further, aggregation models are dependent, to varying degrees, on the content markup approach. SCORM is silent on the makeup of content; however other industries, notably the technical publications field and technologies such as XML (extensible markup language), continue to push the limits and are gaining consensus around fundamental concepts related to markup languages in the learning, education, and training community. Several innovative solutions are maturing within the industry which warrant a deeper analysis from ADL to determine if, and how, they could be applied to SCORM and ADL's future research and development efforts.

For example, the Darwin Information Typing Architecture (DITA) development efforts that are taking place in Organization for the Advancement of Structured Information Standards (OASIS) are very similar to the concepts of S1000D (Gafford & Heller, this volume). Both look at dividing content into small, self-contained reusable "chunks" of information that are described within XML structures. These activities are gaining momentum, and the communities that are using them look to ADL for ways to harmonize the efforts. There may be features and benefits to authoring content at a more granular level, as defined by DITA and S1000D, that could be leveraged within SCORM.

Experimental Capabilities

For a candidate component or capability, such as those described below, to be considered for inclusion in SCORM, they must first be technically proven via prototypes and "one-off" demonstrations, and then scaled. Experimental capabilities provide the proof-of-concept needed before work moves to higher levels of maturity. This ensures that technical validation occurs before significant time and resources are invested in development of a standard.

Software Agents

Software agents and agent technologies have the potential to support the advancement of SCORM to accommodate the diversity of learning use cases that the learning, education, and training community deem important. This will require rethinking the architectural approach, and adoption of a different design focus. Instead of a focus on managed instruction, based on content interoperability, the focus of the potential new design is on the learner engaged in situated learning.

Currently, most SCORM content is static—authored before delivery, or entirely defined for dynamic generation (LSAL, 2003). Learning often includes other types of content, such as collaborative spaces. Here, the content or interaction is not predefined but controlled by the learner, either as a service or dynamically-built content generated and maintained by the service. This allows content to be adaptable—changing and becoming, or being made, suitable to a particular situation or context.

There is a strong foundation to start from as we look more deeply into how these technologies could be leveraged within ADL and SCORM. Some of these advances will enable the provision of more flexible and adaptable environments and solutions. From an ADL/SCORM perspective, there are several issues that need to be resolved to enable some of the adaptable solutions that the learning community is requesting. Some of these needs include:

- A way to represent the learner operating in a particular situation or context.

- A way to represent an individual's goals, learning styles/characteristics, and preferences.

- A way to represent content suitable for a learning event.

- An appropriate set of learning support services.

- The ability to support formal and informal learning activities, including performance support.

- The ability to support role-based interaction among multiple learners as well as others who may be involved in the configuration, execution, or evaluation of learning activities.

Integrating Common Web 2.0 Applications within ADL

Web 2.0 is often described as the next generation of the Web (Downes, 2005). While the Web has not technically changed, the tools and applications that utilize the Web have evolved significantly. Other chapters in this volume address some of these applications—social media (Fowler, this volume), virtual worlds (Gamor, this volume), and serious games (Xu, this volume). Several others applications are mentioned here as possible areas for ADL experimentation.

Social Media/User Generated Content

Social media environments enable anyone with access to contribute, modify, and comment on content. User Generated Content (UGC) is content or media that is publicly available and produced by the end-user community. Organizations are quickly adopting social media environments, such as Wikis, which are primarily used for collaborating with many individuals to collect their knowledge and expertise easily to build a robust information set. ADL could focus attention on several aspects of social media and user generated content.

An interesting aspect of UGC is its potential for enabling instructors, teachers, and instructional designers to utilize a Wiki in the development of various artifacts of the design phases, such as in the training needs analysis, storyboards, or other design artifacts. This would allow instructional designers to collaborate with their peers or, more importantly, with the end user of the learning content, during the design phase. Another possibility is to allow the end user to assist with the development of the learning content. As learners participate in learning experiences with learning content, they can both contribute changes to existing content and contribute new content to facilitate the intended instructional approach.

Social Networks

Social networks focus on building online communities of people who share interests and/or activities, or who are interested in exploring the interests and activities of others (Fowler, this volume). Some believe social networking is the greatest concept of Web 2.0. Social networks can be built around any topic, and can bring in a variety of experts around that topic. These communities of networked individuals often turn into networks of experts, providing a timely and efficient way to share trusted knowledge around a given topic.

Since social networks are proving to be great avenues for sharing information and harnessing the power of collective knowledge, there is interest in determining how social networks can be used with more focus on learning, education, and training. How can instructors, teachers, and instructional designers utilize social networks? Can social network applications such as Facebook and Twitter be used in a formal—or informal—training environment? These are just some of the questions that could be explored by ADL.

SCORM has been developed to support the creation of reusable learning content as instructional objects within a common technical framework. This requires a flexible architecture that can bridge a variety of heterogeneous systems and knowledge bases without forcing them into a single knowledge representation scheme. Additionally, the architecture must allow for extension and modification while maintaining backward compatibility.

As semantic technologies continue to evolve and stabilize, SCORM may need to evolve to support these technologies. The data and metadata components of semantic technologies promise a durable, extensible representation scheme that is flexible enough to allow communication between schemes. Linked data, semantic models, and ontologies provide ways to related data from different representations and vocabularies. Furthermore, semantically enabled automated reasoning can be built upon properly structured metadata to provide better learning repository and registry searches, and more flexible instructional systems.

Imagine a system that can determine that the progress of a learner is not sufficient. Then imagine that system dynamically, at run-time, building a semantic query for supplemental instruction, based on the lack of progress, and including that training within the context of the learning. This tailoring of instruction to make the training flexible and adaptable begins to push the envelope in the sense of the "A" in Advanced Distributed Learning.

Closing Remarks

Standardization works in concert with adoption, commercialization, and communities such as those who implement SCORM. ADL encourages software component, content, and standards developers to adopt similar approaches while recognizing that the ADL SCORM process and maturity model has implications for their work, including:

- Intellectual property rights and business models need to be disclosed, understood and trusted.

- An open, schedule-driven process will drive community expectations for progress and work effort from all contributors. Standardization work will progress according to the standards developer's processes, but work which does not progress (or where progress is not disclosed) will slip from one SCORM release to the next. Thus, given our small community, personnel resources must be used wisely.

- One goal of standardization is to gain adoption and demonstrate maturity to address business needs and work "at scale." Standardization can proceed from known practices, i.e., building from existing systems or prototypes, or building prototypes in parallel with standardization to shorten standards development cycles. Unproven technology will rank low on maturity and thus may not cross the community threshold for inclusion.

- Maturity and inclusion are for specific versions of standards. Technical changes, no matter when introduced in the standardization process, must be fully vetted along all adoption dimensions before being accepted by the community, i.e., changes may take a component backward along one or more maturity dimensions.

While we have described ADL's model and process for SCORM, we believe that any work on standards in our domain shares core issues around maturity, adoption, and process. We see these as three key characteristics that will influence the future of interoperability and standards in education.

This chapter reviewed selected technical considerations for the ADL Initiative to consider as it progresses to the next generation of learning, education, and training technologies. The future course of SCORM parallels the future course of e-learning. The review presented here is by no means exhaustive, and there are numerous paths that ADL may pursue to achieve its long term vision of providing the highest quality training and education, delivered on demand.

References

Downes, S. (2005). e-Learning 2.0. Retrieved from: http://elearnmag.org/subpage.cfm?section=articles&article=29-1

Erl, T. (2006). SOA principles. Retrieved from http://www.soaprinciples.com/

Gibbons, A. S., & Fairweather, P. G. (2000). Computer-based instruction. In S. Tobias & J. D. Fletcher (Eds.), *Training and retraining: A handbook for business, industry, government, and the military* (pp. 410-442). New York: Macmillan Reference USA.

Hurwitz, J., Bloor, R., Baroudi, C., & Kaufman, M. (2007). *Service-oriented architecture for dummies*. New York: John Wiley & Sons.

Learning Systems Architecture Lab [LSAL]. (2003). *Technical evolution of SCORM* (2003). Pittsburgh, PA: Carnegie Mellon University.

Travers, V., Roberts, R. B., Guin, C., Tomlinson, R., & Marks, J. (2007, November). *A Web service architecture for integrating didactic and experiential learning.* Paper presented at the Interservice/Industry Training, Simulation, & Education Conference (I/ITSEC), Orlando, FL.

WorkForce ADL Co-Lab [WFADL]. (2007). Evolving the JADL Integrated Prototype Architecture: Alignment with the e-Framework. Memphis, TN: Author.

Web Resources

ADLnet: www.adlnet.org

DITA: http://www.oasis-open.org/committees/tc_home.php?wg_abbrev=dita

MedBiquitous Consortium: www.medbiq.org

S1000D: www.s1000d.net

The Authors

Angelo Panar is ADL Enterprise Strategist at the ADL Co-Lab Hub in Alexandria, Virginia.

Daniel Rehak, PhD, is Technical Advisor at the ADL Initiative.

Schawn Thropp supports the S1000D Bridge activity.

Chapter 25

ADL and Enterprise Content Management
Wayne Gafford and Miriam Heller

Technologies of all types are evolving at an accelerating rate due to the exponential growth in the power of information technology (Kurzweil, 2009). Included are information technologies that support advanced distributed learning and performance aiding systems as well as technologies ranging from submarines to weapon systems that often serve as the subject matter for these distributed learning systems. As technologies change, the authoritative sources for their specifications, operations, and maintenance are updated to reflect the changes. Ensuring consistency between authoritative source information and the associated content in training and performance aiding systems may require greater levels of data interoperability and integration in the context of enterprise content management.

This chapter describes a path-finding international project conducted by the Advanced Distributed Learning (ADL) Co-Lab's Job Performance Technology Center (JPTC) to demonstrate an effective enterprise content management strategy. Enterprise content management comprises the strategies, methods, and tools used to capture, manage, store, preserve, and deliver content and documents related to organizational processes (AIIM, 2010).

This project offers a far-reaching opportunity to augment the attributes of accessibility, interoperability, durability, and reusability of content afforded by ADL's SCORM (Sharable Content Object Reference Model) environments to address technical data consistency, accuracy, and currency. This is accomplished by committing technical learning content to an enterprise content management strategy shared by related data communities.

The keystone of the project is the standardization of technical data specifications, in this case S1000D™, an industry-based technical documentation specification. The project explores how standard technical specifications can facilitate integration of technical data and learning content, streamline production processes, search for content potentially impacted by proposed equipment changes, and notify subect matter experts of learning-content maintenance needs. Finally, a methodology is developed and tested to evaluate the cost-effectiveness of this content management strategy.

In the context of ADL's business paradigm (Wisher, this volume), the "Bridge Project" extends the interoperability line to the world of technical data acquisition, production, and management. Numerous possibilities present themselves with this extension: new designs of instruction and assessment, new platforms, and new learning environments. One challenge for learning on demand, and job performance aiding, is that the content must be current.

The U.S. military maintains its position at the vanguard of ever-increasing technology intensity and innovation. So it is not surprising that most operating force training is equipment-based (Hammond & Purdy, 2009). Materiel readiness depends on human readiness for skilled operation and maintenance. Human readiness entails training and performance aiding based on assured data readiness. Data readiness, in turn, implies accurate, up-to-date authoritative source information about products, their operation, and maintenance that can be accessed by the right people at the right time and in the right format. Achieving and maintaining data readiness for training in such a rapidly changing technical environment requires transforming historical business processes that delay training content production until after new or modified equipment and systems are deployed. The following sections explain the strengths and weaknesses of the current methods used to manage technical data and provide background that led to a solution that was ultimately undertaken by the JPTC.

SCORM and the Technical Data Gap

The flagship product of ADL is SCORM (Gallagher, this volume). SCORM has become the *de facto* content packaging standard that allows learning content to operate on any SCORM-conformant learning management system (LMS) in the U.S. and around the world: across government, industrial, and academic institutions. It is essentially a *de jure* standard for the Department of Defense (DoD) since DoD Instruction (DoDI) 1322.26 mandated its use for all e-learning products procured by DoD (Freeman, this volume).

Rules and attributes in SCORM are written in Extensible Markup Language (XML), a standard, simple, self-describing, and therefore, extensible, way to electronically encode text and data automatically across diverse hardware, operating systems, and applications. Using XML rules and attributes, SCORM specifies how to communicate training content in units of sharable content objects (SCOs) with e-learning software in a way that is neutral to the LMS vendors, the instructional design, content, content format, and content domain. SCORM also provides sequencing capabilities to allow navigation between SCOs, e.g., within a course.

This neutrality engenders content objects with interoperability, accessibility, durability, and reusability across SCORM-conformant LMSs. However, given that SCORM is employed as a run-time environment, the inability to access and parse content at the data level implies an inability to assess and thereby assure data readiness. Thus, the benefits of these four learning object characteristics afforded by SCORM's content neutrality may fail to impart readiness to the data and humans in the case of rapidly changing technical environments where information products of many types must be efficiently updated.

S1000D – A Rosetta Stone for Technical Data Life Cycle Management

Technical documentation accompanies engineered equipment, machinery, material, and systems (generally referred to as products) to provide information about their design, physical specifications, manufacturing standards, operation, applicable regulations, product liability, handling, function, testing, maintenance, and learning requirements. S1000D is an industry specification for the preparation, production, management, and maintenance of technical documentation. Originated by the predecessor of what is now the Aerospace and Defence Industries Association of Europe (ASD), the specification supports the management of air, land, and sea systems throughout their life cycle from design to operation and maintenance. S1000D also represents industry's consensus for the optimal specification of all technical documentation procured by the DoD (AIA, 2008). See Robson and Richards (this volume) for more information on technical standards.

S1000D uses the XML standard, which provides openness and data neutrality. Data Modules (DMs) logically organize the technical information into coherent information types such as descriptions, procedures, maintenance schedules, fault isolation, crew/operators, testing, and business rules (AIA, 2008). A DM, the smallest addressable unit specified in S1000D, constitutes a complete and independent unit of information with standalone value and meaning. All DMs associated with a particular product are stored and managed in a database, the Common Source Data Base (CSDB). Each DM has a unique data module code (DMC) to prevent data duplication. S1000D links each DMC to a system component using a Standard Numbering System that relates document subcomponents to larger components, ultimately to define a product.

Data neutrality coupled with information compartmentalized into DMs stored in the CSDB allows publication into different output formats such as page-oriented, Interactive Electronic Technical Manuals (IETMs), and generally Interactive Electronic Technical Publications (IETPs). This minimizes duplication while ensuring consistent data delivery, data reuse, and configurability. Finally, S1000D and the CSDB provide for overall life cycle management of technical data by enabling impact analyses of engineering change proposal (ECP) notices on technical documentation.

Paving the Way to Fill SCORM's Data Gap with S1000D Harmonization

While S1000D was evolving to support life cycle management of technical data, the need for integration with technical training content was becoming increasingly apparent in the business processes that also treated technical data and training content separately. Developers of technical training content in this business model are notified after technical publications are updated, sometimes as much as a year after the redesigned system is deployed (AIA, 2008). These built-in time delays propagate into the production, delivery, and life cycle maintenance of learning content, thus jeopardizing the accuracy and currency of the content.

Yet, information to support inclusion of technical content in product operations and maintenance training was absent from S1000D until 2008. Without such information, technical data could not be integrated into technical learning content in a reliable, consistent, and an automated fashion that could draw on the strengths of a CSDB. Without consistent naming, identification, and structure of technical training and technical data content, data interchange between programs and vendors could not be supported and life cycle configuration management would be elusive. Including learning and human performance data into S1000D could constitute one solution to integrating the stove-piped organizational and business processes that separate training from technical documentation production.

In 2004, ADL and the Aerospace and Defence Industries Association of Europe Technical Publications Specification Maintenance Group, that was managing the S1000D, and the Aerospace Industries Association, that was representing U.S. industry, acknowledged this need by signing a Memorandum of Understanding (MoU) to harmonize S1000D and SCORM. The MoUs stated "The Parties wish to co-ordinate their activities to develop an integrated approach to development and distribution of learning and technical data/information (MoU, 2004)."

S1000D Issue 4.0, released in the second half of 2008, began to actualize this MoU by introducing features to support configuration management of technical learning content. This included a learning DM that branches into five information models each with associated DMCs: learning plan, learning overview, learning content, learning summary, and learning assessment (Gafford et al., 2008). Defining the learning models constitutes a necessary and significant first step to creating, configuring, and managing technical training content through its life cycle. S1000D, enhanced with learning DMs, begins to fill SCORM's data specification gap. Moreover, Issue 4.0 provides a mechanism to plan and reuse content stored in a CSDB by defining a SCORM-oriented aggregation model using native S1000D processing, instructional design codes that can be used in S1000D, and guidelines for planning reusable data. Yet closing the gap by integrating the S1000D technical data and the learning content is not possible without a formal link.

The International S1000D-SCORM Bridge Project

The International S1000D-SCORM Bridge Project scope and details were formally developed in a pre-planning project which defined the first operational objective: close the SCORM data gap by developing a formal integration mechanism, a "Bridge," between any SCORM-based learning content authoring environment and CSDBs used by the S1000D technical data community.

The project participants acknowledged as part of a second operational objective that technical data and training are both elements of integrated logistics support (ILS) (ARMYREG, 2009), a military discipline to facilitate system support through the use of a robust logistic concept at the lowest cost and in line with reliability, availability, maintainability, and other requirements as defined for the project (Wikipedia, Military Logistics, 2010). Product Life Cycle Support (PLCS) refers to a joint industry and government initiative that has resulted in the ISO 10303 Standard for the Exchange of Product Model Data (STEP) and so covers the information aspects of ILS (PLCS, 2010). This objective provides for sharing of all technical and learning data across programs, CSDB, and authoring environments. Together these objectives directly address the strategic vision defined by the pre-planning project "to ensure learning data and technical publication data are developed and maintained based on consistent ILS [integrated logistics support for product-specific] data" (Gafford & Jesukeiwicz, 2009, p. 4).

ADL, through JPTC, assumed the lead in this effort as a result of its recognition of the need for and designated responsibility to advance the state-of-the-art in life cycle development, management, and delivery of distributed learning content both generally and as expressed in Department of Defense Instruction 1322.26 (Department of Defense, 2006). ADL's JPTC staff and affiliates had also played key roles in critical activities leading up to the project in identifying the evolving life cycle management needs for distributed learning content and in defining learning data modules schema in S1000D. The Instruction also prescribes complementary pieces of the life cycle content management puzzle that fit within ADL's scope, including SCORM conformance and registration of content for search and discovery of reusable content.

The Blueprint for the Bridge

The focused pre-planning project consisted of three meetings in the last third of calendar year 2008. The team members represented ADL, Naval entities, U.S. industry, and the S1000D specification body as well as international partners—the Swedish Defence Materiel Administration Defence, the Norwegian Logistics Office, and various product companies and vendors from Norway, Sweden, and Italy—all of whom had been actively working in other consortia and community user groups to address misalignments in business processes between training and authoritative source material (Gafford & Jesukiewicz, 2009). Specifically at issue were the impacts to current practices involving learning and technical content.

Production processes. Technical manuals and training courses are not currently produced as part of an integrated process. Although course developers use technical manuals as inputs, they also obtain their own contractor data and Job Task Analyses and then process the data using separate techniques.

Authoring tools. Developers of training course use authoring tools (editors) that are not integrated into CSDBs, in which authoritative source technical data are stored.

Storage formats. The technical and training data are stored in different formats, which hampers data integration and reuse.

Storage repositories. Technical and learning data are usually stored in different, unfederated repositories.

System and equipment upgrading. Equipment upgrades and modifications are managed during acquisition using an engineering change proposal (ECP) tool described in a military handbook (Department of Defense, 1997). Technical manuals and training affected should be cited in ECP documents, however, no common or automated identification system (metadata) or technical and business processes exist to link ECPs to the particular technical data *and to the training content that may require modification.*

The planning team essentially drafted the blue print for the "Bridge Project," starting with a definition of the *project goals* to guide efforts to achieve the vision. Each goal is described below as well as its status or outcome. The *first goal* involved identifying the tactical problem statements that capture the issues associated with the misalignment of life-cycle management of technical data and learning content:

1. Vendor-neutral communication protocols do not exist between content development tools and CSDBs, which would facilitate the life cycle support of S1000D technical content for learning.

2. There are no vendor-neutral tools in place to validate SCORM 2004 conformance at the end of the publishing process.

These two problems are depicted schematically in Figure 25-1 for generalized production of training content based on S1000D specifications. The dashed circular areas encompass components and activities that do not currently exist as integrated processes: the gaps.

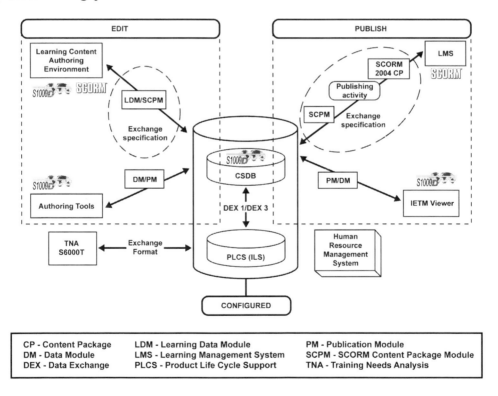

CP - Content Package	LDM - Learning Data Module	PM - Publication Module
DM - Data Module	LMS - Learning Management System	SCPM - SCORM Content Package Module
DEX - Data Exchange	PLCS - Product Life Cycle Support	TNA - Training Needs Analysis

Figure 25-1. Conceptual view of the S1000D-SCORM Bridge Project. The dashed circles indicate the two main focus areas. Tactical Problem Statement 1 identifies the inefficiencies in the Edit Cycle (left in the schematic), and Tactical Problem Statement 2 identifies those in the Publish Cycle (right in the schematic).

The planning team envisioned an Application Programming Interface (API) solution, i.e., software to "bridge" the gaps and enable data exchange between the CSDB and both the learning content authoring environment and the LMS. The "API Bridge" in the *Edit* and *Publish* areas therefore represents the collection of software, technology, and supporting business process solutions that correspond to solutions to the operational problem statements 1 and 2, respectively. The scope of this project, though, is limited to the data exchange requirements in the *Publish* area to a standardized extraction of information when creating a SCORM content package in a CSDB. This project will deliver a "Bridge Toolkit" that supports transformation of S1000D learning data modules from a CSDB into a SCORM content package. The current project does not address automatic delivery of a SCORM package from a CSDB to an LMS.

A *second goal* entailed developing a set of use cases—scenarios developed using systems engineering techniques to define and model system's behavior in response to external requests—to:

- Connect to and work in any S1000D database from any editor.

- Originate learning content in S1000D data modules, and locate and reuse these modules.

- Compile SCORM content packages from S1000D databases.

- Identify data modules, potentially impacted by a proposed product design change.

Eight use cases were devised and served to define twenty-four functional requirements that served as the basis for the S1000D-SCORM Bridge specification.

The *third goal* set out an action plan, a technical development strategy, for the S1000D-SCORM API Bridge, including a description of use cases and functional requirements as input for future projects. High level deliverables were defined as: 1) a community-reviewed consensus-based specification for the API Bridge; 2) beta-implementations of the API Bridge; 3) best practice guides for implementing the API Bridge based on the beta site experiences); and 4) mechanisms for the community to provide feedback about the API Bridge and its implementation. To accommodate the heterogeneity of the community, rather than providing a single way to create a SCORM content package, a guide was recommended for interpreting certain S1000D elements in a SCORM content package and best practices. These community oriented goals may be pursued at a later date.

The *fourth and last goal* required review of S1000D Issue 4.0 to identify potential change requests that enhance SCORM content support.

Complementary Enterprise Perspectives, Sponsorship, and Leadership
The technology-focused pre-planning work expanded to include the enterprise-level objectives of the sponsors of the two-year International S1000D-SCORM Bridge Project. The Bridge project, as it came to be known, commenced in February 2009

under the support of the Office of the Under Secretary of Defense for Acquisition, Technology and Logistics as part of the Reduction of Total Ownership Cost (RTOC) program sponsored by the Office of the Secretary of Defense (OSD). ADL's JPTC manages the project.

At the enterprise level, the Bridge Project focuses on the objective of the RTOC program: to improve system readiness by either improving the reliability of the systems or the efficiency of the processes used to support them (RTOC, 2010). Put in terms of both the technical and enterprise objectives, the Bridge project aims to improve the reliability of technical data and the efficiency of technical training content by extending and improving the Navy's Integrated Logistics Support (ILS). The expected outcomes are a reduction in the total costs of producing technical manuals and training courses in an integrated way, improved capacity for the Navy to implement its policy to ensure appropriate and timely logistics support as new systems and equipment upgrades are fielded, and consequent increased readiness by ensuring technical learning data in these logistics supports are accurate and current.

To complement the use cases and technical development strategy derived in the project's pre-planning phase, a methodology had to be devised to address the enterprise-level RTOC program goal of estimating the total cost of ownership, which the Bridge Project addressed by examining whether the net benefits derived from investing in the implementation and use of the Bridge are compelling and outweigh the costs. However, since the suite of Bridge technologies are not currently fully implemented, the approach taken involved estimating costs and benefits for two cases that reflect different levels of scope and decision making.

The broad adoption and implementation of the suite of Bridge technologies, software, and business processes would reflect the interests of OSD, the sponsor of the Bridge project. To have the estimates grounded in historical data, one case study speaks to the OSD perspective and focuses on all Hull, Mechanical, and Electrical (HM&E) technical manuals produced by the Naval Ship System Engineering Station in Philadelphia, Pennsylvania, and all Computer-Based Training courses delivered by Navy e-Learning (NeL), a part of the Naval Education and Training Command. The HM&E analysis is substantial in terms of percent of total production of all manuals and training and so more closely approximates OSD interests.

The decision to adopt S1000D as the technical specification standard for documentation is a prerequisite for implementing the Bridge and typically occurs at the Navy program level. The program level case study selected for the Bridge project concentrated on the AN/AQS-20A program, which is part of the mine mission package for the Littoral Combat Ships, that involves an underwater towed body containing a high resolution sonar system used to identify bottom mines as well as detect, localize, and classify bottom, close tethered, and volume mines. The "Q-20" case study sought to answer whether the Bridge would lead to reductions in the cost, exclusive of the Bridge project's costs, of producing future Q-20 technical manuals and training courses.

In both of the case studies, the costs and benefits include 1) project investment costs—the personnel and related expenses of the project during the second and 2) implementation costs—the expense of training technical writers and course developers to use the Bridge, plus the site/program license and user fees to cover the additional costs of maintaining the networks and the repositories for storing technical information. To account for potential dependencies on the initially assumed costs, sensitivity analyses were performed with respect to future implementation and development costs, personnel pay rates, and the fraction of training focused on hard skills, which typically demand more authoring time for initial course preparation and are subject to more frequent modifications due to more frequent ECPs expected on more complex systems—factors expected to increase the benefits of integration.

The Cost-Benefit Question: Is the Bridge Project an Attractive Investment?

The RTOC cost-benefit analysis, completed at the end of the first project year, has contributed two important results for future evaluation of life cycle content management using the Bridge: 1) specific case study cost-benefit estimates at two different decision-making levels and 2) a quantitative methodology that accounts for uncertainty to analyze the desirability of the S1000D-SCORM Bridge.

The AN/AQS-20A analysis estimated savings attributable to the benefits at approximately 8.9 percent of the current 10-year present value. This percentage may still overestimate savings if implementation costs scale with the workload.

The cost-benefit analysis associated with applying the Bridge to the production and maintenance of all Navy HM&E manuals and NeL delivered courses estimated the net benefits of the base case at nine times the 10-year implementation costs. The sensitivity of this result with respect to the five most uncertain inputs yields a range of net benefits that vary from 55 percent to 186 percent relative to the base case.

More than $: Data, Human, and Operational Readiness Make Sense
The benefits expected to accrue to the U.S.Navy from the "The Bridge" project fall into four categories. First, acquisition, management, and production of integrated training and technical information in vendor neutral formats eliminates dependence on proprietary tools, while fostering direct and automated data reuse.

Second, without data neutrality, technical and training content integration and configuration management will continue to rely on *manual* methods for responding to ECPs, making it difficult to improve business process inefficiencies, such as delayed updates and data inconsistencies. The Bridge is likely to provide a mechanism to reduce production delays, resulting inconsistencies, and the overall time needed to maintain training content.

Third, linking technical and training content enables synchronous or near-synchronous production of technical and training content to ensure system-wide data consistency, accuracy and currency.

Fourth, the common communication specification established by the Bridge—between learning-content development environments, S1000D CSDB environments, and SCORM packaging tools—will help reduce the time needed to identify technical learning content that proposed equipment changes might impact through automation. An automated process of notifying learning-content developers to review and modify, as needed, potentially impacted learning content could yield significant benefits. The time and effort to isolate learning content requiring update in response to an equipment change would likely be less than those of manual methods. Lag times between proposed equipment changes and technical training content updates would then decrease. Additionally, the need for retraining as learners deploy would likely decline if training is based on current and accurate data in the first place.

The cost-benefit analysis focused on costs avoided through production process improvements. Yet each of these four categories includes benefits associated with the quality of data that are difficult to quantify no less monetize reliably for use in a cost-benefit analysis. For instance, it would be difficult to estimate the total time spent by all instructors rifling through manuals to identify changes and match them to course content that might be impacted or the costs of retraining all learners because the technical content in their courses was not current. If these additional avoided costs could be estimated they would undoubtedly be very significant. In summary, the Bridge lays the foundation for enterprise life cycle management of technical training content in vendor-neutral environments greater efficiency for high quality, accurate and current data that enhances human and operational readiness.

A Brief View from Beyond the Bridge

The S1000D-SCORM Bridge project offers a compelling solution to enterprise content management, a solution that immediately brings to mind extensions that can be applied to several secondary integration problems associated with technical learning content.

Convergence to a Common Source Database

The integration of S1000D and SCORM in a content production environment makes apparent the transferability of the benefits of using a CSDB for S1000D to the common storage of technical learning content in a CSDB. With data integration and reliable easy access to learning content, further future enhancements become possible and desirable, such as: a set of tools to support S1000D and SCORM integration; optimized information flow and business processes across technical manual and technical learning content, such as team collaboration tools and management of resource-demand variations; more efficient mechanisms to align technical data and technical training content security and information assurance. These enhancements would be expected to reduce maintenance cost for technical information as well as overall life cycle costs. Finally, the shared tags and metadata associated with the technical data and training content that will enable improved response to engineering changes and enhanced consistency, accuracy and timeliness of technical training content, will also enhance the ability to find and reuse technical training content.

Repositories to the Rescue or Lost in Registration

The effort and expense of developing training content has made reusability an imperative. Enabling platform-independent reuse of training content and technical data has driven the establishment of standards such as SCORM and S1000D, respectively. Aside from the portability afforded by standards, reuse implicitly requires that data or content can be identified and located. To this end, reuse has driven the use of CSDBs first for S1000D with piloting underway for SCORM-conformant content. As the Bridge project has demonstrated, storing technical data and training content in the same federated database, such as a CSDB, facilitates the development of Web services to identify content potentially impacted by proposed engineering change using metadata. Yet repository metadata from anywhere on the Internet or trusted networks can be used to identify and locate content to enable engineering change impact analysis. A database of such metadata, or registry, can be populated voluntarily by the owner or generator of the metadata. The ADL Co-Lab has developed a registry for e-learning training content in the U.S. military, the ADL-R, discussed in detail in Lannom (this volume) and also in Jerez et al. (2006).

Each approach has strengths and weaknesses. For instance, registries risk not attracting sufficient volunteered metadata and the updates necessary to maintain their currency and accuracy. CSDBs overcome these weaknesses through compulsory deposition by developers in the community of practice and adoption of life cycle content management practices discussed in this chapter. However, with the control afforded by a CSDB comes a potentially parochial view of available reusable content. Metadata search, discovery, harvesting, and folksonomic tagging methods could mitigate this problem for both CSDB and registry strategies. CSDBs and registries do not necessarily compete with one another. They best operate as complementary technologies with CSDBs providing the authority, checks and balances, and quality control needed for time-dependent content, while registries offer a broad view of available content. ADL's current efforts in storing and locating training content in CSDB and registries should provide important insights into the advantages and disadvantages of each strategy in facilitating discovery of, access to, and life cycle management of distributed, heterogeneous learning content.

Extending Life-Cycle Content Management to 3D Objects and Embedded Assessment

Training content comes in many forms. In addition to descriptive, procedural, graphical, video and other types of information, content can include code specifications or the code itself for rendering and interacting with physical systems such as equipment in virtual worlds and games. The games industry has played the role of the bellwether of content longevity, primarily dictated by the lifespan of video game consoles. Game console life cycles of four to five years have defined game asset turnover. The industry has recently deemed this business practice unsustainable, leading some to seek new business models or at least longer console system life cycles (Cole, 2009). ADL initiated a pilot project to demonstrate a repository for 3D object content, which may address this issue by fostering reuse in virtual world and games (Jesukewicz, 2010).

JPTC is currently engaged in an effort that explores the integration of S1000D and X3D to examine the ease with which 3D content can be automatically updated, for example in response to an engineering change proposal, or for rendering in a virtual world or game. This effort is also examining whether embedded assessments can be represented in 3D interactive environments and maintained along with engineering changes. Neither has been investigated as candidates for configurable information.

Data Readiness and Performance Aids

The Bridge project has potentially profound implications for performance aids: technologies, often mobile, that provide on the job in the field support to technicians, operators, warfighters, etc. If the job performance aid content is different and produced separately from technical data, the same issues discussed in this chapter may result: lack of data accuracy and currency as well as redundant business processes. The costs of these issues may be spectacularly high, though, as compared to the costs of technical training content that lacks life cycle content management. Whereas the cost for inaccurate technical data in training content might be limited to the costs of retraining, the costs of inaccurate technical data may represent seriously reduced human and operational readiness on the job in the field. Fletcher (this volume) provides an example cost-benefits evaluation of performance-aiding technologies. The benefits of the job performance training technology include reduced time to *correctly* solve problems. If performance-aiding content is inaccurate, benefits on the job or in the field would be hard to realize and could be overwhelmed by costs. Life cycle management of content is thus an important, if not necessary, condition for the effective use of performance-aiding technologies if the job involves equipment operations or maintenance.

Conclusions

The first year of the Bridge project has highlighted two capabilities that are critically needed to deliver certain types of training content reliably: the integration of technical specifications data with training content and the management of both to ensure content consistency, accuracy, and currency. The results from the Bridge project thus far have clarified the technical requirements, laid the foundation, and demonstrated one solution strategy for enterprise life cycle content management in the context of advanced distributed learning. Additionally, a methodology for evaluating the cost-effectiveness of some specific content management solutions was devised and exercised. The Bridge project's preliminary estimated costs and benefits of instituting a content management system exploiting the S1000D technical specifications and the CSDB appear favorable. The concept, though, of linking training content to standardized specifications derived from authoritative sources and managing both the content and specifications through their life cycles using a repository may have broader applicability and appeal.

As our knowledge increases and technologies improve, the related content in learning, training, and performance-aiding systems may also change. The need, desirability, and decision to manage content in the context of change will depend on the costs associated with delivering content that is no longer accurate or current versus the costs of establishing a content management system. Clear candidates for content management systems are manuals, training courses, and performance aids based on technical data. The Bridge project demonstrates a strategy for enterprise content management of these sorts of content that rests on standardization of technical specifications using the S1000D, a mechanism to search repositories, in this case the CSDBs, or the Web for content referencing those technical data specifications in the event of proposed engineering changes, and an objective structured methodology to evaluate the costs and benefits of instituting such a system. The Bridge project thus addresses the *quality* aspect of ADL's stated purpose of ensuring access to the *highest quality* learning, training, and performance aiding content, delivered cost-effectively, anytime, and anywhere, *in terms of consistency, accuracy, and currency.*

References

AIA (Aerospace Industries Association of America Product Support Technical Publications Sub-Committee). (2008). *A recommendation to the Department of Defense to adopt the S1000D–the international specification for technical documentation: A discussion of the merits and value of S1000D in the context of interoperable data, Version 0.0, April 25, 2008.* Unpublished report.

AIIM (Association for Information and Image Management). (2005). What is ECM? Retrieved April 26, 2010, from http://www.aiim.org/What-is-ECM-Enterprise-Content-Management.aspx.

U.S. Army. (2009). *ARMYREG 700-127 (Army Regulation 700–127), Integrated logistics support, rapid action revision (RAR), 29 April 2009.* Washington, DC: Author.

Cole, D. (2009, September 11). Analysis: The new reality of the video game console business. *Gamasutra.* Retrieved April 19, 2010, from http://www.gamasutra.com/php-bin/news_index.php?story=25223.

Department of Defense. (1997). *MIL-HDBK-61, Military handbook: Configuration Management Guidance (30 SEP 1997).* Washington, DC: Author. Retrieved March 25, 2010, from http://www.everyspec.com/MIL-HDBK/MIL-HDBK+(0001+-+0099)/MIL-HDBK-61_11531/.

Department of Defense. (2006). *Development, management, and delivery of distributed learning* (DoDI 1322.26). Washington, DC: Author.

Gafford, W., Haslam, P., Clem, J., Tedeschi, S., Kieckhefer, C., Malloy, T., & Lucas, L. (2008, December). *New training content and production support in the S1000D technical data specification, ver4.* Paper presented at the 2008 Interservice/ Industry Training, Simulation, and Education Conference, Orlando, FL.

Gafford, W., & Jesukiewicz, P. (2009, November). *A technical development strategy for bridging S1000D™ and SCORM®.* Paper presented at the 2009 Interservice/ Industry Training, Simulation, and Education Conference, Orlando, FL.

Hammond, J., & Purdy, M. (2009). Information assurance—Taking commercial certifications to the operating Forces. *CHIPS—the Department of the Navy Information Technology Magazine*, *27*(1), 38. Retrieved February 15, 2010, from http://www.chips.navy.mil/archives/09_Apr/web_pages/IA_certification.html.

Jerez, H., Manepalli, G., Blanchi, C., & Lannom, L., (2006). ADL-R: The first instance of a CORDRA registry. *D-Lib Magazine*, *12*(2).

Jesukiewicz, P. (2010, March). *ADL 3D Repository—A system for sharing 3D models and related assets* Paper presented at GameTech 2010, Orlando, FL. Retrieved April 26, 2010, from http://www.teamorlando.org/gametech/downloads/ presentations/ADL%203D%20Repository.pdf.

Kurzweil, R. (2009, December 13). Top futurist, Ray Kurzweil, predicts how technology will change humanity by 2020. *New York Daily News*. Retrieved February 10, 2010, from http://www.nydailynews.com/opinions/2009/12/13/2009-12-13_top_futurist_ray_kurzweil_predicts_how_technology_ will_change_ humanity_by_2020.html#ixzz0fAiaCoH7.

Department of Defense. (1997). *MIL-HDBK-61, Military handbook: Configuration Management Guidance (30 SEP 1997).* Washington, DC: Author. Retrieved March 25, 2010, from http://www.everyspec.com/MIL-HDBK/MIL-HDBK+(0001+-+0099)/MIL-HDBK-61_11531/.

MoU (Memorandum of Understanding Between ADL and TPSMG), April 21, 2004. Retrieved March 3, 2010, from cpf.s1000d.org/events/user_forum/clearwater.../ mou_spec1000d_adlv7.pdf.

Eurostep Group. (2005). PLCS (Product life-cycle support). Retrieved April 4, 2010, from http://www.plcs-resources.org/.

Institute for Defense Analyses (n.d.). *Reduction of total ownership costs.* Retrieved March 22, 2010, from http://rtoc.ida.org/rtoc/rtoc.html.

Wikipedia (n.d.) *Military logistics.* Retrieved March 15, 2010, from http://en.wikipedia. org/wiki/Logistics#Military_logistics.

Web Resources

ASD: http://www.asd-europe.org/site/

S1000D: http://www.s1000d.net/

The Authors

Wayne Gafford is the Director of the Job Performance Technology Center at the Advanced Distributed Learning (ADL) Co-Laboratory Hub in Alexandria, Virginia. He is also the government co-chair of the S1000D Learning Standards Harmonization Task Team and ADL liaison to the Naval Postgraduate School's Modeling, Virtual Environments and Simulation Institute.

Miriam Heller, PhD, is Special Projects Consultant to the Job Performance Technology Center at the Advanced Distributed Learning Co-Lab.

Chapter 26

ADL and Global Education
Badrul H. Khan

In the past decade, e-learning and its numerous variations have become commonplace in many countries, for both training and education. Some groups are learning from early adopters. Some implementations are more advanced than others. Some organizations are experimenting with new approaches. But all interested parties from many nations are discovering the advantages that computer and communication technologies bring to the learner and those who provide for the learner.

This chapter represents my attempt to unite the Advanced Distributed Learning (ADL) Initiative's business paradigm as described by Wisher (this volume) with the perspectives I have gained over the past decade and a half concerning the use of the World Wide Web for instruction. Until being commissioned by the ADL Initiative to serve as a co-editor of this book, my dealings with ADL were occasional. I attended ADL open houses, participated in certain activities, and studied ADL publications. All along, I have independently admired the Initiative's vision and goals, and its openness about providing high quality content that is accessible, interoperable, durable, and reusable.

The Emergence of the Web
In the emerging field of information technology, the Web was a new kid on the block during 1993-94. However, its impact as a new medium for sharing information in multimedia format quickly gained enormous attention throughout the world. Corporations, educational institutions, and government agencies found the Web to be an effective and convenient way of providing information about their products and services. In its early form, the Web was used mostly to offer *informational* sites.

After reflecting on various attributes and capabilities of the Web, I started to explore its potential for educational use. With contributions from more than 100 researchers and practitioners worldwide who specialized in technology-mediated learning, I compiled a book entitled *Web-Based Instruction* (Khan, 1997) which provided an organized, coherent framework for Web-based instruction by defining the critical dimensions of this new field of inquiry and practice at all levels of education. *Instructional* sites geared toward using the Web for educational and training purposes began to emerge in the late 1990s.

In the United States, the Department of Defense deserves credit for pursuing early, and on a mass scale, network-based learning that takes advantage of Web features for the training and education of military personnel. In the summer of 1998, a special team composed of educators from each of the military Services interviewed practitioners of online education in academia and industry to benchmark educational technology policies and practices. The goal was to revamp joint professional military education programs to move more instruction to Internet delivery (Goodden, 2001). I was a member of the team of researchers and practitioners who participated, and shared my experience with designing and teaching Web-based courses while on the faculty at the George Washington University.

The new field of Web-based instruction added to the interest in software applications known as learning management systems, or LMSs. At that time, there were no standards for LMSs. In November 1999, the ADL Initiative and *PCWEEK* magazine organized an event entitled "PCWEEK Shootout" where I served as a judge to review LMSs. Summarizing the Shootout, Donston (1999) reported, "Standards for learning management systems are in flux, according to the judges of a recent shoot-out between seven such systems, and the products are not yet able to meet the distributed-learning needs of organizations" (p. 134). Hundreds of learning management systems entered the marketplace over the past three decades, but they lacked interoperability (Wisher, this volume). The impact was that learning content developed on one system could not be shared and used on another system without substantial recoding. The specifications harmonized in ADL's Sharable Content Object Reference Model (SCORM) are intended to speed adoption of distributed learning by allowing organizations to share training and education materials.

ADL Initiative

The ADL Initiative became well known globally for consensus building and promotion of SCORM which, together with content registries (Lannom, this volume), allows LMSs to find, share, import, export, and reuse e-learning content with one another. The contributions of SCORM in e-learning are technical advances that enable interoperability rather than pedagogical contributions (Roberts & Gallagher, this volume). Even though SCORM was not devised to provide pedagogical guidance, the e-learning industry has a vested interest in developing instructionally sound e-learning materials with SCORM.

Since its inception in November 1998, those in the ADL Initiative, other parties, and myself observed steady changes in the attributes and capabilities of emerging technologies, and their implications in education and training. The ADL Initiative continued to provide improved services to the field, as reflected in the *ADL* business paradigm (Wisher, this volume). I, from the academic world, stayed tuned to ADL's activities while continuing to study critical issues of meaningful learning environments using emerging technologies and the Web. The result was a *Global E-Learning Framework* (Khan, 2001), described later.

This chapter provides broader perspectives of e-learning implementation for globally diverse learners by discussing critical issues encompassing various dimensions of global e-learning environments together with aspects of the ADL business paradigm. It discusses, in order, open and distributed learning, global interest in e-learning, global interest in the ADL Initiative, my *Global E-Learning Framework*, and the *Framework's* relationship to the ADL business paradigm for supporting global education. Table 26-2 provides a cross-reference for every chapter in this volume with a dimension in the

Framework, and illustrates the commonalties and overlapping interests between ADL and an independently developed view on global education.

Open and Distributed Learning

With the continual emergence of new technologies offered through the Web, institutions around the world are investing more and more in the development and deployment of *open* (i.e., learning in your own time, pace, and place, Calder & McCollum, 1998) and *distributed* learning (i.e., learning materials located in different locations, Khan, 2001). Distributed learning is used here in the context of learning environments with dispersed instructors and students, including standing alone with no instructor other than the computer itself present (Fletcher, this volume). There are numerous terms that refer to open and distributed learning activities, including E-Learning, Distributed Learning, Advanced Distributed Learning, Web-Based Learning, Web-Based Instruction, Web-Based Training, Internet-Based Training, Distance Learning, Online Learning, Mobile Learning (or m-Learning), Nomadic Learning, Remote Learning, Off-site Learning, a-Learning (anytime, anyplace, anywhere learning), etc. In this chapter, the term **e-learning** is used to represent open and distributed learning (see Figure 26-1).

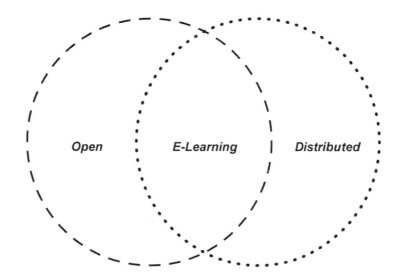

Figure 26-1. Open and distributed learning. This diagram shows an overlapping area between open learning and distributed learning.

Global Interest in E-Learning

In the information society, advances in information and communication technologies (ICTs) have created a digital society and broadened the scope of sharing innovations globally. In this digital society, people use digital devices in almost everything they do in their lives, from brushing teeth, to reading books, to driving a car. In the education and training arenas, an open and distributed digital learning environment provides a flexible form of interactive and facilitated learning environment to anyone, anyplace, anytime by using the attributes and resources of digital technologies along with other forms of learning materials (Khan, 2005a).

E-learning, increasingly enhanced by the availability of more powerful ICTs, is growing globally. Academic institutions, corporations, and government agencies worldwide are increasingly using the Internet and digital technologies to deliver instruction and training. A study of 2,500 U.S. colleges and universities reports that the number of online students more than doubled in five years, growing from 1.6 million students taking at least one online course in the fall of 2002 to 3.94 million in the fall of 2007. This represents a compound annual growth rate of 19.7 percent (Allen & Seaman, 2008). Similar growth trends are seen in other countries.

e-Learning Practices

The prevalence of e-learning practices has been more visible in some western countries than in other parts of the world; however, other nations are not lagging behind. Most nations are increasingly incorporating ICTs into their national agenda to improve efficiency in information and knowledge sharing in education, governance, commerce, health, agriculture, and other sectors. Educational policies are being formulated in various communities worldwide to enable educational institutions to come to terms with new learning technologies. For example, e-learning and the use of ICT tools to deliver educational resources (Kisambira, 2008) is an emerging issue at institutions of higher learning in Africa.

Similar national initiatives are either in place or underway elsewhere. Examples include projects such as ictQATAR and Bangladesh's new initiative called "Digital Bangladesh," which seek to connect people to emerging technologies that enrich their lives with education and support greater economic development (Nahid, 2009). Various national e-learning initiatives for higher education taken by ministries of education or national agencies have been documented. Access to both of these efforts can be found at the Web Resources section at the end of this chapter.

The demand for e-learning continues to grow. However, implementing meaningful e-learning for diverse learners for open and distributed environment is challenging. Designing and delivering instruction and training on the Web requires thoughtful analysis and investigation, combined with an understanding of both the Internet's capabilities and resources and the ways in which instructional design principles can be applied to tap the Internet potential (Ritchie & Hoffman, 1997, cited in Khan, 1997). Also, various factors encompassing the critical issue of ensuring an open and distributed learning environment must be addressed to create meaningful e-learning for learners worldwide.

Global Interest in ADL Initiatives

Since its inception in November 1998, the Advanced Distributed Learning Initiative has been instrumental in empowering the computer-based training industry globally in the large-scale development, implementation, and assessment of interoperable and reusable learning systems. Global interest in ADL is evident. Starting with the United Kingdom in 2002, several nations have volunteered to champion the ADL cause. Canada, Korea, Australia, Norway, Romania, and a consortium of 14 Latin American and Caribbean nations stepped forward as international partners of the ADL Initiative, as described in Section Four of this volume. Some of these efforts translate the ADL documentation into their national languages, others develop internal compliance test centers, and others share content. The most recent addition to the network of international partnership labs is the German Workforce ADL Partnership Laboratory, formed in October 2009.

e-Learning in the Middle East

Although ADL does not have a partnership lab in the Middle East, e-learning practices have been very visible there recently. Academic institutions and corporations are using e-learning for education and training purposes. Because of the tremendous interest in the region, *Educational Technology Magazine* compiled a special issue on "ICT and E-Learning in the Middle East" (Khan & Ally, 2010). Articles in the special issues includes case studies of e-learning practices in Saudi Arabia, Israel, Iran, Lebanon, Jordan, Turkey, Morocco, Oman, Kuwait, Palestine, Bahrain, Qatar, and the United Arab Emirates. In January 2009, Dr. Robert Wisher (former Director, ADL Initiative) was invited to deliver a keynote speech on the ADL Initiative at the 2nd Annual Forum on e-Learning Excellence in the Middle East in Dubai. During my presentations at conferences in several countries in the Middle East, I field many questions about SCORM and ADL. For example, Dr. Abdullah Almegren, the Director General of the National Center for e-Learning & Distance Learning Center in Saudi Arabia, has expressed an interest in using SCORM in an open-source, Arabic LMS, and in the potential for establishing future partnerships.

Metrics on Global Interest

An analysis of visits to ADL's Web site between May 2009 and December 2009 reveals that 58.3 percent of all traffic originated outside of the United States with an average of three page views per visit. Of the 195 countries of the world, 180 have visited the ADL Initiative's Web site. These statistics show that the interest in ADL is truly global. Though a majority of visits are for SCORM-related information, other parts of the Web site are also visited for information containing the ADL Registry, immersive technologies, training evaluation and research, and ADL's Learning Technology Lab. Additionally, 34 percent of all traffic is translated into local languages; these languages include English, Spanish, Chinese, French, German, Portuguese, Italian, and Russian. Thirty-three percent of all visitors are returning to the Web site for additional information (Personal communication, Ryan Proctor, December 15, 2009).

Global interest for ADL services has mostly been limited to designing technical standards for learning content development. However, as the e-learning industry has developed to a solid platform, the industry has tended to seek ADL's guidance and advisement on other issues in learning development, including pedagogical, management, interface design, resource support, evaluation, etc. Conversations with leaders in e-learning around the world (Khan, 2005b) indicate that the ADL Initiative has become a leading resource in the world for harnessing the power of learning and information technologies to standardize and modernize education and training globally, and does so in a way that is open and vendor neutral.

The Global E-Learning Framework

Since 1995, I have researched critical ICT and e-learning issues throughout the world, to answer the question: What does it take to provide flexible learning environments for learners worldwide? As we are accustomed to teaching or learning in a traditional classroom-based closed system, the openness of flexible online learning is new. In order to create effective environments for diverse learners, however, we need to leave our classroom-based, closed system of learning design. We need to be attentive to a variety of new and emerging issues of flexibility and address them in the design of e-learning environments (Khan, 2007; Morrison & Khan, 2003). We need to change our mindset—that is the paradigm shift. In order to facilitate such a shift, and in response to the range of issues I saw in my research, I formulated a *Global E-Learning Framework*. The framework was reviewed by leading academic researchers and practitioners in the field of instructional design and technology from around the globe who provided constructive feedback for its steady improvement. A number of my edited volumes focus on various dimensions of this framework.

Through my research I found that numerous factors contribute to creating a meaningful open and distributed learning environment. Many of these factors are systemically interrelated and interdependent. A systemic understanding of these factors can help us create meaningful learning environments. These factors are clustered into eight dimensions to develop the Global E-Learning Framework: *institutional, pedagogical, technological, management, interface design, resource support, evaluation, and ethical considerations* (Khan, 2001). In this chapter, the eight dimensions of the framework are also referred to as the dimensions of the e-learning environment. E-learning environments can vary by sector (such as education), and by vertical markets within sectors (such as a university system). The dimensions are graphically depicted in Figure 26-2.

Figure 26-2. The global e-learning framework. This figure shows the eight dimensions radiating from a central global e-learning hub.

Dimensions of the E-Learning Environment

The eight dimensions of the e-learning framework define an e-learning environment. No single dimension is more important than others. All dimensions have systemic relationships for interrelatedness. The interrelatedness of the framework dimensions can best be described by their stakes in various issues or factors they share in working toward developing a meaningful e-learning environment. For example, creating a SCORM-conformant learning object is a core issue for the *technological* dimension. As we know, sharable learning content is cost effective (i.e., *institutional*), instructionally useful (*pedagogical*), interoperable in different parts of a course (*interface design*), easily maintainable (*management*), and resourceful (*resource support*). For a comprehensive design for a specific learning environment, we should understand the reality of that particular learning context and address relevant issues encompassing each dimension.

Each dimension has several sub-dimensions. Each sub-dimension generates factors focused on a specific aspect of an e-learning environment. The eight dimensions and their respective sub-dimensions represent areas requiring consideration early in the e-learning development process. These need to be revisited throughout an e-learning project's life cycle as part of a continuous improvement strategy (Gamor, this volume).

Table 26-1 lists the eight dimensions and underlying sub-dimensions of the learning environment.

Table 26-1

Dimensions and Sub-Dimensions of the E-Learning Environment

1. INSTITUTIONAL	**5. EVALUATION**
1.1 Administrative (with 14 factors)	5.1 Assessment of learners
1.2 Academic affairs (with 5 factors)	5.2 Evaluation of instruction & learning
1.3 Student services (with 16 factors)	environment
2. PEDAGOGICAL	**6. MANAGEMENT**
2.1 Content analysis	6.1 Maintenance of learning environment
2.2 Audience analysis	6.2 Distribution of information
2.3 Goal analysis	
2.4 Medium analysis	**7. RESOURCE SUPPORT**
2.5 Design approach	7.1 Online support (with 4 factors)
2.6 Organization	7.2 Resources (with 2 factors)
2.7 Methods and strategies (with 20 factors)	
	8. ETHICAL
3. TECHNOLOGICAL	8.1 Social and political influence
3.1 Infrastructure planning (technology plan,	8.2 Cultural diversity
standards, metadata, learning objects)	8.3 Bias
3.2 Hardware	8.4 Geographical diversity
3.3 Software (LMS, LCMS, SCORM)	8.5 Learner dversity
	8.6 Digital divide
4. INTERFACE DESIGN	8.7 Etiquette
4.1 Page and site design	8.8 Legal issues (with 3 factors)
4.2 Content design	
4.3 Navigation	
4.4 Accessibility	
4.5 Usability testing	

A Unified Approach to Supporting Global Education

Education and training via emerging technologies for diverse learners needs continuous investigation of what works and what does not work. Updated prescriptive and descriptive knowledge from academia and industry are sorely needed to support the design of e-learning. The *Global E-Learning Framework* provides guidance in the design, development, evaluation, and implementation of meaningful e-learning, and the *ADL Business Paradigm* enhances e-learning efforts by providing technical standards, a collaborative framework, and an ensuing, competitive marketplace for continuous improvement. Figure 26-3 represents a view before joining together the components of each.

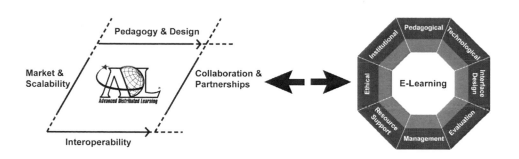

Figure 26-3. Representations of the ADL business paradigm and the e-learning framework. This figure shows the four dimensions of the ADL business paradigm parallelogram and the eight dimensions of the e-learning framework octagon.

The *business paradigm* and the *framework* are complementary and supplementary to each other. A unified view is presented in Figure 26-4. Planners, administrators, and stakeholders at nearly every level can apply this unified view as a diagnostic tool to guide the utility and compatibility of e-learning design and implementation. An overall balance across all components and dimensions reflects an approach to e-learning that is sound, and contributes to the field in a global manner.

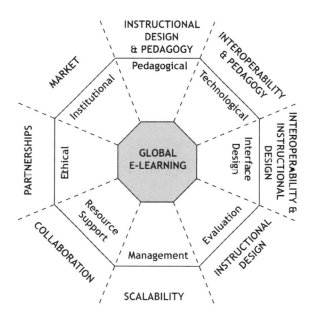

Figure 26-4. Comprehensive approach to e-learning. This figure illustrates a methodology for combining the ADL business paradigm and the global e-learning framework to integrate e-learning design and implementation.

Elements of the ADL business paradigm are shown in the outer rings of Figure 26-4, replicated from the four lines of the parallelogram in Figure 26-3. The message from Figure 26-4 is that the approach that the ADL Initiative has taken, and its overarching requirements for access, interoperability, durability, reuse, and durability, synchronizes with the needs of e-learning environments as identified in the *Global e-Learning Framework*. ADL adds technical knowledge, globally recognized standards and tools, and a long-term perspective on a path to high quality education and training, delivered on demand.

Chapters in this Volume and e-Learning Framework

In Table 26-2, the eight dimensions of the *Global e-Learning Framework* from this chapter are depicted across eight columns. Elements from the ADL Business Paradigm presented in Chapter 1 (this volume) are depicted across eight rows. The twenty-four other chapters in this volume are positioned within the matrix, where they fit best. This correspondence further illustrates coherence between the accomplishments of ADL and the issues that others may face in developing an e-learning environment. A pragmatic look at some issues is offered in the next section.

Table 26-2

Learning on Demand: ADL and the Future of e-Learning, cross-referenced by chapter with the elements of the Framework for e-Learning and the ADL Business Paradigm.

ADL Business Paradigm (Chapter 1)	Global E-Learning Framework (Chapter 26)							
	Pedagogical	Technological	Interface Design	Evaluation	Management	Resource Support	Ethical	Institutional
Instructional Design & Pedagogy	Chapters 5, 7, 12 13, 14, 15							
Interoperability & Pedagogy		3, 4, 8, 24						
Interoperability & Instructional Design			16					
Instructional Design				2, 6				
Scalability					9, 20, 21 22, 23			
Collaboration						10, 11, 25		
Partnerships							18	
Market								17, 19

This section of the chapter addresses specific issues that arise in e-learning design environments, with reference to the relevant components and dimensions of the unified model presented in Figure 26-4. Once we become familiar with the various components and dimensions of an e-learning environment, it is important to identify issues that may require specific attention during various stages of e-learning design. Since each project is unique, it is important to identify as many issues—in the form of questions—as possible for your organization's e-learning project.

One way to identify critical issues is to place each stakeholder group (such as learner, instructor, support staff, etc.) at the center of the framework and raise issues along each of the eight dimensions. Team members can articulate issues and answer questions in a way that can help create a meaningful learning environment for a particular organization or group. By repeating the same process for other stakeholders, it is possible to generate a comprehensive list of issues for the e-learning project.

Examples of e-Learning Issues
Several examples of the issues that frequently arise are discussed below. Many others are not covered here; these are most relevant to the widest audience and to ADL concerns.

Are all learning objects created for the course reusable and shareable? If your institution creates learning objects by following international interoperability standards (such as SCORM), they can be reused and shared by multiple courses within your institution and beyond. Reusable and shareable learning objects not only save money but also promote collaboration among e-learning partner institutions. Administrators would be interested in including this type of issue as part of infrastructure planning within the *technological* dimension. The process used by ADL for registering learning content (Freeman, this volume; Lannom, this volume) provides a good example of policy for content registration.

Does the course make an effort to reduce or avoid the use of jargon, idioms, ambiguous or cute humor, and acronyms? To improve cross-cultural verbal communication and avoid misunderstanding, we should refrain from icons, symbols, jokes, or comments that might be misinterpreted by others. In Bangladesh, the thumbs-up sign means to disregard someone, but in other cultures it often means "excellent" or "job well done." An icon that uses a pointing hand to indicate direction would violate a cultural taboo in certain African cultures because it represents a dismembered body part (this is also true for a pointing finger that indicates a hyperlink). A right arrow to indicate the reader should move to the next page may instead guide Arabic and Hebrew language speakers to return to the previous page, since they read from left to right instead of from right to left. This is an *interface design* concern for learners from many different cultural backgrounds, and thus is an issue relevant to instructional designers creating content for a diverse audience (Deibler & Berking, this volume).

How often is dynamic course content updated? In designing e-learning, we need to consider the stability of course content. Content that does not need to be updated is categorized as static (e.g., historical events, grammar rules, etc.). Content that has the potential to change over time is considered to be dynamic (e.g., laws, policies, technical documentation, etc.). Because dynamic content needs to be revised from time to time, it is necessary to identify such content in a course and establish an ongoing method for timely updating as needed. It can be very frustrating for learners to find outdated or obsolete information (Shanley et al., this volume). This is one example of an issue relevant to the content analysis section of the *pedagogical* dimension. For an example on how to deal with this issue, consult the technical approach to currency and life cycle management of content discussed by Gafford and Heller (this volume).

Are students actually doing the work? How do we know we are assessing fairly and accurately? These are the types of questions that will always be in the minds of online instructors and administrators. Assessment of learners at a distance can be a challenge. Issues related to cheating are a major concern, and an institution offering e-learning should have a mechanism by which a learner can be accurately measured and which detects cheating. This has been a concern of the ADL Initiative and the Department of Defense (Curnow, Freeman, Wisher, & Belanich, 2002), and is relevant to the assessment of learners component of the *evaluation* dimension.

Does the course have encryption (i.e., a secure coding system) available for students to send confidential information over the Internet? All institutions are vulnerable to hackers. Academic networks can be targets of hackers if they lack adequate security. This is a concern for network managers, and is a key aspect of the security measures section of the *management* dimension. The chapter by Camacho, West, and Vozzo (this volume), which describes three levels of security in the Joint Knowledge Online portal, provides one example of an effective approach to security.

The purpose of raising questions within each dimension of the framework is to help us think through our projects thoroughly. Note that there might be other issues not yet known, or not yet encountered. As more and more institutions worldwide offer e-learning, new issues will be raised within the eight dimensions of the framework.

E-Learning Application Continuum

The framework can be applied to e-learning of any scope. This scope refers to a continuum defined by the extent to which instruction and training are delivered on the Internet and it must be planned for systematically. The weight placed on any e-learning dimension or sub-dimension, or on any set of e-learning items, will vary with the scope of the instruction. This continuum is described below, with examples, to show the type and scope of e-learning activities along the continuum, and how their design relates to various categories of the framework.

At the "micro" end of the continuum, e-learning activities and information resources can be designed for face-to-face instruction in educational and training settings. In the high school physics classroom, for example, a teacher may use simulations to support the cognitive work of analyzing data, visualizing concepts, and manipulating models. Further along the continuum, a more comprehensive design is needed for complete academic or training courses that require that all content, activities, interaction, tutorials, project work, and assessment be delivered on the Internet.

At the "macro" end of the continuum, the framework can support the design of complete distance-learning programs and virtual universities without a face-to-face component, such as continuing education programs for accountants or network engineers. For example, designers of Web-based continuing education for accountants dispersed all around the world would have to plan for every dimension of the framework in considerable detail. They would have to work with computer programmers, testing specialists, security professionals, subject-matter experts, and accountants' professional organizations. These designers would have to do everything from planning a secure registration system to considering cultural and language differences among accountants from different countries who are seeking continuing education credit.

As the scope of e-learning design expands, design projects change from one-person operations to complex team efforts. The framework can be used to ensure that all important factors are considered in the design of e-learning, whatever its scope or complexity. It also helps to create the appropriate blend by ensuring that each ingredient, individually and collectively, adds to a meaningful e-learning environment.

E-Learning Key Factors

Once we become familiar with various dimensions of an e-learning environment, we are then able to draw the boundaries of our e-learning environments. We have to ask ourselves: How far do we want to go? Who are our customers (or learners)? Where are they? What and how they want to learn? If our scope of operation is global, then our issues are global. To address all these issues, we have to identify all of the critical factors that are relevant to particular e-learning environments.

Since this chapter focuses on global education, I would like to present an application of how the e-learning framework was used in a study from Curtin University of Technology, Australia. The university used the *Global E-Learning Framework* to identify key factors or issues to be addressed before offering a fully online curriculum. The study investigated the views of four different perspectives (students, IT staff, academic staff, and management). Using a 5-point Likert Scale, participants were asked to rate the list and then to rank in terms of importance the dimensions that were derived from the framework. A three-round Delphi study had produced the 54 factors encompassing the eight dimensions of the e-learning environment (Chin & Kon, 2003). In the Curtin University of Technology study, as one example, the factors of greatest concern under the Pedagogical Dimension of the Framework were: prompt feedback, alternative submission of assignments, interactive course, learning styles, teacher as facilitator, student commitment, multimedia tools/technologies, and agreed time for communication.

Conclusion

E-learning is becoming more and more accepted in workplaces around the world. Institutions are investing heavily in the development and deployment of online programs. Academic institutions, corporations, and government agencies worldwide are increasingly using the Internet and digital technologies to deliver instruction and training. At all levels of these institutions, individuals are being encouraged to participate in online learning activities.

Implementation of e-learning with emerging technologies for global audiences is increasingly dependent on several factors: culturally responsive pedagogy (Frederick, Donnor, & Haltley, 2009), up-to-date interoperability standards for sharing content, globally feasible business approaches for greater return on investment, understanding the attributes of newer technologies and their implication for education and training, and sharing of knowledge and resources. With changes in information technology and in lifestyles, designing *learning on demand* will be increasing challenging. The field of e-learning benefits from expanding the knowledge base to integrate multiple different perspectives. Curtis Bonk points to the convergence of three factors: an enhanced learning infrastructure through the Web; immense quantities of open content within that infrastructure; and a culture of sharing knowledge and participation, that is opening up education, and the world, to everyone (Bonk, 2009).

Many communities around the globe are transforming their educational systems by taking advantage of newer learning technologies with the hope of greater return-on-investment. They need guidance to successfully implement their e-learning programs. Experience from both academia and industry is critical to the successful implementation of e-learning. The *Global E-Learning Framework* is rooted in academia, and the *ADL business paradigm* is based on industry research and analysis supported by a government initiative. The combined knowledge base derived from both approaches provides comprehensive perspectives for designing effective education and training for globally diverse learners in the information society.

References

Allen, I. E., & Seaman, J. (2008). *Staying the course: Online education in the United States, 2008*. Needham, MA: Sloan Consortium.

Banathy, B. H. (1995). Developing a systems view of education. *Educational Technology, 35*(3), 53-57.

Bonk, C. J. (2009). *The world is open: How Web technology is revolutionizing education*. San Francisco: Jossey-Bass.

Kisambira, E. (May 5, 2008). *Interview with Boubakar Barry, Coordinator, Research and Education Networking Unit at AAU*. Retrieved from http://www.elearning-africa.com/newsportal/english/news127.php

Calder, J., & McCollum, A. (1998). *Open and flexible learning in vocational education and training*. London: Kogan Page.

Chin, K., & Kon, P. (2003). Key factors for a fully online e-learning mode: A delphi study. In G. Crisp, D. Thiele, I. Scholten, S. Barker, & J. Baron (Eds.), *Interact, integrate, impact: Proceedings of the 20th Annual Conference of the Australasian Society for Computers in Learning in Tertiary Education*. Retrieved from http://www.ascilite.org.au/conferences/adelaide03/docs/pdf/589.pdf

Curnow, C. K., Freeman, M. W., Wisher, R. A., & Belanich, J. (2002). *Training on the Web: Identifying and authenticating learners* (Study Report No. 2002-7). Alexandria, VA: U.S. Army Research Institute for the Behavioral and Social Sciences.

Donston, D. (1999). From the trenches: Distributed learning is high priority (the judges of the shoot-out between learning management systems). *PCWEEK, 16*(46), 134. Retrieved from https://www.thedacs.com/techs/abstract/298998

Ellis, R. K. (2009). Field guide to learning management systems. *ASTD Learning Circuits*. Retrieved from http://www.astd.org/NR/rdonlyres/12ECDB99-3B91-403E-9B15-7E597444645D/23395/LMS_fieldguide_20091.pdf

Frederick, R., Donnor, J., & Haltley, L. (2009). Culturally responsive application of computer technologies in education. *Educational Technology, 49*(6), 9-13.

Goodden, R. T. (2001). Benchmarking educational technology for military planners. In B. H. Khan (Ed.), *Web-based training* (pp. 399-404). Englewood Cliffs, NJ: Educational Technology Publications.

Khan, B. H., & Ally, M. (Eds.). (in press). ICT and e-learning in the Middle East [Special Issue]. *Educational Technology*.

Khan, B. H. (Ed.). (1997). *Web-based instruction*. Englewood Cliffs, NJ: Educational Technology Publications.

Khan, B. H. (Ed.). (2001). *Web-based training*. Englewood Cliffs, NJ: Educational Technology Publications.

Khan, B. H. (2005a). *Managing e-learning: Design, delivery, implementation and evaluation*. Hershey, PA: Information Science Publishing.

Khan, B. H. (2005b). *Interviews with Badrul Khan* [A regular syndicated column]. Educational Technology. Retrieved from http://asianvu.com/bookstoread/interviews

Khan, B. H. (Ed.). (2007). *Flexible learning in an information society*. Hershey, PA: Information Science Publishing.

Morrison, J. L., & Khan, B. H. (2003). The global e-learning framework: An interview with Badrul Khan. *The Technology Source*. Retrieved from http://www.technologysource.org/article/global_elearning_framework/ and archived at http://www.webcitation.org/5ie1gdNRb.

Nahid, N. I. (2009). Statement by H.E. Mr. Nurul Islam Nahid, Minister for Education, Government of the People's Republic of Bangladesh at the General Policy Debate of the 35th Session of UNESCO General Conference in Paris; 7 October 2009. Thirty-fifth Session of UNESCO General Conference, Paris, 7 October 2009. Retrieved from http://www.unesco.org/fileadmin/MULTIMEDIA/HQ/GBS/35GC/Documents/35VR_PDF/35VR_03/Bangladesh_en.pdf

Singh, H. (2003). Building effective blended learning programs. *Educational Technology*, *44*(1), 5-27.

Web Resources

ictQATAR. http://www.ict.gov.qa/output/Page2.asp

eLearning Africa. http://www.elearning-africa.com/

National Initiatives Worldwide. http://www.virtualcampuses.eu/index.php/Category: National_initiatives

The Author

Badrul Khan, PhD, is a special consultant to the ADL Initiative while co-editing this volume.

AUTHOR INDEX

A

Abramson, L.J., 170, 176

Aimeur, E., 171, 176

Alberts, D.S., 9, 19

Alderman, F.L., 12, 19, 73, 84

Allen, I.E., 336, 346

Ally, M., 217, 337, 347

Alpert, D.I., 23, 36

Anderson, F.J., 18, 19

Anderson, W.G., 117, 244

Anderson, J., 209, 217

Anderson, J.R., 170, 175

Angier, B., 27, 30, 36

Atkinson, R.C., 23, 25, 36, 37

Ausubel, D., 170, 175

B

Banathy, B.H., 346

Baroudi, C., 310, 315

Barritt, C., 12, 19, 73, 84

Bauer, M., 36

Bauer, K., 94, 97

Belanich, J., 160, 167, 344, 347

Bell, B., 7, 20, 92, 97

Bell, M., 178, 192

Bennett, S., 67

Betrancourt, M., 249, 256

Bitzer, D.L., 23, 36

Blanchi, C., 131, 141, 330

Bloom, B.S., 23, 29, 35, 36

Bloor, R., 310, 315

Blunt, R., 201, 205

Boehle, S., 209, 216

Bonk, C.J., 20, 164, 167, 168, 346

Bowman, C., 184, 192, 194

Brown, J., 217

Brown, J.S., 28, 38, 160, 167

Brown, K.G., 88, 94, 96, 97, 217, 264, 290

Bruen. C., 65, 66

Buehl, M., 25, 37

Bunzo, M., 170, 175

C

Cade, W., 34, 38

Calder, J., 335, 347

Calongne, C., 184, 192

Camacho, J., 31, 36

Campbell , J., 185, 186, 193

Canale, R., 65, 67

Carbonell, J.R., 28, 36

Carey, L., 72, 84

Carroll, K., 210, 216

Casper, W.J., 94, 97

Chen, S., 199, 205

Chin, K., 345, 347

Chipman, P., 170, 175

Cho, Y.S., 279, 280, 282

Churchill, D., 67, 102, 108

Clark, R.E., 7, 19, 35, 36, 86, 87, 96, 119, 129

Clark, J., 184, 192

Cohen, A., 163, 167

Coleman, S., 67

349

Collins, A., 160, 167

Colllins, M., 186, 193

Conlan, O., 65, 66

Constantine, L., 148, 155

Corbett, A., 25, 35, 36, 170, 175

Corno, L., 24, 36

Coulson, J.E., 23, 37

Crowder, N.A., 100, 107

Cunningham, D.J., 99, 107

Curnow, C.K., 344, 347

D

Dabbagh, N., 184, 192

Dalsgaard, C., 161, 167

Daugherty, L., 155

Davidson, M., 185, 186, 193

Dawley, L., 187, 194

Dede, C., 184, 192, 194

Dees, J.J., 170, 176

Delwiche, A., 184, 192

Dennis, S., 175

Dick, W., 72, 84

Dirr, P.J., 110, 117

Dochy, F., 25, 37

Dodds, P.V.W., 17, 19, 34, 37, 64, 65, 66, 99, 133, 172, 173, 175

Doerksen, T.L., 54, 66

Donnor, J., 346, 347

Donston, D., 334, 347

Downes, R., 1, 15, 16

Downes, S., 50, 66, 313, 315

Dragan, G., 68

Driskell, J.E., 195, 205

DuBuc, C., 225, 230

Duffy, T.M., 99, 107

Duguid, P., 160, 167

Duval , E., 51, 53, 54, 66, 68, 69

Dyer, J.H., 152, 154

E

Edwards, L., 224, 230

Eggan, G., 170, 175

Ellaway, R., 106, 107

Ellis, R.K., 347

Ely, K., 90, 93, 94, 96, 97

Erl, T., 310, 315

Evangelou, C., 151, 152, 154

F

Faerman, S.R., 153, 154

Fairweather, P.G., 305, 315

Falk, J., 120, 129

Falkiewicz, C., 90, 96

Fiore, S.M., 9, 19

Fletcher, J.D., 19, , 23, 25, 26, 27, 28, 30, 32, 34, 35, 36, 37, 39, 64, 66, 99, 103, 107, 172, 173, 175, 196, 256, 315

Flesher, K., 50, 68

Foltz, D.W., 170, 175

Ford, J.K., 88, 96

Fowler, B.T., 26, 34, 37

Frederick, R., 346, 347

Freeman, M.W., 344, 347

G

Gafford, W., 320, 321, 330

Gagne, R.M., 170, 175

Galanter, E., 23, 37, 107

Gallagher, P.S., 49, 51, 52, 53, 54, 64, 66, 104, 108

Gamor, K.I., 184, 192

Gardner. D., 200, 201, 205

Gargan. M., 65, 66

Garnsey, M., 224, 230

Garris, R., 195, 205

Gettinger, M., 25, 37

Gibbons, A.S., 305, 315

Gilbert, T.F., 35, 38

Goldman. R., 163, 167

Grabinger, R.S., 184, 193

Graesser, A.C., 24, 34, 38, 170, 175, 176

Grafinger, D.J., 71, 84

Greiner, J.M., 29, 38

Guin, C., 311, 315

H

Haag, B.B., 186, 193

Haltley, L., 346, 347

Hammond, J., 318, 330

Han-Bin, C., 216

Hanesian, H., 170, 175

Hannum, W., 6, 19

Hardy, C.R., 18, 19

Harpe, B., 65, 67, 155

Harris, N.D., 107, 184, 193

Hatch, N., 152, 154

Hayes 9, 19

Haynes, R.E., 170, 175

Hodgins, W., 51, 66

Holden, J.J., 233, 244

Hsuan-Pu, C., 216, 217

Hui-huang Hsu, H., 216

Hurwitz, J., 310, 311, 315

I

Ip, A., 65, 67

J

Jackson, G.T., 175, 176

Jackson, P., 178, 181, 193

Jacobs, J., 163, 168

Jerez, H., 131, 141, 327, 330

Jesukiewicz, P.J., 76, 282, 321, 330

Johnson, D.W., 190, 193

Jonassen, D.H., 67, 84, 102, 107, 108, 184, 185, 186, 191, 193

Jordan, 176, 337

Jovanovi, P., 68

K

Kahn, R., 109, 117

Kahn, Ro., 134, 141

Kanar, K., 92, 97

Kaner, C., 120, 129

Karacapilidis, N., 151, 152, 154

Katz, D., 109, 117

Katz, H., 54, 67

Kaufman, M., 310, 315

Kearsly, G., 19

Keller, F.S., 100, 108, 199, 206

Keough, E., 234, 244

Ketelhut, D., 184, 192, 194

Khan, B., 7, 20, 187, 193, 333, 334, 335, 336, 337, 338, 347, 348

Kilby, T., 54, 67

Kilgour, F.G., 22, 38

Kisambira, E., 336, 347

Klerkx, J., 69

Knowles, M.S., 198, 205

Koedinger, K.R., 170, 175

Koehler, M., 184, 193

Kolb, D.A., 185, 186, 190, 194

Kon, P., 345, 347

Kozlowski, S.W., 7, 20

Kraan, W., 64, 67

Kraiger, K., 85, 86, 92, 94, 96, 97, 170, 175

Kulik, J.A., 26, 38

Kumar, K., 153, 154

Kurzweil, R., 317, 330

L

Laham, D., 170, 175

Lajoie, S.P., 170, 171, 175, 176

Landauer, T.K., 170, 175

Lanier J., 107, 108

Lannom, L., 131, 141, 330

Lee, G., 55, 62, 64, 68

Leeson, J., 18, 19

Lesgold, A., 170, 175

Lewis, S., 17, 19

Liber, O., 64, 65, 68

Lickyer, L., 67

Lin, N.H., 212, 216, 217

Lindsey, A.M., 224, 230

Louwerse, M.M., 175

Lu, S., 175

Lukasiak, J., 67

Lynch, C., 176

M

Ma, W.W., 164, 167

Macpherson, D.H., 170, 176

Manepalli, G., 131, 141, 330

Marks, J., 224, 231, 311, 315

Martin, 170, 175

Marvin, D., 224, 225, 230, 231

Mayer, R.E., 28, 37, 38, 256

McCaffrey, D.P., 153, 154

McCollum, A., 335, 347

McKinnon, D.H., 30, 38

McLoughlin, C., 65, 68

Meire, M., 69

Michael, O., 199, 205

Miller, P., 51, 68

Minocha, S., 163, 167

Misanchuk, E., 249, 256

Mitchell, H., 175

Mitrovic, 170, 175

Moore, G., 144, 155

Moore, M.G., 117, 244

Morrison, J.L., 338, 348

Moss-Kanter, R., 153, 155

Murawski, M., 67

N

Nahid, N.I., 336, 348

Najjar, J., 69

Nelson, B., 192, 194

Nelson, M.L., 141, 185

Nguyen, H., 120, 129

Nkambou, R., 171, 176

Nobeoka, K., 152, 154

Noh, J., 184, 193

Noja, G.P., 28, 38

Nolan, C.J., 30, 38

Novak, J., 170, 175

O

Oliver, R., 65, 68

Olivier, B., 64, 65, 68

Olney, A., 34, 38, 170, 175, 176

Olson, T.M., 164, 167

O'Neill, H.F., 39

Orlansky. J., 26, 33, 38, 39

Orvis, K.L., 160, 164, 167

Ostyn, C., 57, 59, 62, 63, 64, 68

P

Pacey, L., 234, 244

Page-Jones, M., 148, 155

Paradise, A., 9, 20, 93, 96

Perez, R., 107, 170, 175, 206

Person, N.K., 24, 38

Phelps, S., 62, 68

Pike, W.Y., 224, 230

Pisel, K., 224, 230

Prensky, M., 195, 206

Purdy, M., 318, 330

R

Ragan. T.J., 72, 84

Rehak, D., 56, 57, 68

Rheingold, H., 184, 194

Robbins, C., 67

Roberts, D., 163, 167

Roberts, R.B., 224, 231, 311, 315

Rose, C.P., 163, 176

Rothenberg, J., 143, 155

S

Salas, E., 9, 19

Sawyer, B., 199, 206

Schwier, R., 249, 256

Scriven, M., 22, 38

Seaman, J., 336, 346

Segers, M., 25, 37

Sheanan, F., 167

Shelby, R.H., 176

Shellnut, B., 199, 206

Shih, T., 216, 217

Shute, V.J., 106, 108

Sinclair, K.E., 30, 38

Sitzmann, T., 86, 90, 92, 93, 94, 96, 97, 170, 175

Sleeman, D., 28, 38

Smith, B., 225, 230

Smith, P., 199, 206

Smith, P.L., 72, 84

Snow, R.E., 24, 36

Spector, M., 106, 108

Stewart, D., 86, 97, 170, 175

Strijker, A.A., 53, 68

String, J., 26, 38

Su, S., 55, 62, 64, 68

Suppes, P., 23, 25, 37, 38, 39

Suraweera, 170, 175

Sutcliffe, A., 50, 53, 68

Szabo, M., 50, 68

T

Taylor, L., 176

Teitelbaum, D., 33, 39

Tennyson, R.D., 197, 206

Thomas, D.L., 32, 39

Thornton, D.M., 170, 176

Tobias, S., 19, 25, 28, 37, 39, 315

Tomlinson, R., 311, 315

Travers, V., 224, 231, 311, 315

Trenholm, S., 160, 167

Tyler-Smith, S.K., 161, 168

V

van Dissel, H.G., 153, 154

VanLehn, K. 170, 172, 176

Van Slyke, D.M., 153, 154

Ventura, M., 175

Verano, M., 26, 39

Verbert, K., 54, 68, 69

Vygotsky, L.S., 160, 168

W

Wade, V., 65, 66

Wagner, E.D., 157, 168

Wainess, R., 94, 97

Walker, V., 184, 194

Ward, K., 224, 230

Weil, S.A., 224, 231

Weinstein, A., 176

Wen Chieh, K., 216

Westfall, P.J., 233, 244

Wetzel-Smith, S.K., 21, 39

Whiteside, A., 177, 183, 194

Wilensky, R., 134, 141

Wiley, D.A., 50, 53, 69, 103, 108

Williams, J.B., 163, 168

Wilson, S., 64, 67

Wisher, R.A., 18, 19, 20, 86, 97, 160, 164, 167, 170, 175, 176, 337, 344, 347

Woolf, B.P., 171, 176

Worsham, S., 67

Wulfeck, W.H., 21, 39

Y

Yourdon, E., 148, 155

Yuen, A.H., 164, 167

Z

Zanotti, M., 25, 39

Zimmerman, R., 94, 97

SUBJECT INDEX

A

Accessibility ...*see "ADL functional requirements"*

Activity tree, 58, 62-64, 173

ADDIE process, 71-72, 76, 186-187

ADL business paradigm, 10, 13-14, 49, 71, 99, 109, 119, 131-132, 143, 152, 169, 177, 195, 207, 219, 233, 247, 272, 275, 283, 295, 297, 305, 334, 341-342, 346

    ADL Co-Labs, 14-15, 133, 220, 248, 250, 262

    Co-Lab Hub, 1, 15, 78, 176, 225, 239-241, 248

    Joint ADL Co-Lab in Orlando, 15, 219, 222, 234

    partnership labs, 15, 262, 283, 337

ADL functional requirements, 112

    accessibility, 9, 12, 46, 52, 57, 73, 86, 101, 112, 120, 141, 165-166, 169, 177, 195, 247, 300, 305, 317-318, 340

    durability, 9-10, 12, 14, 47, 73, 112, 120, 195, 300, 305, 317-318, 342

    interoperability

        and ADL business paradigm, 10-11, 13-15, 107

        benefits of, 300

        and conformance, 119-121, 123-124

        content reuse, 256

        and emerging technologies, 169, 174, 177, 195, 202

        as a functional requirement, 8, 9, 12, 73, 103, 166, 239, 259-260, 284, 288, 295, 299, 305, 317, 342-343

        Implementation, 230, 241, 291, 298

        implementation issues, 5, 6, 7, 220, 280-281

        and learning content, 131-133, 136, 312

        and LMS, 72, 147

        for open source, 297

        and policy, 111-112

        and SCORM, 49, 51, 52, 55, 64, 81, 101, 105, 318, 334

        and standards, 7, 41-42, 46-47, 53-54, 114, 309, 315

        and technical data, 317

    reusability

        and context, 75, 90, 148

        as a functional requirement, 9, 12, 47, 73, 112, 120, 195, 284, 300, 302, 305

        and instructional design, 150, 261

        of learning content, 54, 90

        and learning objects, 50-51

        and SCORM, 52, 103, 105, 165, 260, 267, 290-291, 317-318

ADL-R ...*see "ADL Registry"*

ADL Registry, 17, 34, 76, 78, 93, 111-116, 131-137, 139-141, 220-221, 223-224, 229, 251, 262-263, 272, 327, 337

    CORDRA, 17, 34, 46, 54, 132-133, 135-136, 140, 276, 290

    Federation, 46, 131, 135, 139-140, 181, 248, 253, 276, 287

    handle system, 135, 139

    registry interface mechanism (RIM), 137-138

Aerospace and Defence Industries Association of Europe (ASD), 319

AICC ...*see "Aviation Industry CBT Committee (AICC)"*

Air Force

    Italian Air Force, 28

    U.S. Air Force, 32-33, 93, 164, 200, 212, 224, 229

Application Program Interface (API), 44, 57-62, 123, 158, 203-204, 310-311, 323

Army
>U.K. Royal Army, 213
>U.S. Army, 176, 200, 224, 248

Army National Guard, 234, 239

Artificial intelligence, 171

Asynchronous learning ...*see "Instructional design"*

Asynchronous communication ...*see "Instructional design"*

Attitudes ...*see "Learning outcomes"*

Authoring tools, 2, 72, 121, 125, 144, 150-151, 160, 173, 225, 241, 255, 260, 263-264, 266, 268-269, 298, 321

Avatar, 178

Aviation Industry CBT Committee (AICC,) 41-48, 53, 55 99

B

Blog ...*see "Web 2.0"*

Bologna Process, 266-267

Boolean, 104-105

C

Certification, ...*see "SCORM"*

Cheating, 344

Classroom instruction, 90
>>face-to-face, 21, 161, 178, 188, 228, 268, 296-297, 344-345

Cloud computing, 214-215

Collaborative tool ...*see "Social Media"*

Common source data base (CSDB), 319-321, 323, 326-327, 329

Community of interest, 251, 253

Community of practice, 93, 125, 160, 327

Computer-based instruction, 5-7, 28-29, 50, 103, 251, 305

Computer-based training (CBT), 7, 41-42, 47-48, 53, 80, 86, 99, 100, 165, 169-170, 174, 207, 243, 259, 324, 337

Classroom instruction, 23-24, 26, 31, 85-87, 90-91

Conformance ...*see "SCORM"*

Constructivist, 184, 186

Content Aggregation Model (CAM) ...*see "SCORM"*

Content package ...*see "SCORM"*

Cost-benefit ...*see "ROI"*

Course satisfaction, ...*see "Evaluation"*

Courseware, 12, 50, 90, 99, 148, 163, 165, 223, 249-254, 297

Cyber home learning system, 278-280

D

Darwin Information Typing Architecture (DITA), 311

Data model ...*see "S1000D"*

Data modules ...*see "S1000D"*

Data readiness, 318, 328

Decision aiding ...*see "Job performance"*

Declarative knowledge ...*see "Learning outcomes"*

Defense Acquisition University (DAU), 2, 18, 226, 238, 248, 254

Delivery media
>games
>>as emerging technology, 191
>>and instructional design, 201-202, 204
>>as instructional method, 88-89, 131, 169-170
>>for learning, education, and training, 195-196
>>life cycle of, 327-238
>>and military training, 256

and mobile learning, 211

and SCORM, 11, 102, 106, 125, 202-203, 310

and simulations, 196

taxonomy, of 200

testing, of 225-226

and virtual worlds, 179, 186, 264

immersive technologies, 195, 197, 202, 225, 337

video teleconferencing, 238

virtual worlds, 89, 177-191, 225-226, 256, 264, 290, 313, 327

voice chat, 88

webinars, 15

Digital library, 267

Digital rights management, 149

Use rights, 114

Durability ...see "ADL functional requirements"

E

e-books, 211

Economies of scale ...see "ROI"

EDUCAUSE, 178

Effect size ...see "Evaluation"

Embedded training, 112

Engineering change proposal (ECP), 319, 321, 328

Ethics, 94, 187

Ethical, 338, 340, 342

Euro-Atlantic Partnership Council, 295

Evaluation

and ADDIE process, 71, 76-77, 113, 183

as cognitive skill, 190

comparative studies, 26, 164

of costs, 325, 328

course satisfaction, 94

data interpretation, 93-94

effect size, 26, 28-29

instructional effectiveness, 7, 28, 35, 73, 84

within Khan framework, 187, 340, 342, 344

meta-analysis, 86-87

metrics, 18, 79-80, 85-86, 96, 150, 152, 160, 228, 247, 251, 308, 337

multiple choice, 80, 92, 100, 169

at program level, 80, 223, 338

Rule of Thirds, 5, 23, 35, 86, 233, 251

as software application, 269, 297, 312

of standards, 13, 281, 292

of student model, 173

of training, 85-87, 89-91, 95-96, 337

training effectiveness, 85, 94-96, 143

of training intervention, 92-93

Training efficiency, 85, 89-90

Executive Order 13111, 1, 234, 240, 243

F

Face-to-face, 21, 161, 178, 188, 228, 268, 296-297, 344-345

Federation ...see "ADL-R"

G

Games ...see "Delivery media"

Government Accountability Office (GAO), 219-220, 248

GAO ...see "Government Accountability Office (GAO)"

H

Hand-held devices ...see "Mobile learning"

Handle system, ...see "ADL-R"

Human performance, 219, 320

T

Test logs, 127

Test suite, 2, 14, 52, 64, 78, 121-122, 127-128, 307

Tiger team, 226-227

Training costs ...*see "ROI"*

Training effectiveness ...*see "Evaluation"*

Training efficiency ...*see "Evaluation"*

Training interventions, 13, 91, 146

Transfer ...*see "Learning outcomes"*

Tutorial, 21-25, 28, 34-36, 270, 279

U

U.K. Royal Army ...*see "Army"*

United Nations, 207, 213, 296

U.S. Air Force ...*see "Air Force"*

U.S. Army ...*see "Army"*

United States Distance Learning Association, USDLA 233, 242

Use rights, 149

User generated content ...*see "Web 2.0"*

V

Video teleconferencing ...*see "Delivery media"*

Virtual worlds ...*see "Delivery media"*

Vocational training, 280-281

Voice chat ...*see "Delivery media"*

W

Web 2.0, 34, 157, 166, 208, 210, 305, 313
    Blog, 163-166
    user generated content, 211, 313
    wiki, 313

Webinars ...*see "Delivery media"*

Wiki ...*see "Web 2.0"*

X

Extensible Markup Language (XML), 55, 138-139, 225, 298, 311, 311, 318-319